Issues and Trends in Literacy Education

Fourth Edition

Richard D. Robinson
University of Missouri at Columbia

Michael C. McKenna
University of Virginia

Boston   New York   San Francisco
Mexico City   Montreal   Toronto   London   Madrid   Munich   Paris
Hong Kong   Singapore   Tokyo   Cape Town   Sydney

Executive Editor and Publisher: Aurora Martínez Ramos
Series Editorial Assistant: Lynda Giles
Executive Marketing Manager: Krista Clark
Production Editor: Mary Beth Finch
Editorial-Production Service: Omegatype Typography, Inc.
Composition Buyer: Linda Cox
Manufacturing Buyer: Linda Morris
Electronic Composition: Omegatype Typography, Inc.
Cover Administrator: Joel Gendron

For related titles and support materials, visit our online catalog at www.ablongman.com.

Between the time website information is gathered and then published, it is not unusual for some sites to have closed. Also, the transcription of URLs can result in typographical errors. The publisher would appreciate notification where these errors occur so that they may be corrected in subsequent editions.

ISBN-13:   978-0-205-52031-2
ISBN-10:   0-205-52031-6

Library of Congress Cataloging-in-Publication Data

Issues and trends in literacy education / [edited by] Richard D. Robinson, Michael C. McKenna. — 4th ed.
     p. cm.
  Includes bibliographical references and index.
  ISBN-13: 978-0-205-52031-2
  ISBN-10: 0-205-52031-6
  1. Language arts. 2. Reading. 3. English language—Composition and exercises.
4. Literacy. I. Robinson, Richard David II. McKenna, Michael C.
  LB1576.I87 2008
  428.4'071—dc22

                                        2007010234

Printed in the United States of America

10 9 8 7 6 5 4 3 2 1   11 10 09 08 07

*This book is dedicated to those teachers
who have inspired in their students
an undying love for reading and writing*

About the Authors

Richard Robinson is currently a professor of education in the Department of Learning, Teaching, and Curriculum at the University of Missouri–Columbia. He received his Ed.D from the University of Georgia in the area of literacy education. He has authored over 150 articles and book chapters on the history of literacy, content reading instruction, and teacher training in reading education. Dr. Robinson is the author of 25 books including *Issues and Trends in Literacy, Issues and Innovations in Literacy Education: Readings From "The Reading Teacher," Readings in Reading Instruction: Its History, Theory, and Development*, and *Teaching Through Text: Reading and Writing in the Content Areas*. His current research and teaching interests are particularly related to the history of literacy, the teaching of reading in the content areas in the middle and secondary schools, and teacher training in reading in the elementary school. He received the Albert Kingston Award for service from the National Reading Conference in 1996. In his personal life he is an avid railfan and is interested in all aspects of railroads.

Michael C. McKenna is Thomas G. Jewell Professor of Reading at the University of Virginia. He has authored, coauthored, or edited 15 books and more than 100 articles, chapters, and technical reports on a range of literacy topics. His books include *The Literacy Coach's Handbook, Assessment for Reading Instruction, Help for Struggling Readers, Teaching through Text, Issues and Trends in Literacy Education*, and others. His research has been sponsored by the National Reading Research Center (NRRC) and the Center for the Improvement of Early Reading Achievement (CIERA). He is the cowinner of NRC's Edward Fry Book Award and ALA's Award for Outstanding Academic Books. He serves on the editorial board of *Reading Research Quarterly*, and his articles have appeared in that journal as well as the *Journal of Educational Psychology, Educational Researcher, The Reading Teacher*, and others. He has coedited themed issues of the *Peabody Journal of Education* and *Reading and Writing Quarterly*. His research interests include comprehension in content settings, reading attitudes, technology applications, needs-based instruction, literacy coaching, and beginning reading.

Contents

Preface

Reading is the sole means by which we slip, involuntarily, helplessly, into another's skin, another's voice, another's soul.

—Joyce Carol Oates

The primary purpose of this book is to help you better study and understand the field of literacy education. What was once a rather limited discipline is today a vast and complicated body of knowledge and field of inquiry, frequently drawing on information from many diverse areas such as psychology, sociology, and linguistics. The individual wishing to investigate a question or topic in literacy today may find the experience a daunting one.

For example, a recent computer search on the subject "reading comprehension" identified over 12,000 references to this one topic. Ranging across a broad spectrum of subtopics, the results of this search clearly showed the diversity that is typical of the literacy field. These results included data-based research studies, classroom observational inquiries, theoretical research papers, as well as personal opinion articles. These references represented the work of university faculty, classroom teachers, commercial publishers, and private individuals. Complicating the situation is the fact that there is not only a great deal of information currently available, but many different opinions and perspectives as well. These viewpoints often range between a single individual's position on a topic and a national movement reflecting the philosophies and attitudes of many thousands of people.

It is with these circumstances in mind that this book was written. We have attempted to identify the most significant issues and trends facing literacy educators today and to locate sources that explain principal viewpoints on these issues. Beyond selecting sources and providing textual aids to promote comprehension and engagement, our contribution has been minimal. We prefer to let the authors speak for themselves.

We have assumed that most readers of this book have had at least some introduction to the study of literacy education. The book has been developed with practicing teachers in mind—practitioners interested in extending their own thinking about the important issues they face in classrooms. We have not attempted to produce an introductory text, but assume that the foundations of literacy instruction—its purposes, concepts, and methods—have already been laid by means of prior coursework and teaching experience.

Organization of the Text

Each chapter consists of six sections: (1) a brief introduction to the topic, (2) a guidance section that suggests important ideas to keep in mind while reading, (3) the articles themselves, (4) questions about classroom implications, (5) suggested print sources for further reading, and (6) a few key online sources.

Chapter Introductions

Each topic is first summarized in a brief section designed both to provide necessary background and to help stimulate thinking related to the topic. Many readers of this book will have—either through previous education classes or classroom teaching experiences—ideas and feelings about the topics discussed in this book. We challenge you to keep an open mind about what you currently believe concerning literacy instruction. In many literacy areas, either because of recent research or relevant classroom experiences, instructional strategies that were once considered appropriate are now being challenged by new ideas and pedagogy.

Each chapter introduction concludes with a list of important questions designed to guide your reading and organize your thinking. Actively considering them should give you a better understanding of your current knowledge, beliefs, and feelings about a particular literacy issue.

As You Read

This brief section in each chapter should provide you with some specific guidance as you read the individual articles. You might keep these ideas and suggestions in mind as you consider the material presented on these various literacy topics.

Articles

Following the introduction are the selections. Our intent is that this section will help familiarize you with important, though sometimes incompatible, views on the chapter topic. Of particular note is the presentation of differing points of view. For some topics, where there is little disagreement or controversy, you will find a general discussion of the literacy trend. You should understand that the selections are never intended to be all-inclusive but rather to introduce the topic and encourage you to pursue further study on your own.

Classroom Implications

It is an important goal of this book to provide the reader information that is applicable to the effective teaching of classroom literacy. In this section are presented ideas and suggestions for the implementation of the chapter contents to your instruction. While these thoughts are general in nature they are provided in this format so that you can readily apply them to your own particular classroom setting and individual students.

For Further Reading

The materials presented here have been selected to support and in some cases challenge the ideas and thoughts of the articles in the chapter. If you would like to expand your thinking on a particular literacy topic you might use these references for further reading. They also are good suggestions if you wish to write a paper on these literacy issues.

Online Resources

In some of the chapters is a list of useful online references where appropriate. These individual listings were current at the time this book was published but in many cases become obsolete relatively rapidly.

MyLabSchool

mylabschool is a collection of online tools for your success in this course, on your licensure exams, and in your teaching career.

Visit www.mylabschool.com to access the following:

- Video footage of real-life classrooms, with opportunities for you to reflect on the videos and offer your own thoughts and suggestions for applying theory to practice
- An extensive archive of text and multimedia cases that provide valuable perspectives on real classrooms and real teaching challenges
- Allyn & Bacon's Lesson and Portfolio Builder application, which includes an integrated state standards correlation tool
- Research paper assistance using Research Navigator™, which provides access to three exclusive databases of credible and reliable source material: EBSCO's ContentSelect Academic Journal Database, The New York Times Search-by-Subject Archive, and "Best of the Web" Link Library
- Career Center with resources for Praxis exams and licensure preparation, professional portfolio development, and job search and interview techniques

Acknowledgments

We wish to take this opportunity to thank the following reviewers for their helpful comments: Richard Bates, SUNY Potsdam; Debby Deal, Loyola College of Maryland; Clarissa Gamble Booker, Prairie View A&M University; Michael Moore, Georgia Southern University; and Carolyn Ann Walker, Ball State University.

....

Chapter 1

Word Recognition

To teach reading as mere combinations of letters which do not teach anything,
which are often unintelligible to young persons and which leave minds
in states of listless curiosity and total ignorance is a waste of time.
—David Blair (1806)

There is not argument over the question of whether phonics should be taught,
for the answer is an unqualified 'yes.' Sharp differences do arise among those
representing various approaches to instruction over 'what' and 'when.'
—A. Sterl Artley (1962)

We believe that learning the relationship between letters and sounds—the way in
which the written language represents the spoken language—is absolutely
crucial to becoming an accomplished and lifelong reader.
—Michael F. Graves, Connie Juel, & Bonnie Graves (2007)

Of all the areas of literacy education there is perhaps no more contentious issue than that of word recognition, particularly as it relates to phonics. The debate on phonics instruction through the years has been controversial and seemingly never ending, as reflected in the following three statements. Horace Mann in 1838 wrote, "It can hardly be doubted therefore that a child would learn to name 26 unfamiliar words sooner than the unknown, unheard of letters of the alphabet" (Mann, 1838, p. 17). Rudolf Flesch, over a century later, took a much different approach to the teaching of phonics. He said, "if a child isn't taught the sounds of the letters, then he has absolutely nothing to go by when he tries to read a word. All he can do is guess. . . . Systematic phonics is *the* way to teach reading." (Flesch, 1955, pp. 21, 121). More recently, Allington and Cunningham (2007) have noted, "Phonics instruction is clearly important because one big task of beginning readers is figuring out how our alphabetic language works" (p. 68).

A research synthesis by the National Reading Panel (NICHHD, 2000) makes a strong case for the role of word recognition as one of the key aspects of literacy education. The three papers included in this section discuss various aspects of this report. Although it is possible, in theory at least, to argue that reading instruction should be "all phonics" or "no phonics," these are extreme positions that few would take very seriously. For most educators, there is a middle stance—namely, that phonics is important in a total classroom literacy program but that other aspects are crucial as well.

The "Reading Wars"

Why has word recognition instruction—and phonics in particular—occasioned such controversy. The situation has often been likened to warfare, with the two sides generally characterized as (1) those who believe that explicit instruction in decoding is profitable for most students and (2) those who believe that a meaning emphasis will lead naturally to proficient decoding. At the heart of the argument is what good readers do as they make their way through text. The first view posits that virtually every letter of every word is recognized, even in the case of words known at sight, whereas the second view holds that readers use context to predict each word and then merely sample the letters to test their predictions. Though there are several variations of these ideas, we can generally describe the first view as "bottom-up," because the letters of a word tell the brain how to identify it. We can describe the second view as "top-down," because the brain decides which portions of a word are useful for recognizing it. Let's look at these models in more detail.

As you read these words, you are not likely to be cognizant of exactly how it is happening. As a proficient reader, you merely take for granted that you can effortlessly bring meaning to any print you are likely to encounter. In recent decades, educators have taken a special interest in precisely how this process occurs and what subprocesses may be involved. Their interest goes beyond theoretical curiosity. Understanding how the mature reading process takes place can be very useful in addressing the problems experienced by some students. Now let's contrast the two competing models of how reading occurs.

The Top-Down Model

A persuasive model of the reading process was proposed by Kenneth Goodman (1969) and Frank Smith (1966, 1972) in the late 1960s and early 1970s. The brain, they contended, is largely incapable of processing the huge volume of data contained in the letters on a page. Good readers therefore make this process as efficient as possible by continually forming hypotheses about the next word they will encounter. Consider the following partial sentence:

> She combed her long blond _____.

When you reach the blank, you are able to form a reasonable guess about what the next word will be. The guess is based on all the words that have gone before. That is, you used the context of the next word in order to help identify it. In real reading, of course, you are not faced with blanks but with actual words. This means that your guess can be aided by the letters of the word you are trying to identify. To continue with our example, if you suspected that the next word was *hair*, you might simply notice that the first letter of that word was an *h*. This would be enough to confirm your prediction and allow you to keep reading quickly and efficiently.

> She combed her long blond h_____.

Goodman and Smith therefore viewed reading as a process of continually forming predictions about upcoming words and of confirming them—not by fully decoding those words but by merely *sampling* enough letters to confirm each prediction. When the prediction is wrong, the reader would need to slow down and take a closer look at the actual letters of the word. What if the original sentence had been a bit different?

> She combed her long blond tresses.

Expecting the word *hair*, the reader would sample one or more letters in the word *tresses* and realize that this prediction was incorrect. The reader would therefore need to slow down and take a closer look.

This model of reading is often called the "top-down" model because higher-level mental processes are very much in control of word recognition. The conscious thoughts of the reader are directing the lower-level process of letter and word recognition. In other words, the brain is telling the eye what to look for. Teachers tend to find this model very attractive because it gives a central role to comprehension. It is meaning oriented and is sometimes referred to as a "concept-driven" model.

The trouble with this model is that it is completely wrong, and a large number of studies have put it to rest. Let's look now at the model that has replaced it.

The Bottom-Up Model

The competing model now accepted as an accurate description of how reading takes place is often called the "bottom-up" model. At first, it may seem counterintuitive. According to this model, a proficient reader processes nearly every letter of every word. For the most part, this is done unconsciously and automatically. In fact, some psychologists have suggested that the process of recognizing words is conducted through an independent "module" of the mind. Like a conveyor belt, this module continually supplies a reader's conscious thoughts with the words encountered on the page. There is no need for the reader to make predictions about upcoming words because they are rapidly and efficiently supplied through the module. The brain does not need to tell the eyes what information is needed. Rather, this information is simply supplied when the reader needs it.

You may have had the experience of reading to a young child and allowing your mind to wander. Even though you were thinking about other matters, you were able to continue your oral reading and the child may not have known the difference. You were able to do so because your word recognition "module" is capable of working automatically, and you are free to ignore the words it supplies.

The Role of Context

This is not to say that context plays no role in proficient reading. For one thing, when you came to the word *tresses* in our earlier example, studies show that you recognized it a few milliseconds more quickly having read the preceding context than if you had encountered the word *tresses* in isolation (on a flashcard, perhaps). However, this modest difference in time is merely the result of certain portions of your word memory (which psychologists call your *lexicon*) having been "primed" by the context. That priming is an unconscious process and is a far cry from making conscious predictions about what the next word will be. (Here's an example of priming. A friend makes a passing reference to *Gone with the Wind*. An hour later, as if out of nowhere, the theme from the movie runs through your mind.)

Context plays another important role in reading as well. Consider the following sentence:

The Braves scored a run in the first inning.

An unabridged dictionary gives more than thirty definitions of the word *run*. However, you had no difficulty choosing the right one, and you did so on the basis of context. Without context, you would have been unable to arrive at the intended meaning. Because most words have more than a single meaning, context utilization is a vital skill that all readers must acquire.

The bottom-up model (also called a "text-driven" model) suggests that context has no role in locating the word *run* in your lexicon. Instead, context comes into play *after* the word has been located. It is used to suppress all meanings of the word *run* except the one that makes sense in context. Again, you are scarcely aware of this process. When you read the sentence, the idea that the word *run* might refer to a flaw in a woman's stocking did not enter your conscious thinking at all. Context was useful in suppressing this idea. And thankfully so! Imagine how cumbersome reading would be if it involved consciously sorting through all possible meanings of every word encountered.

The "Simple View" of Reading

Phillip Gough and his colleagues have suggested that understanding the reading process is really quite simple. Reading entails two components: listening comprehension and word recognition. Anyone proficient in both of these areas is likely to be a good reader. Although Stahl and Hayes have pointed out that it is also necessary to be motivated to read in the first place, it is generally accepted that these two components are a good way of reducing the reading process to its essentials. Of course, Gough and his colleagues were a bit tongue-in-cheek in suggesting that this view is simple. Each of these two components is highly complex; as an overview, however, it is a good way of envisioning the process.

It is also a good starting point from which to assess the difficulties a child may have. For example, a child may be a weak decoder with strong comprehension skills. Another child may have achieved oral reading fluency and yet have limited capacity to understand what is read. Still another child may have deficiencies in both areas. Effective reading teachers must conduct the battle on two fronts: decoding and comprehension.

Stages of Reading Development

The bottom-up model provides an accurate depiction of proficient reading, but precisely how does an individual get to this point? The process of learning to read can profitably be described as a child's progress through discernible stages of development. The most widely accepted stage model is that of Jeanne Chall (1983/1996), who describes the following stages (I have taken the liberty of updating her terminology slightly).

Emergent Literacy. Beginning in the preschool years, children acquire a foundation of oral language, learn the alphabet, and gain an early notion of how books and the print they contain are laid out. They also develop an awareness of the sounds of spoken language, which will serve them well as they learn to read.

Decoding. Children learn next that letters and groups of letters represent the sounds they hear in spoken words. Instruction in letter–sound correspondences is what we call *phonics*. In an alphabetic language like English, children soon come to grasp a fundamental idea called the "alphabetic principle." According to this principle, a limited number of letters are used to represent the basic sounds of spoken language. These basic sounds, called *phonemes*, are the building blocks of words. Of course, there are other decoding skills as well, including recognition of affixes, roots, and so forth. Depending on the curriculum the decoding stage may begin in kindergarten or first grade.

Fluency. Children who have learned a great many specific decoding skills will be able to decode most unfamiliar words, but their oral reading is likely to be halting for a time and characterized by poor phrasing. This is because their decoding skills are not yet automatic. Their word recognition "module" is still in the formative stages. With practice, however, their oral reading will become more proficient and will sound more adultlike. They will have attained oral reading fluency. Generally, this occurs during second grade.

Learning the New.   Once oral reading fluency is attained, a child's mental resources can be trained on comprehension. A reader who must devote conscious attention to too many words will not be able to adequately comprehend. But when word recognition becomes automatic, thinking about the content of what one reads becomes an attainable goal. There is a truism in reading: First a child learns to read and then the child reads to learn. When the child reaches the stage of learning the new, reading can become a real tool. One of the dangers of an overemphasis on decoding in the primary grades, however, may be that some readers become excellent "word callers" but have only a limited ability (or inclination) to comprehend what they decode.

As You Read

The following questions summarize some of the major issues in the current discussion of word recognition instruction. Prior to reading the articles in this section, consider your views as a teacher about these questions. After you have read the material, note how you may have modified your opinions about the role of word recognition in an effective classroom literacy program.

1. Why has the role of word recognition, especially phonics, been such a controversial area in literacy education?
2. What are some of the principal approaches to the teaching of word recognition skills?
3. In your opinion what should be the primary role of phonics in your classroom reading program?

In the first article of this section Shanahan (2005) discusses the current thinking among literacy experts on the appropriate role of word recognition in an effective classroom literacy program. This discussion is based on the work of the National Reading Panel (NICHHD, 2000). What is reported here is only one section of a much longer paper on the conclusions of this important research project. Although somewhat controversial in the literacy community, Shanahan presents a valuable review of this work. Wilson, Martens, Arya, & Atwater continue the discussion of the report, with emphasis on its relevance for classroom literacy instruction. As you read these first two articles note how they are similar and how they differ on their reporting of the NRP conclusions. In the third article on word recognition, Camilli and Wolfe (2004) also deal with the National Reading Panel's work. These authors seriously disagree with the results of the report, noting that in their opinion the research paradigm was flawed and thus the conclusions are open to question.

References

Allington, R. L., & Cunningham, P. M. (2007). *Schools that work: Where all children read and write* (3rd ed.). Boston: Allyn & Bacon.

Artley, A. S. (1962). Phonic skills in beginning reading. *Education, 82,* 529.

Blair, D. (1806). *The class book.* London: R. Taylor & Company.

Camilli, G., & Wolf, P. (2004). Research on reading: A cautionary tale. *Educational Leadership, 61,* 26–30.

Flesch, R. (1955). *Why Johnny can't read—and what you can do about it.* New York: Harper.

Graves. M. F., Juel, C., & Graves, B. (2007). *Teaching reading in the 21st century.* Boston: Allyn & Bacon.

Mann, H. (1838). *The Common School Journal, 1,* 17.

National Institute of Child Health and Human Development (NICHHD). (2000). *Report of the National Reading Panel. Teaching children to read: An evidence-based assessment of the scientific research literature on reading and its implications for reading instruction: Report of the subgroups* (NIH Publication No. 004754). Washington, DC: Government Printing Office.

Shanahan, T. (2005). *The National Reading Panel Report: Practical Advice for Teachers. Phonics* (pp. 11–17, 41–42). Naperville, IL: North Central Regional Educational Laboratory Learning Point Associates.

Wilson, G. P., Martens, P., Arya, P., & Altwerger, B. (2004). Readers, instruction, and the NRP. *Phi Delta Kappan, 86,* 242–246.

Phonics

TIMOTHY SHANAHAN

● ● ● ● ●

Some Definitions and Distinctions

Phonics instruction teaches students to use the relationship between letters and sounds to translate printed text into pronunciation. . . . It includes the teaching of letter sounds, how complex spelling patterns are pronounced, and how to use this information to decode or sound out words. Throughout most of the history of American schooling, phonics was widely seen as a unique method of teaching—like basal readers or computerized instruction. However, it should be thought of more properly as part of the content of reading instruction. No matter what instructional approach is taken to learning to read, the ability to use phonics should be one of the outcomes.

The National Reading Panel examined the impact of systematic phonics instruction. *Systematic phonics* is the teaching of phonics with a clear plan or program, as opposed to more opportunistic or sporadic attention to phonics in which the teacher must construct lessons in response to the observed needs of children. During the years leading up to the National Reading Panel Report, some reading authorities claimed phonics should be taught through minilessons based on individual student learning needs (Moustafa, 1997). The way this was intended to work was that teachers would note that some children needed help with a particular sound-symbol relationship or spelling pattern and would then provide appropriate "just in time" lessons; only giving the children what they needed at the time they needed it. The authorities claimed that this kind of responsive teaching would be more effective than a well-planned daily sequence of phonics instruction. The National Reading Panel examined the value of phonics instruction and the effectiveness of the different approaches in meeting the learning needs of children.

Another important distinction is between *synthetic phonics* and *analytic phonics*. In synthetic phonics—sometimes called *explicit phonics*—children are taught the individual

Shanahan, T. (2005). *The National Reading Report: Practical advice for teachers.* Naperville, IL: North Central Regional Educational Laboratoty Learning Point Associates. 11–17; 41–42. Reprinted with permission.

sounds of words and how to blend these individual sounds into word pronunciations, while analytic—also called *word analogy* phonics—emphasizes larger units of pronunciation. For a long time, experts have argued about the merits of synthetic and analytic phonics, and commercial programs have tended to be either synthetic or analytic in their approaches. The National Reading Panel set out to determine which of these approaches helped children more. (Although *systematic* and *synthetic* are very different concepts, some observers have interchanged them, which has resulted in some confusing and misleading interpretations of the National Reading Panel findings. Synthetic and analytic phonics can both be taught either systematically—that is, with a predetermined daily plan of instruction—or responsively, based on teacher observations of student need.)

Does Phonics Instruction Improve Reading?

The National Reading Panel found 38 studies in which children were given a special emphasis on phonics instruction to evaluate the value of this type of teaching (NICHD, 2000). The summary of these studies led to a definite conclusion that systematic phonics instruction gave children a faster start in learning to read than responsive instruction or no phonics instruction. Phonics instruction improved kindergarten and first-grade children's word recognition and spelling skills and had a positive impact on their reading comprehension. Phonics for second-grade students (and older struggling readers) also improved their word recognition skills, but without any measured improvement in reading comprehension. (After the report was published, some researchers questioned whether these results were correct, and they reworked the entire phonics section of the report—searching for articles again, recoding the variables, and providing some very different analyses of these data [Camilli, Vargas, & Yurecko, 2003]. Despite all of these changes, the value of phonics instruction was still evident—though the positive impact was smaller than reported by the panel.)

Systematic phonics instruction clearly and convincingly outperformed the more responsive or opportunistic approaches to phonics in which teachers were expected to improvise instruction as needed. The synthesis of these studies suggested that systematic approaches provided teachers with support for teaching more phonics more thoroughly to more children. Although phonics instruction that was not systematic was better than no phonics instruction, it was not as effective as systematic phonics programs; perhaps because it is too difficult to juggle this amount of individual diagnosis, teaching, and review within the demands of a regular classroom.

Of course, the fact that it is a good idea to use some type of phonics curriculum or program to guide phonics teaching leads teachers and parents to wonder which phonics programs are best. Although more than a dozen different programs of phonics instruction were used in these 38 studies, it was impossible to determine which programs were most effective. None of these programs were used in sufficient numbers of studies to permit that kind of evaluation. But it should be noted that generally all of the phonics programs used in these studies seemed to work. The National Reading Panel findings are not specific enough to guide the choice of programs, but these findings should encourage the adoption of such programs and suggest that most programs of this type will be better than having no program or having teachers trying to improvise this kind of teaching.

For many years, reading authorities have argued whether it is best to teach synthetic phonics or analytic phonics. Those who favor synthetic approaches emphasize the ease with which the individual sounds are learned, while those who favor analytic approaches claim children can better apply the analogy approach to word recognition. Although these 38 studies examined various versions of synthetic and analytic phonics, there were no significant differences among them in terms of effectiveness. Both synthetic and analytic phonics were effective, and neither significantly outperformed the other. (Scores were somewhat higher for synthetic phonics, but this superiority was not statistically significant; that is, the differences were due to chance alone.)

Teachers should know how to deliver both kinds of instruction. For some children, sounds are too difficult to distinguish within the context of words and being able to simplify this by providing explicit single-sound teaching can make it easier to convey the concept to young children. However, children sometimes have difficulty blending together each individual sound without adding other sounds (because it is impossible to pronounce most consonants without attaching a vowel; for example, children trying to sound the individual letters in *cat* may end up with something more like /cuh/ /ă/ /tuh/). Reliance on known words as analogies can make this a more manageable task. If teachers are able to make these types of modest adjustments to phonics instruction as needed, they might increase its effectiveness.

Studies of phonics teaching suggest that kindergarten phonics instruction provides children with an early advantage in learning to read, and that additional phonics instruction in Grades 1 and 2 builds on and increases this advantage. This means children should receive phonics instruction for about three years, though some struggling learners will need to continue longer until they can successfully decode. One study estimated the proportion of children who fail to understand phonics sufficiently even with systematic instruction to be one quarter of the students (Torgesen et al., 1999). Even with this additional time for struggling readers, the short length of time for which phonics instruction is useful is surprising to some teachers and parents who presume phonics will be delivered at all grade levels for all students. Systematic phonics instruction needs to be provided beyond that only for struggling readers, though more proficient learners still can benefit from occasional reviews and with help in the sounding of more complex words or with spelling patterns not common until these grade levels, such as *-tion* or *-able*.

Advice for Teachers on Teaching Phonics

Why did phonics instruction have no impact on reading comprehension as children age? It is evident that teaching phonics to first graders has an immediate impact on reading comprehension but that is not the case with older children. This may be due to the nature of the English language and how school textbooks are constructed (Foorman, Francis, Davidson, Harm, & Griffin, 2004; Hiebert, 2002). When children are beginning to learn to read, their oral-language vocabularies far surpass the numbers of words they can read. This means that when a young child sounds out a word, there is a very good chance it will already be in his or her oral vocabulary, and therefore that decoding (translating from one form of a message to another) will be a good match for comprehension. However, as children progress through school, their oral language starts to lag behind the large number of words that may be included in increasingly technical materials from social studies, science, and mathematics (Biemiller, 1999). At those higher grade levels, when students sound out a word, there is a very good chance they would not already know the meaning of the word, and so decoding would not lead directly to meaning (just as correctly sounding out words in a foreign language would not lead to an understanding of their meanings). Phonics can only help foster improved comprehension when it leads students to pronunciations of words that are in their oral language, a process that is less likely as text grows more difficult (one basic measure of text difficulty is how uncommon the words are in oral and written language [Hiebert, 2002]). This means phonics can help older readers but only to the extent that the reading instruction is building up knowledge of word meanings.

Earlier, a distinction was made between phonemic awareness and phonics. The importance of teaching phonemic awareness prior to or early in the phonics sequence was noted. However, it should be pointed out that because the National Reading Panel wanted to determine if each of these forms of instruction was beneficial, it only considered studies in which these aspects of teaching were examined separately. This does not mean that it is best to teach them separately; in fact, the panel itself cautioned against this misinterpretation. Some programs of instruction provide young children with a heavy dose of phonemic-awareness teaching and then follow it with phonics; others mix the two together, emphasizing the phonemic awareness of particular sounds, or for these sounds, in particular parts of words (it is usually easier, for instance, to hear an /f/ sound at the beginning of a word than in the middle of it). The research does not distinguish between such approaches, and both are likely effective. The key is teaching phonemic awareness until students can easily segment words completely, and teaching phonics until students can easily decode words.

With phonemic awareness instruction, it was clear that small-group instruction was the most effective. With phonics, the group organization did not seem to matter; tutoring, small-group, and whole-class instruction all worked equally well. This does not mean that for children who are struggling, it would not be beneficial to provide a more intensive experience either through tutoring or small-group instruction; they may still be useful. Because not everyone understands particular phonics concepts when they are first presented, it seems to be a good idea to continually monitor student success and give some students additional, more intensive phonics instruction in groups as small as is practical.

It is easy for most teachers to conceive of letter-sound teaching as the hallmark of phonics. In a synthetic approach, this might take the form of saying to the children, "Listen to the s sound. S makes a /sssssssssss/. Now you make an s sound: /sssssssss/."

Alternatively, in an analytic approach the form might be, "Listen to these words: sack, sent, sip, sock, sun. Do you hear that they sound the same at the beginning: *sss-ack, sss-ip, ssss-ock, sss-un?* Can you think of any other words that begin like *ssss-ack* or *sss-un?*" However, it is important that phonics instruction accomplish more than only teach students which letters are associated with which sounds. It also is imperative that they learn to use this information to decode words that they cannot yet read. As soon as children know enough letters or spelling patterns to allow the decoding of new words, instruction should include opportunities to practice applying phonics knowledge to decoding words the students cannot yet read (Pflaum, Walberg, Karegianes, & Rasher, 1980), and this was a common feature of many of the phonics approaches examined by the panel.

Sometimes this demand for decoding practice as part of phonics instruction raises the possibility of using nonsense words for this practice. For example, the teacher may want the child to try to decode words such as *tab, tad, tag, tan, tap,* and *tax.* This pool of words can easily be expanded with some nonsense syllables—or words that will seem like nonsense because they will be unknown by young children—such as *tac, taf, taj, tak, tam, tas, tat,* and *taz.* Many of the programs examined in the research used such nonsense syllables for practice decoding or dictation (in which the teacher reads the words or nonsense words to the children who then try to spell them). This approach displeases some educators who worry it might confuse children. The benefit of this approach is that it expands the amount of practice that is possible, and while these syllables might not be words, often they are common syllables within other words so it is beneficial to be able to read them quickly and easily (Rozin & Gleitman, 1977). Phonics programs that use nonsense syllables are as effective as phonics programs that avoid such practice.

If nonsense syllables are to be used as part of the practice exercises, it seems prudent to minimize their use, to explain to children that they are not real words, and to explain why they are being used. Even when they are not used in teaching, it has become common practice to evaluate students' decoding using nonsense syllables (Elliott, Lee, & Tollefson, 2001). This kind of assessment is valuable as it allows decoding to be evaluated without the confusion of prior student knowledge of particular words (because children can memorize a word that they may not be able to decode otherwise, it is impossible to separate this kind of knowledge from decoding on tests that use only real words). Unfortunately, teachers sometimes try to improve performance on such tests by teaching students to memorize the nonsense words, which should be avoided under any circumstances.

Decoding practice definitely should be a part of phonics instruction, and at least part of this practice should take place outside of the context of textual reading. The reason for this is students need to learn to use the letters and their sounds alone to arrive at word pronunciations. Good readers examine every letter and resolve every word (Rayner & Pollatsek, 1989). When a word is used in the context of a sentence or picture, then students do not necessarily need to use the letters to do the decoding. This does not mean that children should avoid reading text, only that some decoding practice should take place outside of context—and programs usually try to provide children with both kinds of practice.

An issue of frequent concern is about the nature of the text reading practice for decoding: Should it focus on what are described as *decodable texts?* Decodable texts are specially written to give children plenty of practice with particular sounds or patterns. For example: "Mig and Tig saw the pig. The pig was big. Mig put a wig on the pig. Tig danced a jig with the pig. The pig can dig. So can Mig and Tig. Mig and Tig and the pig dig." Obviously that kind of text allows students an abundance of practice, in this case with the *ig* spelling pattern, in a very brief time. Although some of the programs studied by the National Reading Panel used text like that, there was no way to determine whether it provided any benefit. Since the publication of the report, there have been some studies of the use of decodable text within a phonics program and the results were not promising (Jenkins, Peyton, Sanders, & Vadasy, 2004). Apparently, this level of decodability is not necessary as there were equal outcomes for the use of texts that ranged from 15 percent to 85 percent decodable. Students need reading practice, and this practice should include the sound-symbol correspondences and spelling patterns being taught, but the text can be fairly natural and certainly does not have to repeat the patterns to such a thorough extent. It also is fair to say, however, that none of the studies showed any problems resulted from brief uses of decodable text either. So small amounts of such practice may not be absolutely necessary, but they do not appear to be damaging either. The earlier advice seems appropriate here as well: If decodable text is to be used, then children should receive an explanation of why it is being used and why, unlike other text, it may not make much sense.

The role of spelling in phonics instruction is interesting. The value of having students attempting to spell words through dictation was seen in several of the studies examined by the National Reading Panel (e.g., Blachman, Tangel, Ball, Black, & McGraw, 1999; Bond, Ross, Smith, & Nunnery, 1995; Lum & Morton, 1984; Santa & Hoien, 1999). Similarly, the National Reading Panel concluded that invented-spelling activities, in which students are encouraged to spell words as they think they should be spelled, was supportive of phonemic awareness development (NICHD, 2000). Phonics instruction provides children with knowledge of the aural patterns and correspondences, while spelling activities provide practice in applying this knowledge through writing. Encouraging young children to attempt to spell words based on their sounds is an effective approach to supporting phonics learning.

One of the more difficult challenges in the teaching of phonics is students' dialects, especially when teachers and students speak different dialects. English language users can vary in their pronunciations of words, and this means that sound-symbol correspondences are likely to vary as well. These dialect differences are associated with region, race, and ethnicity, and it is important that we prevent these differences from interfering with student progress in learning to read. The key for the teacher is to be observant about the dialect differences that exist in the classroom and to adjust phonics teaching accordingly. The key for students is to match the letters to their usual pronunciations of the words. In one particular dialect, words like *yard* and *park* have very definite *r*-sounds, while in a New England dialect these words are spoken as if there were no *r* at all (*y-ah-d, p-ah-k*). If a person is teaching phonics to children in Boston who speak that dialect, it is important for them to learn how to read words with the *ar* spelling in their own dialect but not for the students to learn the teacher's dialect.

Phonics Summary

Students in Grades K–2 and older remedial readers all benefit from being taught how to use letter sounds and spelling patterns to decode words. The use of systematic approaches or programs of phonics instruction were found to be more effective than more opportunistic or responsive approaches. Activities like dictation or invented spelling, in which students try to write or spell words based on the sounds, have been found to help children learn phonics.

References

Adams, M., Foorman, B., Lundberg, I., & Beeler, T. (1997). *Phonemic awareness in young children: A classroom curriculum.* Baltimore: Brookes.

Allington, R. L. (2002). *Big brother and the national reading curriculum.* Portsmouth, NH: Heinemann.

Bryant, P., MacLean, M., Bradley, L., & Crossland, J. (1990). Rhyme and alliteration, phoneme detection and learning to read. *Developmental Psychology, 26,* 429–438.

Hu, C. F., & Catts, H. W. (1998). The role of phonological recoding in early reading ability: What we can learn from Chinese. *Scientific Studies of Reading, 2,* 55–80.

Murray, B. A. (1998). Gaining alphabetic insight: Is phoneme manipulation skill or identity knowledge causal? *Journal of Educational Psychology, 90,* 461–475.

National Institute of Child Health and Human Development (NICHD). (2000). Report of the National Reading Panel. *Teaching children to read: An evidence-based assessment of the scientific research literature on reading and its implications for reading instruction: Reports of the subgroups* (NIH Publication No. 00-4754). Washington, DC: U.S. Government Printing Office. Retrieved November 11, 2005, from www.nichd.nih.gov/publications/nrp/report.htm

Shanahan, T. (2003). Research-based reading instruction: Myths about the National Reading Panel report. *The Reading Teacher, 56,* 646–655.

Shanahan, T. (2004). Critiques of the National Reading Panel Report: Their implications for research, policy, and practice. In P. McCardle & V. Chhabra (Eds.), *The voice of evidence in reading research.* Baltimore: Paul H. Brookes Publishing.

Torgesen, J. K., & Mathes, P. G. (2000). *A basic guide to understanding, assessing, and teaching phonological awareness.* Austin, TX: Pro-Ed.

TABLE 1   Phonemic Awareness Skills

PHONEMIC AWARENESS SKILL	EXAMPLE OF INSTRUCTION
Phoneme isolation	Teacher: What sound do you hear first in **cat**? **Student: /k/**
Auditory discrimination	Teacher: Which of these words doesn't belong: **bag, bear, can**? **Student: Can** doesn't belong—it doesn't begin like **bag** and **bear**. **–Or–** Teacher: What sound is the same in **jar, jam, jet**? **Student: /j/**
Phoneme blending	Teacher: What word is **/p/ /i/ /n/**? Student: **/p/ /i/ /n/** is **pin**
Phoneme segmentation	Teacher: Break this word into its sounds: **sock.** **Student: /s/ /o/ /k/** **-Or-** Teacher: How many sounds are in **tie**? **Student: /t/ /I/** There are two sounds in **tie**.
Phoneme deletion	Teacher: Say **chin** without the **/ch/** **Student: in**
Phoneme addition	Teacher: Add a **/s/** to the end of **duck** **Student: Ducks** **-Or-** Teacher: Add **/b/** to the beginning of **ring** **Student: Bring**
Phoneme substitution	Teacher: Change the last sound you hear in **pig** to **/n/** **Student: Pin**

TABLE 2   Comparison of Synthetic and Analytic Phonics

SYNTHETIC OR EXPLICIT PHONICS	ANALYTIC OR WORD ANALOGY PHONICS
1. Teacher teaches children some simple consonant sounds (e.g., /b/, /n/, /p/, /s/).	1. Teacher teaches words (e.g., cat, pig, man, Dad).
2. Teacher teaches a vowel sound (e.g., the short /a/—the sound in *cat*).	2. Teacher then shows students how to use this word knowledge to sound out new words (e.g., can, pan, Dan): This word starts like the first sound in /c/ *cat* and it ends like *man* /an/ . . . It is *can*.
3. Teacher teaches children how to sound out words, and perhaps nonsense words, using these letter sounds: bab, ban, bap, bas, nab, nan, nap, nas, pab, pan, pap, sab, san, sap, sas	3. Teaching continues developing new words and understandings of the sound-symbol relationships based on known words.
4. Teaching continues letter by letter and sound by sound.	

TABLE 3   Summary of Phonics Content

CONTENT OF PHONICS INSTRUCTION	EXAMPLES
Consonants	b, d, f, g, h, k, l, m, n, p, q, r, s, t, v, w, x, y, z
Consonant blends or clusters	bl, br, cl, cr, dr, dw, fl, fr, gl, gr, pl, pr, sc, sk, sl, sm, sn, sp, st, sw, tr, tw, scr, str
Consonant digraphs	sh, th, ch, ph, ng, gh
Short vowels	cat, bet, fit, dot, but, myth
Long vowels	ate, beat, pipe, road, use
Vowel digraphs	oo, ew, aw, au, ou, ow, oi, oy
R-influenced vowels	ar, er, ir, or
Some common spelling patterns and complex rules	Consonant-Vowel-Consonant-Silent E (CVCe), CVC, CV, CVVC, CVCCe, hard c, hard g
Silent consonants	kn, wr

Readers, Instruction, and the NRP

G. PAT WILSON, PRISCA MARTENS, POONAM ARYA, AND BESS ALTWERGER

Jessica, a second-grader in an urban school with a low socioeconomic profile, reads: "But the nighttime tried to stand back down the stairs. So I caused it."[1] Like her classmates, Jessica has learned to read words through systematic and explicit phonics instruction. She comes up with words that look and sound similar to the words on the page, but they do not always make sense in the sentence. She accepts this, seemingly unaware that the text is supposed to make sense. Jessica's repertoire of reading strategies is limited, and her comprehension is poor. Is this the kind of reading that we wish to promote?

The pressure on schools to use programs of systematic and explicit phonics instruction is tremendous. The report of the National Reading Panel (NRP), a keystone resource for the Reading First program of the No Child Left Behind (NCLB) Act, used 38 studies to determine that explicit and systematic phonics instruction in the early grades is necessary.[2] Though it is not clear how long lessons should run, how many letter/sound relationships should be learned, how much phonics should be covered, or the type of instruction needed, phonics is deemed necessary. The federal government severely restricts the range of reading programs that it will fund through NCLB to those that demonstrate a systematic and predominant emphasis on phonics. Only programs that are considered to be research-based, using a narrow medical model, are acceptable. Those who use other kinds of instruction that are based on other kinds of research risk forgoing federal funds.

A case in point is New York City's run-in with federal agencies in which the phonics program the city tested in its schools was not considered "research-based."[3] In order to ensure funding, school districts are adopting or mandating single commercial programs, such as Direct Instruction or Open Court, which, at the core of instruction, impose extensive systematic and explicit skill approaches on all children.

Wilson, G. P., Martens, P., Arva, P., & Altwerger, B. (2004). Readers, instruction, and the NRP. *Phi Delta Kappan*, *2004*, 242. Reprinted with permission.

Studying Readers

Much of the research used by the NRP and approved by NCLB measures reading achievement by means of word lists, short passages with blanks, and lists of non-words. Such research does not study the actual process of students reading "real" texts, which would make it possible to determine the impact of phonics instruction on the strategies young readers use, on how they comprehend, or on how they perceive the reading process. We developed a study to do just that. We examined the impact of three different reading programs used in our metropolitan area on the reading processes of second-graders who had been instructed with these programs since at least first grade. Two were commercial programs that used explicit and systematic phonics instruction as a central piece in early reading learning: Direct Instruction (DI)[4] and Open Court (OC).[5] The third was a literature-based program, labeled Guided Reading (GR), wherein students were taught to use multiple strategies to focus on the meaning of what they read. This program was an adaptation of work by Irene Fountas and Gay Su Pinnell.[6]

The 84 students in our study live in urban settings and are of low socioeconomic status, but they are not coded for special education or for receiving ESL (English as a Second Language) services. To study the reading processes of these students, we asked the second-graders to read books to us aloud. We studied their reading using "miscue analysis," an established research tool that analyzes oral reading "miscues" or divergences from the text to reveal a reader's use of phonics cues, language structure cues, and meaning-based cues.[7] Thus we learned about the students' reading strategies, as well as their skill in comprehending as they read. To measure the students' comprehension, we had them retell the story they had read. These retellings were analyzed for inclusion of characters, setting, plot episodes, inferences and connections, and general cohesion (smoothness and completeness of the retelling).[8] From an interview with the students, which included questions such as "When you are reading and you come to something you don't know, what do you do?"[9] we determined their awareness of reading strategies and their perceptions of reading. In addition, the children took a phonics test from the *Woodcock Johnson Psycho-Educational Battery*, wherein they "read" a list of non-words.[10] We observed language arts instruction in the children's classrooms and interviewed principals and teachers to learn their perceptions of the reading program in use. These observations of language arts instruction allowed us to compare what the students said with what they did while reading and with what was going on during their reading instruction. In this manner, we built a comprehensive picture of the students' actual understanding and practice of reading.

Instruction and the Reader

The instruction provided by DI and OC is similar in many ways. In addition to incorporating systematic, explicit phonics instruction, both programs include reading anthologies for the second grade. The DI anthology is written by program authors, while the OC series uses stories from other published sources. The DI program is heavily scripted, while the OC program provides teachers with detailed lessons.

The profiles of the readers at both the DI and OC schools were also similar.[11] At both sites, the students tended to rely heavily on phonics cues. At the DI site, the students often substituted non-words for text words; at the OC site, the words were usually real words that often did not make sense, as we saw with Jessica in the opening of this article. In fact, almost half the miscues at both sites did not make sense. The students' retellings showed moderate comprehension, with strength in identification of character and setting but a lack of coherence and inference. In both schools, the students did well reading the non-words of the phonics test, scoring within the average range for their grade. Finally, the interviews showed that the students employ a limited number of strategies while reading. "Sounding out" and asking for help dominated the students' understanding of how to figure out the unknown in the text. In summary, the readers at the DI and OC schools tended to be "word readers" who focused on phonics without attending to whether the words they read actually made sense.

In contrast, at the third site of our study, phonics instruction was integrated into reading and writing. At the GR school, students learn phonics in the context of reading and writing. During reading instruction, teachers used experiences such as shared reading, read aloud, guided reading, independent reading, literature discussions, strategy discussions, interactive writing, guided writing, and independent writing to focus the children on constructing meaning by drawing on their knowledge of language and of the world. The material the teachers used did not come from an anthology but rather consisted of literature and collections of "leveled" books that increased in difficulty of language and complexity of story.[12]

The profile that emerged from the GR school reveals that the students use phonics while reading in ways similar to the students at the DI and OC sites (no significant difference in measures of phonics use in and out of context), but with a definite concern for meaning. The mean percentage of miscues not acceptable in terms of meaning or language usage is statistically lower at the GR school than at the other sites, and there is a higher incidence of attempts at correction. Within this instructional approach, the students generally are unwilling to continue reading when their reading doesn't make sense or sound grammatical.

Figure 1 presents an example of Latisha's reading. Latisha was designated by her teacher as a "low" reader; she is reading from *Bear Shadow*.[13] The willingness of the GR students to take risks and use a variety of cues and correction strategies is particularly evident in lines 0901 and 0902. After several attempts, Latisha reads "Nearby," but she has trouble with "cliff." She uses a "blank" strategy and continues reading, correcting her omission of "to." When she reads "cliff" in line 0902, she realizes that this is the word she "blanked" in the previous line and goes all the way back to reread those lines correctly.

In addition to describing setting and characters, the GR students' retellings are cohesive, and they reflect a tendency toward forming inferences and making connections. In the interviews, the students named a repertoire of strategies, including sounding out words, asking the teacher, "look for little words," "come back to it," and "break it apart." As at the DI and OC sites, the GR students performed in the average range for second-graders on the phonics test.

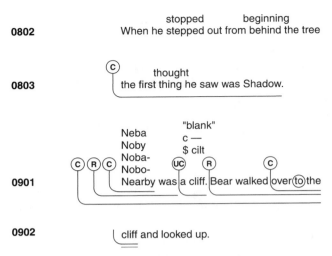

FIGURE 1   Sample of Reading at Guided Reading Site

Notations for miscue analysis: Student's substitutions are written above the text; $ means the substitution was a non-word; omitted words are circled. A circle connected to a line under a portion of text indicates a regression, and the letter in the circle indicates what occurred; C indicates the miscue was corrected; R indicates a straight repetition; UC means an unsuccessful attempt to correct the miscue was made.

Contrary to the NRP

Our findings run contrary to what would be expected given the NRP's determinations. The NRP Report concludes that systematic early phonics instruction (kindergarten and first grade) has a significant positive effect on students' skills in phonics, compared to programs that do not use this type of instruction. We did not find this to be the case. The students at the DI and OC sites had such phonics instruction in the first and second grades, yet we found no statistically significant differences between their use of phonics, either within the reading process or in isolation, and that of the GR students

The NRP Report also states that systematic and explicit phonics instruction is important for comprehension. In fact, a publication disseminating the report emphatically and unequivocally states, "Systematic and explicit phonics instruction significantly improves children's reading comprehension."[14] The basis for this conclusion is the NRP's theory that systematic and explicit phonics instruction influences word reading and thus enhances comprehension.

In our study, however, the students at the DI and OC site did not have an advantage over the students at the GR site in their ability to construct meaning during reading or in their overall comprehension of the texts after reading. In fact, our data indicate that, in addition to not improving students' reading and comprehension, the systematic, explicit phonics instruction takes students' focus and concern away from constructing meaning. While the phonics-related scores of the students in DI and OC were not significantly different from those of the students in GR, the results did reveal statistically significant differences in several meaning-based scores. But these differences favored the GR students. Instead of teaching phonics more effectively, the DI and OC sites in our study created readers for whom constructing meaning had become less important than noting phonic similarity—an outcome that can lead students to read the way Jessica did at the beginning of this article.

Conclusions

The students in this study had similar demographic backgrounds. However, their reading profiles did differ: the DI and OC students were limited by the program instituted in their school. And these were programs that met NCLB requirements. Yes, the students using DI and OC tested well on phonics, and they demonstrated literal comprehension of characters and setting. Thus their performance would look strong on "scientifically based" measures. But as former teachers and now teacher educators, we want more. By looking at readers' actual reading process, we can see deeper weaknesses as well as greater possibilities. Thus we return to the question, What kind of readers do we want to develop? For us, the answer is readers who intentionally use strategies to read for meaning. In order to help students learn to read in this way, we offer the following conclusions.

The blanket adoption of commercial phonics-based programs will not automatically create effective readers. Teaching to a curriculum makes the curriculum, rather than the learners, the center of decision making. Instruction that is based on students' strengths and needs is a necessity; teachers need to be able to draw on solid and broad knowledge of effective reading instruction. In their study of instruction, Michael Pressley and his colleagues identified the following characteristics of instruction by exemplary first-grade teachers: literature is emphasized, there is much reading and writing, tasks are matched to student competence, skills are explicitly taught, self-regulation is encouraged, connections are made across the curriculum throughout the day, the environment is positive with an emphasis on cooperation, and excellent classroom management is demonstrated.[15]

Instruction in skills can be taught in meaning-filled contexts through literature and writing. Students can be provided the tools (strategies) they need to make meaning a priority. One such tool is self-monitoring during reading to make sure that the text makes sense. Teachers model this tool through "think alouds," wherein they periodically tell students what they are thinking while they are reading. They then guide the students to monitor their own reading through such questions as, Did that make sense? Something doesn't seem quite right, take a closer look at _____.[16]

Literature motivates, provides rich vocabulary for learning, and suggests a variety of concepts to explore. Leveled literature allows knowledgeable teachers to control the complexity of the text and to gradually introduce more difficult text features. Teachers must know how to match students to texts, as well as how to use a text to teach skills and strategies. Such instruction requires extensive teacher decision making that is founded on a solid understanding of reading processes.

Effective decision making by teachers requires continued support and development. Elliot Eisner viewed researchers as the instruments of research in that they "engage the situation and make sense of it . . . interpreting significance."[17] To do this well, researchers must build their skill, knowledge, and judgment. Similarly, teachers are the instruments of teaching, and so they must build deep knowledge of effective instruction, reading processes, and the content of the language arts.

We believe that teachers should continue to study the impact of instruction on students' actual reading. To do this well, teachers need to rely on a broad database that draws on multiple sources, not just on standardized testing that samples isolated reading skills. Teachers also need to analyze students' oral reading and retellings to see how they integrate information in meaningful ways. We, as teachers, need to pay attention to students' actual reading and have the authority to change our instruction based on what each student is doing. Otherwise, we may not get the kind of readers we want.

References

1. The text actually read: "But the nightmare tried to sneak back down the stairs. So I chased it." It comes from Mercer Mayer, *There's Something in My Attic* (New York: Penguin Putnam Books for Young Readers, 1992).
2. National Institute of Child Health and Human Development, *Report of the National Reading Panel: Teaching Children to Read: An Evidence-Based Assessment of the Scientific Research Literature on Reading and Its Implications for Reading Instruction* (Washington, D.C.: U.S. Government Printing Office, 2000).
3. Abby Goodnough, "Bush Adviser Casts Doubt on the Benefits of Phonics Program," *New York Times,* 24 January 2003, p. B-1.
4. Siegfried Engelmann et al., *Reading Mastery* (Columbus, Ohio: SRA/McGraw-Hill, 1995).
5. *Open Court Teacher Edition* (Columbus, Ohio: SRA/McGraw-Hill, 2000).
6. Irene C. Fountas and Gay Su Pinnell, *Guided Reading: Good First Teaching for All Children* (Portsmouth, N.H.: Heinemann, 1996).
7. Yetta Goodman, Dorothy J. Watson, and Carolyn L. Burke, *Reading Miscue Inventory: Alternative Procedures* (Katonah, N.Y.: Richard Owen, 1987).
8. Leslie Mandel Morrow, *Literacy Development in the Early Years: Helping Children Read and Write,* 3rd ed. (New York: Allyn and Bacon, 1997).
9. Goodman, Watson, and Burke, op. cit.
10. Richard Woodcock and W. Bonner Johnson, *Woodcock Johnson Psycho-Educational Battery-R* (Itasca, Ill.: Riverside, 1990).
11. Bess Altwerger et al., "When Research and Mandates Collide: The Challenges and Dilemmas of Teacher Education in the Era of NCLB," *English Education,* vol. 36, 2004, pp. 119–33; and G. Pat Wilson et al., *The Impact of Four Reading Programs on Children's Reading Strategies: Research Summary Report* (Towson, Md.: Towson University Literacy Research Center, 2003).
12. Fountas and Pinnell, op. cit.
13. Frank Asch, *Bear Shadow* (Englewood Cliffs, N.J.: Prentice-Hall, 1985).
14. Bonnie B. Armbruster, Fran Lehr, and Jean Osborn, *Put Reading First: The Research Building Blocks for Teaching Children to Read,* 2nd ed. (Washington, D.C.: Center for the Improvement of Early Reading Achievement, Partnership for Reading, 2003), p. 14.
15. Michael Pressley et al., *Learning to Read: Lessons from Exemplary First-Grade Classrooms* (New York: Guilford Press, 2003).
16. Fountas and Pinnell, op. cit.
17. Elliot W. Eisner, *The Enlightened Eye: Qualitative Inquiry and the Enhancement of Educational Practice* (New York: Macmillan, 1991), p. 34.

Research on Reading:
A Cautionary Tale

GREGORY CAMILLI AND PAULA WOLFE

• • • • • ▬▬

Research on reading has generated much controversy and confusion. In an attempt to clarify the situation, education policymakers sought a research method that would offer the final word on what works in reading instruction. Meta-analysis—a statistical procedure that synthesizes the data from a number of existing studies to determine important programmatic effects—appeared to offer great potential for objectivity and even-handedness. Disputes could be resolved by making the fullest use of the research literature. The National Reading Panel (2000) likewise attempted to conduct a meta-analysis to review the best evidence available to guide instruction in reading. Unfortunately, the scientific method used in the Panel's report is flawed.

Flawed Science

The National Reading Panel's most important conclusion is that its findings "provide solid support" for the idea that systematic phonics instruction is more effective than alternatives in teaching children to read. But Camilli, Vargas, and Yurecko (2003) reanalyzed the same data, also using meta-analysis, and found that the effect size of programs using systematic phonics was only half as large as that reported by the National Reading Panel. This effect, moreover, was substantially smaller than the facilitative effect of one-to-one instruction. Additional analyses have shown that the combined effect of a number of literacy activities appears to be larger than the effect of systematic phonics instruction alone.

    The huge discrepancies between the National Reading Panel study and the analysis by Camilli and colleagues are due largely to differences in the scientific methods used to analyze the data. In our view, defensible studies of reading outcomes must take into account the multiple influences on reading ability and provide accurate descriptions of experimental effects.

Specifically, the process of extracting quantitative information from previous studies requires a more systematic approach. The National Reading Panel researchers decided to compare studies that had "more active" phonics interventions (experimental groups) with studies that had "less active" interventions (control groups). Yet this choice resulted in the experimental groups of some studies resembling the control groups of others. In other words, the *more/less* principle created a sliding scale and compromised the rigor of the Panel's report. The many influences on a student's reading ability cannot be reduced to such a *more/less* dimension.

Research studies of reading typically do not compare a pure treatment group to a pure control group. For example, even direct instruction in explicit decoding can be embedded within a comprehensive, meaning-based literacy program. This is why Fletcher and Lyon (1998) noted that gains in reading skills are reinforced by an emphasis on good literature, reading for enjoyment, and a meaning-based context. Unfortunately, the National Reading Panel analysis was designed to ignore the effects of literacy activities, and consequently it confounds the effects of systematic phonics with those of literacy-oriented treatments.

To justify this design decision, some researchers (Archibald, 2003) have assumed that the literacy effect can simply be added to the systematic phonics effect to arrive at the "true" effect of the latter. But assuming that the phonics effect is the sum of all instructional efforts is the equivalent of false advertising. Such an assumption ignores questions like these: Was there a print-rich environment offering extended opportunities for writing practice? Did the treatment supplement or supplant classroom instruction? A scientific approach to reading research does not automatically attribute to systematic phonics the effects of other factors.

Untangling the Terminology

The small effect for systematic phonics, which was the focus of the National Reading Panel's report, is a less important finding than one might think. Neither the report nor its reanalysis addressed phonics in general. Rather, both focused on *systematic phonics*, an approach that introduces letter-sound correspondences in a predetermined schema. This is different from phonics as *decoding*—that is, using the sound and look of a word to figure out what it means in context.

We know of no mainstream researcher or teacher who thinks that decoding is unimportant. But the National Reading Panel's report has confused many consumers of research who loosely mix the terms *decoding*, *phonics*, and *systematic phonics*. The authors of a recent editorial, for example, argued that the study by Camilli and colleagues placed "even greater weight on the importance of phonics than did the National Reading Panel" (Editorial, 2003). It is difficult to determine whether the author of the editorial understood the difference between decoding skills and systematic phonics instruction. But the issue is not whether "phonics," or decoding skills, is important. The issue is *how to teach* decoding skills.

Beyond the "Phonics" Debate

In an attempt to answer the question, What works in reading instruction?, some have argued for a balance of methods that would incorporate both direct instruction and meaning-based approaches (McIntyre & Pressley, 1996; Morrow & Tracey, 1997; Pearson, 1995). Pressley, Rankin, and Yokoi (1996) surveyed the practices of effective reading teachers and concluded that teachers' educations should "include exposure to a number of approaches and practices intermingling different types of instruction" (p. 380). However, there is no secret formula that will address the needs of every reader. One unfortunate connotation of the balance approach is that the teacher may devise a single curriculum with a mix-and-match strategy to "catch" all students. This approach eliminates the teacher's professional power and responsibility for instructional decision making.

Even the most reductive, scripted reading programs can make the claim of "balance." We prefer the term *differentiation*, which implies a different scenario. Using this strategy, the teacher assesses students' needs, determines the appropriate methods to address those needs, and creates individual and group experiences accordingly. Perhaps some students need direct instruction in decoding skills; perhaps none do. With differentiation in mind, a clearer interpretation of the National Reading Panel's findings on phonics instruction may be this: Direct instruction in phonics is necessary for certain at-risk kindergartners, but only if embedded in a print-rich, comprehensive literacy program and delivered in brief, individualized lessons.

Needed: Better Science

Unless researchers describe *literacy, language,* and *phonics* within a comprehensive framework, they may continue to conduct studies that have no clear implications for instructional practice. It seems noncontroversial to argue that there is no useful one-dimensional model of reading instruction. Consequently, scientific studies should be sensitive to the mosaic of effects present in any reading environment.

As researchers (Baumann, Hoffman, Moon, & Duffy-Hester, 1998; Morrow & Tracey, 1997) have shown, most teachers think decoding skills are important; these teachers provide daily phonics instruction in their classrooms. In a survey by Pressley and colleagues (1996), 95 percent of teachers reported explicitly teaching phonics. These studies indicate that most students receive phonics instruction, and Camilli and colleagues (2003) found that adding systematic phonics instruction to this base appears to have a small impact for certain groups of students.

The important recommendation here is that systematic phonics instruction may be valuable for selected students when added to a comprehensive literacy program, but it imparts little value when used as the *only* reading instruction for all students. The efficacy of phonics instruction depends on how teachers use their class time. If a teacher delivers 10 minutes of systematic phonics instruction each day to those students who need it, such instruction may have a high benefit-cost ratio. If phonics activities displace literature-rich and meaning-oriented instruction, however, the benefit of systematic phonics instruction will be greatly diminished.

As educators look for practical guidance about what works in reading instruction, they should know that some findings of "evidence-based research" have been greatly exaggerated. The complexity of classroom-relevant understandings of reading instruction may seem overwhelming, but this is why teachers should make curricular decisions. Effective teachers must understand the particular needs and situations of their students as well as a range of contextualized, evidence-based practices. Questions of whether direct instruction in decoding or phonics is necessary are less important than the questions of when, why, how, and to whom teachers should provide such instruction. These are core questions in the scientific study of reading.

References

Archibald, G. (2003, June 10). Researchers verify reading ability gets a boost from phonics. *Washington Times*. Available: www.washtimes.com/national/20030610-125708-5569r.htm

Baumann, J. F., Hoffman, J. V., Moon, J., & Duffy-Hester, A. M. (1998). Where are teachers' voices in the phonics/whole language debate? Results from a survey of U.S. elementary classroom teachers. *Reading Teacher, 51*(8), 636–650.

Camilli, G., Vargas, S., & Yurecko, M. (2003). Teaching children to read: The fragile link between science and federal education policy. *Education Policy Analysis Archives, 11*(15). Available: http://epaa.asu.edu/epaa/v11n15

Editorial. (2003, June 12). Sounding phonics. *Richmond Times-Dispatch*.

Fletcher, J. M., & Lyon, G. R. (1998). Reading: A research-based approach. In W. Evers (Ed.), *What's gone wrong in America's classrooms* (pp. 49–90). Stanford, CA: Hoover Institute Press.

McIntyre, E., & Pressley, M. (1996). *Strategies and skills in whole language: An introduction to balanced teaching*. Boston: Christopher-Gordon.

Morrow, L. M., & Tracey, D. H. (1997). Strategies used for phonics instruction in early childhood classrooms. *Reading Teacher, 50*(8), 644–651.

National Reading Panel. (2000). *Teaching children to read: An evidence-based assessment of the scientific research literature on reading and its implications for reading instruction. Reports of the subgroups*. Washington, DC: National Institute of Child Health and Human Development.

Pearson, P. D. (1995, November). *Reclaiming one center: A reading curriculum for all students and teachers*. Presentation at the meeting of the California Reading Association, Anaheim, California.

Pressley, M., Rankin, J., & Yokoi, L. (1996). A survey of instructional practices of primary teachers nominated as effective in promoting literacy. *Elementary School Journal, 96*(4), 363–384.

Classroom Implications

1. Now that you have read the materials in this chapter on word recognition, consider your beliefs on this aspect of classroom literacy instruction. How has your current definition of reading changed based on your views concerning word recognition? Or has it?

2. What specific changes might you make in your classroom instructional program in literacy based on the material you have read in this chapter?

For Further Reading

Christensen, C. A., & Bowey, J. A. (2005). The efficacy of orthographic rime, grapheme-phoneme correspondence, and implicit phonics approaches to teaching decoding skills. *Scientific Studies of Reading, 9,* 327–349.

Cooper, H. (2005). Reading between the lines: Observations on the report of the National Reading Panel and its critics. *Phi Delta Kappan, 86,* 456–461.

Darling, S. (2005). Strategies for engaging parents in home support of reading acquisition. *The Reading Teacher, 58,* 476–479.

Davenport, D., & Jones, J. M. (2005). The politics of literacy. *Policy Review, 130,* 45–57.

Glazer, S. M. (2005). To phonic or not to phonic? *Teaching PreK–8, 36,* 71.

Goodman, K. S. (1969). Let's dump the uptight model in English. *Elementary School Journal, 70,* 1–13.

Goswami, U. (2005). Synthetic phonics and learning to read: A cross-language perspective. *Educational Psychology, 21,* 273–282.

Hiebert, E. H., Leigh, A., & Menon, S. (2005). Are there alternatives in reading textbooks? An examination of three beginning reading programs. *Reading & Writing Quarterly, 21,* 7–32.

Manning, M. (2005). Phonemic awareness. *Teaching PreK–8, 36,* 68–69.

Mesmer, H. A. (2005). Text decodability and the first-grade reader. *Reading & Writing Quarterly, 21,* 61–86.

Pogorzelski, S., & Wheldall, K. (2005). The importance of phonological processing skills for older low-progress readers. *Educational Psychology in Practice, 21,* 1–22.

Rasinski, T., & Oswald, R. (2005). Making and writing words: Constructivist word learning in a second-grade classroom. *Reading & Writing Quarterly, 21,* 151–163.

Roy, K. (2005). On sense and nonsense: Looking beyond the literacy wars. *Journal of Philosophy of Education, 39,* 99–111.

Smith, F. (1966). *The genesis of language: A psycholinguistic approach.* Cambridge, MA: M.I.T. Press, Massachusetts Institute of Technology.

Smith, F. (1972). Limitations on reading and learning to read. *English Quarterly, 5,* 1–2; 45–47.

White, T. G. (2005). Effects of systematic and strategic analogy-based phonics on grade 2 students' word reading and reading comprehension. *Reading Research Quarterly, 40,* 234–255.

Wilson, P., Martens, P., & Arya, P. (2005). Accountability for reading and readers: What the numbers don't tell. *The Reading Teacher, 58,* 622–631.

Online Resources

International Reading Association. (Posted 1997). The Role of Phonics in Reading Instruction. Position Statement.
www.reading.org/downloads/positions/ps1018_phonics.pdf

National Reading Panel Report.
www.nationalreadingpanel.org

Chapter 2

Fluency

Selections made to blend the 'moral and useful' with pleasing and ornamental, at the same time to give a flowery and animating [oral] language, instead of that dry and formal style, which is generally disgusting to young people.

—W. Pinnock (1810)

It is this capability of automatic processing [fluency] which we consider critical for the successful operation of multicomponent, complex skills such as reading.

—David LaBerge & S. Jay Samuels (1974)

The National Reading Panel (2000) concluded that fluency, defined in terms of speed, accuracy, and proper expression, is a critical part of proficient reading.

—Elfrieda Hiebert & Charles W. Fisher (2005)

It has only been since the 1980s that literacy educators have became interested in fluency as a basic component of an effective reading program. However, it is important to be clear exactly what is meant by fluency. Technically, fluency can refer to any language skill that is so thoroughly learned that it can be applied with little conscious thought. A reader can be fluent in segmenting a spoken word into phonemes or in decoding regularly spelled words. In this chapter, we use the word *fluency* to denote fluent oral reading, but we note that this result is dependent on a reader's ability to fluently apply the specific word recognition skills that contribute to oral reading. Fluent oral reading has three aspects:

1. Word recognition accuracy
2. Word recognition speed
3. Prosody (naturalness in terms of phrasing, pitch, etc.).

The importance of fluency has nothing to do with "performance" as one reads aloud. After all, the goal of fluency instruction is not to create newscasters. Reading is now seen as a limited resource system, one in which the reader's cognitive powers can only go so far. Dysfluent readers are forced to train their attention on word recognition, leaving little thinking capacity for comprehension. Fluent readers, in contrast, recognize words so rapidly that they are able to attend to meaning to a far greater extent (Kuhn, 2003; Stahl & McKenna, 2006). Moskal and Blachowicz (2006) recently described fluent reading as "flowing, smooth, and effortless" (p. 3). We agree and would add that the more effortless word recognition is, the more effort can be directed toward understanding what one reads.

To put it somewhat differently, oral reading fluency can be described as the ability to read a text, both orally and silently, with appropriate speed, accuracy, and expression (Samuels, 2002; Johns & Berglund, 2005; Rasinski, 2004). However, fluency does not guarantee comprehension. Although the relationship between fluency and comprehension is not fully understood, it is probably reasonable to suggest at this point that fluency is necessary but not sufficient for comprehension to occur.

As You Read

The following issues and teaching guidelines related to fluency are of particular importance to classroom literacy teachers.

1. Do teachers adequately understand the role and importance of fluency in reading development?
2. In your experience, do teachers provide sufficient opportunities for repeated readings and other evidence-based approaches for developing fluency?
3. Is fluency instruction accompanied by assessments designed to monitor students' progress?

References

Hiebert, E. H., & Fisher, C. W. (2005). A review of the National Reading Panel's studies on fluency: The role of text. *The Elementary School Journal, 105,* 443–444.

Hudson, R. F., Lane, H. B., & Pullen, P. C. (2005). Reading fluency assessment and instruction: What, why, and how? *The Reading Teacher, 58,* 702–714.

Johns, J. L., & Berglund, R. L. (2005). *Fluency* (2nd ed.). Dubuque, IA: Kendall Hunt.

Kuhn, M. R. (2003). Fluency in the classroom: Strategies for whole class and group work. In L. M. Morrow, L. B. Gambell, & M. Pressley (Eds.), *Best practices in literacy instruction* (pp. 127–142). New York: Guilford.

LaBerge, D., & Samuels, S. J. (1974). Toward a theory of automatic information processing in reading. *Cognitive Psychology, 6,* 295.

Moskal, M. K., & Blachowicz, C. (2006). *Partnering for fluency.* New York: Guilford.

Pinnock, W. (1810). *An introduction to the Universal Explanatory Reader.* London: Alton Publishers.

Rasinski, T. (2004). Creating fluent readers. *Educational Leadership, 61,* 46–51.

Samuels, S. J. (2002). Reading fluency: Its development and assessment. In S. J. Samuels & A. E. Farstrup (Eds.), *What research has to say about reading instruction* (3rd ed., pp. 166–183). Newark, DE: International Reading Association.

Stahl, K. A., & McKenna, M. C. (2006). *Reading research at work: Foundations of effective practice.* New York: Guilford.

Therrien, W. J., & Kubina, R. M. (2006). Developing fluency with repeated reading. *Intervention in School and Clinic, 41,* 156–160.

Creating Fluent Readers

TIMOTHY RASINSKI

• • • • •

Fifth grade has turned into a difficult year for Jonah. He is a bright student, but he has difficulty reading. Although he can accurately sound out the words he encounters, he plods along word-by-word, often hesitating at challenging vocabulary. His oral reading shows little attention to punctuation and phrasing, and it lacks expression and enthusiasm. Jonah can, however, understand material read to him. His difficulty seems to lie somewhere on the path from decoding to comprehension—in reading fluency.

Since the publication of the National Reading Panel report (2000) and other recent scholarly reviews of scientific research (Chard, Vaughn, & Tyler, 2002; Kuhn & Stahl, 2000; Rasinski & Hoffman, 2003), reading fluency has taken a front seat in discussions about student reading success and effective instruction in reading. Yet programs and materials addressing reading instruction and teacher training seldom tackle reading fluency (Rasinski & Zutell, 1996). This lack may be due to the fact that fluency has long been associated with oral reading, a form of reading traditionally viewed as having little importance in learning to read (Gibson & Levin, 1975; Smith, 2002).

Three Dimensions of Reading Fluency

Defining reading fluency may help clarify the issue. Successful reading requires readers to process the text (the surface level of reading) and comprehend the text (the deeper meaning). Reading fluency refers to the reader's ability to develop control over surface-level text processing so that he or she can focus on understanding the deeper levels of meaning embedded in the text.

Reading fluency has three important dimensions that build a bridge to comprehension. The first dimension is *accuracy in word decoding*. Readers must be able to sound out the words in a text with minimal errors. In terms of skills, this dimension refers to phonics and other strategies for decoding words. The second dimension is *automatic processing*. Readers need to expend as little mental effort as possible in the decoding aspect of reading so that they can use their finite cognitive resources for meaning

Rasinski, T. (2004). Creating fluent readers. *Educational Leadership, 61*, 46–51. Reprinted with permission. The Association for Supervision and Curriculum Development is a worldwide community of educators advocating sound policies and sharing best practices to achieve the success of each learner. To learn more, visit ASCD at www.ascd.org.

making (LaBerge & Samuels, 1974). The third dimension is what linguists call *prosodic reading* (Schreiber, 1980, 1991; Schreiber & Read, 1980). The reader must parse the text into syntactically and semantically appropriate units. If readers read quickly and accurately but with no expression in their voices, if they place equal emphasis on every word and have no sense of phrasing, and if they ignore most punctuation, blowing through periods and other markers that indicate pauses, then it is unlikely that they will fully understand the text.

Assessing Reading Fluency

Teachers can easily assess each of the three dimensions of reading fluency. To determine proficiency in decoding connected text, calculate the percentage of words a reader can accurately decode on grade-level material. An accuracy level of 90–95 percent is usually considered adequate. Thus, a 3rd grader who is progressing normally in decoding accuracy should be able to read a 100-word text written at a 3rd grade level with no more than 10 uncorrected decoding errors. More than 10 uncorrected errors per 100 words indicates that decoding is a concern, one that requires additional instruction and practice.

Teachers can normally assess automaticity in decoding by looking at the student's reading rate. Reading rates increase as students mature, so the target reading rate increases as students move through school. An easy method for determining reading rate, and thus automaticity, involves having students orally read a grade-level passage for 60 seconds and then calculating the number of words read correctly (corrected errors count as words read correctly) (Deno, 1985). Compare students' scores with target rates (oral fluency norms) for each grade level (Rasinski, 2003). Readers who fall 20–30 percent below the target rate will normally require additional instruction.

The best way to assess prosodic reading is to listen to a student read a grade-level passage and to then judge the quality of the reading using a rubric that scores a student on the elements of expression and volume, phrasing, smoothness, and pace (see Figure 1). Students who score poorly may be considered at risk in this dimension of reading fluency.

By having students read one or two grade-level passages for one minute each, teachers can get a quick sense of their students' level of decoding accuracy, automaticity, and prosodic reading. Although such quick assessments may not be definitive, they do provide teachers and school administrators with a method for screening new students, tracking students' ongoing progress in the various dimensions of reading fluency, and identifying the students who may require additional assessment and instruction.

Teaching Reading Fluency

Instruction in reading fluency depends on the area in which students require the most help. Students with difficulties in accuracy require instruction in learning how to decode words. Although teachers are familiar with this kind of instruction, which develops skills in phonics and decoding, they may not be as familiar with methods for developing students' strength in automaticity and prosodic reading.

FIGURE 1   Multidimensional Fluency Scale

Use the following rubric (1–4) to rate reader fluency in the areas of expression and volume, phrasing, smoothness, and pace.

Expression and Volume

- Reads words as if simply to get them out. Little sense of trying to make text sound like natural language. Tends to read in a quiet voice.
- Begins to use voice to make text sound like natural language in some . . . areas of the text but not in others. Focus remains largely on pronouncing the words. Still reads in a quiet voice.
- Makes text sound like natural language throughout the better part of the passage. Occasionally slips into expressionless reading. Voice volume is generally appropriate throughout the text.
- Reads with good expression and enthusiasm throughout the text. Varies expression and volume to match his or her interpretation of the passage.

Phrasing

- Reads in monotone with little sense of phrase boundaries; frequently reads word-by-word.
- Frequently reads in two- and three-word phrases, giving the impression of choppy reading; improper stress and intonation fail to mark ends of sentences and clauses.
- Reads with a mixture of run-ons, mid-sentence pauses for breath, and some choppiness; reasonable stress and intonation.
- Generally reads with good phrasing, mostly in clause and sentence units, with adequate attention to expression.

Smoothness

- Makes frequent extended pauses, hesitations, false starts, sound-outs, repetitions, and/or multiple attempts.
- Experiences several "rough spots" in text where extended pauses or hesitations are more frequent and disruptive.
- Occasionally breaks smooth rhythm because of difficulties with specific words and/or structures.
- Generally reads smoothly with some breaks, but resolves word and structure difficulties quickly, usually through self-correction.

Pace

- Reads slowly and laboriously.
- Reads moderately slowly.
- Reads with an uneven mixture of fast and slow pace.
- Consistently reads at conversational pace; appropriate rate throughout reading.

Scores range 4–16. Generally, scores below 8 indicate that fluency may be a concern. Scores of 8 or above indicate that the student is making good progress in fluency.

Adapted from Zutell & Rasinski, 1991. Used with permission.

In my own instructional efforts to develop automaticity and prosodic reading, I use *assisted readings* and *repeated readings*, two methods that research has shown to improve reading fluency (Kuhn & Stahl, 2000; National Reading Panel, 2000; Rasinski & Hoffman, 2003). Students need to hear what fluent reading sounds like and how fluent readers interpret text with their voices.

Hearing fluent reading, however, is not the same as being a fluent reader. Fortunately, assisted readings can help. After reading a passage aloud to students, I ask them to follow along with me, first silently and then aloud, as a group. Sometimes I ask students to orally read a passage with a partner who is at the same reading level. At other times, I ask more fluent readers to read with students who are having difficulty with reading (Eldredge & Quinn, 1988; Topping, 1987a, 1987b, 1995) or I have students silently read while listening to a fluent rendering of the passage on tape (Carbo, 1978; Pluck, 1995). Such practices constitute a powerful strategy for improving fluency and comprehension.

Developing fluency in reading requires practice; this is where the method of repeated readings comes in (Samuels, 1979). Research indicates that repeated readings lead not only to improvement in reading the passage but also to improvement in decoding, reading rate, prosodic reading, and comprehension of passages that the reader has not previously seen (Dowhower, 1994; Koskinen & Blum, 1986; Kuhn & Stahl, 2000; National Reading Panel, 2000).

Passages meant to be read aloud as a performance—poetry, for example, or scripts, speeches, monologues, dialogues, jokes, and riddles—are perfect texts for developing fluency. I see many teachers converting their classrooms into poetry cafés and readers' theater festivals on Friday afternoons to give students the opportunity to perform the assigned texts that they have diligently practiced during the week.

The teacher plays a key role in developing prosodic reading skills by modeling prosodic reading in classroom read-aloud sessions and then discussing the specific oral interpretation that he or she chose. Coaching provides another opportunity for developing these skills by making students aware of their own interpretation of the text and moving readers toward deeper levels of interpretation and meaning.

Here are some comments I have heard teachers make while coaching students in oral interpretation.

- "You got all the words right, Thomas, but you read too fast. It was hard for me to follow what you were trying to tell me."
- "Eliza, the way you made each character sound different in this dialogue was fantastic. It was easy and fun to listen to these characters arguing."
- "I really like how you paused between sentences. This gave me a chance to think about the author's message. Now think about finding places to pause for just a second more inside longer sentences."
- "I loved how you made your voice strong and loud in this section. It really told me that this section of the passage was important."
- "Try slowing down here and making your voice a bit softer. Remember, you're trying to tell me about something mysterious. Tell the story with your voice as well as with the words."

As assisted and repeated reading, coupled with coaching, become part of the classroom routine, teachers can track changes in students' accuracy, reading rate, and prosodic reading. Jonah, our struggling 5th grade reader, originally read a 4th grade-level passage at 60 words correct per minute and a 5th grade-level passage at 52 words correct per minute. A 5th grader, however, should be reading approximately 100–125 words correct per minute during the first half of the school year. After just two months of working in small groups with a reading teacher for three 40-minute sessions each week, Jonah's reading rate on 5th grade-level passages increased to 84 words correct per minute. His accuracy, prosodic reading, and comprehension improved as well.

Several instructional routines for developing reading fluency show promise for improving reading in all readers. Fluency-Oriented Reading Instruction (Stahl & Heubach, in press) has students engage in modeled, repeated, and assisted reading of passages from basal readers. The Fluency Development Lesson (Rasinski, Padak, Linek, & Sturtevant, 1994) uses poetry, monologues, dialogues, speeches, and other performance texts to promote reading fluency. Fast Start (Rasinski, 1995; Stevenson, 2002) promotes early reading fluency through parental involvement.

Confusing Fast with Fluent

The new focus on reading fluency has great potential for improving the reading achievement of all students, particularly those who have not met with great success in reading. I am, however, concerned about how some schools define reading fluency and how some teachers teach it. In some schools, where improvement of the reading rate has become the chief goal of fluency instruction, teachers admonish students to "pick up the pace," regularly time them on their reading to encourage them to beat their previous scores, and engage students in daily reading exercises that emphasize speed over meaning.

This is a corruption of the concept of reading fluency. If we emphasize speed at the expense of prosodic and meaningful reading, we will end up with fast readers who understand little of what they have read. Fluency instruction leads to impressive gains when it provides regular opportunities for expressive reading through assisted and repeated readings coupled with coaching; it doesn't require explicit reference to reading for speed. Students' reading rates will improve as they become naturally more efficient and confident in their ability to decode words.

Fluency Into the Future

Research (Pinnell et al., 1995) suggests that reading fluency is a crucial factor among 4th grade students, but it can also be an important issue beyond the elementary grades. I recently worked with a group of colleagues from Kent State University to examine the fluency of high school students in an urban setting. We found that variations in the reading fluency of these students accounted for approximately 30 percent of the variance in their performance on Ohio's High School Graduation Test. Clearly, this finding suggests that fluency may be an issue that goes well into the high school years, especially among students from less advantaged backgrounds.

If teachers and school leaders are truly committed to leaving no child behind in reading, then they must actively pursue the goal of reading fluency in elementary and middle school classrooms. Existing scientific research on reading fluency indicates that it is an important factor in reading education and thus should be part of any comprehensive and effective reading curriculum.

References

Allington, R. L. (1983). Fluency: The neglected reading goal. *The Reading Teacher, 36,* 556–561.

Carbo, M. (1978). Teaching reading with talking books. *The Reading Teacher, 32,* 267–273.

Chard, D. J., Vaughn, S., & Tyler, B. (2002). A synthesis of research on effective interventions for building fluency with elementary students with learning disabilities. *Journal of Learning Disabilities, 35,* 386–406.

Deno, S. L. (1985). Curriculum-based measurement: The emerging alternative. *Exceptional Children, 52,* 219–232.

Dowhower, S. L. (1994). Repeated reading revisited: Research into practice. *Reading and Writing Quarterly, 10,* 343–358.

Eldredge, J. L., & Quinn, W. (1988). Increasing reading performance of low-achieving second graders by using dyad reading groups. *Journal of Educational Research, 82,* 40–46.

Gibson, E. J., & Levin, H. (1975). *The psychology of reading.* Cambridge, MA: MIT Press.

Koskinen, P. S., & Blum, I. H. (1986). Paired repeated reading: A classroom strategy for developing fluent reading. *The Reading Teacher, 40,* 70–75.

Kuhn, M. R., & Stahl, S. A. (2000). *Fluency: A review of developmental and remedial practices* (CIERA Rep. No. 2-008). Ann Arbor, MI: Center for the Improvement of Early Reading Achievement.

LaBerge, D., & Samuels, S. A. (1974). Toward a theory of automatic information processing in reading. *Cognitive Psychology, 6,* 293–323.

National Reading Panel. (2000). *Teaching children to read: An evidence-based assessment of the scientific research literature on reading and its implications for reading instruction. Reports of the subgroups.* Washington, DC: National Institute of Child Health and Human Development.

Pinnell, G. S., Pikulski, J. J., Wixson, K. K., Campbell, J. R., Gough, P. B., & Beatty, A. S. (1995). *Listening to children read aloud.* Washington, DC: U.S. Department of Education, Office of Educational Research and Improvement.

Pluck, M. (1995). Rainbow Reading Programme: Using taped stories. *Reading Forum, 1,* 25–29.

Rasinski, T. V. (1995). Fast Start: A parental involvement reading program for primary grade students. In W. Linek & E. Sturtevant (Eds.), *Generations of literacy: 17th Yearbook of the College Reading Association* (pp. 301–312). Harrisonburg, VA: College Reading Association.

Rasinski, T. V. (2003). *The fluent reader.* New York: Scholastic.

Rasinski, T. V., & Hoffman, J. V. (2003). Oral reading in the school reading curriculum. *Reading Research Quarterly, 38,* 510–522.

Rasinski, T. V., Padak, N. D., Linek, W. L., & Sturtevant, E. (1994). Effects of fluency development on urban second-grade readers. *Journal of Educational Research, 87,* 158–165.

Rasinski, T. V., & Zutell, J. B. (1996). Is fluency yet a goal of the reading curriculum? In E. G. Sturtevant & W. M. Linek (Eds.), *Growing literacy: 18th Yearbook of the College Reading Association* (pp. 237–246). Harrisonburg, VA: College Reading Association.

Samuels, S. J. (1979). The method of repeated readings. *The Reading Teacher, 50*(5), 376–381.

Schreiber, P. A. (1980). On the acquisition of reading fluency. *Journal of Reading Behavior, 12,* 17–186.

Schreiber, P. A. (1991). Understanding prosody's role in reading acquisition. *Theory Into Practice, 30,* 158–164.

Schreiber, P. A., & Read, C. (1980). Children's use of phonetic cues in spelling, parsing, and—maybe—reading. *Bulletin of the Orton Society, 30,* 209–224.

Smith, N. B. (2002). *American reading instruction* (Special ed.). Newark, DE: International Reading Association.

Stahl, S., & Heubach, K. (in press). Fluency-oriented reading instruction. *Elementary School Journal.*

Stevenson, B. (2002). *Efficacy of the Fast Start parent tutoring program in the development of reading skills of first grade students.* Unpublished doctoral dissertation, The Ohio State University, Columbus.

Topping, K. (1987a). Paired reading: A powerful technique for parent use. *The Reading Teacher, 40,* 604–614.

Topping, K. (1987b). Peer tutored paired reading: Outcome data from ten projects. *Educational Psychology, 7,* 133–145.

Topping, K. (1995). *Paired reading, spelling, and writing.* New York: Cassell.

Zutell, J., & Rasinski, T. V. (1991). Training teachers to attend to their students' oral reading fluency. *Theory Into Practice, 30,* 211–217.

Developing Reading Fluency with Repeated Reading

WILLIAM J. THERRIEN AND RICHARD M. KUBINA, JR.

• • • • •

Reading, a complex process some have likened to rocket science (Moats, 1999), has become less of a mystery in recent years. Reports, such as that from the National Reading Panel (NRP, 2000), have highlighted extensive research that details how to best teach beginning reading. Topics in the NRP report include phonemic awareness, phonics instruction, comprehension, computer technology, and reading fluency. Fluency, in particular, has received an increasing amount of attention.

Kuhn and Stahl (2003) reviewed the literature for fluency used during developmental and remedial instruction and concluded that teachers should use fluency instruction more often because of the benefits to reading. Fluency serves as a bridge between decoding words and comprehension (Carnine, Silbert, Kame'enui, & Tarver, 2004). Moreover, oral reading fluency has been shown to predict comprehension better than such direct measures of reading comprehension as questioning, retelling, and doze (Fuchs, Fuchs, & Hosp, 2001).

How can teachers best provide fluency instruction for their students? One answer lies in a technique called *repeated reading*. Repeated reading represents an educational strategy for building reading fluency in which a student rereads a passage until meeting a criterion level (Dahl, 1977; Samuels, 1979). Research shows that repeated reading can facilitate growth in reading fluency and other aspects of reading achievement (Adams, 1990; NRP, 2000; Therrien, 2004). We present four elements to consider when deciding whether and how to implement repeated reading.

Determine If Students Have the Necessary Prerequisite Skills

Regardless of present grade level, repeated reading appears beneficial for students who read between a first- and third-grade instructional level. The intervention may also be useful for students who, although able to decode words above a third-grade level, read

Therrien, W. J., & Kubina, R. M. (2006). Developing reading fluency with repeated reading. *Intervention in School and Clinic, 41*, 156–160. By Pro-Ed, Inc. Reprinted with permission.

in a slow, halting manner. Repeated reading is not recommended for students who read below a first-grade level, as they have yet to acquire foundational reading skills (e.g., letter–sound correspondences, blending words).

The research base for repeated reading covers nondisabled students (Bryant et al., 2000; O'Shea, Sindelar, & O'Shea, 1985; Rasinski, Padak, Linek, & Sturtevant, 1994), students with learning disabilities (Bryant et al., 2000; Freeland, Skinner, Jackson, McDaniel, & Smith, 2000; Gilbert, Williams, & McLaughlin, 1996; Mathes & Fuchs, 1993; Mercer, Campbell, Miller, Mercer, & Lane, 2000; O'Shea, Sindelar, & O'Shea, 1987; Rashotte & Torgesen, 1985; Sindelar, Monda, & O'Shea, 1990; Vaughn, Chard, Bryant, Coleman, & Kouzekanani, 2000), high-functioning students with autism (Kamps, Barbetta, Leonard, & Delquadri, 1994), and students with low vision (Koenig & Layton, 1998). The intervention has also been used successfully with students in second (Dowhower, 1987) through eighth (Mercer et al., 2000) grades who have an instructional reading level between first (Weinstein & Cooke, 1992) and fifth grade (Homan, Klesius, & Hite, 1993).

It is instructive to think of repeated reading within the context of stages of learning. Mercer and Mercer (2001) described stages of learning as levels through which a student progresses. As the student advances through the stages of learning, the skill or behavior becomes increasingly more functional. The stages of learning progress as follows:

1. Entry level
2. Acquisition
3. Proficiency
4. Maintenance
5. Generalization
6. Adaptation

Teachers provide instruction in the acquisition stage and help foster an accurate performance of a skill. At the proficiency stage, the aim is to develop fluency or a behavior that can be performed with both accuracy and speed (Mercer & Mercer, 2001). Thus, repeated reading can be thought of as a well-organized practice strategy resulting in sharpened decoding skills.

Choose an Appropriate Format for the Intervention

Repeated reading has been effectively implemented in a variety of formats. Interventions have been successfully conducted by teachers (Dowhower, 1987; O'Shea et al., 1987), paraprofessionals (Mercer et al., 2000), and peer tutors (Rasinski et al., 1994; Stoddard, Valcante, Sindelar, O'Shea, & Algozzine, 1993). Repeated reading has also been conducted as both a whole-class activity (Homan et al., 1993; Simmons, Fuchs, Fuchs, Mathes, & Hodge, 1995) and a pull-out program (O'Shea et al., 1985; Sindelar et al., 1990). Whole class administration can be accomplished with a peer-tutoring format. Peer-tutoring has been demonstrated to be both flexible and empirically sound (Miller, Barbetta, & Heron, 1994). Intervention sessions should be conducted with sufficient frequency ranging from 3 to 5 times a week. Administration of repeated reading requires a time commitment between 10 to 20 min per session.

Implement Essential Instructional Components

Figure 1 shows that there are three essential instructional components to include in a repeated reading intervention (Therrien, 2004). First, passages should be read aloud to a competent tutor. Carefully selecting and preparing competent tutors is imperative because monitoring students' oral reading and providing feedback is directly tied to program success. A recent meta-analysis (Therrien, 2004) found that repeated reading interventions conducted by adults or well-trained peer tutors were, on average, three times more effective. Teachers must, therefore, ensure that all tutors are taught the skills needed to monitor tutees' oral reading and provide effective and timely feedback. Additionally, teachers should closely monitor peer groups during repeated reading sessions. If students have difficulty monitoring peers' oral reading and providing feedback, additional instruction should be given or adjustments made to the peer groupings.

The second instructional component is providing corrective feedback. Feedback on word errors and reading speed needs to be communicated to students. Depending on the type of word error, tutors should either give immediate or delayed corrective feedback. If the student hesitates on a word for 3 s or omits a word, error correction should be given immediately. Otherwise, error correction should be provided after the passage has been read but prior to having the tutee reread the passage. Error correction in both cases can be as simple as providing the word and asking the student to repeat it. After each passage reading, tutors should provide performance feedback to

FIGURE 1   Repeated Reading Essential Instructional Components

1. Passages should be read aloud to a competent tutor.

- Tutors must be trained to monitor students' oral reading and provide feedback.

2. Corrective feedback should be provided.

Feedback on word errors

- Student hesitates for 3 seconds: provide word and have student repeat it.
- Student mispronounces/omits word: provide word after reading is complete but prior to rereading.

Performance feedback

- Provide student with feedback on reading speed and accuracy after each passage reading.

3. Passages should be read until a performance criterion is reached.

- Read passages until student reaches a predetermined fluency level.

tutees on their reading speed and accuracy. For example, upon reaching the goal on the fourth reading, the tutor could say, "Great job, Sarah, You made the goal! You read 118 words and only made 1 mistake. That was 11 more words and 3 fewer errors than the last time you read it!" Providing performance feedback often motivates students as it allows them to explicitly see their progress.

The third instructional component is to reread passages until a performance criterion is reached. To ensure that students receive sufficient practice to become fluent, each passage should be reread until the student attains a performance criterion goal. Appropriate performance criterion should be selected based on the student's instructional reading level. Here are examples of performance criteria based on grade levels: second grade, 94 correct words per minute; third grade, 114 correct words per minute (Hasbrouck & Tindal, 1992). Although the use of a performance criterion is recommended, passages should, in general, be at a difficulty level where the student can achieve the goal in a reasonable amount of time. If a student consistently needs to reread passages for extended periods of time to meet the criterion, easier passages should be used. Similarly, if a tutee is consistently able to reach criterion in a few readings, more challenging passages should be used.

Select Appropriate Reading Material and Obtain Additional Supplies

Three items are necessary to conduct a repeated reading intervention: instructional-level reading passages, a timer, and data-tracking sheets. Passages within students' instructional level (i.e., passages read with 85% to 95% word accuracy) that can be read by students in 1 to 2 min are preferable. Many teachers may find that their schools already have suitable reading materials. If materials are not available, teachers may purchase commercially prepared passages. A digital countdown timer or stopwatch is needed for tutors to be able to track the reading rate of the tutee. If unavailable, tutors can be taught to time readings using the classroom clock. A tracking sheet should be designed and used to record progress through the intervention (see Figure 2 for an example).

Follow Repeated Reading Instructional Sequence

Repeated reading can become a routine for students each day during reading instruction. Steps involved with repeated reading may occur with a teacher or paraprofessional assuming the permanent role of tutor or following in the peer–tutor format procedure:

1. Students pair up and gather their reading material. Materials consist of the reading passage (100- to 200-word passages) at the instructional level, a copy of the passage or a transparency and dry-erase marker, and a data sheet.

FIGURE 2   Sample Repeated Reading Tracking Sheet

Tutee's name: **Sarah A.**
Tutor's name: **Tasha S.**

DATE	GOAL	PASSAGE #	REREADING #	WORDS READ	ERRORS	CORRECT WORDS	GOAL MET?
5-4	114	12	1	74	10	64	no
5-4	114	12	2	87	7	80	no
5-4	114	12	3	98	4	94	no
5-4	114	12	4	118	1	117	yes

2. One student begins as the reader and the other student acts as the counter. The student who is the counter may also be the timer, depending on whether the teacher starts the timing for the group or has the students time each other.
3. When the timer begins, the reader reads and the counter marks incorrect or missed words on the reading passage. Should a reader hesitate on a word for 3 s or more, the counter should provide the word and have the reader repeat it and continue reading. If using a transparency, the reader puts the transparency over her copy of the passage and places an X on missed words with the dry-erase pen.
4. After the timer or teacher indicates the 1-min interval has ended, the counter provides feedback and has the reader repeat the correct pronunciation for words she missed.
5. The counter records the number of words read, errors, and correct words per minute on the data tracking sheet.
6. The student engages in another repeated reading by rereading the passage and receiving feedback. Students can reread a passage up to 4 times per session (Rashotte & Torgesen, 1985).
7. Students switch roles, and Steps 2 through 5 are repeated.
8. The teacher and students end the repeated reading procedure on a positive note.

Conclusion

A call has been made for incorporating techniques to develop reading fluency in the classroom (Kuhn & Stahl, 2003; NRP, 2000; Rasinski, 2000). Repeated reading directly targets oral reading fluency and can easily be integrated in an existing reading program. Previous research has shown that repeated reading is effective with a variety of students, including students with disabilities. Using essential instructional components and selecting appropriate materials maximizes the effectiveness of repeated reading. Following the guidelines suggested in this article, teachers can easily incorporate repeated reading into their existing classroom routines.

References

Adams, M. J. (1990). *Beginning to read: Thinking and learning about print.* Cambridge, MA: MIT Press.

Bryant, D. P., Vaughn, S., Linan-Thompson, S., Ugel, N., Hamff, A., & Hougen, M. (2000). Reading outcomes for students with and without reading disabilities in general education middle-school content area classes. *Learning Disability Quarterly, 23,* 238–252.

Carnine, D. W., Silbert, J., Kame'enui, E. J., & Tarver, S. G. (2004). *Direct instruction reading* (4th ed.). Upper Saddle River, NJ: Prentice Hall/Merrill.

Dahl, P. R. (1977). An experimental program for teaching high speed word recognition and comprehension skills. In J. E. Burton, T. Lovitt, & T. Rowland (Eds.), *Communications research in learning disabilities and mental retardation* (pp. 33–65). Baltimore: University Park Press.

Dowhower, S. L. (1987). Effects of repeated reading on second-grade transitional readers' fluency and comprehension. *Reading Research Quarterly, 22*(4), 389–406.

Freeland, J. T., Skinner, C. H., Jackson, B., McDaniel, C. E., & Smith, S. (2000). Measuring and increasing silent reading comprehension rates: Empirically validating a repeated reading intervention. *Psychology in the Schools, 37*(5), 415–429.

Fuchs, L. S., Fuchs, D., & Hosp, M. K. (2001). Oral reading fluency as an indicator of reading competence: A theoretical, empirical, and historical analysis. *Scientific Studies of Reading, 5*(3), 239–256.

Gilbert, L. M., Williams, R. L., & McLaughlin, T. F. (1996). Use of assisted reading to increase correct reading rates and decrease error rates of students with learning disabilities. *Journal of Applied Behavior Analysis, 29*(2), 255–257.

Hasbrouck, J. E., & Tindal, G. (1992). Curriculum-based oral reading fluency norms for students in grades 2 through 5. *Teaching Exceptional Children, 24*(3), 41–44.

Homan, S. P., Klesius, J. P., & Hite, C. (1993). Effects of repeated readings and nonrepetitive strategies on students' fluency and comprehension. *The Journal of Educational Research, 87*(2), 94–99.

Kamps, D. M., Barbetta, P. M., Leonard, B. R., & Delquadri, J. (1994). Classwide peer tutoring: An integration strategy to improve reading skills and promote peer interactions among students with autism and general education peers. *Journal of Applied Behavior Analysis, 27*(1), 49–61.

Koenig, A. J., & Layton, C. A. (1998). Increasing reading fluency in elementary students with low vision through repeated reading. *Journal of Visual Impairment and Blindness, 92*(5), 276–292.

Kuhn, M. R., & Stahl, S. A. (2003). Fluency: A review of developmental and remedial practices. *Journal of Educational Psychology, 95*(1), 3–21.

Mathes, P. G., & Fuchs, L. S. (1993). Peer-mediated reading instruction in special education resource rooms. *Learning Disability Research and Practice, 8*(4), 233–243.

Mercer, C. D., Campbell, K. U., Miller, M. D., Mercer, K. D., & Lane, H. B. (2000). Effects of a reading fluency intervention for middle schoolers with specific learning disabilities. *Learning Disability Research and Practice, 15*(4), 179–189.

Mercer, C. D., & Mercer, A. R. (2001). *Teaching students with learning problems* (6th ed.). Upper Saddle River, NJ: Prentice Hall/Merrill.

Miller, A. D., Barbetta, P. M., & Heron, T. A. (1994). START tutoring: Designing, training, implementing, adapting, and evaluating tutoring programs for school and home settings. In R. Gardner, D. Sainato, J. Cooper, T. Heron, W. Heward, J. Eshleman, & T. Grossi (Eds.), *Behavior analysis in education: Focus on measurably superior instruction* (pp. 265–282). Belmont, CA: Brooks-Cole.

Moats, L. C. (1999). *Teaching reading is rocket science: What expert teachers of reading should know and be able to do.* Washington, DC: American Federation of Teachers.

National Reading Panel. (2000). *Report of the National Reading Panel: Teaching children to read* [Online]. Available: http://www.nichd.nih.gov/publications/nrp-pubskey.cfm [2000, November, 10].

O'Shea, L. J., Sindelar, P. T., & O'Shea, D. J. (1985). The effects of repeated readings and attentional cues on reading fluency and comprehension. *Journal of Reading Behavior, 17*(2), 129–141.

O'Shea, L. J., Sindelar, P. T., & O'Shea, D. J. (1987). The effects of repeated reading and attentional cues on the reading fluency and comprehension of learning disabled readers. *Learning Disabilities Research, 2*(2), 103–109.

Rashotte, C. A., & Torgesen, J. K. (1985). Repeated reading and reading fluency in learning disabled children. *Reading Research Quarterly, 20,* 180–188.

Rasinski, T. V. (2000). Speed does matter in reading. *The Reading Teacher, 54*(2), 146–151.

Rasinski, T., Padak, N., Linek, W., & Sturtevant, E. (1994). Effects of fluency development on urban second-grade readers. *The Journal of Educational Research, 87*(3), 158–165.

Samuels, S. J. (1979). The method of repeated readings. *The Reading Teacher, 41*, 756–760.

Simmons, D. C., Fuchs, L. S., Fuchs, D., Mathes, P., & Hodge, J. P. (1995). Effects of explicit teaching and peer tutoring on the reading achievement of learning-disabled and low-performing students in regular classrooms. *The Elementary School Journal, 95*(5), 387–408.

Sindelar, P. T., Monda, L. E., & O'Shea, L. J. (1990). Effects of repeated readings on instructional- and mastery-level readers. *The Journal of Educational Research, 83*(4), 220–226.

Stoddard, K., Valcante, G., Sindelar, P. T., O'Shea, L., & Algozzine, B. (1993). Increasing reading rate and comprehension: The effects of repeated readings, sentence segmentation, and intonation training. *Reading Research and Instruction, 32*(4), 53–65.

Therrien, W. J. (2004). Fluency and comprehension gains as a result of repeated reading: A meta-analysis. *Remedial and Special Education, 25*(4), 252–261.

Vaughn, S., Chard, D. J., Bryant, D. P., Coleman, M., & Kouzekanani, K. (2000). Fluency and comprehension interventions for third-grade students. *Remedial and Special Education, 21*(6), 325–335.

Weinstein, G., & Cooke, N. L. (1992). The effects of two repeated reading interventions on generalization of fluency. *Learning Disability Quarterly, 15*, 21–28.

Reading Fluency Assessment and Instruction: What, Why, and How?

ROXANNE F. HUDSON, HOLLY B. LANE, AND PAIGE C. PULLEN

• • • • •

Reading fluency is gaining new recognition as an essential element of every reading program, especially for students who struggle in reading. Reading fluency is one of the defining characteristics of good readers, and a lack of fluency is a common characteristic of poor readers. Differences in reading fluency not only distinguish good readers from poor, but a lack of reading fluency is also a reliable predictor of reading comprehension problems (Stanovich, 1991). Once struggling readers learn sound–symbol relationships through intervention and become accurate decoders, their lack of fluency emerges as the next hurdle they face on their way to reading proficiency (Torgesen et al., 2001; Torgesen, Rashotte, Alexander, Alexander, & MacPhee, 2003). This lack of fluent reading is a problem for poor readers because they tend to read in a labored, disconnected fashion with a focus on decoding at the word level that makes comprehension of the text difficult, if not impossible.

The speed with which text is translated into spoken language has been identified as a major component of reading proficiency (Adams, 1990; Allington, 1983; Fuchs, Fuchs, Hosp, & Jenkins, 2001; Hasbrouk & Tindal, 1992; Samuels, Schermer, & Reinking, 1992). Many struggling readers may not gain reading fluency incidentally or automatically. In contrast to skilled readers, they often need direct instruction in how to read fluently and sufficient opportunities for intense, fluency-focused practice incorporated into their reading program (Allinder, Dunse, Brunken, & Obermiller-Krolikowski, 2001). The National Research Council (Snow, Burns, & Griffin, 1998) recommended that reading fluency be regularly assessed in the classroom and effective instruction be provided when dysfluent reading is detected. Despite the importance of reading fluency and the need for direct teaching (National Institute of Child Health and Human Development [NICHD], 2000), it is often neglected in reading instructional programs (Allington, 1983; Kame'enui & Simmons, 2001). Teachers who are concerned about meeting the needs of all students in their classrooms should consider

Hudson, R. F., Lane, H. B., & Pullen, Paige C. (2005, May). Reading fluency assessment and instruction: What, why, and how? *The Reading Teacher, 58*(8), 702–714. Reprinted with permission of the International Reading Association.

whether they know who their dysfluent readers are and what types of instruction they plan to provide for those readers.

What Is Reading Fluency and Why Is It Important?

Fluent reading comprises three key elements: *accurate* reading of connected text at a conversational *rate* with appropriate *prosody* or expression (Hudson, Mercer, & Lane, 2000). A fluent reader can maintain this performance for long periods of time, can retain the skill after long periods of no practice, and can generalize across texts. A fluent reader is also not easily distracted and reads in an effortless, flowing manner.

The most compelling reason to focus instructional efforts on students becoming fluent readers is the strong correlation between reading fluency and reading comprehension (Allington, 1983; Johns, 1993; Samuels, 1988; Schreiber, 1980). Each aspect of fluency has a clear connection to text comprehension. Without accurate word reading, the reader will have no access to the author's intended meaning, and inaccurate word reading can lead to misinterpretations of the text. Poor automaticity in word reading or slow, laborious movement through the text taxes the reader's capacity to construct an ongoing interpretation of the text. Poor prosody can lead to confusion through inappropriate or meaningless groupings of words or through inappropriate applications of expression.

Automaticity and Working Memory

LaBerge and Samuels (1974) suggested that there is a limited capacity of attention and working memory in cognitive processing and that learning one aspect of reading (word identification) to a criterion of automaticity frees the processing space for higher order thinking (comprehension). Attentional capacity is limited, so more resources are available for comprehension if word identification processes occur relatively effortlessly. Because comprehension requires higher order processes that cannot become automatic, word identification must become the automatic process. The only other option (and the one most commonly attempted by beginning readers) is to switch attention rapidly back and forth from identifying words on the page to constructing meaning, thus limiting the ability to do either one well.

Quick and effortless word identification is important because when one can read words automatically, one's limited cognitive resources can be used for comprehension (e.g., NICHD, 2000), and many times the differences in comprehension between good and poor readers can be attributed to differences in the level of automatic decoding (Perfetti & Hogaboam, 1975; Torgesen, 1986). Fawcett and Nicholson (1994) hypothesized that the difficulties experienced by students with dyslexia are due to an underlying deficit in automaticity (i.e., processing speed deficits). Fluent readers are better at seeing a word in a single eye fixation and do not need as many refixations or regressions. The placement and overlap of the eye fixations of fluent readers are more efficient than those of less skilled readers. Faster readers also make shorter fixations, longer jumps between fixations, and fewer regressions than slow readers (NICHD, 2000).

Link between Reading Accuracy and Reading Proficiency

Word-reading accuracy refers to the ability to recognize or decode words correctly. Strong understanding of the alphabetic principle, the ability to blend sounds together (Ehri & McCormick, 1998), and knowledge of a large bank of high-frequency words are required for word-reading accuracy. Poor word-reading accuracy has obvious negative influences on reading comprehension and fluency. A reader who reads words incorrectly is unlikely to understand the author's intended message, and inaccurate word reading can lead to misinterpretations of the text. In the 2002 Oral Reading Fluency Study, conducted as part of the National Assessment of Educational Progress (NAEP), researchers found that when children made errors that changed the meaning of the text, there was a more direct relationship to reading comprehension than the errors that did not result in a change of meaning (National Assessment Governing Board, 2002). They also noted that errors that do not affect meaning are rare.

When words cannot be read accurately from memory as sight words, they must be analyzed. Thus it is important to teach word-identification strategies, such as decoding and use of analogy (Ehri, 2002), to figure out unknown words. Decoding is a sequentially executed process where the reader blends sounds to form words from their parts. This can take place by blending individual phonemes (beginning decoding) or phonograms (a more advanced form of decoding; Ehri, 2002). In order to accurately decode words, readers need to be able to accurately (a) identify the sounds represented by the letters or letter combinations, (b) blend phonemes, (c) read phonograms (common patterns across words), and (d) use both letter–sound and meaning cues to determine exactly the pronunciation and meaning of the word that is in the text (e.g., knowing how to correctly pronounce *bow* in two different sentences: The dog had *a bow* tied around her neck. The *bow* of the ship was tall). Instruction in all of these subprocesses is necessary for the first part of reading fluency: accurate word identification.

> Because the ability to obtain meaning from print depends so strongly on the development of word recognition accuracy and reading fluency, both should be regularly assessed in the classroom, permitting timely and effective instructional response when difficulty or delay is apparent. (NICHD, 2000, p. 7)

Link between Reading Rate and Reading Proficiency

Reading rate comprises both word-level automaticity and the speed and fluidity with which a reader moves through connected text. Automaticity is quick and effortless identification of words in or out of context (Ehri & McCormick, 1998; Kuhn & Stahl, 2000). The automaticity with which a reader can decode or recognize words is almost as important as word-reading accuracy. It is not enough to get the word right if a great deal of cognitive effort is required to do so; automaticity frees up cognitive resources that can be devoted to text comprehension (LaBerge & Samuels, 1974).

Most educators quantify rate in terms of reading speed—either the number of words read correctly per minute or the length of time it takes for a reader to complete a passage. Poor readers are often characterized by slow, laborious reading of connected text. Many fluency interventions focus on increasing reading rate, because slow reading can result in weakened comprehension (Mastropieri, Leinart, & Scruggs, 1999). Students who read slowly often fail to complete their work, lose interest in school, and seldom read for pleasure (Moats, 2001).

There is strong correlational evidence that increased reading rate is related to higher levels of comprehension in average and poor readers (Breznitz, 1987; Deno, Marston, Shinn, & Tindal, 1983; Dowhower, 1987; Perfetti & Hogaboam, 1975; Rasinski, 1989, 1990; Tenenbaum & Wolking, 1989), as well as in students with reading disabilities (Breznitz, 1991; Chard, Vaughn, & Tyler, 2002; Fuchs, Fuchs, & Maxwell, 1988). Fuchs et al. (2001) proposed that "oral reading fluency [i.e., rate and accuracy] represents a complicated, multifaceted performance" (p. 239) that captures a variety of processes related to reading: using sound–symbol relationships to translate text to sound, accessing word meanings, making connections between words and sentences, relating textual meaning to prior knowledge, and making inferences. Oral reading rate is also related to teacher judgments of proficiency; is correlated with criterion-referenced tests in basal curricula; and differentiates between students in special, compensatory, and general education programs (Deno et al., 1983). Thus, oral reading rate is considered an important measure of reading proficiency and a tool for progress monitoring, just as a thermometer can be used to measure the current temperature and ongoing changes (Deno, Mirkin, & Chiang, 1982; Fuchs & Fuchs, 1992; Fuchs et al., 1988; Hasbrouk & Tindal, 1992; Shinn, Good, Knutson, & Tilly, 1992).

Link between Prosody and Reading Proficiency

Prosody is a linguistic term to describe the rhythmic and tonal aspects of speech: the "music" of oral language. Prosodic features are variations in pitch (intonation), stress patterns (syllable prominence), and duration (length of time) that contribute to expressive reading of a text (Allington, 1983; Dowhower, 1991; Schreiber, 1980, 1991). These elements signal question, surprise, exclamation, and other meanings beyond the semantics of the words being spoken. When these features are present and appropriate in oral reading, the reader is reading prosodically, or "with expression." A fundamental task of fluent reading is to supply the prosodic features in a text, although they are not graphically represented (Schreiber, 1980). Schreiber suggested that fluent readers use the other cues (i.e., morphemic, syntactic, semantic, and pragmatic) present in text to organize the text into meaningful phrases and read with correct prosody (i.e., reading that sounds like speaking). Struggling readers are often characterized as reading in a monotone without expression or with inappropriate phrasing. Because prosody and reading comprehension seem to have a reciprocal relationship, prosody is an important area of focus for fluency instruction.

Prosodic reading provides evidence that the reader understands what is being read (Kuhn & Stahl, 2000). Despite this connection, little research has been conducted exploring the relationship between prosody and reading comprehension, and what little research has been done has found an unclear relationship. While studying repeated readings, Dowhower (1987) found that as the students' reading rate, accuracy, and comprehension increased, so did their prosodic reading on practiced and unpracticed passages, but she could not determine which caused the other. Pinnell et al. (1995) rated a representative sample of fourth graders according to a prosody scale.

They found that higher levels of prosody were associated with higher scores on the main NAEP reading proficiency scale and concluded that decisions about the causal relationships are unclear. It is unclear whether prosody is a cause or result of comprehension (Kuhn & Stahl, 2000) or if the relationship is reciprocal; however, it is clear that the amount of correct expression indicates to a trained ear how much the reader comprehended the text.

Assessing Reading Fluency

Teachers need to listen to students read aloud to make judgments about their progress in reading fluency (Zutell & Rasinski, 1991). Systematic observation helps assess student progress and determine instructional needs. Teachers observing students' oral reading fluency should consider each critical aspect of fluent reading: word-reading accuracy, rate, and prosody. Table 1 provides a summary of assessments for oral reading fluency, including standardized assessments and assessments for monitoring student progress.

Assessing Accuracy

Measurement of students' word-reading accuracy can take numerous forms. Simply listening to oral reading and counting the number of errors per 100 words can provide invaluable information for the selection of appropriate text for various instructional purposes for an individual or group of students. A running record and miscue analysis (Clay, 1984, 1993) provides more detailed information about the student's accuracy. Through careful examination of error patterns, a teacher can determine which strategies the student is using and which strategies the student is failing to use. For example, observation of a student's attempts to figure out an unknown word might yield evidence of phonemic blending, guessing based on context, or a combination of decoding and contextual analysis. These observations can provide information about areas in need of further instruction to improve word-reading accuracy.

Assessing Rate

Contextual reading rather than reading words in a list (Jenkins, Fuchs, van den Broek, Espin, & Deno, 2003) and oral reading rather than silent reading (Fuchs, Fuchs, Eaton, & Hamlet, 2000 cited in Fuchs et al., 2001) were both found to be the best measures of reading rate. Measuring reading rate should encompass consideration of both word-reading automaticity and reading speed in connected text. Assessment of automaticity can include tests of sight-word knowledge or tests of decoding rate. Tests of decoding rate often consist of rapid decoding of nonwords. Measurement of nonword reading rate ensures that the construct being assessed is the student's ability to automatically decode words using sound–symbol knowledge.

Measurement of reading speed is most typically accomplished through timed readings. Timings of a student's reading of connected text allows a teacher to observe the number of words read correctly and the number of errors made in a given time period. Data from timed readings are usually recorded on a timing chart (see Figure 1 for an example).

TABLE 1 Reading Fluency Assessments

ASSESSMENT	PUBLISHER	DESCRIPTION
AIMSweb Standard Reading Assessment Passages (RAPs)	Edformation	AIMSweb RAPs provide teachers with passages for quick but accurate formative assessment of students' oral reading fluency. These assessments are a Curriculum Based Measurement (CBM) system that is intended to assist teachers in making instructional decisions and monitoring student progress. RAPs have been field-tested and validated. The AIMSweb system includes a Web-based software management system for data collection and reporting.
Dynamic Indicators of Basic Early Literacy Skills (DIBELS)	University of Oregon and Sopris West	DIBELS contains a subtest of Oral Reading Fluency and Retell Fluency for students in the first through third grades. The Oral Reading Fluency is standardized and individually administered. Students read a passage aloud for one minute. The number of correct words per minute is determined to provide the oral reading fluency rate. The Retell Fluency is a measure of comprehension that accompanies the Oral Reading Fluency assessment.
Gray Oral Reading Test, Fourth Edition (GORT-4)	PRO-ED	The GORT-4 is a norm-referenced measure of oral reading performance. Skills assessed include rate, accuracy, fluency (rate and accuracy combined), comprehension, and overall reading ability (rate, accuracy, and comprehension combined).
National Assessment of Educational Progress (NAEP) Fluency Scale	National Center for Education Statistics (NCES)	The NAEP Fluency Scale provides a descriptive guide for oral reading performance based on the student's "naturalness" of reading. The student's performance is rated on a four-point scale, with emphasis placed on phrasing of words, adherence to syntax, and expressiveness (Pinnell et al., 1995). Accuracy and rate are measured and determined by calculating the correct words read per minute.
Reading Fluency Monitor by Read Naturally	Read Naturally	The Reading Fluency Monitor is an assessment instrument that allows teachers to monitor student progress. Fall, winter, and spring administrations are recommended. Grade-level passages are available for grades 1–8, as well as a software program for reporting and record keeping.

Timed readings (Samuels, 1979) can be used to measure and increase word-reading accuracy and passage-reading rate. Timed readings are conducted using books or passages the student has read before that are at an independent reading level (i.e., books the student can read with 95% accuracy or above). To conduct timed readings, follow these steps:

1. Record a baseline rate on a new passage by having the student read the passage without knowing that he or she is being timed. The number of words read correctly for that minute are recorded as the baseline.

Timed Reading Record

Student _____   Tutor _____   Goal _____

Week of   2/6   2/13   2/20   _____   _____   _____

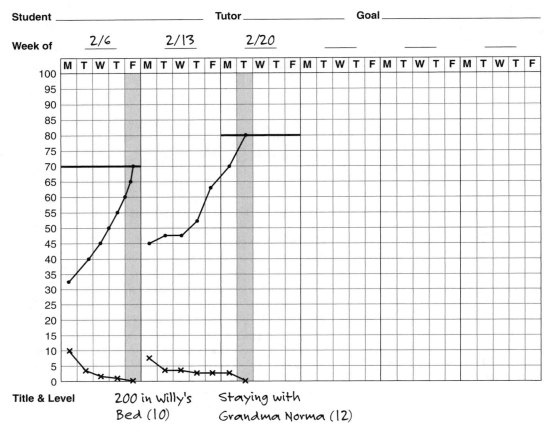

Title & Level   200 in Willy's   Staying with
                 Bed (10)   Grandma Norma (12)

FIGURE 1   Timing Chart

2. Note the errors as the student reads. After the reading, discuss any errors and work on them by rereading the parts that were difficult or by doing word-study activities.
3. Set a goal for the next reading by asking the student to read five or six more words, or maybe another line. The goal should be a reasonable one that can be attained within the next few attempts. If the student made three or more errors in the first attempt, the goal may be to decrease the errors and keep the correct word per minute (CWPM) the same.
4. Record the goal on the graph with a highlighter.
5. Time the student again for one minute and record the CWPM and errors.
6. Discuss the errors; set another goal and repeat the process.
7. Timings should be done at least three times per week in order to build consistency.
8. When the student levels off and is no longer increasing the CWPM, it is time to select a new passage.

9. Select a new passage and begin the process again by taking a baseline reading.
10. Once students become familiar with the procedures involved in timed readings, they can record their own progress on the timing chart, record an audiotape of their own oral reading and chart their progress, or work in pairs to listen and record the reading rate and accuracy of their peers.

Assessing Prosody

A student's reading prosody can be measured only through observation of an oral reading of a connected text. During the reading of a passage, a teacher can listen to the student's inflection, expression, and phrase boundaries. The following is a simple checklist of oral reading prosody observation:

1. Student placed vocal emphasis on appropriate words.
2. Student's voice tone rose and fell at appropriate points in the text.
3. Student's inflection reflected the punctuation in the text (e.g., voice tone rose near the end of a question).
4. In narrative text with dialogue, student used appropriate vocal tone to represent characters' mental states, such as excitement, sadness, fear, or confidence.
5. Student used punctuation to pause appropriately at phrase boundaries.
6. Student used prepositional phrases to pause appropriately at phrase boundaries.
7. Student used subject–verb divisions to pause appropriately at phrase boundaries.
8. Student used conjunctions to pause appropriately at phrase boundaries.

A more quantifiable scale that provides a score that can be used to compare a student against him or herself across time or between students in a class or school can be found in Zutell and Rasinski (1991). Prosody in oral reading should signal reading comprehension of the reader and enhance listening comprehension of the listener. That is, prosodic readers understand what they read and make it easier for others as well.

Evidence-Based Instructional Methods to Develop Fluency

Fluency instruction is not a reading program itself, but it is part of a comprehensive reading program that emphasizes both research-based practices and reading for meaning. As teachers consider integrating fluency instruction into that program, questions often arise. Once they know who the students in their classrooms with fluency problems are, what should they do? There are several research-based general recommendations for how to provide reading instruction to build fluency with struggling readers. Research with average, struggling, and learning-disabled students indicates that teachers should take the following steps:

● Model fluent oral reading (Blevins, 2001; Rasinski, 2003) using teacher read-alouds and as part of repeated reading interventions (Chard et al., 2002).

- Provide direct instruction and feedback to teach decoding of unknown words, correct expression and phrasing, the return-sweep eye movement, and strategies that fluent readers use (NICHD, 2000; Snow et al., 1998).
- Provide oral support and modeling for readers (Rasinski, 2003) using assisted reading, choral reading, paired reading, audiotapes, and computer programs.
- Provide students with plenty of materials at their independent reading level to read on their own (Allington, 2000).
- Offer many opportunities for practice using repeated readings of progressively more difficult text (Chard et al., 2002; Meyer & Felton, 1999; Rasinski, 2003; Samuels, 1979).
- Encourage prosody development through cueing phrase boundaries (Rasinski, 2003; Schreiber, 1980).

Instructional Methods Primarily Focused on Rate and Accuracy

Repeated Readings

The repeated readings technique (Samuels, 1979) has many different approaches that vary in levels of support and emphasis on building speed. Repeated readings emphasizes practice as a way of working on all of the areas of reading fluency—accuracy, rate, and prosody—and is one of the most-studied methods for increasing reading fluency (Kuhn & Stahl, 2000; Meyer & Felton, 1999; NICHD, 2000).

Timed Repeated Readings.   Samuels (1979) was the first to describe the repeated readings method that is used so often today. It consists of (a) selecting a short passage at the student's instructional level, (b) setting a rate criterion, and (c) having the student read and reread the passage over time until the rate criterion is reached. The oral reading rate is determined by timing the student for one minute and then counting how many correct words were read. Charting of the rate is recommended as a means of record keeping and of maintaining motivation with the student (Figure 1). Timed repeated readings are the basis for several methods available to develop reading fluency. These methods, which focus on increasing rate and accuracy, typically measure the number of words correctly read in one minute and involve the student in charting data. For example, Great Leaps Reading uses phonics timings to increase decoding automaticity, sight-phrase timings to increase recognition of high-frequency words, and story timings to increase the rate of reading connected text. (See Table 2 for more information.) In a study with middle school students, Great Leaps was found to have significant positive effects on reading achievement (Mercer, Campbell, Miller, Mercer, & Lane, 2000). Other timed reading programs include Jamestown Timed Readings Plus, which includes both narrative and related expository passages, and QuickReads, which focuses on nonfiction text (Table 2).

Repeated Readings with Recorded Models.   Using audiotaped text to support repeated readings is an efficient method because it provides the student with a fluent

TABLE 2   Instructional Resources for Developing Reading Fluency

PROGRAM/ RESOURCE	PUBLISHER	DESCRIPTION
Carbo Recorded Books	National Reading Styles Institute	Carbo Recorded Books are audiotaped literature for children and adolescents. These materials provide a resource for audio-assisted repeated reading.
Great Leaps Reading	Diarmuid, Inc.	Great Leaps is a tutorial program for students with reading problems. Programs are available for students in Grades K–12 and adults. In the K–2 edition, fluency practice is provided for sound awareness, letter recognition, phonics, sight words and phrases, and stories. The editions for beyond grade 2 are divided into phonics, sight phrases, and reading fluency
Jamestown Timed Readings Plus	Jamestown Education, Glencoe/ McGraw-Hill	Jamestown Timed Readings Plus is a program designed to help secondary struggling readers increase their reading rate and fluency with 400-word nonfiction passages followed by related fiction passages and comprehension questions.
Phonics Phones	Crystal Springs Books	Whisper phones or Phonic Phones are pieces of PVC pipe elbows connected to form a telephone shape. This shape amplifies the sound of the student's voice, which focuses the student's attention on reading and allows the student to evaluate prosody and rate.
QuickReads	Modern Curriculum Press	QuickReads is a reading fluency program for students in grades 2–4. The lesson requires approximately 15 minutes and includes short nonfiction passages. The program has been field-tested and has shown positive effects on students' reading fluency and comprehension.
Read-Along Radio Dramas	Balance Publishing Company	This program includes a recording of a radio play with full cast and sound effects, a word-for- word read-along script and annotated script of the original story, and a variety of student activities.
Read Naturally	Read Naturally	Read Naturally is an individually paced program for improving students' reading fluency. A software version is available that guides students through lessons and tracks individual progress. An audio version is also available on CD or cassette tape with accompanying passage blackline masters.
Soliloquy Reading Assistant	Soliloquy Learning	Soliloquy Reading Assistant is a software program designed to increase students' opportunities for oral reading practice. The computer guides the reader by highlighting the words to be read and changing the color as they are read correctly. If a student hesitates on a word too long, Soliloquy supplies the challenging word. The computer also prompts the student to reread a sentence if it was read with poor fluency and includes a progress-monitoring feature that the student or teacher can use.

model without requiring individual teacher assistance. In a comparison of assisted (audiotape) and unassisted repeated readings, Dowhower (1987) found that both resulted in significantly higher word reading accuracy, comprehension, fluency, and prosody. The assisted condition seemed to affect prosody more than the unassisted. There are several methods of repeated readings with recorded models.

Most recorded books found in classroom listening centers are designed for listening rather than for reading along. They are read too fast for struggling readers to keep up, and the addition of music or other sound effects can be distracting. Therefore, although a listening center may be useful for developing skills such as listening comprehension, vocabulary, or sense of story, it is unlikely to improve reading fluency, especially for struggling students. Marie Carbo developed a method of recording books that makes it possible for a developing reader to read along with the recording. Carbo Recorded Books are recorded at a much slower pace than listening center books, yet they maintain the expression and inflection necessary for understanding (see Table 2). Using this method, Carbo (1981, 1992) reported reading gains among struggling readers. Thus, adding a read-along center to a classroom reading program can promote reading fluency.

Read Naturally (Table 2) is a repeated reading method that includes both audiotaped and computer models. Read Naturally combines supported oral reading and independent repeated reading. The student begins with a one-minute "cold" reading to the teacher or computer. Then, the student practices reading the same passage three or four times while listening to a recorded fluent model. The student then continues independent practice without the recording. Finally, the student reads to the teacher or computer again. In the computer version, the student can receive feedback during the independent reading by clicking on difficult words and noting where they stopped during each timed reading. Hasbrouk, Ihnot, and Rogers (1999) found encouraging improvements in reading fluency from Read Naturally with both beginning readers and struggling older readers.

Soliloquy Reading Assistant (Table 2) is a software program designed to increase students' opportunities for oral reading practice. Soliloquy employs speech recognition software to record what a student reads and to measure progress over time and offers a variety of text genres, including fiction, poetry, biographies, and folktales. Although Soliloquy was developed on a solid research base, as of this writing, no studies of its effectiveness have been published.

Common Instructional Questions Related to Developing Reading Rate

What Type of Text Should I Use?   We recommend practicing with text at an independent level (95–100% accuracy). We also suggest using relatively short passages, texts from a variety of genres, and text that is motivating to the individual student. The accuracy, speed, and expressiveness of poor readers are more affected by text difficulty than average readers (Young & Bowers, 1995), and making proper text selection is much more critical when working with struggling readers. The number of shared words facilitates transfer from practiced text to unpracticed text (Dowhower, 1987; Rashotte & Torgesen, 1985). Rashotte and Torgesen found that passages that shared many of the same words led to transfer of training from repeated readings to another passage.

How Do I Know When to Move My Student to a New Passage? A question many teachers ask is "How fast should they have their students read?" Another is "How much progress should they expect?" These questions do not have definitive answers and depend on the student's age, the type of text the student is reading, and the purpose for which he or she is reading. However, Howell and Lorson-Howell (1990) suggested that fluency aims be determined by sampling the performances of successful students working in the target setting. Using similar reasoning, reading rates were established in "norming" studies designed to determine how varying fluency rates related to levels of reading achievement among large samples of students (Good, Simmons, & Kame'enui, 2001; Hasbrouk & Tindal, 1992; School Board of Alachua County, 1997). Recommendations from these studies should serve as a general guide for determining students' goals for oral reading rate (Table 3).

Fuchs, Fuchs, Hamlett, Walz, and Germann (1993) suggested that an essential step in assessing reading fluency was to establish how much weekly growth a teacher should expect. A standard for weekly improvement helps teachers decide whether a student's rate of progress is sufficient or whether an adjustment in teaching strategies is needed. Using data from their norming study, Fuchs et al. (1993) suggested that on average, the following are reasonable expectations for improvement among average, poor, and disabled readers:

- First grade: 2–3 words per week increase in CWPM
- Second grade: 2.5–3.5 words per week increase in CWPM

TABLE 3   Recommended Reading Fluency Rates in Connected Text

GRADE		CORRECT WORDS PER MINUTE
First grade	Winter	39
	Spring	40–60
Second grade	Fall	53
	Winter	72–78
	Spring	82–94
Third grade	Fall	79
	Winter	84–93
	Spring	100–114
Fourth grade	Fall	90–99
	Winter	98–112
	Spring	105–118
Fifth grade	Fall	105
	Winter	110–118
	Spring	118–128

Note: Adapted from Good, Simmons, & Kame'enui (2001); Hasbrouk & Tindal (1992); and the School Board of Alachua County (1997).

- Third grade: 1–3 words per week increase in CWPM
- Fourth grade: .85–1.5 words per week increase in CWPM

Is Isolated Word Reading Practice a Good Idea?   Single-word training, either in a list or on flashcards, appears to be valuable for helping struggling readers develop reading fluency. Several researchers (e.g., Levy, Abello, & Lysynchuk, 1997; Tan & Nicholson, 1997; van den Bosch, van Bon, & Schreuder, 1995) have found that with poor readers, practice reading words in isolation led to improved reading fluency in context; the practice of the words generalized to textual reading.

Instructional Methods Focused on Prosody

In addition to reading with recorded books, several methods have been designed with the specific goal of improving prosody. These methods emphasize how a student's reading sounds—its inflection, expression, and phrasing.

Repeated Reading Practice for Performance

Readers Theatre.   Readers Theatre is a popular method of reading practice that can be a powerful way to increase prosody. For Readers Theatre, the teacher creates scripts from selections of children's literature that are rich in dialogue. The teacher begins by reading aloud the story on which the script is based and leads a discussion of the characters' emotions and how they might sound at different points in the story. Students then practice reading the entire script before the teacher assigns roles. Rehearsing and performing the play for peers provides an authentic purpose for rereading the text multiple times. Readers Theatre can help students develop accuracy, rate, and prosody.

Radio Reading.   Radio reading is a variation of Readers Theatre for older students that adds sound effects to make the performance sound like an old-time radio show. Groups of students can create recorded versions of their "radio shows" that can become listening center readings for their classmates. Students can even generate questions to pose to listeners at the end of the recording. Radio reading reinforces the importance of prosody, because so much information from the story must be communicated through vocal variation. National Public Radio has an old-time radio show called Theatre of the Mind. From these radio shows, an instructional program called Read-Along Radio Dramas was developed. This program includes a recording of a radio play with full cast and sound effects, a word-for-word read-along script, an annotated script of the original story, and a variety of student activities (see Table 2).

Reader as Fluent Model

Self-Recordings.   Hearing one's own voice on audiotape can be an eye-opening experience. For struggling readers, having the opportunity to record, listen, and rerecord can be a powerful method for increasing reading fluency. This approach promotes independent judgment and goal setting, along with ownership of the process.

Amplification.   Whisper phones or phonic phones are a low-tech method of amplifying one's own voice. Whisper phones are pieces of PVC pipe elbows connected to form a telephone shape. This shape amplifies the sound of the student's voice, but only to the student. The whisper phone also masks other extraneous noises for the distractible reader. Whisper phones can be modified by twisting one end to form an *S* shape. With this modification, the whisper phone can be used for quiet partner reading. One student reads into the mouthpiece of the phone while the other student listens in the other end.

Calling the Reader's Attention to Phrase Boundaries

Appropriate placement of pauses around phrase boundaries can contribute substantially to meaning. For example, Rasinski (2003) used the following example of a sentence that can convey meaning or appear as a nonsensical string of words: The young man the jungle gym. Most readers pause after *man*, which results in nonsense. By pausing after *young*, the reader can construct meaning from those words.

The concept of phrase boundaries can be taught by cueing pauses in text with slashes. Single slashes represent shorter pauses, and double slashes indicate longer pauses. Table 4 illustrates a passage cued for phrase boundaries.

Assisted Reading Methods

There are several effective methods for improving prosody through assisted reading with fluent models. For example, echo reading is a technique in which the teacher reads a phrase or sentence and the student reads the same material just behind him or her. In unison reading, the teacher and student read together, and in assisted cloze reading, the teacher reads the text and stops occasionally for the student to read the next word in the text.

Explicit Teaching of Intonation

Blevins (2001) suggested a variety of ways to teach appropriate intonation. For example, students can be taught to recite the alphabet as a conversation, using punctuation to cue inflection (e.g., ABCD? EFG! HI? JKL. MN? OPQ. RST! UVWX. YZ!). By reciting the same sentence using different punctuation (e.g., Dogs bark? Dogs bark! Dogs bark.), students learn the importance of punctuation to meaning. A similar activity, in which the student places stress on different words in the same sentence (e.g., *I* am tired. I *am* tired. I am *tired.*), emphasizes the importance of inflection.

TABLE 4   **Example of Phrase Boundaries**

My favorite season / of the year / is summer.//
I am so glad / we don't have school / in the summer.//
I would rather / spend my time / swimming, / playing, / and reading.//

An Essential Skill

Research has clearly demonstrated the significance of fluency in the development of reading proficiency, and a variety of effective methods for assessment and instruction of reading fluency have been developed. Opportunities to develop all three areas of reading fluency are important for all readers, but teachers of struggling readers in particular must recognize the importance of incorporating explicit fluency-based instruction into their reading programs. Reading fluency has long been acknowledged as an essential skill that proficient readers need to have, and now is the time to focus attention on all areas to be developed—accuracy, rate, and prosody—for truly effective, comprehensive reading instruction for all children.

References

Adams, M. J. (1990). *Beginning to read: Thinking and learning about print.* Cambridge, MA: MIT Press.

Allinder, R. M., Dunse, L., Brunken, C. D., & Obermiller-Krolikowski, H. J. (2001). Improving fluency in at-risk readers and students with learning disabilities. *Remedial and Special Education, 22*(1), 48–54.

Allington, R. L. (1983). Fluency: The neglected reading goal. *The Reading* Teacher, *36*, 556–561.

Allington, R. L. (2000). *What really matters for struggling readers: Designing research-based programs.* Boston: Longman.

Blevins, W. (2001). *Building fluency: Lessons and strategies for reading success.* Scranton, PA: Scholastic.

Breznitz, Z. (1987). Increasing first graders' reading accuracy and comprehension by accelerating their reading rates. *Journal of Educational Psychology, 79*, 236–242.

Breznitz, Z. (1991). The beneficial effect of accelerating reading rate on dyslexic readers' reading comprehension. In M. Snowling & M. Thomson (Eds.), *Dyslexia: Integrating theory and practice* (pp. 235–243). London: Whurr.

Carbo, M. (1981). Making books talk to children. *The Reading Teacher, 35*, 186–189.

Carbo, M. (1992). Eliminating the need for dumbed-down textbooks. *Educational Horizons, 70*, 189–193.

Chard, D. J., Vaughn, S., & Tyler, B. J. (2002). A synthesis of research on effective interventions for building reading fluency with elementary students with learning disabilities. *Journal of Learning Disabilities, 35*, 386–406.

Clay, M. M. (1984). *Observing the young reader.* Auckland, New Zealand: Heinemann.

Clay, M. M. (1993). *Reading Recovery: A guidebook for teachers in training.* Portsmouth, NH: Heinemann.

Deno, S. L., Marston, D., Shinn, M. R., & Tindal, G. (1983). Oral reading fluency: A simple datum for scaling reading disability. *Topics in Learning and Learning Disabilities, 2*(4), 53–59.

Deno, S. L., Mirkin, P. K., & Chiang, B. (1982). Identifying valid measures of reading. *Exceptional Children, 49*, 36–45.

Dowhower, S. L. (1987). Effects of repeated reading on second-grade transitional readers' fluency and comprehension. *Reading Research Quarterly, 22*, 389–406.

Dowhower, S. L. (1991). Speaking of prosody: Fluency's unattended bedfellow. *Theory Into Practice, 30*, 165–175.

Ehri, L. C. (2002). Phases of acquisition in learning to read words and implications for teaching. In R. Stainthorp & P. Tomlinson (Eds.), *Learning and teaching reading* (pp. 7–28). London: British Journal of Educational Psychology Monograph Series II.

Ehri, L. C., & McCormick, S. (1998). Phases of word learning: Implications for instruction with delayed and disabled readers. *Reading and Writing Quarterly: Overcoming Learning Difficulties, 14*(2), 135–164.

Fawcett, A. J., & Nicolson, R. I. (1994). Naming speed in children with dyslexia. *Journal of Learning Disabilities, 27*, 641–646.

Fuchs, L. S., & Fuchs, D. (1992). Identifying a measure for monitoring student reading progress. *School Psychology Review, 21*(1), 45–58.

Fuchs, L. S., Fuchs, D., Eaton, S., & Hamlet, C. L. (2000). [Relations between reading fluency and reading comprehension as a function of silent versus oral reading mode]. Unpublished raw data.

Fuchs, L. S., Fuchs, D., Hamlett, C. L., Walz, L., & Germann, G. (1993). Formative evaluation of academic progress: How much growth can we expect? *School Psychology Review, 22*(1), 27–48.

Fuchs, L. S., Fuchs, D., Hosp, M. D., & Jenkins, J. (2001). Oral reading fluency as an indicator of reading competence: A theoretical, empirical, and historical analysis. *Scientific Studies of Reading, 5*, 239–259.

Fuchs, L. S., Fuchs, D., & Maxwell, L. (1988). The validity of informal reading comprehension measures. *Remedial and Special Education, 9*(2), 20–28.

Good, R. H., Simmons, D. C., & Kame'enui, E. J. (2001). The importance and decision-making utility of a continuum of fluency-based indicators of foundational reading skills for third-grade high-stakes outcomes. *Scientific Studies of Reading, 5*, 257–288.

Hasbrouk, J. E., Ihnot, C., & Rogers, G. H. (1999). "Read Naturally": A strategy to increase oral reading fluency. *Reading Research and Instruction, 39*(1), 27–38.

Hasbrouk, J. E., & Tindal, G. (1992). Curriculum-based oral reading fluency norms for students in grades 2 through 5. *TEACHING Exceptional Children, 24*(3), 41–44.

Howell, K. W., & Lorson-Howell, K. A. (1990). What's the hurry? Fluency in the classroom. *TEACHING Exceptional Children, 22*(3), 20–23.

Hudson, R. F., Mercer, C. D., & Lane, H. B. (2000). *Exploring reading fluency: A paradigmatic overview.* Unpublished manuscript, University of Florida, Gainesville.

Jenkins, J. R., Fuchs, L. S., van den Broek, P., Espin, C., & Deno, S. L. (2003). Accuracy and fluency in list and context reading of skilled and RD groups: Absolute and relative performance levels. *Learning Disabilities: Research & Practice, 18*, 237–245.

Johns, J. L. (1993). *Informal reading inventories.* DeKalb, IL: Communitech.

Kame'enui, E. J., & Simmons, D. C. (2001). Introduction to this special issue: The DNA of reading fluency. *Scientific Studies of Reading, 5*, 203–210.

Kuhn, M. R., & Stahl, S. A. (2000). *Fluency: A review of developmental and remedial practices.* Ann Arbor, MI: Center for the Improvement of Early Reading Achievement.

LaBerge, D., & Samuels, S. J. (1974). Toward a theory of automatic information processing in reading. *Cognitive Psychologist, 6*, 293–323.

Levy, B. A., Abello, B., & Lysynchuk, L. (1997). Transfer from word training to reading in context: Gains in reading fluency and comprehension. *Learning Disabilities Quarterly, 20*, 173–188.

Mastropieri, M. A., Leinart, A., & Scruggs, T. E. (1999). Strategies to increase reading fluency. *Intervention in School and Clinic, 34*, 278–283, 292.

Mercer, C. D., Campbell, K. U., Miller, M. D., Mercer, K. D., & Lane, H. B. (2000). Effects of a reading fluency intervention for middle schoolers with specific learning disabilities. *Learning Disabilities Research & Practice, 15*, 179–189.

Meyer, M. A., & Felton, R. H. (1999). Repeated reading to enhance fluency: Old approaches and new directions. *Annals of Dyslexia, 49*, 283–306.

Moats, L. C. (2001). When older students can't read. *Educational Leadership, 58*(6), 36–40.

National Assessment Governing Board. (2002). Reading Framework for the 2003 National Assessment of Educational Progress. Retrieved July 9, 2004, from http://www.nagb.org/pubs/reading_framework/toc.html.

National Institute of Child Health and Human Development. (2000). *Report of the National Reading Panel. Teaching children to read: An evidence-based assessment of the scientific research literature on reading and its implications for reading instruction* (NIH Publication No. 00-4769). Washington, DC: U.S. Government Printing Office.

Perfetti, C. A., & Hogaboam, T. (1975). Relationship between single word decoding and reading comprehension skill. *Journal of Educational Psychology, 67*, 461–469.

Pinnell, G. S., Pikulski, J. J., Wixson, K. K., Campbell, J. R., Gough, P. B., & Beatty, A. S. (1995). *Listening to children read aloud.* Washington, DC: U.S. Department of Education, National Center for Educational Statistics.

Rashotte, C. A., & Torgesen, J. K. (1985). Repeated reading and reading fluency in learning disabled children. *Reading Research Quarterly, 20,* 180–188. doi:10.1598/RRQ.20.2.4

Rasinski, T. V. (1989). Fluency for everyone: Incorporating fluency instruction in the classroom. *The Reading Teacher, 42,* 690–693.

Rasinski, T. V. (1990). Investigating measures of reading fluency. *Educational Research Quarterly, 14*(3), 37–44.

Rasinski, T. V. (2003). *The fluent reader: Oral reading strategies for building word recognition, fluency, and comprehension.* New York: Scholastic.

Samuels, S. J. (1979). The method of repeated readings. *The Reading Teacher, 32,* 403–408.

Samuels, S. J. (1988). Decoding and automaticity: Helping poor readers become automatic at word recognition. *The Reading Teacher, 41,* 756–760.

Samuels, S. J., Schermer, N., & Reinking, D. (1992). Reading fluency: Techniques for making decoding automatic. In S. J. Samuels & A. E. Farstrup (Eds.), *What research has to say about reading instruction* (2nd ed., pp. 124–144). Newark, DE: International Reading Association.

School Board of Alachua County. (1997). *Curriculum-based assessment in Alachua County, Florida: Vital signs of student progress.* Gainesville, FL: Author.

Schreiber, P. A. (1980). On the acquisition of reading fluency. *Journal of Reading Behavior, 7,* 177–186.

Schreiber, P. A. (1991). Understanding prosody's role in reading acquisition. *Theory Into Practice, 30,* 158–164.

Shinn, M. R., Good, R. H., Knutson, N., & Tilly, W. D. (1992). Curriculum-based measurement of oral reading fluency: A confirmatory analysis of its relation to reading. *School Psychology Review, 21,* 459–479.

Snow, C., Burns, S., & Griffin, P. (1998). *Preventing reading difficulties in young children.* Washington, DC: National Academy Press.

Stanovich, K. E. (1991). Word recognition: Changing perspectives. In R. Barr, M. L. Kamil, P. Mosenthal, & P. D. Pearson (Eds.), *Handbook of reading research* (Vol. 2, pp. 418–452). New York: Longman.

Tan, A., & Nicholson, T. (1997). Flashcards revisited: Training poor readers to read words faster improves their comprehension of text. *Journal of Educational Psychology, 89,* 276–288.

Tenenbaum, H. A., & Wolking, W. D. (1989). Effects of oral reading rate on intraverbal responding. *The Analysis of Verbal Behavior, 7,* 83–89.

Torgesen, J. K. (1986). Computers and cognition in reading: A focus on decoding fluency. *Exceptional Children, 53,* 157–162.

Torgesen, J. K., Alexander, A. W., Wagner, R. K., Rashotte, C. A., Voeller, K., Conway, T., & Rose, E. (2001). Intensive remedial instruction for children with severe reading disabilities: Immediate and long-term outcomes from two instructional approaches. *Journal of Learning Disabilities, 34,* 33–58.

Torgesen, J. K., Rashotte, C., Alexander, A., Alexander, J., & MacPhee, K. (2003). Progress towards understanding the instructional conditions necessary for remediating reading difficulties in older children. In B. Foorman (Ed.), *Preventing and remediating reading difficulties: Bringing science to scale* (pp. 275–298). Baltimore: York Press.

van den Bosch, K., van Bon, W., & Schreuder, P. R. (1995). Poor readers' decoding skills: Effects of training with limited exposure duration. *Reading Research Quarterly, 30,* 110–125.

Young, A., & Bowers, P. G. (1995). Individual difference and text difficulty determinants of reading fluency and expressiveness. *Journal of Experimental Child Psychology, 60,* 428–454.

Zutell, J., & Rasinski, T. V. (1991). Training teachers to attend to their students' reading fluency. *Theory Into Practice, 30,* 211–217.

Classroom Implications

1. For many literacy educators the recent emphasis placed on fluency is a new aspect of their instruction. Based on what you have read in this chapter, what do you believe should be the role of fluency in your daily literacy instruction? You might consider specific instructional practices that will enhance fluency in your students.

2. Do you think fluency is primarily an oral aspect of literacy, or can it also be associated with silent reading? In what ways can the teacher determine fluency when students are reading silently?

For Further Reading

Blevins, W. (2005). The importance of reading fluency and the English language learner. *The Language Teacher, 29*, 13–16.

Kuhn, M. (2005). A comparative study of small group fluency instruction. *Reading Psychology, 26*, 127–146.

Moskal, M. K., & Blachowicz, C. (2006). *Partnering for fluency. Tools for teaching literacy series.* New York: Guilford.

National Reading Panel. (2000). *Teaching children to read: An evidence-based assessment of the scientific research literature on reading and it implications for reading instruction.* Washington, DC: National Institute of Child Health and Human Development.

Rasinski, T. (2006). Reading fluency instruction: Moving beyond accuracy, automaticity, and prosody. *The Reading Teacher, 59*, 704–706.

Rasinski, T., Blachowicz, C., & Lems, K. (2006). *Fluency instruction: Research-based best practices.* New York: Guilford.

Rasinski, T., & Stevenson, B. (2005). The effects of fast start reading: A fluency-based home involvement reading program, on the reading achievement of beginning readers. *Reading Psychology, 26*, 109–125.

Stahl, S., & Heubach, K. (2006). Fluency-oriented reading instruction. In K. D. Stahl & M. McKenna (Eds.), *Reading research at work: Foundations of effective practice.* New York: Guilford Publications.

Online Resources

Fluency in Beginning Reading (University of Oregon)
http://reading.uoregon.edu/flu

Fluency Instruction (National Institute for Literacy)
www.nifl.gov/partnershipforreading/publications/reading_first1fluency.html

Chapter 3

Comprehension

The difficulty of making comprehension keep pace with utterances, has been experienced by every one who has superintended the education of children; and this difficulty must be carefully removed, or continue to present a powerful obstacle to good reading.

—W. Pinnock (1813)

In earlier days reading was often taught with emphasis on word recognition and oral reading. . . . Under this system children may have been 'barking at words' but they were not reading in the modern sense: that is in the sense of understanding and interpreting what is read.

—David Russell (1956)

Comprehension—thinking about and responding to what you are reading—is 'what it is all about!' Comprehension is the reason and prime motivator for engaging in reading. . . . Reading comprehension—and how to teach it—is probably the area of literacy about which we have the most knowledge and the most consensus. It is also probably the area that gets the least attention in the classroom.

—Patricia M. Cunningham & Richard L. Allington (2007)

To understand what one reads is the fundamental purpose for reading. Unhappily, this is one of the few statements about comprehension on which everyone agrees. Past debates have framed both the issues and trends in what comprehension is and how we can best foster it in children. Let's start by posing some of the central issues as a series of questions.

Is Comprehension the Construction or Reconstruction of Meaning?

A traditional view of reading comprehension is that the reader attempts to discern what the writer has attempted to convey through print. According to this view, reading is all about intended meaning. When the principal writes an email, the teacher's task is to infer the principal's thoughts. Clarity in writing will help, of course, but so will an understanding of the school context, an appreciation of the principal's philosophy of leadership, a knowledge of previous emails the principal may have sent, and so forth. Other teachers will be attempting to achieve the same goal, and although teachers may differ as to what the principal intended to express, the comprehension process is a convergent one. But consider a different reading task. The following lines were written by William Blake, an English Romantic poet:

> To see a world in a grain of sand
> Or a heaven in a wild flower,
> To hold infinity in the palm of your hand
> And eternity in an hour.

Should comprehension of these lines also be viewed as an attempt to *reconstruct* in the reader's mind Blake's intended meaning? Or should we view the reader as free to *construct* any meaning that is based, however loosely, on the lines but filtered through one's own experience, cultural perspectives, emotional sensibilities, and aesthetic tastes? We believe that there is room for both views of comprehension but that the nature of the text and one's purpose for reading are considerations. Regardless of one's view, it is important for teachers to come to terms with the distinction.

Are There Levels of Comprehension?

The cognitive processes associated with comprehension range across the entire spectrum of thought from the simple remembering of facts to sophisticated dynamic processes such as critical reading and arriving at inferences about the content of the text. What at first glance may seem a relatively easy process is in fact a complex and difficult undertaking that even today is not fully understood. E. L. Thorndike in a classic study now nearly a century old noted,

> It seems to be a common opinion that reading (understanding the meaning of printed words) is a rather simple compounding of habits. . . . In educational theory, then, we should not consider the reading of a textbook or reference as a mechanical, passive, undiscriminating task, on a totally different level from the task or evaluating or using what is read. While the work of judging and applying doubtless demands a more elaborate and inventive organization and control of mental connections, the demands of mere reading are also for the active selection that is typical of thought. It is not a small or unworthy task to learn "what the book says" (Thorndike, 1917, pp. 323, 332).

What are the implications of this complexity for teaching students to comprehend? Some authorities have argued that comprehension is profitably viewed as occurring at multiple levels. A popular approach has been to define at least three such levels: (1) the *literal* level, at which the reader extracts explicitly stated information; (2) the *inferential* level, at which the reader arrives at implicit facts by using prior knowledge and explicit information; and (3) the *critical* level, at which the reader makes value judgments about the text. The practicality of this view is that it facilitates activities and questioning strategies. It also helps guide test developers, who tend to be more interested in assessments at certain levels of comprehension, especially the inferential.

Should We Teach Skills or Strategies?

Another benefit of delineating comprehension into levels is that each level can be further subdivided into specific skills. For example, the inferential level is sometimes partitioned into skills like inferring the main idea, inferring cause-and-effect relationships, inferring a sequence of events, predicting an outcome, and so forth. This approach can make comprehension instruction seem concrete, manageable, and testable. It has grounded core reading programs for decades, as an inspection of any scope and sequence of comprehension skills will reveal. But does teaching isolated skills to mastery necessarily lead to proficient comprehenders? A more recent view is that these skills are like tools. One needs to be accomplished in how to apply them, to be sure, but it is also important to know when and how to use them to achieve a particular purpose. For example, a carpenter needs to know how to use a drill, a hammer, a saw, and so forth, but when the task is to install a window, the carpenter must be able to apply these skills strategically. Comprehension strategies therefore involve a variety of skills. Proficient readers are able to monitor their understanding as they read and to make repairs when they do not comprehend, by rereading, reading ahead, or seeking outside clarification. They can summarize what they read and make reasoned predictions before and during reading. Such strategies require more than a single skill, and their use will vary with the demands of the specific reading task. As educators have realized the importance of children becoming more strategic as they read, changes in what constitutes best practice have evolved (Shanahan, 2005). Strategy instruction, endorsed by the report of the National Reading Panel (NICHHD, 2000) has taken several forms, such as direct explanation (see Duffy, 2002) and transactional strategy instruction (Pressley et al., 1992).

As You Read

The articles selected for this chapter on literacy comprehension represent recent research and commentary on this topic. Each has been included here with the primary purpose of showing the depth and breadth of this topic. Hopefully these authors will stimulate you to read further in the extensive material that is currently available on the important task of fostering comprehension proficiency.

The first selection is a chapter from the RAND Reading Study Group's report on comprehension. It provides an excellent overview of how we now conceptualize this elusive construct. Smolkin and Donovan speak to issues of comprehension instruction prior to the attainment of fluency. Their solution to this dilemma may surprise you. Cunningham and Shagoury expand on this discussion, noting that even with the youngest students the importance of building "community" is vital to developing an effective basis for comprehension. Their suggestions, although directed at those who teach beginning readers, have important implications for teachers at all levels of literacy instruction. Ivey and Fisher then use the tactic of negative research, building on what we know is unlikely to work, in order to learn from past failures. They provide a summary of good comprehension practices. They identify a number of "ineffective comprehension strategies" that unfortunately are on display in many classrooms today; they then discuss appropriate corrective measures.

As you read, consider the following questions, which address some primary issues concerning the role of comprehension in the reading process:

1. In what ways might a teacher's definition of the reading process shape the teaching of comprehension? For instance, if the teacher believes that "effective reading is saying all the words correctly," how would this belief influence that teacher's comprehension instruction?
2. Does meaning reside in the reader's background of experience or in what the author intended when writing the material? Are these views of comprehension the same or are they different? If the two perspectives differ, can they be reconciled?
3. Are there identifiable comprehension skills or instructional strategies that can be taught and, if so, what are they?
4. In what ways can comprehension be measured, either through formal or informal assessments, and how effective are these various approaches?

References

Cunningham, P. (2006). What if they can say the words but don't know what they mean? *The Reading Teacher, 59*, 708–711.

Cunningham, P. M., & Allington, R. L. (2007). *Classrooms that work: They can all read and write* (3rd ed.). Boston: Allyn & Bacon.

Duffy, G. G. (2002). The case for direct explanation of strategies. In C. C. Block & M. Pressley (Eds.), *Comprehension instruction: Research-based best practices* (pp. 28–41). New York: Guilford.

National Institute of Child Health and Human Development (NICHHD). (2000). Report of the National Reading Panel. *Teaching children to read: An evidence-based assessment of the scientific research literature on reading and it implications for reading instruction: Reports of the subgroups.* (NIH Publication No. 00-4754). Washington, DC: Government Printing Office.

Pinnock, W. (1813). *The universal explanatory English reader.* Winchester, UK: James Roberts.

Pressley, M., El-Dinary, P. B., Gaskins, I., Schuder, T., Bergman, J., Almasi, L., & Brown, R. (1992). Beyond direct explanation: Transactional instruction of reading comprehension strategies. *Elementary School Journal, 92*, 511–554.

Russell, D. H. (1956). *Children's thinking.* Boston: Ginn & Company.

Shanahan, T. (2005). *The National Reading Panel report: Practical advice for teachers.* Naperville, IL: North Central Regional Educational Laboratory, Learning Point Associates.

Thorndike, E. L. (1917). Reading as reasoning. A study of mistakes in paragraph reading. *Journal of Educational Psychology, 8*, 323–332.

Defining Comprehension

RAND READING STUDY GROUP

We define reading comprehension as the process of simultaneously extracting and constructing meaning through interaction and involvement with written language. We use the words *extracting* and *constructing* to emphasize both the importance and the insufficiency of the text as a determinant of reading comprehension. Comprehension entails three elements:

- The *reader* who is doing the comprehending
- The *text* that is to be comprehended
- The *activity* in which comprehension is a part.

In considering the reader, we include all the capacities, abilities, knowledge, and experiences that a person brings to the act of reading. Text is broadly construed to include any printed text or electronic text. In considering activity, we include the purposes, processes, and consequences associated with the act of reading.

These three dimensions define a phenomenon that occurs within a larger *sociocultural context* (see Figure 1) that shapes and is shaped by the reader and that interacts

It should be noted that we are using terms that others have also used in defining reading comprehension, sometimes in similar and sometimes in slightly different ways. Galda and Beach (2001), for example, define context in a way that is not dissimilar from ours, whereas Spiro and Myers (1984) use context in a way that emphasizes culture less and task or purpose more. Many authors identify much the same list of attributes (purpose, interest, text, knowledge, strategy use, etc.) as we do, but Blachowicz and Ogle (2001), for example, distribute these attributes over the categories of individual and social processes rather than group them as we do. Pearson (2001) and Alexander and Jetton (2000) identify reader (learner), text, and context as key dimensions, without including activity as a separate dimension at the same level of analysis. The National Reading Panel report focuses on text and reader as sources of variability (NRP, 2000). Gaskins, in analyses with a variety of colleagues (e.g., Gaskins, 1998; Gaskins et al., 1993; Gaskins & Elliot, 1991), has identified comprehension as requiring the reader to take charge of text, task, and context variables, presumably an implicit acknowledgment that text, task, and context are all important in defining reading comprehension and can be obstacles to comprehension, while at the same time the reader is seen as the most central element.

Snow, C. (2002). *Reading for understanding: Toward an R&D program in reading comprehension.* Santa Monica, CA: RAND Corporation. Reprinted with permission.

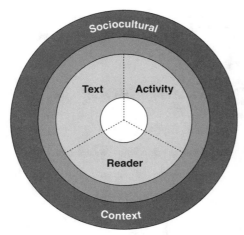

FIGURE 1   A Heuristic for Thinking about Reading Comprehension

with each of the three elements. The identities and capacities of readers, the texts that are available and valued, and the activities in which readers are engaged with those texts are all influenced by, and in some cases determined by, the sociocultural context. The sociocultural context mediates students' experiences, just as students' experiences influence the context. We elaborate on each element in subsequent sections.

Reader, text, and activity are also interrelated in dynamic ways that vary across pre-reading, reading, and post-reading. We consider each of these three "microperiods" in reading because it is important to distinguish between what the reader brings to reading and what the reader takes from reading. Each act of reading is potentially a microdevelopmental process. For example, in the pre-reading microperiod, the reader arrives with a host of characteristics, including cognitive, motivational, language, and non-linguistic capabilities, along with a particular level of fluency. During the reading microperiod, some of these reader characteristics may change. Likewise, during the post-reading micro-period of the same reading event, some of these same reader characteristics, or other reader characteristics, may change again. Much research related to reading comprehension has focused on specific factors (e.g., vocabulary knowledge) without specifying either that the effect of that factor reflects a relationship among reader, text, and activity or that the factor may change from pre-reading to reading to post-reading.

The process of comprehension also has a macrodevelopmental aspect. It changes over time, as the reader matures and develops cognitively, as the reader gains increasing experience with more challenging texts, and as the reader benefits from instruction. From among the many factors influencing the macrodevelopment of comprehension, we have selected instruction, particularly classroom instruction, for special attention as we sketch the research agenda needed to improve comprehension outcomes.

The Reader

To comprehend, a reader must have a wide range of capacities and abilities. These include cognitive capacities (e.g., attention, memory, critical analytic ability, inferencing, visualization ability), motivation (a purpose for reading, an interest in the content being read, self-efficacy as a reader), and various types of knowledge (vocabulary, domain and topic knowledge, linguistic and discourse knowledge, knowledge of specific comprehension strategies). Of course, the specific cognitive, motivational, and linguistic capacities and the knowledge base called on in any act of reading comprehension depend on the texts in use and the specific activity in which one is engaged.

Fluency can be conceptualized as both an antecedent to and a consequence of comprehension. Some aspects of fluent, expressive reading may depend on a thorough understanding of a text. However, some components of fluency—quick and efficient recognition of words and at least some aspects of syntactic parsing—appear to be prerequisites for comprehension.

As a reader begins to read and completes whatever activity is at hand, some of the knowledge and capabilities of the reader change. For example, a reader might increase domain knowledge during reading. Similarly, vocabulary, linguistic, or discourse knowledge might increase. Fluency could also increase as a function of the additional practice in reading. Motivational factors, such as self-concept or interest in the topic, might change in either a positive or a negative direction during a successful or an unsuccessful reading experience.

Another important source of changes in knowledge and capacities is the instruction that a reader receives. Appropriate instruction will foster reading comprehension, which is defined in two ways—the comprehension of the text under current consideration and comprehension capacities more generally.

Thus, although teachers may focus their content area instruction on helping students understand the material, an important concurrent goal is helping students learn how to become self-regulated, active readers who have a variety of strategies to help them comprehend. Effective teachers incorporate both goals into their comprehension instruction. They have a clear understanding of which students need which type of instruction for which texts, and they give students the instruction they need to meet both short-term and long-term comprehension goals.

The Text

The features of text have a large effect on comprehension. Comprehension does not occur by simply extracting meaning from text. During reading, the reader constructs different representations of the text that are important for comprehension. These representations include, for example, the surface code (the exact wording of the text), the text base (idea units representing the meaning), and a representation of the mental models embedded in the text. The proliferation of computers and electronic text has led us to broaden the definition of text to include electronic text and multimedia documents in addition to conventional print. Electronic text can present particular challenges to comprehension, such as dealing with the non-linear nature of hypertext, but it also offers the potential for supporting the comprehension of complex texts, for example, through hyperlinks to definitions or translations of difficult words or to paraphrasing of complex sentences.

Texts can be difficult or easy, depending on factors inherent in the text, on the relationship between the text and the knowledge and abilities of the reader, and on the activities in which the reader is engaged. For example, the content presented in the text has a critical bearing on reading comprehension. A reader's domain knowledge interacts with the content of the text in comprehension. In addition to content, the vocabulary load of the text and its linguistic structure, discourse style, and genre also interact with the reader's knowledge. When too many of these factors are not matched to a reader's knowledge and experience, the text may be too difficult for optimal comprehension to occur. Further, various activities are better suited to some texts than to others. For example, electronic texts that are the product of Internet searches typically need to be scanned for relevance and for reliability, unlike assigned texts that are meant to be studied more deeply. Electronic texts that incorporate hyperlinks and hypermedia introduce some complications in defining comprehension because they require skills and abilities beyond those required for the comprehension of conventional, linear print.

The challenge of teaching reading comprehension is heightened in the current educational era because all students are expected to read more text and more complex texts. Schools can no longer track students so that only those with highly developed reading skills take the more reading-intensive courses. All students now need to read high-level texts with comprehension to pass high-stakes exams and to make themselves employable.

The Activity

Reading does not occur in a vacuum. It is done for a purpose, to achieve some end. Activity refers to this dimension of reading. A reading activity involves one or more purposes, some operations to process the text at hand, and the consequences of performing the activity. Prior to reading, a reader has a purpose, which can be either externally imposed (e.g., completing a class assignment) or internally generated (wanting to program a VCR). The purpose is influenced by a cluster of motivational variables, including interest and prior knowledge. The initial purposes can change as the reader reads. That is, a reader might encounter information that raises new questions that make the original purpose either incomplete or irrelevant. When the purpose is externally mandated, as in instruction, the reader might accept the purpose and complete the activity; for example, if the assignment is "read a paragraph in order to write a summary," the compliant student will accept that purpose and engage in reading operations designed to address it. If the reader does not fully accept the mandated purpose, internally generated purposes may conflict with the externally mandated purpose. Such conflicts may lead to incomplete comprehension. For example, if students fail to see the relevance of an assignment, they may not read purposively, thus compromising their comprehension of the text.

During reading, the reader processes the text with regard to the purpose. Processing the text involves, beyond decoding, higher-level linguistic and semantic processing and monitoring. Each process is more or less important in different types of reading, including skimming (getting only the gist of text) and studying (reading text with the intent of retaining the information for a period of time).

Finally, the consequences of reading are part of the activity. Some reading activities lead to an increase in the *knowledge* a reader has. For example, reading the historical novel *Andersonville* may increase the reader's knowledge about the U.S. Civil War, even though the reader's initial purpose may have been enjoyment. The American history major who reads an assigned text about the Civil War may experience similar consequences, although the reading activity was undertaken for the explicit purpose of learning. Another consequence of reading activities is finding out how to do something. These *application* consequences are often related to the goal of the reader. Repairing a bicycle or preparing bouillabaisse from a recipe are examples of applications. As with knowledge consequences, application consequences may or may not be related to the original purposes. Finally, other reading activities have *engagement* as their consequences. Reading the latest Tom Clancy novel might keep the reader involved while on vacation at the beach. We are not suggesting, however, that engagement occurs only with fiction. Good comprehenders can be engaged in many different types of text.

Knowledge, application, and engagement can be viewed as direct consequences of the reading activity. Activities may also have other, longer-term consequences. Any knowledge (or application) acquired during reading for enjoyment also becomes part of the knowledge that a reader brings to the next reading experience. Learning new vocabulary, acquiring incidental knowledge about Civil War battles or bouillabaisse ingredients, or discovering a new interest might all be consequences of reading with comprehension.

The Context

One important set of reading activities occurs in the context of instruction. Understanding how the reader's purpose for reading and operations are shaped by instruction, and how short- and long-term consequences are influenced by instruction, constitutes a major issue within the research agenda we propose.

When we think about the context of learning to read, we think mostly of classrooms. Of course, children bring to their classrooms vastly varying capacities and understandings about reading, which are in turn influenced, or in some cases determined, by their experiences in their homes and neighborhoods. Further, classrooms and schools themselves reflect the neighborhood context and the economic disparities of the larger society. The differences in instruction and in the availability of texts, computers, and other instructional resources between schools serving low-income neighborhoods and those serving middle-income neighborhoods are well documented.

Sociocultural and sociohistorical theories of learning and literacy describe how children acquire literacy through social interactions with more expert peers and adults. According to Vygotsky (1978), with the guidance and support of an expert, children are able to perform tasks that are slightly beyond their own independent knowledge and capability. As they become more knowledgeable and experienced with the task, the support is withdrawn, and the children internalize the new knowledge and experiences they have acquired, which results in learning. From a sociocultural perspective, both the process (the ways the instruction is delivered and the social interactions that contextualize the learning experience) and the content (the focus of instruction) are of major importance.

Tharp and Gallimore (1988) explain that children's acquisition of knowledge (and literacy) is influenced by five characteristics of the sociocultural context, which they call activity settings: the identity of the participants, how the activity is defined or executed, the timing of the activity, where it occurs, and why children should participate in the activity, or the motivation for the activity. Clearly, all five characteristics are likely to vary as a function of both economic and cultural factors.

The effects of contextual factors, including economic resources, class membership, ethnicity, neighborhood, and school culture, can be seen in oral language practices, in students' self-concepts, in the types of literacy activities in which individuals engage, in instructional history, and, of course, in the likelihood of successful outcomes. The classroom-learning environment (such as organizational grouping, inclusion of technology, or availability of materials) is an important aspect of the context that can affect the development of comprehension abilities.

References

Tharp, R. G., & Gallimore, R. (1988). *Rousing minds to life: Teaching learning, and schooling in social context.* Cambridge: Cambridge University Press.

Vygotsky, L. S. (1978). *Mind in society: The development of higher psychological processes.* Cambridge, MA: Harvard University Press.

"Oh Excellent, Excellent Question!"

Developmental Differences and Comprehension Acquisition

LAURA B. SMOLKIN AND CAROL A. DONOVAN

• • • • •

There is much we have learned from past research on comprehension instruction. From summaries provided by Pressley and his colleagues (Pressley, Johnson, Symons, McGoldrick, & Kurita, 1989) and Pearson and his colleagues (e.g., Dole, Duffy, Roehler, & Pearson, 1991; Pearson & Fielding, 1991; Pearson, Roehler, Dole, & Duffy, 1992), we know there are eight important cognitive acts that teachers should encourage their students to perform. These are activating their prior knowledge, monitoring comprehension (and employing "fix-up" strategies such as rereading when reading goes awry), generating questions, answering them, drawing inferences between and among pieces of text, creating mental imagery, bringing knowledge of text structure to bear, and, both during and after reading, creating summaries of what they have read. We have come, too, to understand the crucial role of teacher modeling in children's comprehension development (e.g., Beck, McKeown, Hamilton, & Kucan, 1997; Duffy, Roehler, & Herrmann, 1988; Pressley & Harris, 1990; Pearson, 1996). However, despite all we have learned, there are important points raised in prior research that we seem to have forgotten. For us, a critical need in this time when phonemes rule is to remind ourselves that comprehension is developmental in nature and to address the question of what type of comprehension-related work should be done at what grade levels.

So that we can move forward to frame and ultimately answer this question, we first look backward, attending to the findings and comments of researchers writing in the 1970s and 1980s (and some in the 1990s) as they discussed developmental aspects of comprehension, cognition, and language learning. We then shift our discussion to application of this knowledge and a particular context we have studied, the interactive information book read-aloud, that supports what we have come to call comprehension

Laura B. Smolkin and Carol A. Donovan. Oh Excellent, Excellent Question: Developmental Differences and Comprehension Acquisition. From *Comprehension Instruction: Researched-Based Practices*. Reprinted with permission of Guilford Press.

acquisition. Finally, we consider what remains to be learned about children's developing abilities to comprehend various types of texts.

Research on the Developmental Nature of Comprehension, Cognition, and Language Learning

In the following sections, we consider the major research we believe forms the foundation for thinking about the development of abilities to comprehend written text, research that seems to us to have been forgotten, put aside in our current intensive interest in phonological awareness. We start with a look at the developmental nature of comprehension. Next, we look at issues of cognitive and language development that affect comprehension acquisition. We then consider implications of this research for comprehension instruction.

The Developmental Nature of Comprehension

When research on reading comprehension strategy instruction began, those working in cognition had already established that children's comprehension was developmental in nature (e.g., Flavell, Speer, Green, & August, 1981; Markman, 1977, 1979). Paris, in a series of articles written with various colleagues (Cross & Paris, 1988; Paris, Cross, & Lipson, 1984; Paris, Lipson, & Wixson, 1983; Paris & Jacobs, 1984), addressed this developmental aspect of reading comprehension as he researched informed strategies for learning (ISL). Paris argued (e.g., Paris & Jacobs, 1984) that metacognitive and reasoning abilities continue developing throughout the elementary grades. Although Paris and Jacob's third graders and fifth graders both improved in their comprehension abilities as a result of direct instruction in comprehension strategies, fifth graders "exhibited greater reading awareness and comprehension than 8-year-olds" (p. 2091). Based on his various findings, Paris and colleagues specifically addressed the need to consider appropriate ages for reading comprehension instruction (e.g., Paris, Saarnio, & Cross, 1986). They suggest that a certain threshold of decoding (and memory) would need to be exceeded before strategies such as skimming, rereading, using context, planning, paraphrasing, and summarizing could "play [a significant role] in children's reading comprehension" (Paris et al., 1986, p. 121). This threshold would likely be passed when children's reading had become fluent enough for comprehension to occur (LaBerge & Samuels, 1974).

Young Children Operate in Cognitively Different Ways from Older Children

Paris and colleagues' attention to memory reflected the discoveries of their contemporary developmental psychologists. In 1983, Brown, Bransford, Ferrara, and Campione's work indicated that young children's use of strategies, a planning effort requiring memory, could be enhanced through instruction; however, they noted, these gains were seldom sustained beyond the training sessions. This same point had been and would be repeatedly made by many working in the field of cognitive development. As early as 1965, Sheldon White had described the "five-to-seven shift" in children's cognition, a time when children moved from unidimensional thinking to the multidimensional thinking that comprehension strategy application would require. The classic balance-scale experiment (Siegler, 1976) is useful in distinguishing unidimensional and multidimensional thinking. This experiment has two variables—amount of weight on either side of a fulcrum and the distance of that weight from the fulcrum—that determine whether the scale will balance. Younger children tend to rely on one dimension—weight alone—in making their predictions of whether the scale would balance; by age 9, children comfortably consider two dimensions, weight and distance, in predicting the outcome of the task. Although in 1996 Siegler would acknowledge the many studies that did and did not indicate that young children could reason multidimensionally, he still felt it necessary to comment: "[D]emonstrating that 5-year-olds can reason multidimensionally does not explain why they fail to do so in many situations in which older children and adults do" (p. 77). A more appropriate "explanation for 5-year-olds' frequent unidimensional reasoning," suggested Siegler, "is that they encode situations more narrowly than do older children" (p. 80). White (1996), too, came to see the shift in cognition in relation to contexts: What happens to children between 5 and 7 is not the acquisition of an absolute ability to reason; it is an ability to reason with others . . . to learn how to act in . . . [various] behavior settings" (pp. 27–28).

Contemplating Routes to Knowledge

Second-language researcher and theorist Stephen Krashen (1976, 1981) proposed his monitor theory of language acquisition and learning. Krashen suggested that there exist two separate knowledge systems underlying language performance. The first he termed "acquisition"; this he saw as operating in a largely subconscious fashion. The second which he deemed less important in ultimately mastering a language, was the "learned" system, created during periods of formal instruction. To clarify his distinction, it may help to look at examples of 4-year-old girls of two different cultures learning dances. Young Pueblo girls can be seen dancing in the harvest dance either by the sides of their mothers or in the group of children who dance at the rear of the larger group's circle. They have received no explicit training in preparing to participate; they simply accompany parents to practice events, watching and sometimes imitating, acquiring the steps of the dance. Young Anglo girls can be seen carefully counting beats and steps as they dance sugarplum fairies in ballet recitals. They receive explicit training for these events, attending hours of after-school classes in which teachers focus on pointed toes, proper positioning of bodies, and careful attention to the point in the music at which particular actions will be performed. In Krashen's presentation, the Pueblo girls are acquiring the steps of the harvest dance, whereas the Anglo girls are learning the steps of the sugarplum-fairy dance.

As recast by Gee (1990), acquisition could be seen as resulting from exposures to models and through practice in social groups, accomplished without formal instruction. By contrast, learning occurred through conscious effort, a gaining of knowledge through a teacher, in which a task had been analyzed into useful parts. In contrast to Krashen, Gee recognized that these two processes were often mixed and that the balance would be different at different developmental stages.

These contrasting cognitive operations bear a remarkable resemblance to the "low roads" and "high roads" to transfer described by Salomon and Perkins (1989). Low roads to transfer, which would result in "the acquisition of habitual behavior patterns" and "cognitive strategies and styles" (p. 122), involved socialization and depended on "practice that occurs[ed] in a variety of somewhat related and expanding contexts" (p. 120). High roads to transfer depended on "the mindful abstracting of knowledge from a context" (p. 115). The key here was the notion of a decontextualizing of cognitive elements, resulting in abstractions that sometimes took the forms of rules or principles, something seen in virtually every form of strategy instruction.

Cazden (1992) discussed the socialization of attention in learning to read and chose to recast Krashen's terminology, borrowing her terms from Donaldson (1978), as "revealing" and "telling." Revealing, she suggested, might be particularly useful for young children, in that "told" information seemed often to be "indigestible for later use" and that abstractions often oversimplified a complex reality. However, for older children, telling was particularly useful in discussing previous actions or approaches, allowing a more critical look (more "mindful" would be Salomon and Perkins' term) at the phenomenon being advocated.

Revisiting Paris's Decoding Emphasis Suggestion

Given that young children have trouble thinking multidimensionally, given that they do not easily retain strategies, and given the preponderance of evidence that phonemic awareness has been shown to be critical to young children's reading success (see Snow, Burns, & Griffin, 1998), it would seem sensible to follow Paris and colleagues' (1986) suggestion to focus young children's attention on the associative learning tasks of attaching phonemes to letters and names to symbols. However, we now have some evidence that early reading instruction that stresses decoding but that fails to attend in some substantive fashion to children's concurrent growth in the comprehension of a range of texts may unintentionally put children in peril. In their 1996 chapter, Morrison, Griffith, and Frazier, examining the issue of transfer of literacy skills, suggested that instruction in decoding does not "naturally produce spin-off benefits in vocabulary skills and general knowledge" (p. 179). In their preliminary investigation of the effects of schooling, they examined two groups of students, distinguished from each other by school entry cutoff dates that placed 10 of their participants in kindergarten and the other 10 in first grade. Their results indicated that the "young" first-grade group made far more substantive progress in phonemic awareness than the "old" kindergarten group. In vocabulary, general knowledge, and narrative skills, both groups made significant gains from fall to spring testing; however, the two groups' gains were found to be equal. The researchers explained, "no evidence was revealed that unique experiences in schooling improved growth" (p. 179) in the three areas. These results call into question the assumption that primary grade instruction that focuses on decoding will necessarily lead to success in comprehension, which is so heavily dependent on all three of these areas of knowledge.

Looking for Guidance on Comprehension Building for Our Youngest Scholars

We take the various scholarly findings and suggestions we have reviewed to indicate that there is likely a developmentally "better" time to begin actual comprehension strategy instruction, telling, or learning, perhaps during children's second-grade year as children's ability to reason multidimensionally grows closer to adult forms. This leaves us with the important question of what types of comprehension activities will supply primary grade students with the "vocabulary skills and general knowledge," critical components in background knowledge, to which Morrison, Griffith, and Frazier (1996) alluded.

The answer, we believe, lies in the thoughtful creation of the social contexts and situations that shape children's cognition, a point stressed by author after author in the preceding review. From our review, we have come to see two elements as critical in the comprehension building period that we are calling "comprehension acquisition" (see Smolkin & Donovan, 2000, in press). For the first, we look to White (1996), who stressed that during the five-to-seven shift, children are *learning to reason with others*. For the second, we find it helpful to consider Salomon and Perkins's (1989) emphasis on practice. They stressed that social practice of the desired behavior (in our case, comprehension of texts) must occur in a *variety of contexts*, as it is the contrast in contexts that yields "more transfer by exercising a wider variety of related complexes" (p. 120) of procedures.

If we want children to reason their ways through texts during a time when they cannot yet read, then the social context for comprehension acquisition must be read-aloud of text. We now have now many years of research documenting the benefits of reading loud to children. From Cohen's (1968) study to Wells's (1986) longitudinal study, research has almost universally supported the idea that reading aloud to children leads to improved reading comprehension (but see Meyer, Stahl, Wardrop, & Linn, 1994, for a cautionary note on the amount of read-aloud time). If children are to learn to reason with others and later to reason for themselves, then these read-alouds must entail child-involved analytical interactions in discussions of the text being read (Dickinson & Smith, 1994). If the social practice must occur in contrasting contexts, then there must be a variety of texts that are read.

Comprehension Acquisition: Applying What We Know

In the sections that follow; we further elucidate and demonstrate the key principles and acts involved in the settings we see as most supporting comprehension acquisition, so that teachers might put them into practice. To this end, we draw on examples from our own work (Smolkin & Donovan, 1993, 2000, in press), gathered when one of us (Donovan) was a first-grade teacher, first at a low to middle socioeconomic status (SES) elementary school and then at a middle to upper SES school, to show how comprehension can be supported and revealed for children as their first-grade teacher extends their reasoning efforts. First, we look at the role of the teacher and the nature of the discussions that support children's reasoning. Next we consider the variations in texts that should lead to greater transfer of comprehension ability. Then we supply examples of interactive information book read-alouds, showing how the cognitive acts identified through comprehension instruction research are put into play.

The Adult in the Reasoning Building Context: Interaction and the Read-Aloud

Since Cazden's (1965) dissertation, we have understood that, in terms of verbal inter-actions, different adult responses to children's verbal contributions produce differ-ent language outcomes. In that research on African American preschoolers, Cazden found that meaning-oriented adult extensions of children's meaning-making offerings yielded greater gains on six measures of syntactic development, including a sentence-imitation test and mean length of utterance, than did adult responses, termed expan-sions, that supplied Standard English syntactic forms. By 1983, Cazden had further considered adult "input," noting three types that occurred as parents communicated with young children in contexts that would ultimately allow the child to complete the same task (Cazden, 1983). Scaffolds, borrowed from Wood, Bruner, and colleagues (Wood, Bruner, & Ross, 1976; Wood, Wood, & Middleton, 1978), enabled children to complete tasks beyond their present capabilities. Models demonstrated a mature behavior deemed important in our larger society. Direct instruction occurred when an adult not only modeled but then also directed "the child to *say* or *tell* or *ask*" (1983, p. 14). Drawing on Cazden, we see that interactive read-alouds (see Oyler, 1996) in which children's initiations, efforts at meaning are *extended* and key points of compre-hension *revealed* by their teachers provide the rich cases from which younger learners can reason with others in particular behavior settings.

Considering the Interactive Read-Aloud.   Presently, several researchers use the term "interactive" to describe read-aloud practices. Unlike Barrentine (1996), who used the term to describe a situation in which teachers carefully examined texts to determine at what point to insert their well-placed questions, we use the term as did Oyler (1996), to indicate a genuine sharing of authority. In this situation, which we distinguish from other types of read-aloud interactions in the next section, teachers can "gain insight into the connections students are making between the text" (Oyler, 1996, p. 150) and their lives, schemas, and other texts, building on those connections to extend and shape children's reasoning. Like Oyler, we are not describing a situation in which teachers abandon their authority but a situation in which the adult can reveal the way texts and information work at the very moment children are attempting to reason their way through these points.

What Happens during an Interactive Read-Aloud?   Consider this interchange between Donovan and her students. The underlining indicates text, in this instance, Tomie dePaola's *The Popcorn Book* (1978). This dual-purpose (see Donovan & Smolkin, in press-a, in press-b; Smolkin, Donovan, & Lomax, 2001) book consists of two texts. The first, a simple story displayed through cartoonlike characters with speech balloons, is about two brothers who have decided to make popcorn. The second is informational; one of the boys wonders why their mother keeps popcorn in the refrigerator, and he reads aloud to his brother from a hefty, encyclopedic tome to find his answer. Underlining indicates the actual text of the book.

> **Teacher:** In 1612, French explorers saw some Iroquois people popping corn in clay pots. They would fill the pots with hot sand, throw in some popcorn and stir it with a stick. When the corn popped, it came to the top of the sand and made it easy to get.
>
> **Child:** Look at the bowl!
>
> **Teacher:** (*providing an oral commentary on the "story"*): Okay, now it's hot enough [for the brothers] to add a few kernels.
>
> **Child:** What's a kernel?
>
> **Child:** Like what you pop.
>
> **Teacher:** It's a seed.
>
> **Annie:** What if you, like, would you think [of] a popcorn seed? Like a popcorn seed. Could you grow popcorn?
>
> **Teacher:** Oh, excellent, excellent question. Let's read and we'll see if this [book] answers that question, and if not, we'll talk about it at the end.

Note that the teacher provides her students a context that supports and extends their reasoning efforts. Within this context, in which meaning is being co-constructed, Annie (a pseudonym) feels free to pose her question—if you plant a popcorn seed, will popcorn grow? In response, the teacher compliments Annie's question (one of the eight cognitive acts we earlier noted), then directly instructs children in a method for answering questions ("let's read . . ."). Her interactive style in no way diminishes her right to supply correct information ("It's a seed"), nor to reveal how good comprehenders approach a text. This sharing, this co-construction indicates to children that they need to be actively processing text and pictures as books are read aloud.

This interactive style contrasts sharply with "interactive" examples supplied by Barrentine (1996, p. 40).

> **Teacher:** Can you think of a way that Little Sal and Little Bear are alike? Bart?
>
> **Bart:** They're both little.
>
> **Teacher:** They're both little. Yes, they are. Matt, what do you think?
>
> **Matt:** They're both brown.
>
> **Teacher:** Okay. Um, somebody in the back. Ben. Do you want to look at the picture, Ben? Here's Little Sal, and here's Little Bear.
>
> **Ben:** They're both girls.
>
> **Teacher:** Okay. Maybe so.

We see clearly that Barrentine's teacher is working toward enabling her students to compare and contrast the two stories simultaneously developing in Robert McCloskey's *Blueberries for Sal,* a major component of the humor of this text. However, their interchange is clearly marked with the standard I-R-E (teacher initiation, student response, teacher evaluation) instructional pattern so common in schools (see Cazden, 1988). In part, this may be due to the fact that the text is a story, a genre that we have found, as we discuss later, less supportive of comprehension-related acts than are information book read-alouds. Still, an approach such as Barrentine's, in our opinion, provides considerably less opportunity for a teacher to seize, extend, and support a child-posed reasoning effort than does Donovan's read-aloud.

Working toward Interactive Read-Alouds.   A co-constructive, interactive style is not something that comes naturally to all of us. Anne Barry, a Chicago teacher who worked, with both Christine Pappas and her student Cynthia Oyler (Oyler, 1996; Oyler & Barry, 1996; Pappas & Barry, 1997), acknowledged that for her the move to an interactive style entailed hard work (Pappas & Barry, 1997). However, making this effort was worthwhile, for Barry then was better able to support, extend, and scaffold her students' verbal points as they reasoned their ways through various types of texts. And this process, she believed, ultimately allowed her to know both her students and their cognition better.

Variations in Texts: What We Think Teachers Should Know

Recently, Duke (1999, 2000) established the minimal presence of information books in first-grade classrooms. Having no reason to assume that the situation is different in pre-school and kindergarten classrooms, we believe this absence of information books to be an extremely important problem. First, as the literature on transfer suggests, varied types of practice are critical for children's transfer of particular types of reasoning. Duke's (1999) study and Kamberelis's (1999) work clearly establish the dominance of story texts in young children's school lives. This early story dominance appears to have long-term results. It has, for example, been established that even good third-grade readers recall more information from, generate more connectors, and maintain the original ordering better in readings of narrative texts than they do in their readings of expository text (e.g., Bridge & Tierney, 1981). Certainly, this is not a surprising finding if we remind ourselves of the conditions for low-road transfers.

Storybook and Information Book Read-Alouds Are Different.   For some time, we have been thinking our way through the differing natures of story and information book read-alouds. Strongly influenced by Pappas (1991), we decided to conduct a study in which one of us (Donovan) read aloud to her first-grade students. The books, quality trade literature named in Children's Choices in *The Reading Teacher,* included six information books and six storybooks. We decided to focus our attention on the discussion that occurred during the read-aloud itself and accordingly recorded from the time the actual reading began until the book was finished. Because Donovan transferred from a lower-middle-class school to a middle-upper-class school at the end of the year, we decided to replicate the study. Transcribing the tapes, we analyzed both teacher and student contributions through the reader response categories of Martinez, Roser, Hoffman, and Battle (1992).

In our first coding pass (Smolkin & Donovan, 1993), we placed children's responses into 17 different categories that ranged from children's *bids for turns* ("Mrs. Donovan!") to *literary associations* ("It could be like *Look, Look, Look*") to *predictions* ("They're gonna make a mess in there") to *wondering outside the text* ("Did God put the color on those eggs or how did it get there?") to *literary evaluations* ("This is getting weird"). In our next analysis (Smolkin & Donovan, 2000) we combined the categories titled *interpreting, telling, personal associations,* and *literary associations* into an overarching category that we called *comprehension.* (Since that publication, we have reexamined our thinking and our computations; the correct figures are as reported here.) As we noted in that Center for the Improvement of Early Reading Achievement report, there were considerable differences in these particular comprehension-related moves made by Donovan's students during information book read-alouds as contrasted with story read-alouds. At the lower-middle-class school, the students produced 256 comprehension-coded moves when listening to information books (83% of their total) as contrasted with their 52 moves in this category when they were listening to the six storybooks (17% of their total). The percentages in the transcripts from the upper-middle-class school looked quite similar—253 comprehension moves during the information book read-alouds (87% of the total), contrasted with 38 moves during the read-aloud of fiction (13% of the total).

In our most recent analyses (Smolkin & Donovan, in press), we have extended our comprehension category to include the additional subcategories of *elaborations* ("Look at that little baby. He's screaming"), *predictions* (demonstrated previously), and *wondering* (demonstrated previously). With all categories included, at the lower-middle-class school, Donovan's students produced 395 comprehension-coded moves while listening to information books (70% of their total) as contrasted with their 170 moves in this enlarged category while they were listening to the six storybooks (30% of the total). These percentages in the transcripts from the upper-middle-class school show a similar orientation—421 comprehension moves during the information book read-alouds (78% of their total) contrasted with 118 moves during the read-aloud of fiction (22% of their total).

Regarding teacher discourse categories, we have combined our earlier categories (Martinez et al., 1992) of *informing* ("You can plant it as long as you haven't cooked it"), *summarization* ("They were just eating plants"), *fostering predictions* ("The best thing about popcorn is . . ."), and *thinking about text* ("I think the book's going to tell us"). In our most recent analyses, Donovan produced 226 comprehension-related moves in the information book read-alouds with her lower-middle-class students as contrasted with 60 such moves during read-alouds of storybooks (79% vs. 21%). With her upper-middle-class students, she produced 254 meaning-oriented moves during the information read-alouds as contrasted with only 34 such moves during the storybook read-alouds (88% vs. 12%).

Our findings are by no means unique. Mason, Peterman, Powell and Kerr (1989), Kerr and Mason (1994), and Oyler (1996), to name a few, have all observed that genre influences the types of discourse produced by participants in read-alouds.

Comprehension Activity Called for in Story and Information Book Read-Alouds Differs.   It is our contention that these different types of texts call for different types (and amounts) of comprehension activity, whether they are read aloud or read silently. Consider the types of comprehension occurring in this excerpt from Donovan's read-aloud of Joanna Cole's folktale *It's Too Noisy*.

> **Teacher:**   <u>The wiseman closed his eyes. He thought and thought. "Here is what to do," he said. "Bring your rooster and your chickens into the house." "That is a funny thing to do," thought the farmer. But he did what the wiseman told him. He got his rooster and his chickens. He put them in the house.</u>
>
> **C:**   The wiseman wants him to make it more noisy!
>
> **Teacher:**   Will that make it better for the farmer?
>
> **C:**   (*many, in unison*): NO!
>
> **C:**   It's gonna get real noisy.

Stories contain much with which children are already familiar—people, their actions, and outcomes. Their structures are almost always similar; someone's problem is established and various episodes occur as the individual works to solve the problem (e.g., Hasan, 1984; Stein & Glenn, 1979). This is clearly not the case with informational or expository text. These texts not only come in a variety of structures (e.g., Donovan & Smolkin, in press-a, in press-b; Meyer, 1975; Taylor & Taylor, 1983) but they also contain numerous new concepts (and their attendant vocabulary). Moreover, their linguistic features vary considerably, stressing nominalization (e.g., Martin, 1993; Unsworth, 1999), a transformation of form virtually confined to written texts. For us, it is no stretch at all to accept the hypothesis suggested by Chall, Jacobs, and Baldwin (1990) that a contributing factor to the fourth-grade slump might be children's lack of familiarity with expository text.

We do not wish our message to be mistaken. We are not saying that teachers should not read stories aloud; far from that. Even our own prior research (Yaden, Smolkin, & Conlon, 1989) has clearly shown the benefits of reading stories aloud. We do, however, stress the importance for teachers of gaining greater familiarity with the varied types of informational texts, a task with which we hope our explorations may provide some assistance. Our analyses (Donovan & Smolkin, in press-a) have revealed, for instance, three separate subgenera of information books—*narrative*, *nonnarrative*, and *dual-purpose* texts. We also ask that teachers accept that, although it may at first be "hard to read aloud without a story line" (Chittenden, 1991, p. 13), their young students will gain much from learning to reason in these important contextual variations.

Comprehension Activity during Information Book Read-Alouds

In the sections that follow, we present examples of Donovan's modeling, scaffolding, and explicitly instructing children as they worked interactively to co-construct the meanings of expository text. First, we consider some links that texts require. Second, we present a consideration of the role of text structure in comprehension. Finally, we focus on a type of explicit instruction that resulted from a comprehension failure.

Linking Pieces of Text Together

The examples in this section are taken from two texts that we classify as *narrative information texts*. All three examples indicate the ways links are formed, from the level of a word and its meaning in a sentence to the creation of causal inferences.

Linking a Word to Contexts.   As we indicated earlier, information books exist to acquaint children with new concepts in which vocabulary figures importantly. In our first example, the teacher (Donovan) reads from Gibbons' (1988) *Sunken Treasure*. This book, by noted information book writer Gail Gibbons, makes great use of the narrative, time-dependent structures (*now*, *next*, and *then*) that children have learned from story exposures. The teacher pauses to make sure the children comprehend the meaning of a particular word in the text.

> **Teacher:** *Now the treasure can be brought to the surface. Salvage boats are moved in. Divers descend and crewmembers lower baskets over the side to them.* What does descend mean? We learned this word when we talked about hot air balloons. Pete?
>
> **Pete:** It's like . . .
>
> **Child:** Lifting it up . . .
>
> **Child:** Lifting it up . . .
>
> **Teacher:** Say what you were going to say, Pete.
>
> **Pete:** It goes down.
>
> **Teacher:** Excellent. Down. That's right. And, you can tell that by the meaning of the sentence: *Divers descend and crewmembers lower baskets over the side to them.* So, they're going down.

In this example, the teacher clearly has moved into the role of authority on text as she demonstrates and discusses a number of important comprehension strategies. Concerned that the children will not understand the word *descend*, she first leads the children through a consideration of their prior knowledge, their previous experiences with this word. She also explicitly tells her students that they can double-check that information by examining it in the context of the sentence in which the word appeared, demonstrating Gee's (1990) point that acquisition and instruction are often mixed.

Linking Pieces of Text Information to Consider Cause.   In the following example from *Sunken Treasure*, Donovan works to scaffold the children's construction of an inference in a section of text that does not make a causal connection explicit.

> **Teacher:** All right, it hit the reef. Why did it hit the reef? Because it got. . . . (*No response from children*). What did it [the book] say? It said there was . . .
>
> **Child:** A storm.
>
> **Teacher:** Storm, right.
>
> **Child:** They couldn't see.
>
> **Teacher:** Right, it did [say that]. Because they couldn't see, and if they were out
>
> **Child:** Were the people surprised?
>
> **Child:** The storm blew it into the rocks.
>
> **Teacher:** Exactly.

Using scaffolding, the teacher guides the children backward in the text to the pieces of text information critical in understanding the cause of the shipwreck. The ascertaining of cause (Trabasso, 1994; Trabasso & Magliano, 1996) is critical in narratives, whether they constitute stories studied by Trabasso and Magliano or the recountings of factual events in narrative informational texts.

Our two examples thus far featured teacher-initiated comprehension activities. The information book read-alouds were genuinely interactive, allowing children to put forth their concerns. In the next example, a student initiates the comprehension effort, after carefully studying the picture in another narrative information book, Cole and Wexler's (1976) *A Chick Hatches*.

> **Child:** That yellow stuff wasn't there. [Why did it disappear?]
>
> **Teacher:** Well, it might have dried up, or it might be a little bigger. Let's keep reading and see. *Inside the membrane, the fetus looks more and more like a chick. Notice how much of the yolk has been used up. Every day now until hatching some of the yolk will be drawn into the chick's body.*
>
> **Child:** Why?
>
> **Child:** Why? Does he eat the egg?
>
> **Child:** Oh, gross.
>
> **Teacher:** Well, remember, remember the blood vessels are in the yolk and they get the food from the yolk, so yeah, it uses it up. He doesn't eat it with his mouth, but he eats it through his blood vessels.
>
> **Child:** (*whispering*) Wow.

Between them, the teacher and the children put a number of cognitive acts and strategies into play. Like a good adult comprehender, the child poses a problem (an implied question). The teacher responds with two possible answers, then suggests that they try reading further to find their answer, a strategy we noted earlier in the example from *The Popcorn Book* (de Paola, 1978).

Further supporting the children's comprehension, the teacher models the formation of inferences, linking the current information on the yolk absorption to previously presented information on the location and function of the blood vessels. To accomplish this end, she directly indicates that the metacognitive act of remembering might be instantiated to locate an important piece of text information.

Attending to Text Structure

As comprehension research has shown repeatedly, awareness of text structure aids readers' comprehension. In the excerpt that follows, the teacher pauses to discuss the way de Paola's *The Popcorn Book* is structured.

> **Teacher:** *And 100-year-old popcorn kernels were found in Peru that could still be popped.* Now. This guy is doing different . . . [It's] kind of like two stories [are] going on. What is this part giving us?
>
> **Children:** *(together)* Information.
>
> **Teacher:** It is. And what is this doing?
>
> **Child:** It's telling you.
>
> **Teacher:** It's giving us, right, the steps of how to make the popcorn.
>
> **Child:** And he has a big ole speech bubble.
>
> **Teacher:** Yes, because he's reading about this, remember? And so, his speech bubble is him reading from this book about this *(pointing to pictures of native peoples)*.

By interrupting to comment on the way this book "works," the teacher models attention to text structure and then scaffolds her children in noting that a text's structure may be critical in understanding its presentation of ideas. In this particular *dual purpose informational text*, all information regarding the history of popcorn appears speech bubbles, whereas the narrative describes the steps the two brothers engage in as they prepare popcorn.

Modeling Fix-Up Strategies When Comprehension Failure Occurs

Monitoring comprehension, as we noted at the beginning of the chapter, is an important comprehension strategy. In the following example, Donovan reads from *Tree Trunk Traffic* (Lavies, 1989), a book that we classify as *nonnarrative informational text*. Reading amidst the many comments her students are offering, the teacher suddenly pauses and begins again.

> **Teacher:** *Insects live on the tree, too. This big cicada just crawled out of its brown, shell-like skin. For several years. . . . (Teacher pauses. The next word in the text is "it.")* Let's start back here. *Insects live on the tree, too. This big cicada just crawled out of its brown, shell-like skin.*
>
> **Child:** *(interrupting):* We already read this.
>
> **Teacher:** I know, but see, sometimes if you stop, it helps [to reread the previous sentences]. It didn't make sense just reading [further in the text].

This particular example seems very important for us. Opportunities to hear an adult speak of a comprehension failure are quite few. This particular opportunity arises because the teacher's genuinely interactive style allows her children to comment freely. Like many children, the child wants the reading of the text simply to move forward and complains when it doesn't. The teacher doesn't talk about the source of her comprehension difficulty, the distance between a noun ("skin") and its pronoun ("it"), but she does inform her students that when we have to stop during reading, it truly is helpful for comprehension to reread the previously read section.

What Remains to Be Learned about Comprehension Building in the Earliest Grades

Our notion of comprehension acquisition contains within it many questions for future research. In this section, we pose six questions that we feel merit further attention to enhance our understanding of supporting young children's comprehension.

   1. *What are the distinctions in the comprehension of stories and informational texts?* The first point we make is that our view of the distinctions between story and information book read-alouds need additional validation. Although we carefully studied both other researchers' reports and our own data, we believe that studies involving larger numbers of teachers are needed to support what we have found. We wish, ultimately, to substantiate our assertion that information book read-alouds contribute in some substantively different way from storybook read-alouds to children's long-term comprehension abilities.

   2. *How do the subgenera of informational texts impact comprehension strategies used?* Within those studies, we would also like to address the types of comprehension fostered by the different subgenera of informational texts to which we have referred in this chapter. We are quite interested in teacher read-alouds of dual-purpose texts such as de Paola's (1978) *The Popcorn Book* and Joanna Cole and Bruce Degen's various "Magic School Bus" books. We have observed that read-alouds of normative informational texts such as Lavies's (1989) *Tree Trunk Traffic* produce many questions to which the authors have supplied no answer. This inevitably leads teachers and children to a consideration of where to read or look next to find the answer to those questions, emphasizing the important strategies of both asking and answering questions during reading. And, as we noted previously, narrative informational texts seem to produce many efforts toward establishing causal links. We believe that knowing what types of books support particular comprehension processes will facilitate both comprehension acquisition and comprehension instruction.

   3. *What are the cognitive demands of different comprehension strategies?* We are also keenly interested in considering which of the eight identified cognitive acts place lesser and greater demands on younger renders in terms of cognitive abilities. Knowing this would be very important in designing developmental-comprehension curricula to follow and support the period of comprehension acquisition.

4. *What support would teachers need to move toward interactive read-alouds?* We need to know what types of teacher support are needed to move toward interactive read-alouds that highlight comprehension. Since the early 1990s (e.g., El-Dinary, Pressley, & Schuder, 1992; Rich & Pressley, 1990), we have known that teachers resist using instructional approaches that strike them as either too disembedded or too complex. We also understand, as was established earlier in this chapter, that not all teachers feel comfortable reading interactively with their students. Clearly, research that seeks to determine appropriate contexts for comprehension acquisition must attend carefully to teacher needs.

5. *What are the benefits of interactive information book read-alouds over time?* In that informational texts are deliberately instructive in concepts and vocabulary, we are interested in the long-term benefits of information book read-alouds. What impact will a greater early acquaintance with these texts offer in terms of children's vocabulary and concept knowledge? What impact might this have in terms of text structure knowledge or ease of comprehending lexico-grammatical structures particular to expository text?

6. *What are the long-term effects of establishing a comprehension acquisition approach?* Ultimately, this is the most important question to be addressed. Research to answer this question and the others posed here will require longitudinal studies. These studies will need to contrast children's reading comprehension progress over the course of their elementary years, comparing groups for whom a comprehension acquisition period was addressed with those whose school literacy diets have consisted virtually exclusively of decoding emphases in their primary grade instruction.

Conclusion

In this chapter, we have argued for increasing our research attention to young children's development of text comprehension. We suggest strongly that cognitive development occurring between the ages of 5 to 7 needs to be considered as part of this equation. To us, this seems particularly important in determining the types of situations that will ultimately lead children to transfer, through low roads and revealed information, the comprehension activities demonstrated by adult models to their own future text encounters. We have supplied a possible model for "comprehension acquisition instruction"—the interactive information book read-aloud—but stress that this model needs future research validation. We argue for attention to the situations and texts that will ultimately enable upper-grade elementary students to remark to themselves as they read, "Oh, excellent, excellent question! I wonder if it's answered in here?"

References

Barrentine, S. J. (1996). Engaging with reading through interactive read-alouds. *Reading Teacher, 50,* 36–43.

Beck, I. L., McKeown, M. G., Hamilton, R. L., & Kucan, L. (1997). *Questioning the author: An approach for enhancing student engagement with text.* Newark, DE: International Reading Association.

Bridge, C. A., & Tierney, R. J. (1981). The inferential operations of children across text with narrative and expository tendencies. *Journal of Reading Behavior, 13,* 201–214.

Brown, A. L., Bransford, J. D., Ferrara, R. A., & Campione, J. C. (1983). Learning, remembering, and understanding. In J. H. Flavell & E. M. Markman (Eds.), *Cognitive development* (4th ed., pp. 77–166). New York: Wiley.

Cazden, C. B. (1965). *Environmental assistance to the child's acquisition of grammar.* Unpublished doctoral dissertation, Harvard University, Cambridge, MA.

Cazden, C. B. (1983). Adult assistance to language development: Scaffolds, models, and direct instruction. In R. P. Parker & F. A. Davis (Eds.), *Developing literacy: Young children's use of language* (pp. 3–18). Newark, DE: International Reading Association.

Cazden, C. B. (1988). *Classroom discourse: The language of teaching and learning.* Portsmouth, NH: Heinemann.

Cazden, C. B. (1992). Revealing and telling: The socialization of attention in learning to read. *Educational Psychology, 12,* 305–313.

Chall, J. S., Jacobs, V. A., & Baldwin, L. E. (1990). *The reading crisis: Why poor children fall behind.* Cambridge, MA: Harvard University Press.

Chittendon, E. (1991). The role of science books in primary classrooms. In W. Saul & S. A. Jagusch (Eds.), *Vital connections: Children, science, and books: Papers from a symposium sponsored by the Children's Literature Center* (pp. 127–141). Washington, DC: Library of Congress.

Cohen, D. (1968). The effect of literature on vocabulary and reading achievement. *Elementary English, 45,* 209–213, 217.

Cole, J. (1989). *It's too noisy.* New York: Crowell.

Cole, J., & Wexler, J. (1976). *A chick hatches.* New York: William Morrow.

Cross, D. R., & Paris, S. G. (1988). Developmental and instructional analyses of children's metacognition and reading comprehension. *Journal of Educational Psychology, 80*(2), 131–142.

de Paola, T. (1978). *The popcorn book.* New York: Holiday House.

Dickinson, D. K., & Smith, K. W. (1994). Long-term effects of preschool teachers' book readings on low-income children's vocabulary and story comprehension. *Reading Research Quarterly, 29,* 104–122.

Dole, J. A., Duffy, G. G., Roehler, L. R., & Pearson, P. D. (1991). Moving from the old to the new: Research on reading comprehension instruction. *Review of Educational Research, 61,* 239–264.

Donaldson, M. C. (1978). *Children's minds.* New York: Norton.

Donovan, C. A., & Smolkin, L. B. (in press-a). Considering genre, content, and other features important in the selection of trade books for science. *Reading Teacher.*

Donovan, C. A., & Smolkin, L. B. (in press-b). Genre and other factors influencing teachers' book selections for science instruction. *Reading Research Quarterly.*

Duffy, G. G., Roehler, L. R., & Herrmann, B. A. (1988). Modeling mental procedures helps poor readers become strategic readers. *Reading Teacher, 41,* 762–767.

Duke, N. K. (1999). *The scarcity of informational texts in first grade* (CIERA Report #1-007). Ann Arbor: CIERA/University of Michigan.

Duke, N. K. (2000). 3.6 minutes per day: The scarcity of informational texts in first grade. *Reading Research Quarterly, 35,* 202–224.

El-Dinary, P. B., Pressley, M., & Schuder, T. (1992). Teachers learning transactional strategies instruction. In C. K. Kinzer & D. J. Leu (Eds.), *Literacy research, theory, and practice: Views from many perspectives. 41st yearbook of the National Reading Conference* (pp. 453–462). Chicago, IL: National Reading Conference.

Flavell, J. H., Speer, J. R., Green, F. L., & August, D. L. (1981). The development of comprehension monitoring and knowledge about communication. *Monographs of the Society for Research in Child Development, 46*(5)[192], 1–65.

Gee, J. P. (1990). *Social linguistics and literacies: Ideology in discourses.* New York: Falmer.

Gibbons, G. (1988). *Sunken treasure*. New York: Harper Trophy.

Halliday, M. A. K. *An introduction to functional grammar* (2nd ed.). London: Arnold.

Hasan, R. (1984). The nursery tale as a genre. *Nottingham Linguistic Circular, 13*, 71–102.

Kamberelis, G. (1999). Genre development and learning: Children writing stories, science reports, and poems. *Research in the Teaching of English, 33*, 403–460.

Kerr, B. M., & Mason, J. M. (1994). Awakening literacy through interactive story reading. In F. Lehr & J. Osborn (Eds.), *Reading, language, and literacy: Instruction for the twenty-first century* (pp. 133–148). Hillsdale, NJ: Erlbaum.

Krashen, S. (1976). Formal and informal linguistic environments in language acquisition and language learning. *TESOL Quarterly, 10*, 157–168.

Krashen, S. (1981). *Second language acquisition and second language learning*. Oxford, England: Pergamon Press.

LaBerge, D., & Samuels, S. J. (1974). Toward a theory of automatic information processing in reading. *Cognitive Psychology, 6*, 293–323.

Lavies, B. (1989). *Tree trunk traffic*. New York: Dutton.

Markman, E. M. (1977). Realizing that you don't understand: A preliminary investigation. *Child Development, 48*, 986–992.

Markman, E. M. (1979). Realizing that you don't understood: Elementary school children's awareness of inconsistencies. *Child Development, 50*, 643–655.

Martin, J. R. (1993). Life as a noun: Arresting the universe in science and humanities. In M. A. K. Halliday & J. R. Martin (Eds.), *Writing science: Literacy and discursive power* (pp. 166–202). London: Falmer.

Martinez, M., Roser, N. L., Hoffman, J. V., & Battle, J. (1992). Fostering better book discussions through response logs and response framework; A case description. In C. K. Kinzer & D. J. Leu (Eds.), *Literacy research, theory, and practice: Views from many perspectives. 41st yearbook of the National Reading Conference* (pp. 303–311). Chicago: National Reading Conference.

Mason, J. M., Peterman, C. L., Powell, B. M., & Kerr, B. M. (1989). Reading and writing attempts by kindergartners after book reading by teachers. In J. M. Mason (Ed.), *Reading and writing connections* (pp. 105–120). Boston: Allyn & Bacon.

Meyer, B. J. (1975). Identification of the structure of prose and its implications for the study of reading and memory. *Journal of Reading Behavior, 7*(1), 7–47.

Meyer, L. A., Stahl, S. A., Wardrop, J. L., & Linn, R. L. (1994). Effects of reading storybooks aloud to children. *Journal of Educational Research, 88*(2), 69–85.

Morrison, F. J., Griffith, E. M., & Frazier, J. A. (1996). Schooling and the 5 to 7 shift: A natural experiment. In A. J. Sameroff & M. Haith (Eds.), *The five- to seven-year shift: The age of reason and responsibility* (pp. 161–186). Chicago: University of Chicago Press.

Oyler, C. (1996). Sharing authority: Student initiations during teacher-led read-alouds of information books. *Teaching and Teacher Education, 12*, 149–160.

Oyler, C., & Barry, A. (1996). Intertextual connections in read-alouds of information books. *Language Arts, 73*, 324–329.

Pappas, C. C. (1991). Is narrative "primary"? Some insights from kindergartners' pretend readings of stories and information books. *Journal of Reading Behavior, 25*, 97–129.

Pappas, C. C., & Barry, A. (1997). Scaffolding urban students' initiations: Transactions in reading informational books in the read-aloud curriculum. In N. J. Karolides (Ed.), *Reader response in elementary classrooms: Quest and discovery* (pp. 215–236). Mahwah, NJ: Erlbaum.

Paris, S. G., Cross, D. R., & Lipson, M. Y. (1984). Informed strategies for learning: A program to improve children's reading awareness and comprehension. *Journal of Educational Psychology, 76*, 1239–1252.

Paris, S. G., & Jacobs, S. E. (1984). The benefits of informed instruction for children's reading awareness and comprehension skills. *Child Development, 55*, 2083–2093.

Paris, S. G., Lipson, M. Y., & Wixson, K. K. (1983). Becoming a strategic reader. *Contemporary Educational Psychology, 8*, 293–316.

Paris, S. G., Saarnio, D. A., & Cross, D. R. (1986). A metacognitive curriculum to promote children's reading and learning. *Australian Journal of Psychology, 38*(2), 107–123.

Pearson, P. D. (1996). Reclaiming the center. In M. F. Graves, P. van den Broek, & B. M. Taylor (Eds.), *The first R: Every child's right to read* (pp. 259–274). New York: Teachers College Press.

Pearson, P. D., & Fielding, L. (1991). Comprehension instruction. In R. Barr, M. L. Kamil, P. Mosenthal & P. D. Pearson (Ed.), *Handbook of reading research* (Vol. 2, pp. 815–860). New York: Longman.

Pearson, P. D., Roehler, L. R., Dole, J. A., & Duffy, G. G. (1992). Developing expertise in reading comprehension. In S. J. Samuels & A. E. Farstrup (Eds.), *What research has to say about reading instruction* (pp. 145–199). Newark, DE: International Reading Association.

Pressley, M., & Harris, K. R. (1990). What we really know about strategy instruction. *Educational Leadership, 48*, 31–34.

Pressley, M., Johnson, C. J., Symons, S., McGoldrick, J. A., & Kurita, J. A. (1989). Strategies that improve children's memory and comprehension of text. *Elementary School Journal, 90*, 3–32.

Rich, S., & Pressley, M. (1990). Teacher acceptance of reading comprehension strategy instruction. *Elementary School Journal, 91*, 43–64.

Salomon, G., & Perkins, D. N. (1989). Rocky roads to transfer: Rethinking mechanisms of neglected phenomenon. *Educational Psychologist, 24*(2), 113–142.

Siegler, R. S. (1976). Three aspects of cognitive development. *Cognitive Psychology, 8*, 481–520.

Siegler, R. S. (1996). Unidimensional thinking, multidimensional thinking, and characteristic tendencies of thought. In A. J. Sameroff & M. Haith (Eds.), *The five- to seven-year shift: The age of reason and responsibility* (pp. 63–84). Chicago: University of Chicago Press.

Smolkin, L. B., & Donovan, C. (1993, December). *Responses of first graders to information and picture storybooks within a classroom context.* Paper presented at the annual meeting of the National Reading Conference, Charleston, SC.

Smolkin, L. B., & Donovan, C. A. (2000). *The contexts of comprehension: Information book read alouds and comprehension acquisition* (CIERA Report #2-009). Ann Arbor: CIERA/University of Michigan.

Smolkin, L. B., & Donovan, C. A. (in press). The contexts of comprehension: The information book read aloud, comprehension acquisition, and comprehension instruction in a first grade classroom. *Elementary School Journal.*

Smolkin, L. B., Donovan, C. A., & Lomax, R. G. (2001). Is narrative primary? Well, it depends. In T. Shanahan & F. Rodriguez-Brown (Eds.), *National Reading Conference Yearbook, 49*, 511–520.

Snow, C. E., Burns, M. S., & Griffin, P. (Eds.). (1998). *Preventing reading difficulties in young children: Report of the Committee on the Prevention of Reading Difficulties in Young Children.* Washington, DC: National Academy Press.

Stein, N. L., & Glenn, C. G. (1979). An analysis of story comprehension in elementary school children. In R. O. Freedle (Ed.), *Advances in discourse processes, Vol. 2: New directions in discourse processing* (pp. 53–120). Norwood, NJ: Ablex.

Taylor, I., & Taylor, M. M. (1983). *The psychology of reading.* New York: Academic Press.

Trabasso, T. (1994). The power of narrative. In F. Lehr & J. Osborn (Eds.), *Reading language, and literacy: Instruction for the twenty-first century* (pp. 187–200). Hillsdale, NJ: Erlbaum.

Trabasso, T., & Magliano, J. P. (1996). How do children understand what they read and what can we do to help them? In F. Graves, P. van den Broek, & B. M. Taylor (Eds.), *The first R: Every child's right to read* (pp. 160–188). New York: Teachers College Press.

Unsworth, L. (1999). Developing critical understanding of the specialised language of school science and history texts: A functional grammatical perspective. *Journal of Adolescent and Adult Literacy, 42*(7), 508–521.

Wells, G. (1986). *The meaning makers: Children learning language and using language to learn.* Portsmouth, NH: Heinemann.

White, S. H. (1965). Evidence for a hierarchical arrangement of learning processes. *Advances in Child Behavior and Development, 2*, 187–220.

White, S. H. (1996). The child's entry into the age of reason. In A. J. Sameroff & M. Haith (Eds.), *The five- to seven-year shift: The age of reason and responsibility* (pp. 18–30). Chicago: University of Chicago Press.

Wood, D., Bruner, J., & Ross, G. (1976). The role of tutoring in problem solving. *Journal of Child Psychology and Psychiatry, 17*, 89–100.

Wood, D., Wood, H., & Middleton, D. (1978). An experimental evaluation of four face-to-face teaching strategies. *International Journal of Behavioural Development, 1*, 131–147.

Yaden, D. B., Jr., Smolkin, L. B., & Conlon, A. (1989). Preschoolers' questions about pictures, print conventions, and story text during reading aloud at home. *Reading Research Quarterly, 24*, 188–214.

The Sweet Work of Reading

ANDIE CUNNINGHAM AND RUTH SHAGOURY

Andie, a kindergarten teacher, sits before her class of 5- and 6-year-olds and holds up the book *Owl Moon* (Yolen, 1987) for the students to see.

"Open up the part of your brains that's brilliant," Andie tells them. "We're learning a new strategy today. You're going to use your brains to make a picture of the book. Ready?"

Andie directs her students' attention toward the fresh piece of butcher paper on the easel. She points out the sticky notes and pens. "It's time to read *Owl Moon*," she says. "As I read, pay attention to the place in your brain that makes a picture of the part of the book that's most important to you."

She starts to read, and the class enters the hushed night of owl-calling. Faces turn to the book; from time to time, the students use their "owl voices" to hoot with the owls in the story.

When she finishes, Andie asks the students to decide on the one picture in their heads that's most important to them. "When you're ready," she says, "get your pen and paper and draw your *one* picture. Be specific and detailed."

Slowly and intentionally, Megan picks up a sticky note and pen and walks to a table to draw her picture. Austin looks up at the ceiling, smiles, picks up his pen, and settles down to work. Lacey scrunches up her face, squeezing her eyes shut. "I'm still thinkin'," she says. "I gotta choose 'cuz I got five in my head."

This kindergarten is a workshop of readers and thinkers who take seriously the work of making meaning from books. Andie has set the tone for their comprehension work through deliberate instructions and by providing her students with the tools they need. Students are writing about their reading. They use fine-line black pens to make meaningful marks on large sticky notes that serve as placeholders for their thinking.

This lesson is not reproduced from a published reading program, nor is it a yearly unit trotted out for every new group of kindergartners. This particular book

Cunningham, A., & Shagoury, R. (2005). The sweet work of reading. *Educational Leadership, 63*, 53–57. Reprinted with permission. The Association for Supervision and Curriculum Development is a worldwide community of educators advocating sound policies and sharing best practices to achieve the success of each learner. To learn more, visit ASCD at www.ascd.org.

choice was in response to Carrie's interest in becoming an expert in trees and Kenya's desire to learn more about big birds and where they live.

Building on Interests

As a kindergarten teacher-researcher and a university researcher, we have been investigating what is possible for young children as they acquire literacy skills. Educators concerned with kindergarten curriculum are all asking the same questions: What reading comprehension skills do today's kindergartners truly require? What skills do they need to become avid learners in school and in the world, active and compassionate citizens, and their best selves?

Contemporary researchers (Harvey & Goudvis, 2000; Keene & Zimmermann, 1997; Miller, 2002) have shown how readers can explore comprehension using a range of strategies. The students in Andie's class are teaching us that kindergartners can use these important comprehension strategies to bring their home knowledge into school. Some students realize for the first time that their understanding of a book is important. As they make text-to-self connections in books that the teacher reads to them, students learn the importance of schema—what they bring to a text in terms of their background knowledge and life experiences. As they tap into their knowledge of the world and make connections, they are more prepared to go on to other important reading comprehension skills, such as text-to-text connections, inferences, questioning, and synthesis. For example, when we read *Too Many Tamales* (Soto, 1993), with its central theme of losing an important object, the students made bridges from the book to each of their schemas. Daniel remembered misplacing a screw for a toy truck headlight; Ryan relived the memory of losing a ring in a swimming pool; Bao Jun detailed her loss of a cat in China.

Student interests create our reading curriculum. Nathaniel's interest in pumpkins led to our decision to read *Pumpkin Circle* (Levenson, 1999). We read *Miss Twiggly's Treehouse* (Fox, 1966) to focus on Bianca's interest in studying friendships. Building on their interests helps students make their own authentic connections, the foundation of our work together. The lesson on making mental pictures from *Owl Moon* is not isolated from the rest of the students' lives. They paint what they know, write and tell stories, and read books that link their background knowledge to this new academic world.

A Community of Learners

Andie's classroom is in a K–3 school in Portland, Oregon, that has the highest number of families living in poverty in the district. Of its 540 students, more than 85 percent receive free or reduced-price breakfasts and lunches. There are six half-day kindergarten classes, each with 20–25 students. Students speak at least 13 languages other than English; the school employs two full-time, in-house translators for Spanish and Russian families.

Many languages swirl through the classroom. During daily calendar work, for example, we usually count in Russian, Spanish, and English, thanks to the help of parents who are teaching us to count in their home languages. Sharing our home languages, experiences, knowledge, and questions is an important element of becoming a community. Comprehension and community go hand in hand as the students learn to work together and do the hard work that goes along with making meaning out of difficult texts.

Bringing each student's schema to the classroom discussion is challenging. It requires thoughtful planning on the part of the teacher and ample time for learners to grapple with meaning so they can contribute their ideas to the community.

Mind Pictures

This morning, the students wrestle with important "mind pictures" that they have in their heads as a result of listening to *Owl Moon*. Lacey shows her completed picture to Ruth, a university researcher. "This is a big tree where the man was calling out," she says.

Benjamin shows his drawing to Andie. "This is the guy who is telling her to be quiet," he says, pointing to the two figures on the sticky note. Benjamin shows her the arrow between the two figures, indicating from which direction the voice is coming. He points to two large orbs hovering over the people. "This is the owl's eyes," he says. As the students finish drawing on their sticky notes, they carry them to Andie, who records their words on the notes and sticks them on the butcher paper.

Together we look at and read the individual writing and drawing on the sticky notes, noticing first the differences. For example, Carrie has drawn a picture of an owl landing on a branch, whereas Ivan focused on one of the characters, the Grandpa. Andie reinforces the idea that although everyone is bringing a different schema to the story, they have all drawn owls, trees, and people. The chart has stimulated rich new discussions of the story. With contributions from each class member secured, conversations have a grounded place in which to flourish.

Digging Deep

Readers who care about making sense of the books they read don't give up on stories when meaning eludes them. They come back and struggle with the text until they make sense of it. There is an excitement to uncovering layers of meaning when we spiral back to difficult texts. Few kindergartners are taught how to experience this kind of "hard fun" when they read. But when we give them a chance to play with it, they rise to the challenge.

When Andie finishes reading *Almost to Freedom* (Nelson, 2003), Austin's first words are, "There were a lot of words in there!" This book is challenging. Besides having "lots of words," it tells the painful story of a young girl fleeing slavery on the Underground Railroad.

"Yeah," Nathaniel piggybacks, "like a hundred million words. I want to keep it in the room and read it the next day and the day after that and the day after that."

Nathaniel understands that the more we revisit those tough reads with millions of words, the better our chances of discovering their riches. Throughout the year, we explore such provocative books as *The Three Questions* (Muth, 2002), a retelling of a philosophical tale by Leo Tolstoy; *The Cats of Krasinsky Square* (Hesse, 2004), set in Poland during World War II; *Where Is Grandpa?* (Barron & Soentpiet, 2001), a story of one family dealing with death and loss; and *Visiting Day* (Woodson, 2002), in which a little girl tells of looking forward to her weekly visits to her dad in prison.

Kindergartners are capable of far more sophisticated reading strategies than educators often suspect. As they write, draw, paint, and move their bodies to the stories, they dig deep to make sense. Students might use clay to portray their mental images, dramatize what is important to them in a book, or paint watercolors of their inferences. With these strategies, they have a firm foundation for building reading success.

Synthesizing Meaning

Synthesizing is one of the most complex strategies that readers use to spiral into deeper layers of meaning. Readers "hold their thinking" as they progress through a book. In other words, they keep track of how their thinking is evolving, using their schemas to make inferences. They come to view the book and the world through new lenses.

This week, we dig into synthesizing with the clever picture book *No Such Thing* (Koller, 1997), in which a human child and a monster child are repeatedly assured by their mommies that the other doesn't exist—that there is "no such thing." It's a perfect book for seeing the world through another's eyes and gaining insights about perceptions other than one's own.

Early in the week, the students hold their thinking by writing and making drawings on sticky notes of what they remember from the book. When they finish, they place their notes on Andie's anchor chart. Later in the week, on the third reading of the book, Andie tells her students to use a new lens as they read the book:

> Decide who you are going to think like. The boy? His mom? The monster? Or the monster's mom? You'll be bringing your schema and using it to think like that person.

At the end of the reading, Carrie and Megan crawl under one of the tables and pretend they're lying in bed. Some boys head to the coat rack where they peer back over their shoulders. Around us, we see children pretending to be the little monster and the little boy. Bianca behaves as though she were the mother, looking in the door at her little boy.

After a few moments, the chime ringer rings the bell and the students return to the circle area. Andie tells the students that they can act out their characters for the class and that everyone will try to guess who they are.

Austin volunteers to start. He lies on the floor in the middle of the circle. It turns out he is being the monster screaming "AAAAHHHHH!" When it's his turn, José also lies in the middle of the floor, but he shakes his head *no* to all the guesses. He explains, "I was the boy at the end of the book when he was under the bed."

"Did that actually happen in the book?" Andie asks.

"No," José tells us. "They were just *gonna* switch when the book ends."

"José made a great inference!" Andie exclaims. "He used clues to figure out what was going to happen next—even after the book ends. Sweet work!"

The students take turns acting out different roles. Shy Bianca walks slowly to the center of the circle and hugs her arms tight around herself, rocking from side to side. We guess that she's the monster or the boy being scared.

"No," she says. "I'm huggin' the boy. I'm the mom huggin' the boy."

Bianca lived the book through the mom's eyes, sharing two different parts of the book as she moved: the mother looking at the boy through the doorway and the mother hugging her son. She spiraled deeper as she synthesized meaning.

Too many educators think that there's "no such thing" as kindergartners making sophisticated inferences that help them synthesize what they read. These students show what is possible.

A Nourishing Environment

Kindergartners face enormous challenges. Most of the students in Andie's class have little or no alphabet knowledge when they enter the classroom in the fall. English is a second or third language for many of the families in this impoverished working-class community. Instead of viewing kindergarten as a garden of children, we prefer the metaphor of a tide pool:

> Kindergartens, like tide pools, are a meeting place of two systems. The land and the sea meet at tide pools, and organisms in tide pools must adapt to adjust to the drastic changes in environment that come with the changing of the tides each day. (Barnhart & Leon, 1994, p. 7)

This image helps remind us of the way in which children must adjust to the differing environments of home and school at the cultural meeting place that is kindergarten. Kindergartners need specific learning tools. They need honor and respect to thrive. They need similar souls nearby, without the threat of predators. They need a climate that invites and supports their learning, and they need plenty of time to link literacy with their lives in the challenging world of school (Cunningham & Shagoury, 2005).

Building bridges between the books in the classroom and what students have learned in their first five years takes work. A publisher-designed curriculum might not connect to these children's lives at all. By incorporating students' interests into the curriculum, we can create a community in which we learn together. Within that community, students can learn the kind of reading comprehension skills that will help them become readers who turn to books for meaning, understanding, reflection, and pleasure.

Reading Comprehension Strategies

- *Making connections*—between texts, the world, and students' lives (sometimes called text-to-text, text-to-world, and text-to-self connections). Readers bring their background knowledge and experiences of life to a text.
- *Creating mental images.* These "mind pictures" help readers enter the text visually in their mind's eye.
- *Asking questions.* Readers who use this strategy actively ask questions of the text as they read.
- *Determining importance.* This strategy describes a reader's conscious and ongoing determination of what is important in a text.
- *Inferring.* When readers infer, they create new meaning on the basis of their life experiences and clues from the book.
- *Synthesizing.* Although this strategy is sometimes considered a retell, synthesizing is a way of spiraling deeper into the book. Readers might explore the text through the perspective of different characters to come to new understandings about the character's life and world.

References

Barnhart, D., & Leon, V. (1994). *Tidepools: The bright world of the rocky shoreline.* Upper Saddle River, NJ: Pearson Educational.

Cunningham, A., & Shagoury, R. (2005). *Starting with comprehension: Reading strategies for the youngest learners.* Portland, ME: Stenhouse Publishers.

Harvey, S., & Goudvis, A. (2000). *Strategies that work: Teaching comprehension to enhance understanding.* Portland, ME: Stenhouse Publishers.

Keene, E., & Zimmermann, S. (1997). *Mosaic of thought: Teaching comprehension in a reader's workshop.* Portsmouth, NH: Heinemann.

Miller, D. (2002). *Reading with meaning: Teaching comprehension in the primary grades.* Portland, ME: Stenhouse Publishers.

Learning from What Doesn't Work

GAY IVEY AND DOUGLAS FISHER

• • • • •

Educators are flooding the professional learning community with requests for strategies that work to improve reading comprehension in the upper-elementary and secondary grades. In these achievement-driven times, we want to know what works best to raise test scores, improve comprehension, and motivate students to read. The answers are not simple for most students, particularly for older students still learning about literacy. The needs of adolescent readers are complex and varied (Ivey, 1999), even within specific cultural groups (Alvermann, 2001) and linguistic groups (Rubinstein-Avila, 2003–2004). To make blanket assertions about what works for *all* students would be misguided and shortsighted.

Getting to the bottom of older readers' comprehension and motivation difficulties requires careful, ongoing assessment of instructional practices and students' literacy needs. We believe, like Guthrie and Wigfield (1997), that real engagement in reading is not the product of strategies alone but a fusion of self-efficacy, interest, and strategic knowledge.

What we can report with more certainty are common practices that create barriers to engaged reading and comprehension development. We invite you to consider five ineffective strategies for developing reading comprehension in older students. Before asking "What works?", it might help to ask "What *doesn't* work?"

Ineffective Strategy 1: Don't Let Students Read

A new high school principal "put an end to reading" and gave back to teachers time formerly used for Sustained Silent Reading. He warned teachers that students should be "focused on the instruction at hand" rather than "sitting around reading" during class time. In a discussion about these policy changes, the principal explained, "Students have to be taught. We need more time focused on direct instruction."

Ivey, G., & Fisher, D. Learning from what doesn't work. Reprinted by permission. The Association for Supervision and Curriculum Development is a worldwide community of educators advocating sound policies and sharing best practices to achieve the success of each learner. To learn more, visit ASCD at www.ascd.org.

During the next two years, book circulation rates at the high school library plummeted, and the school's overall achievement on the content standards tests declined. Teachers understood why taking away students' time to "just read" might have resulted in a decline in reading scores, but they were shocked that scores sagged in history and science as well.

Compare this with the approach of principal Doug Williams, a former math teacher. He announced to the faculty of Hoover High School, "If we are going to teach our students to read, we need to provide them with *opportunities* to read." He allocated 20 minutes each day for Sustained Silent Reading and provided his staff with the resources and professional development necessary to ensure that students had time to read books of their choice (Fisher, 2004).

The result? Hoover has met state accountability targets, and students' average reading level as measured by the Gates-MacGinitie Reading Test has risen from 4.3 to 7.2. Although the independent reading initiative cannot take full credit for this, Hoover teachers credit the Sustained Silent Reading time with a significant portion of the increased achievement.

In addition to such schoolwide approaches as a formal Sustained Silent Reading period (Pilgreen, 2000), providing students with time for independent reading during content-area classes increases their motivation, background knowledge, and vocabulary. In fact, students report that having time to read actually affords them the opportunity to think and comprehend (Ivey & Broaddus, 2001). Consequently, we cannot imagine initiatives designed to improve comprehension that do not prioritize time with text. Although some have suggested that providing students with practice does not improve their reading (Shanahan, 2004), we cannot think of a single case in which a poor reader became a better reader without having substantial opportunities to read. How many years of piano, tennis, or driving practice do we need to excel at those skills?

We often hear the argument that we should focus on the basic skills, even in high school, before using valuable instructional time to let students read. We know of programs for struggling readers that emphasize word-level reading skills for several years to the exclusion of real reading. This kind of instruction certainly helps students read words more accurately, but it doesn't necessarily equate to improved reading comprehension, nor does it increase student motivation to read. Students need instruction, but mostly they need opportunities to negotiate real texts for real purposes. For example, 7th grader Manuel struggled to read materials above the 2nd grade level, but he became more skilled and motivated to read when his teacher found easy books for him to read and Web sites for him to peruse on platypuses and leopards, two animals that had piqued his interest in science class.

Ineffective Strategy 2: Make Students Read What They Don't Know About and Don't Care About

Insisting that every student needs to read enduring works of literature, Ms. Prewitt distributes a copy of *Things Fall Apart* (Achebe, 1958) to each of her students, along with a packet that requires the students to summarize each chapter, identify the characters, and respond to specific prompts.

With no background knowledge and little interest in the book, students read one chapter each night for homework. They complete the assigned section of the packet before discussing the chapter in class. The book takes several weeks to complete; students rush to catch up on the packet work on the final day. One student uses *CliffsNotes* to hurriedly complete his packet; another student copies from a peer. When asked about the book, Anthony admits, "I don't know what it was about, really. All we had to do was this" (he shows the packet). When asked, "Did you make any connections between this book and your own life?", Anthony confesses, "I barely read it. I just searched for the answers. Man, it's not like I need to know this."

Alternatively, Mr. Jackson, a history teacher, was discussing the Reformation with his students. Each student had selected a book from a wide range of texts on the topic and appeared interested in the subject at hand. When asked how he engaged his students, Mr. Jackson replied,

> You build on what they know *and* on what they care about. You also give them books to choose from so they can extend what they know.

Observing this classroom at work revealed a number of practices ensuring that students comprehended the content. First, Mr. Jackson used a wide range of texts and media to inundate students with intriguing information about the topic, drawing also from contemporary issues that would help students see connections between history and events currently happening in their world and in their personal lives. As students worked on generating questions for a game simulation, they reviewed their individual readings from the textbook and several trade books as well as their notes from class lectures, discussions, and a video that they had watched.

One page of Daveen's notes focused on the role of the Pope. Daveen's conversation with us confirmed his interest in and comprehension of the subject. After Daveen explained to us the role of the Catholic Church during the Reformation and the process of selecting a Pope, we asked whether he realized that the Pope had just died. "Yeah," he said. "I watched it on TV. I'm not Catholic, but it was cool to see history being repeated." When asked whether he planned to watch the Pope's funeral on television the next day, Daveen grinned and said, "Oh yeah, I'll watch it. You know, Elvis holds that record [for the biggest funeral in history]. I hope the Pope doesn't beat out the King."

Students *can* find curriculum-based topics interesting, and they *can* comprehend what they read in school. Unfortunately, we do not always use texts and methods that highlight what is interesting about the subjects that we teach. Think about how much more compelling students would find a study of genetics, for example, if we used trade books to connect the topic to the fascinating details of solving crimes (*Silent Witness*, Ferllini, 2002) or of multiple births (*Twin Tales: The Magic and Mystery of Multiple Birth*, Jackson, 2001).

Teachers generally ask students to read about a topic before they actually know enough about it to become interested. As adults, we rarely choose to read about unfamiliar topics, and we find it difficult to pay attention when we need to do so. But think about how your inclination to read increases when new information piques your interest. Take the phenomenon of the tsunami, for instance. Before late 2004, would you have been inclined to read about this natural disaster on your own? After the devastating tsunami in Asia, however, perhaps your sympathy for the many victims or your concern about a recurrence caused you to seek out more information on the subject.

We are not saying that students shouldn't read the great, enduring works of literature, nor that they should read only adolescent fiction. We are simply wondering whether a whole class needs to read the same book at the same time and whether this practice tends to produce engaged, interested students who are extending their knowledge.

Teachers who understand their students' backgrounds, prior knowledge, interests, and motivations are much more likely to make the connections that adolescents crave. Although volumes have been written on the importance of and strategies for building background knowledge (Marzano, 2004), good teachers understand that making their content relevant also matters. Studies further suggest that we must provide students with opportunities to draw from what they already know—popular culture and media, for example—so they can more easily learn new information (Goodson & Norton-Meier, 2003).

Ineffective Strategy 3: Make Students Read Difficult Books

Four students of various reading levels sit in a cluster to read together Camus' *The Guest* from their 12th grade literature anthology. Three of these students take turns reading; one follows along. When they reach predetermined places in the story, they stop to take stock of their understanding using the guidelines set forth in a popular strategy known as *reciprocal teaching* (Palincsar & Brown, 1984), in which students (1) summarize the section, (2) clarify confusing parts, (3) ask questions, and (4) predict what will come next.

Each student takes responsibility for one part of the process. The three students who volunteered for the oral reading fulfill their roles productively in the intermittent discussions. This strategy appears to help these students make sense of what they read as they move through the text. The fourth student, who is designated as the person to ask a clarification question, seems timid and confused when it is her turn to talk.

When she is finally convinced to take a turn reading aloud, it is clear that the text is far beyond her comfort level. In a paragraph of roughly 150 words, she misreads *mused, circumstances, alliance, fraternized, fatigue, essential,* and *musings,* and she takes a substantial amount of time to figure out *fluttered, presence, imposing, ancient, community, armor,* and *heavier.* Even with such solid scaffolding as reciprocal teaching, the difficulty of this text makes comprehension too much of a challenge for this student.

Like this high school senior, 7th grader Renee is part of the 25 percent of students in her school who are reading below grade level and failing to achieve passing scores on the state achievement test. However, Renee's social studies teacher knows that she cannot learn from books that are too difficult for her (Allington, 2002).

Instead of assigning one book for the whole class to read during a study of westward expansion in the United States during the mid-1800s, he provides reading choices. A week or so into the unit and after reading aloud from *The Perilous Journey of the Donner Party* (Calabro, 1999), *Hurry Freedom: African Americans in Gold Rush California* (Stanley, 2000), and several other complex but compelling books, he invites Renee and her classmates to select a text from more than 50 different books related to the topic, which vary in genre and level of difficulty. Renee, who has an identified learning disability, and two of her friends who are English language learners select *Kit Carson: A Life of Adventure* (Mercati, 2000), which they read nearly effortlessly on their own. Afterward, they create a fact poster to share with their classmates who have been learning from a host of other books on westward expansion. Renee, who sits in other classes seemingly confused during whole-class readings of difficult texts, has learned so much from this accessible book that she must use the flip side of the poster board to include everything she now has to say.

If we want students to comprehend what they read, we must begin by letting them experience texts that make sense to them. Unfortunately, we hear of school districts that have declared that to get students reading at grade level, all students must practice reading in grade-level texts exclusively: "The test is written at an 8th grade level, so students have to learn how to read 8th grade passages!" We know of no student who got better at reading by reading books that were too difficult for him, and we know of no student reading at a 4th grade level who learned to read at an 8th grade level by reading only 8th grade-level books.

Ineffective Strategy 4: Interrogate Students about What They Read

An 8th grade English teacher begins class with the proclamation. "Today, we are focusing on comprehension." Any observer can see that this is indeed the intention because one of the state curriculum standards dealing with comprehension is written prominently on the chalkboard. "You need to know how to comprehend what you read on the state test coming up in April," the teacher explains. With no further discussion, she asks for a volunteer to begin reading aloud from *I Had Seen Castles* (Rylant, 1993).

Some students follow along as their classmate reads, while others stare out the window, work on assignments for other classes, or whisper to a neighboring student. After several paragraphs, the teacher interrupts: "Can somebody explain what is happening so far?" After three students fail to adequately summarize the story, the teacher throws out a series of literal-level comprehension questions. Facing blank stares from the students, she ends up giving her own summary. This cycle of assigning the reading, questioning, coming up short, and summarizing continues for the rest of the class period.

Now consider a 6th grade small-group reading of *Welcome to Dead House* (Stine, 1995). As students read, the teacher interrupts with, "I wonder what those noises are in the house? When I have questions like this, it sometimes helps me to look back in the chapter." Before she can finish her thought, several students yell out, "The voices are from dead people!" The teacher goes on to tell students that she has seen movies in which the ghost of a person who once lived in a house communicates with the current residents. A student muses, "I wonder whether this ghost will be like Casper." Students and teacher negotiate the text together.

Despite the long-standing practice of literal-level questioning after reading, we have no reason to believe it actually creates better readers. People often confuse *teaching* comprehension skills with *testing* comprehension. This common practice persists in schools despite decades of research indicating that comprehension is a proactive, continual process of using prior knowledge, metacognitive awareness, and reflection to make sense of a text.

When adults think back to what reading comprehension meant when they were in elementary school, they may recall workbook pages that required them to "find the main idea" for a series of unrelated short passages. If you were asked to find the main idea enough times on your own, the thinking went, you would eventually figure out how to do it. We now realize that specific strategies can help students determine what is important in the texts they read and how they can be more strategic before, during, and after the reading so that understanding texts is not such a mystery (Duffy, 2002).

In our work across the United States, we consistently find that many teachers have not yet had the opportunity to study the nature of reading comprehension, even their own. Most new curriculum materials for teaching reading include a focus on strategies, but these materials may not always provide teachers with the theoretical underpinnings of reading processes and of effective comprehension instruction. A good start in the shift from interrogation to teaching would be a schoolwide professional development study of reading comprehension.

Ineffective Strategy 5: Buy a Computer Program and Let It Do All the Work

Enter the skills lab. Students wearing headphones sit at their terminals. They look engaged in the task at hand, and they click away on the keyboard and mouse as their teacher wanders around the room. The school recently purchased a reading comprehension program that promises a "complete solution" to the reading needs of struggling adolescents. During the sales presentation, the administrator was told that the program was "teacher-proof" and that students would improve their test scores in a matter of weeks.

But let's take a closer look. As we join Taheen at his monitor, we see that he has the reading program running in one window and a chat room running in another. He periodically glances up from the chat room to answer a computer-generated comprehension question. He gets all the answers right and doesn't seem to be trying. At the computer across from Taheen, Fernando is getting frustrated. He doesn't know the answer, and the computer is unable to offer him any help.

In another classroom, we join Ryan and Clay, two 8th grade students who are most comfortable reading 1st grade-level texts, such as *Spider Names* (Canizares, 1998) and *Tiny Terrors* (Kenah, 2004). Although these books are easy-to-read nonfiction, they nevertheless include information that even older readers would find fascinating.

The teacher capitalizes on the students' background knowledge by having them talk as they work on their current project. They are dictating to her a story to accompany an intriguing illustration from the wordless picture book *The Mysteries of Harris Burdick* (Van Allsburg, 1984). They debate the most interesting word choices (for example, *hurt* as opposed to *devastated*) while their teacher acts as scribe. They are eager and able to reread this lengthy and complex story—written in their own words—and revise it to make it more interesting and grammatically accurate. Their teacher explains certain conventions of language and draws their attention to literary devices that other authors use as they write. For example, when the boys decide that they need to let readers know early in the story that something bad is going to happen, the teacher locates several picture books that include examples of foreshadowing. This not only gives the students ideas for their own writing but also inspires them to recognize this tool in their strategic reading. This teacher is indispensable.

Although computers and Web sites may reinforce skills, they can't provide the specific feedback that students require. Intervention programs need to increase, not decrease, teacher involvement (Ivey & Fisher, in press). In addition, intervention programs—computerized or not—must be based on assessment information and provide students with reading comprehension instruction rather than focus on a single aspect of reading or writing, such as phonics, fluency, or spelling.

What It Will Take

Improving reading comprehension and instruction in the upper-elementary and secondary grades will require a great deal of time and effort. There is no magical set of strategies you can get from an inservice workshop. Real changes in literacy learning and teaching will most likely result from a schoolwide literacy plan and strong leadership (Ivey & Fisher, in press).

Bringing about such a change means devoting resources to literacy-related personnel and to large volumes of high-quality, diverse, multileveled reading materials in all subject areas. It requires a commitment to providing literacy assessments of all students for the purpose of designing purposeful and appropriate instruction. It means creating a culture of collaboration and peer coaching. Finally, it requires that professional development focus on building teacher knowledge and expertise.

Is this a tall order for schools when the immediate need is to improve their current students' reading comprehension? Absolutely. But we are doing struggling students no favor when we perpetuate strategies that do not work.

References

Allington, R. L. (2002). You can't learn much from books you can't read. *Educational Leadership, 60*(3), 16–19.

Alvermann, D. E. (2001). Reading adolescents' identities: Looking back to see ahead. *Journal of Adolescent & Adult Literacy, 44,* 676–690.

Duffy, G. G. (2002). *Explaining reading: A resource for teaching concepts, skills, and strategies.* New York: Guilford Press.

Fisher, D. (2004). Setting the "opportunity to read" standard: Resuscitating the SSR program in an urban high school. *Journal of Adolescent and Adult Literacy, 48,* 138–150.

Goodson, F. T., & Norton-Meier, L. (2003). Motor oil, civil disobedience, and media literacy. *Journal of Adolescent & Adult Literacy, 47,* 258–262.

Guthrie, J. T., & Wigfield, A. (Eds.). (1997). *Reading engagement: Motivating readers through integrated instruction.* Newark, DE: International Reading Association.

Ivey, G. (1999). A multicase study in the middle school: Complexities among young adolescent readers. *Reading Research Quarterly, 34,* 172–192.

Ivey, G., & Broaddus, K. (2001). "Just plain reading": A survey of what makes students want to read in middle school classrooms. *Reading Research Quarterly, 36,* 350–377.

Ivey, G., & Fisher, D. (in press). *Reading, writing, and thinking in secondary schools.* Alexandria, VA: ASCD.

Marzano, R. (2004). *Building background knowledge for academic achievement: Research on what works in schools.* Alexandria, VA: ASCD.

Palincsar, A. S., & Brown, A. L. (1984). Reciprocal teaching of comprehension-fostering and comprehension-monitoring activities. *Cognition and Instruction, 1*(2), 117–175.

Pilgreen, J. (2000). *The SSR handbook.* Portsmouth, NH: Boynton/Cook.

Rubinstein-Avila, E. (2003–2004). Conversing with Miguel: An adolescent English language learner with later literacy development. *Journal of Adolescent & Adult Literacy, 47,* 290–301.

Shanahan, T. (2004). Improving reading achievement in secondary schools: Structures and reforms. In D. S. Strickland & D. E. Alvermann (Eds.), *Bridging the literacy achievement gap grades 4–12* (pp. 43–55). New York: Teachers College Press.

Classroom Implications

1. How has your concept of reading comprehension changed after reading this chapter? In what specific ways might you modify your current approach to teaching comprehension?

2. The readings in this chapter detail a number of teaching strategies. Which strategy do you think might be most important in your own instruction? What problems might you need to consider before these changes could be effectively implemented?

For Further Reading

Allen, K., & Ingulsrud, J. E. (2005). Reading manga: Patterns of personal literacies among adolescents. *Language and Education, 19*, 265–280.

Cragg, L., & Nation, K. (2006). Exploring written narrative in children with poor reading comprehension. *Educational Psychology, 26*, 55–72.

Cris, T. (2005). The power of purposeful reading. *Educational Leadership, 63*(2), 48–51.

Dieterich, S. E., et al. (2006). The impact of early maternal verbal scaffolding and child language abilities on later decoding and reading comprehension skills. *Journal of School Psychology, 43*, 481–494

Ehren, B. J. (2005, Oct–Dec.). Looking for evidence-based practice in reading comprehension instruction. *Topics in Language Disorders*, 310–321.

Manning, M. (2005). Celebrations in reading and writing: An end to pseudo-reading. *Teaching Pre K–8, 35*, 78–79.

Pearson, P. D., Ferdig, R. E., Blomeyer, R. L., & Moran, J. (2005). *The effects of technology on reading performance in the middle-school grades: A meta-analysis with recommendations for policy.* Naperville, IL: North Central Regional Educational Laboratory.

Salinger, T., & Fleischman, S. (2005). Teaching students to interact with text. *Educational Leadership, 63*(2), 90–92.

Walker, B. J. (2005). Thinking aloud: Struggling readers often require more than a model. *The Reading Teacher, 58*, 688–692.

Vaughn, S., & Edmonds, M. (2006). Reading comprehension for older readers. *Intervention for School & Clinic, 41*, 131–137.

Wolf, M. K., Crossen, A. C., & Resnick, L. B. (2005). Classroom talk for rigorous reading comprehension instruction. *Reading Psychology, 26*, 27–53.

Online Resources

Comprehension in Beginning Reading (University of Oregon)
http://reading.uoregon.edu/comp

Reading Comprehension (Southwest Regional Development Laboratory)
www.sedl.org/reading/framework/nonflash/reading.html

Text Comprehension Instruction (National Institute for Literacy)
www.nifl.gov/partnershipforreading/publications/reading_first1text.html

National Reading Panel Report
www.nationalreadingpanel.org

• • • • •

Chapter 4

Adolescent Literacy

It is one of the great pleasures of a student's life to buy a heap of books at the beginning of the autumn. Here, he fancies, are all of the secrets.

—Robert Lynd (1923)

The impact of even one good book on a young person's mind is surely an end in itself, a valid experience which helps him form standards of judgment and taste at the time when his mind is most sensitive to impressions of every kind.

—Lillian H. Smith (1953)

Adolescent literacy—the reading and writing of middle and high school students —is critical to student success in all areas of the curriculum.

—Implementing the No Child Left Behind Act: Using Student Engagement to Improve Adolescent Literacy (2005)

Many adolescents do not see reading and an important aspect of their daily lives and this is a major concern today to educators as well as the general public. The results in the recent report of the National Assessment of Educational Progress, *The Nation's Report Card: Reading 2005* (Perie, Grigg, & Donahue, 2005), support this serious situation:

- 36 percent of fourth-graders performed below the "Basic" level in reading, which is characterized by "partial mastery of the knowledge and skills that are fundamental for proficient work at a grade level."
- 27 percent of eighth-graders performed below the "Basic" level in reading.
- 43 percent of ethnic minorities scored below the "Basic" level in reading.
- No state had a higher average reading score in 2005 than in previous national assessments and seven had a lower score.
- Between 1988 and 2005, the percentage at or above "Basic" level in reading increased in four states and decreased in eleven states.
- The national average reading score was one point lower in 2005 than in 2003.

The causes of these dire statistics are complex. To gain a more nuanced perspective, we will next examine the situation in middle schools.

The Middle School Problem

A visitor to Oglethorpe Academy in Savannah, Georgia, is not likely to be alarmed. Standardized test scores in reading and content subjects are high, disciplinary referrals are few, and teacher morale is good. Such a visitor might find it difficult to believe that a substantial literacy problem exists in U.S. middle schools. After all, Oglethorpe Academy is a public school, its physical facilities are modest, and its parents do not pay tuition. The fact is, however, that Oglethorpe is not a typical middle school. Its parents tend to be well educated and, through a state charter, agree to volunteer extensively. Most of its students had strong academic records at the elementary level before entering Oglethorpe and are college bound as they move on to high school. Nearly all of them speak English as their first language, and only 30 percent qualify for free or reduced-price lunches.

To gain an understanding of the problem, let us visit a middle school that is more representative of the nation. Rather than single out a real school, we will create a composite—Jefferson Middle School—based on national data. Jefferson serves 605 students in grades 6–8. Although many of them are good readers, 27 percent of the eighth-graders cannot read at even a basic level, as defined by the National Assessment of Educational Progress. Their reading problems did not begin when they entered Jefferson. As fourth graders, a similar percentage were experiencing problems. Poverty levels at Jefferson are relatively high; about 27 percent of the students qualify for free or reduced-price lunches. Parents often have limited education and find it difficult to volunteer extensively at the school. Many of these parents do not harbor fond memories of Jefferson and feel uncomfortable when they visit the school. Girls at Jefferson tend to be better readers than boys, and whites, as a group, outperform blacks and Hispanics. Test scores at Jefferson have allowed the school to demonstrate adequate yearly progress in reading and other areas, but Jefferson is currently flirting with the state's needs-improvement list and is unlikely to make AYP for much longer.

It is easy to see that Jefferson and Oglethorpe are not very similar. In fact, we might joke that the only thing they have in common is the age of the students. Tragically, however, even that is not quite true; the average age of Jefferson students is higher than the students at Oglethorpe because of frequent retentions.

For these reasons, success stories like Oglethorpe's are rarely if ever exportable to struggling schools. The faculty at Jefferson must work for changes that will realistically address the challenges posed by the students they serve. They would do well to begin by studying the factors that led to the literacy crisis in their school.

What Has Caused the Middle School Literacy Problem?

False Causes.   Let's start by dispelling two "causes" that have no direct bearing on middle school literacy achievement. The first is race. Because in the United States race happens to be *correlated* with reading achievement, it is falsely believed by some educators to be a *cause* of low achievement. But when we account for factors such as income level and parental education, we find that race is a very poor predictor of achievement.

For example, children of well-educated, middle-income black parents are just as likely to succeed in school as children of well-educated, middle-income white parents.

The other false factor is technology. Many educators (particularly language arts teachers) lament the proliferation of video gaming, Internet access, cell phones, and the like, which they perceive to be attractive nuisances that relegate literacy to a lower priority for the nation's youth. Similar charges were leveled at television at the time of its advent during the 1950s and 60s. A "displacement" theory was proposed, suggesting that the time available for recreational reading was displaced by watching television. While NAEP findings do indeed show that extreme amounts of televiewing (six or more hours per day) are associated with poor reading achievement, it has never been clear that heavy watchers would be likely to reach for a book if the plug were pulled. Nor does the displacement theory seem very likely in the case of recent technology applications. This is true for two reasons. First, the percentage of eighth-graders who have performed poorly on the NAEP test has remained relatively constant over nearly four decades since the test was first given—long before microchips began to transform the lives of adolescents. Second, many of these technology applications involve some level of literate activity. Whether a student is surfing the Internet, reading clues in a video game, or sending text messages to friends via cell phone, there is no doubt that technology is changing what counts as literacy. But these changes can work to the advantage of middle grades teachers, as we shall see. In the meantime, let's identify the true causes of the middle school literacy problem.

Education and Culture.   Literacy is an attainment that is not universally valued. Its importance is viewed differently by individuals and groups within the U.S. population. The value of literacy is reflected in one's level of education and tends to be acquired from parents and peers. Children who witness literate activity being modeled and valued tend to acquire those values themselves. Children who are not exposed to these influences often develop different views.

Poverty.   Because individuals of limited education tend to earn less, a vicious cycle develops from one generation to the next. Parents of limited education find it difficult to foster high levels of literacy in their children, who grow up at risk of school failure and eventually take jobs for which the literacy demands are low. We believe that literacy is the key to the cycle of poverty, but it is a key that usually must be turned from the outside by dedicated educators. We are not suggesting that literacy is perfectly correlated with income. There are many literate people of modest means. However, extreme poverty makes the attainment of literacy doubtful, for it frequently goes hand-in-glove with one's level of education.

Text Demands.   Jeanne Chall (1983/1996) spoke of a "fourth-grade slump," the point where she believed reading achievement began to flag. Chall attributed this decline in part to the failure of many students to attain prerequisite skills, such as automatic word recognition and fluency. Another factor is the nonfiction text that children encounter. These texts gradually increase in difficulty, but they are still within the reach of most fluent fourth-graders. But their complexity and abstractness do not level off. Robert Calfee, longtime editor of the *Journal of Educational Psychology*, concluded, based on data from the Stanford Achievement Test, that a major slump occurs around grade seven, when the cumulative demands of vocabulary pose considerable challenges. It is in middle school that the conceptual demands of content textbooks become truly troublesome, which is why it is imperative that teachers of science and social studies employ instructional methods that facilitate their students as they wrestle with assigned materials.

Lack of Instruction.   In most middle schools, reading instruction falls in the language arts program, with the exception of remedial and special services. The focus of language arts teachers is split among competing standards. They must teach grammar and mechanics, literature, and composition. There is little time left for what struggling middle schoolers need most: systematic instruction in vocabulary and comprehension strategies. The frequent result is that no one takes responsibility for these prerequisites of reading success.

Profiles of Striving Middle School Readers

Students experiencing reading problems vary considerably, but most of them reflect several basic patterns. To understand these patterns, it helps to contrast them with normal reading development. Chall (1983/1996) proposed a series of stages through which students pass on their way to becoming proficient readers. These stages were

STAGE	NAME	DESCRIPTION	GRADES
0*	Emergent Literacy	Oral language develops; children learn how print functions; they acquire phonological awareness and knowledge of the alphabet	
1	Decoding	Children grasp the alphabetic principle and learn to decode most unfamiliar words quickly; many words now recognized automatically	K–1
2	Fluency	Oral reading of grade-level text becomes relatively rapid, marked by natural phrasing and intonation	2–3
3	Reading to Learn (Learning the New)	Children can purposefully extract and interpret information from grade-level nonfiction text	3–8
4	Multiple Viewpoints	Students recognize that authors embrace different views; they learn to discern differences in perspective	9–12
5	A World View	Students interpret text in terms of their own perspectives, noting differences among authors and between authors and themselves	College

FIGURE 1

The emergent literacy stage involves a very gradual approach to literate activity, and it cannot truly be called a stage. For this reason, Chall designated it as "Stage Zero"!

explained earlier, but the following chart summarizes them. (We have altered her labels slightly and adjusted the typical grade levels according to present-day instructional practice.)

Chall speculated that most striving readers experience difficulties because they do not acquire key skills at certain stages. Her idea is now strongly supported by research findings (see Spear-Swerling & Sternberg, 1997). According to Chall, normally progressing middle grades children should be able to read grade-appropriate nonfiction with good comprehension. Of course, we know that many cannot. Chall's stages help us understand why. Although a very small percentage of middle schoolers exhibit symptoms of developmental dyslexia, most can trace their problems back to a particular stage of development where they went "off track." Let's examine the patterns that result.

- Jamal is a fluent reader, who can read textbook passages aloud at reasonable speeds and with natural phrasing. However, he has little understanding of what he reads even when he reads silently and is not concerned about his public performance as a reader. Rick has passed through the fluency stage successfully but has not acquired the vocabulary and comprehension strategies he needs to gain meaning from text.
- Joanne reads aloud haltingly. She can decode nearly every word, given enough time, but lacks a large sight vocabulary. She has passed through the decoding stage but has not attained fluency. As a result, her attention is on word identification at the expense of comprehension.
- Jack finds reading extremely difficult. He often stops at unfamiliar words and lacks the decoding skills to pronounce them. His instructional reading level is several years below his grade placement. He has never successfully passed through the decoding stage.

Although precise statistics are not available, striving readers like Jamal are clearly the most numerous; there are far fewer readers like Joanne and (fortunately) still fewer like Jack. Determining which of these patterns best fits a particular student is not difficult, and it is a necessary first step towards meeting their instructional needs. These readers cannot attain proficiency unless they progress from their current stage through reading to learn.

Appreciating the nature of these stages and gaining a notion of the percentage of students at each of them are important if the literacy status of a particular middle school is to be understood. Thinking of achievement in terms of developmental stages gets us past the point of trying to analyze mere test scores and helps us gain a better sense of where we need to go.

How Do We Address the Problem of Adolescent Literacy?

The critical question becomes how to change the current situation in adolescent literacy. A report to the Carnegie Corporation, *Reading Next: A Vision for Action and Research in Middle and High School Literacy* (Biancarosa & Snow, 2004) suggested a number of essentials for educators to enhance adolescent literacy instruction, including the following points:

1. *Direct, explicit comprehension.* Instruction makes reading comprehension strategies explicit to students through modeling and explanation and gives students ample opportunities for practice.

2. *Effective instructional principles embedded in content.* Instruction is embedded and reinforced across content areas, with attention paid to content-specific texts and tasks.

3. *Motivation and self-directed learning.* Instruction promotes engagement and self-regulated learning for the development of motivated and flexible literacy skills.

4. *Text-based collaborative learning.* Instruction enables students to engage in guided interactions with texts in groups in order to foster learning of new knowledge.

5. *Strategic tutoring.* Individualized instruction is more intense for struggling readers and focuses on instilling independence.

6. *Diverse texts.* Students have access to, and experience with, texts at a variety of difficulty levels that vary in the styles, genres, topics, and content areas they cover.

7. *Intensive writing.* Instruction should integrate writing as a vehicle for learning and as a measure of comprehension and learning across content areas.

8. *A technology component.* Technology is used to leverage instruction time to provide additional support and practice for students as well as prepare students for the ways different technology alters the reading and writing experience.

9. *Ongoing formative assessment of students.* Instruction should be determined by the use of ongoing assessment of students that helps teachers target instruction.

10. *Extended time for literacy.* Reading and writing instruction takes place for longer than a single language arts period and is extended through integration and emphasis across curricula. Extended time may also include additional time devoted to literacy instruction, especially for learners more than two grade levels behind.

11. *Professional development.* Teachers participate in professional development experiences that are systematic, frequent, long-term, and ongoing to improve their ability to teach reading and writing across the curriculum

12. *Ongoing summative assessment of students and programs.* Students' progress is monitored and tracked over the long term.

13. *Teacher teams.* Infrastructure supports teachers working in small interdisciplinary teams to allow for coloration and more consistent and coordinated instruction and professional development.

14. *Leadership.* Principals and administrators participate in professional development and foster teachers taking leadership roles.

15. *A comprehensive and coordinated literacy program.* Instruction encompasses all aspects of literacy in ways that allow all facets of the program to complement one another and is consistent with professional development as well as the chosen materials and approaches for learning (p. 9).

In a Position Statement entitled *Supporting Young Adolescent Literacy Learning,* (International Reading Association, 2001) four specific recommendations were made for classroom teachers to help their students with their various literacy activities. They included the following:

- Engage in whole-school planning to implement components of a successful school or districtwide literacy learning plan that is integrative and interdisciplinary.
- Collaborate with administrators, librarians, guidance counselors, intervention specialists, and other school-based educators to improve reading instruction and achievement.
- Interpret assessment data and make information available to other teachers and school-based educators.
- Provide opportunities for students to read material they choose and to be read to each school day.

As You Read

The four selections in this chapter represent some of the current thinking by literacy educators on this topic. Darwin and Fleischman discuss specifics about how classroom teachers can help encourage young people to see reading as a part of their lives. The following two articles are concerned with the implications of the No Child Left Behind legislation and its application to adolescent literacy. The last article, by Schofield and Rogers, presents an alternative approach to a classroom literacy program for adolescents. Their many interesting ideas should challenge educators to reevaluate their current literacy programs.

References

Biancarosa, G., & Snow, C. E. (2004). *Reading Next: A vision for action and research in middle and high school literacy.* Washington, DC: Alliance for Excellence Education.

Chall, J. (1983/1996). *Stages of reading development.* New York: McGraw-Hill.

Lynd, R. (1923). *Solomon in all his glory.* New York: G. P. Putnam.

Implementing the No Child Left Behind Act: Using student engagement to improve adolescent literacy. (2005). Naperville, IL: North Central Regional Laboratory.

International Reading Association. (2001). *Supporting young adolescents' literacy learning: A joint position statement of the International Reading Association and the National Middle School Association.* Newark, DE: International Reading Association. Available at www.reading.org/downloads/positions/ps1052_supporting.pdf

Perie, M., Grigg, W. S., & Donahue, P. L. (2005). *The nation's report card: Reading 2005* (NCES 2006-451). U.S. Department of Education, Institute of Education Sciences, National Center for Education Statistics. Washington, DC: Government Printing Office.

Reading to achieve: A governor's guide to adolescent literacy. (2005). Washington, DC: National Governors Association.

Smith, L. H. (1953). *The unreluctant years: A critical approach to children's literature.* Chicago: American Library Association.

Spear-Swerling, L., & Sternberg, R. J. (1997). *Off track: When poor readers become "learning disabled."* Boulder, CO: Westview.

Strickland, D. S., & Alvermann, D. (2004). Learning and teaching literacy in grades 4–12. In D. S. Strickland & D. Alvermann (Eds.), *Issues and challenges in bridging the literacy achievement gap: Grades 4–12.* New York: Teachers College Press.

Research Matters/Fostering Adolescent Literacy

MARLENE DARWIN AND STEVE FLEISCHMAN

A sophomore high school student asked the reading specialist to look at the answers the student had written to questions in her world history textbook as she studied for a chapter test. In response to the question, "What was Robespierre's role in the Reign of Terror?" the student had copied the sentence from the textbook: "Robespierre was the architect of the Reign of Terror." When the reading specialist asked what this meant, the student responded, "Oh yeah, he must have built something." She could read the words, but she was unable to get at the passage's meaning.

What We Know

This student's struggle illustrates a typical challenge that many adolescents face in comprehending content textbooks. Middle and high school students who encounter difficulties in reading generally fall into one of three groups (Schoenbach, Greenleaf, Cziko, & Hurwitz, 1999). Some have severe deficits in reading that can be traced back to weak decoding skills. A second group may know enough phonics to laboriously sound out words, but they become so focused on decoding that they lose all sense of the meaning of the words and sentences.

But most struggling adolescent readers have no trouble decoding words. These students' difficulties are caused by the fact that they have limited vocabularies or lack broad background knowledge to apply to their reading, and thus they cannot create meaning. Such students, although often not recognized as struggling readers by content teachers, are found in most middle and high school classrooms across the country.

Recent data indicate that adolescents in the United States are not keeping pace with current literacy demands. These data also underscore disparities among racial and ethnic groups and among students from different socioeconomic levels. Reading scores of 12th grade students on the National Assessment of Educational Progress (NAEP) have remained flat for 20 years. Since 1988, the gap between the scores of white and black students has widened in 8th and 12th grade (U.S. Department of Education, 2000). At the same time, schools continue to rely on textbooks as the main printed source of curriculum delivery—even in the face of evidence showing that the average student in secondary classrooms is reading below the level of many content-area texts (Allington, 2002).

When teachers become aware that students cannot read their textbooks, they sometimes respond by providing students with all key ideas and concepts through in-class lectures. This practice may actually circumvent students' need to improve their literacy skills, thus avoiding the problem rather than addressing it (Schoenbach et al., 1999).

The nature of secondary school teacher training programs and of the secondary schools themselves may exacerbate the problem (Alvermann & Moore, 1991; Vacca & Vacca, 2005). At most, secondary teachers are required to take one course in content reading strategies. In addition, secondary schools are departmentalized, and each department focuses on its core content rather than on more general skills. We often hear a high school math or social studies teacher say, "I don't have time to teach reading or writing. That's the job of the English teachers."

This is a common misconception. English teachers have specific content to teach and do not have any more time than other content-area teachers do to teach students how to read to learn (Irvin, Buehl, & Klemp, 2003).

What You Can Do

A recent study published by the Comprehensive School Reform Quality Center (2005), *Works in Progress: A Report on Middle and High School Improvement Programs*, surveyed widely adopted programs and approaches, including those that address the diverse needs of adolescent readers. The models surveyed include Accelerated Reader, Student Team Reading and Writing, SRA Corrective Reading, the Reading Apprenticeship framework, and many others. Because the current base of research on secondary school improvement models is sparse, the report does not endorse the adoption of any specific program but instead presents these programs as "promising" and demonstrates that schools have many external programs from which to choose.

No one program or approach, however, will meet the needs of all adolescent readers. Secondary schools should also consider making comprehensive instructional and infrastructure changes. In *Reading Next: A Vision for Action and Research in Middle and High School Literacy*, Biancarosa and Snow (2004) suggest that principals and teachers address the diverse literacy needs of adolescents through a comprehensive approach encompassing the following strategies:

- Develop a schoolwide literacy focus, including targeted professional development and strong instructional leadership.

- Adopt a set of research-based instructional strategies, including such techniques as reciprocal teaching, graphic organizers, prompted outlines, and questioning the author, to foster reading growth across all content areas.
- Offer focused intervention classes taught by a trained reading specialist for students with severe reading deficits.
- Increase opportunities for students to choose books for pleasure reading during the school day.
- Use complementary trade books that present content textbooks' key facts and concepts in a more engaging style.
- Conduct assessments, both formal and informal, to help teachers understand the literacy needs of their students.
- Emphasize prereading activities, during-reading strategies, and graphic organizers to guide students in building background knowledge and creating meaning during the reading process.

When designing this kind of schoolwide approach, educators should take advantage of the many useful resources that have been published in response to the growing concern about adolescent literacy. Two good examples are *Adolescent Literacy Resources: Linking Research and Practice* (Meltzer, Smith, & Clark, 2001) and *Building Reading Proficiency at the Secondary Level: A Guide to Resources* (Peterson, Caverly, Nicholson, O'Neal, & Cusenbary, 2000).

Educators Take Note

To meet the daunting challenge of improving adolescents' literacy skills, teachers, administrators, and policymakers must move beyond a collection of effective programs. We must embrace a new attitude regarding adolescent literacy, recognizing that reading is not a static skill, but one that needs to grow along with the individual. The problem of older students who struggle with reading comprehension is urgent, and we must address it with systematic approaches that help schools focus on literacy growth for all students across all subject areas.

References

Allington, R. L. (2002). You can't learn much from books you can't read. *Educational Leadership*, *60*(3), 16–19.

Alvermann, D. E., & Moore, D. W. (1991). Secondary school reading. In R. Barr, M. Kamil, P. Mosenthal, & P. Pearson (Eds.), *Handbook of reading research* (2nd ed., pp. 951–983). New York: Longman.

Biancarosa, G., & Snow, C. E. (2004). *Reading next: A vision for action and research in middle and high school literacy. A report from Carnegie Corporation of New York*. Washington, DC: Alliance for Excellent Education.

Comprehensive School Reform Quality Center. (2005). *Works in progress: A report on middle and high school improvement programs*. Washington, DC: American Institutes for Research. Available: www.csrq.org/worksinprogress.asp

Irvin, J. L., Buehl, D. R., & Klemp, R. M. (2003). *Reading and the high school student.* Boston: Allyn and Bacon.

Meltzer, J., Smith, N. C., & Clark, H. (2001). *Adolescent literacy resources: Linking research and practice.* Providence, RI: Brown University, Northeast and Islands Regional Educational Laboratory.

Peterson, C. L., Caverly, D.C., Nicholson, S. A., O'Neal, S., & Cusenbary, S. (2000). *Building reading proficiency at the secondary level: A guide to resources.* Austin, TX: Southwest Educational Development Laboratory.

Schoenbach, R., Greenleaf, C., Cziko, C., & Hurwitz, L. (1999). *Reading for understanding.* San Francisco: Jossey-Bass.

U.S. Department of Education, National Center for Education Statistics. (2000). *NAEP 1999 trends in academic progress: Three decades of student performance.* Washington, DC: Author.

Vacca, R. T., & Vacca, J. L. (2005). *Content area reading: Literacy and learning across the curriculum* (8th ed.). Boston: Pearson Education.

No Child Left Behind: What It Means for U.S. Adolescents and What We Can Do about It

MARK W. CONLEY AND KATHLEEN A. HINCHMAN

• • • • •

Through considerable effort over the past decades, researchers have contributed a great deal to our understanding of adolescents and adolescent literacy learning. Reviews in the *Handbook of Reading Research* have provided useful syntheses of this research (see Alvermann & Moore, 1991; Bean, 2000), as has the International Reading Association's *Summary of Adolescent Literacy: A Position Statement* (Moore, Bean, Birdyshaw, & Rycik, 1999).

Despite these advancements, the U.S. federal government recently launched an unprecedented push for an overhaul of early literacy education in the form of the *No Child Left Behind Act of 2001*. In signing this legislation, President George W. Bush optimistically declared,

> Today begins a new era, a new time for public education in our country. Our schools will have higher expectations—we believe every child can learn. From this day forward, all students will have a better chance to learn, to excel, and to live out their dreams. (Committee on Education and the Workforce, 2002)

At first glance, with its emphases on early literacy and early intervention, No Child Left Behind (NCLB) seems unconnected to adolescents and their needs, despite assertions that this new legislative approach will improve the performance of the United States' elementary and secondary schools (Bush, 2001). However, comparisons between adolescent literacy research and the new U.S. federal policies provide a unique opportunity to review what we have learned about adolescent literacy, reconfirming and strengthening some of our insights and raising questions about future directions.

This article explores the connection between what we know about adolescent literacy and No Child Left Behind. Our purpose is to consider ways in which research,

Conley, M. W., & Hinchman, K. A. (2004, September). No Child Left Behind: What it means for U.S. adolescents and what we can do about it. *Journal of Adolescent & Adult Literacy, 48*(1), 42–50. Reprinted with permission of the International Reading Association.

policy, and classroom practice could be more forcefully directed toward supporting adolescents and their literacy learning.

The New Legislation and Adolescent Literacy

With No Child Left Behind, President George W. Bush captured the frustration felt by many about the progress, or lack of progress, in U.S. schools. President Bush noted,

> As America enters the 21st Century full of hope and promise, too many of our neediest students are being left behind. Today, nearly 70 percent of inner city fourth graders are unable to read at a basic level on national reading tests. Our high school seniors trail students in Cyprus and South Africa on international math tests. And nearly a third of our college freshmen find they must take a remedial course before they are able to even begin regular college level courses. (Bush, 2001, p. 1)

These claims are especially disturbing considering that the federal government spends US$120 billion each year, while states and local communities spend additional untold billions, on elementary and secondary education. In short, for the amount being spent, many politicians argue, the U.S. public has not been getting its money's worth.

In January 2002, the principles of NCLB were incorporated into the reauthorization of the Elementary and Secondary Education Act (ESEA). The reauthorized ESEA

> redefines the federal role in K–12 education and will help close the achievement gap between disadvantaged and minority students and their peers. It is based on four basic principles: stronger accountability for results, increased flexibility and local control, expanded options for parents, and an emphasis on teaching methods that have been proven to work. (www.ed.gov/programs/readingfirst/legislation.html)

This legislation suggests that greater accountability is to be gained through increased attention to results of annual assessments in grades 3 through 8. Parents, administrators, and policymakers are more able to pressure schools to make needed improvements, closing the achievement gap between disadvantaged students and other groups of students. Reduction of bureaucracy is to result in greater local control. More options are to be available for parents of children from failing schools, such as school choice and vouchers.

The bill authorizes US$900 million in funds to be spent on early literacy instruction grounded in scientifically based reading research. Funds are also targeted to improve literacy education for limited English proficient students and others at risk of failure due to lack of understanding of essential elements of reading.

The principles of the NCLB legislation, embodied in the reauthorization of ESEA, represent the most sweeping national education reforms since the Sputnik-inspired reforms of the 1960s. Given the political concerns underlying the legislation and the principles inherent in the legislation itself, it is critical to discover what effect NCLB has on U.S. adolescents. Evidence exists of deepening crises for our older youth, especially with respect to literacy-related concerns (Carnegie Council on Adolescent Development, 1998; U.S. Department of Education, 1997, 1999a, 1999b, 2000). Will NCLB offer support for adolescents who face increasingly complex learning, health, social, and emotional issues?

Reviewing What We Know

Before considering whether or how NCLB might be helpful to adolescents and those who work on their behalf, it is important to review the findings and implications of the wealth of research that has been conducted in adolescent literacy. We used metaethnography (Noblit & Hare, 1988), that is, an interpretive synthesis, to review recent research and reviews of research on adolescent literacy. We used this strategy, as opposed to a statistical review, because much of the recent work in adolescent literacy has been qualitative in nature. Also, this approach allowed us to examine the implications of both qualitative and quantitative studies.

Our review considered research from the past 10 years in *Reading Research Quarterly* and *Journal of Literacy Research*. Two recent compilations of adolescent literacy research (Alvermann, Hinchman, Moore, Phelps, & Waff, 1998; Moje & O'Brien, 2001) and various more focused reviews from the *Handbook of Reading Research* were considered (e.g., Alexander & Jetton, 2000; Alvermann & Moore, 1991; R. C. Anderson & Nagy, 1991; T. H. Anderson & Armbruster, 1984; Bean, 2000; Beck & McKeown, 1991; Blachowicz & Fisher, 2000; Nagy & Scott, 2000; Paris, Wasik, & Turner, 1991; Pearson & Fielding, 1991; Pressley, 2000; Tierney & Cunningham, 1984; Tierney & Shanahan, 1991; Wade & Moje, 2000). Recent national assessment reports and statistical analyses (Carnegie Council on Adolescent Development, 1998; U.S. Department of Education, 1997, 1999a, 1999b, 2000) were also included. The goal of this review was to identify a set of categories or themes that reflect the most common concerns and recommendations for NCLB. Categories that emerged from this analysis include the problems faced by adolescents; developmental issues; and recommendations for literacy practices, schooling, funding, and parent choices and involvement.

We compared this review with topics and themes within NCLB, including the reauthorized Elementary and Secondary Education Act, White House white papers, and government websites. Ways in which NCLB could support our efforts with adolescent literacy were identified, along with places where the legislation explicitly leaves adolescents out. Finally, using our comparisons between adolescent literacy and NCLB, new areas for research and questions about classroom practice were conceived. The following sections outline the results of our analyses.

NCLB and Adolescent Literacy: Areas of Convergence

There are a number of recommendations in No Child Left Behind that confirm recommendations from research on adolescent literacy. These include attention to three important areas of emphases.

Continuous Reading Instruction with an Emphasis on Developing Strategic Knowledge for Dealing with Unknown Words and Comprehension.   Those interested in adolescent literacy have long recommended reading instruction that continues in content areas across grades, especially as adolescents are required to read more demanding materials while responding to increasingly complex tasks. These recommendations usually include special attention to vocabulary and comprehension instruction that helps students to be successful reading various types of texts (e.g., Moore, Readence, & Rickelman, 1983). Recent, well-respected reviews by the National Institute of Child Health and Human Development (2000) and the Rand Reading Study Group (Snow, 2002) confirm the importance of direct and incidental vocabulary development (and teaching comprehension) through activating prior knowledge, determining importance, imagery, and summarization, across age groups.

Another significant insight concerns the need for developing students' strategic understandings of how they read (e.g., Greenleaf, Schoenbach, & Cziko, 2001; Palincsar & Brown, 1986). Not only do adolescents need to work on developing comprehension, but they must also understand where, when, and how to apply varied comprehension strategies.

Individually Appropriate Reading Instruction, Anchored in Assessment of Individuals and Programs.   One of the joys of working with adolescents is that they can contribute immeasurably to diagnoses of their literacy-related needs. Recent work suggests that individual teenagers can recognize the sources of their difficulties and, from this recognition, can learn to strategize and move forward to the reading of increasingly complex texts. Indeed, such attention can heighten teens' sense of self-efficacy in important ways (Capella & Weinstein, 2001; Pajares, 1996; Schunk & Rice, 1993).

In similar ways, research suggests that we need to ensure that our schoolwide literacy programs are also self-diagnosing. Research on schoolwide reform suggests there is value in ongoing attention to program outcomes coinciding with the use of reliable evaluation measures (Fullan, 2001). Schools seriously concerned with their own effectiveness often build their capacity to set and recognize the achievement of small reform goals. Chief among the more successful reforms for adolescents is developing greater capacity for heightened attention to individual students, which is fueled by ongoing individual and programmatic assessment (Sizer, 1996). Just as adolescents can serve as guides to their own learning, they are also key to determining the appropriateness and impact of secondary literacy programs.

Multiple Opportunities to Use a Variety of Texts within a Context of Comprehensive Schoolwide Reform.   Some vestige of attention to literacy across the curriculum has been apparent in the literature since just after the turn of the last century (see explanation in Moore et al., 1983). The renaissance for this idea occurred in the 1970s and 1980s with the publication of a variety of texts recommending teaching reading in content areas (e.g., Herber, 1970; Readence, Bean, & Baldwin, 1981; Vacca & Vacca, 1981), all of which were anchored in a schema-theoretic approach to supporting reading organized around pre-, during-, and after-reading heuristics.

Recent attention in the last decade to schoolwide reform (Darling-Hammond, Ancess, & Falk, 1995; Freedman, Simons, Kalnin, Casareno, & The M-Class Teams,

1999; Meier, 1995; Sizer, 1996), especially in urban schools, has reignited efforts to promote literacy across the curriculum. But the contexts and recommendations are different from the past, placing more attention on urban and rural disadvantaged students. This new thrust also involves promoting subject-area study accompanied by increased attention to problem solving and learning to read and write within and across subject-specific discourse communities (Daniels, Bizar, & Zemelman, 2001).

What No Child Left Behind Fails to Say about Adolescent Literacy

Most of the program money in No Child Left Behind is targeted for contexts up to third grade. Moneys that are allocated for adolescent literacy are earmarked for developing accountability systems, for supporting reform for schools that fail to make adequate yearly progress, and, to a more limited extent, for providing interventions for those who struggle beyond grade 3. Three specific areas, critical in the recommendations from adolescent literacy research, are not mentioned: contexts for teaching and learning in content areas, teacher preparation and ongoing education, and adolescents' interests and needs.

Limited Attention to Contexts within which Literacy Strategies are Developed. The research base cited for NCLB emphasizes individuals' development of alphabetic knowledge, fluency, and comprehension strategies. The last of these is most important for adolescent literacy, partly because most teens have developed alphabetic knowledge and some measure of fluency and partly because new contexts of content area study present new contexts for developing reading comprehension strategies.

However, little, if any, of the research cited for NCLB reflects the varied literacy contexts within which adolescents find themselves (National Institute of Child Health and Human Development, 2000; Snow, Burns, & Griffin, 1998). One study even suggested that the narrow criteria for research recognized by these reviews and NCLB made it nearly impossible to say much about strategies across varied subject-matter domains (Alexander & Jetton, 2000).

Research on teaching for adolescents emphasizes the importance of social constructivism and context for literacy strategies (Bean, 2000). Skilled content area teachers are those adept in understanding their students' individual motivations and needs while creating conditions through discussion and strategy, for literacy success in multiple contexts (Alvermann, 2001; Kos, 1991; McCray, Vaughn, & Neal, 2001). This image of creating conditions for comprehension in content areas contrasts starkly with methods for building phonemic awareness and fluency identified as promoting the literacy of young children in NCLB.

Unfortunately, through its emphasis on the details of literacy (e.g., alphabetic knowledge, phonemic awareness, fluency) and accountability, one might hypothesize that NCLB could usher in a new era of lecture-driven practices that conflict with the adoption and use of known content area literacy strategies; teens will not need to learn to read or write richly if their task is simply to learn the facts. Given what we have learned through adolescent literacy research, it would be wise to resist any move away from embracing strategies that help adolescents use literacy to solve the problems posed by complicated content and contexts.

Limited Attention to Those Who Teach.   The kind of research cited as most credible by those who authored NCLB has not examined teacher learning in detailed, replicable ways. It says little about how teachers are to learn best practices or to adapt practices to different kinds of learners. The legislation authorizes staff development in scientifically based methods of reading instruction but does not acknowledge that many important questions remain about how best to contribute to teachers' ongoing learning.

NCLB mentions that classroom paraprofessionals and special education teachers should receive staff development as providers of instruction for those who struggle with literacy in grades 3 through 12. No role is specified for content teachers who might provide developmentally appropriate instruction in comprehension strategies to all youth throughout these same grades, despite a long history of recommendations in this area. No recommendation is made for reading specialists at these grade levels, despite attention to such recommendations in the literature (Moore et al., 1999).

Implied Attention to Adolescents' Varying Needs and Interests.   NCLB's attention to schoolwide reform, drop-out prevention, and technology may be very important to adolescent literacy, at least in implicit ways. However, increasing amounts of qualitative research have focused attention on adolescents' varying constructions of literacy in and out of school, given social concerns related to gender, race, class, and ability (Alvermann et al., 1998; Hinchman & Moje, 1998; Moje & O'Brien, 2001). Sometimes adolescents who are quite skilled in some contexts are viewed as deficient in academic contexts that promote narrow, even disconnected notions of what it means to know (Alvermann, 2001). An example concerns adolescents who are sophisticated users of technology while rejecting effort in math, science, English, or social studies. Researchers have only begun to explore the roles technologies will play in adolescent literacy development into the next century (Alvermann, 2002).

NCLB and its legislation say nothing about the dilemmas posed by adolescents who fail because they choose not to play the game of academics or about school systems that favor some forms of literacy (such as print based) over others (such as technology). The legislation is also silent about the implications of an increasingly technological world for adolescent literacy learning.

Questions Raised for Adolescent Literacy by NCLB

No Child Left Behind represents a unique initiative to reshape the entire educational system around a set of research-based, early literacy principles and practices. As such, the legislation holds potential for influencing educational practices of all kinds, including those in adolescent literacy. One strong implication from NCLB concerns the use of scientifically based reading research for program development and evaluation. This prompts the following question:

Should Those Interested in Adolescent Literacy Invest More in the Kinds of Research and Classroom Practices Promoted by NCLB?   As has already been noted, NCLB rests on a mantra of scientifically based reading research. This raises important questions for those who are interested in adolescent literacy, an area where much recent research and some implications for practice have been derived from qualitative approaches. NCLB does not give the qualitative perspective much credence, despite the fact that many important generalizations about contexts, teachers, and, most important, adolescents, can be drawn from considering this body of work in its entirety.

If researchers in adolescent literacy would like to make more forceful instructional recommendations, to get federal funding or funding that is sensitive to federal priorities, the answer to the question is probably, "Yes." In many cases, guided by NCLB, funding proposals at the national and state levels require practices and evaluations grounded in experimental research. It would be a mistake to ignore the message that standards are important and reliable and that valid measures of accountability are essential as the basis for instructional conclusions. The exclusion of qualitative research as a source of evidence is unfortunate, given the insights about context, teachers, and adolescents that have emerged through this type research in the past several decades. It becomes tragic when one considers that many of the schools that are not making adequate yearly progress could greatly benefit from the recommendations of qualitative research in adolescent literacy when making individual child and program evaluation decisions. Moreover, a heavy reliance on experimental research could instigate a return to an overemphasis on narrowly prescribed accountability measures and accompanying instructional practices that stress fitting adolescents to standards, when alternative strategies and flexibility would be more desirable and have a greater chance of success. Thus, the answer to the question of whether adolescent literacy researchers and secondary teachers should be influenced by NCLB's methodology is "Yes"—but only if more inclusive constructions of adolescent literacy can also be considered such as those nuances that have been discovered through qualitative research.

Missing Pieces from Research and Current Legislation

We have available a number of resources from which to draw in order to attend to adolescents' proclivities and needs. Comparing the research on adolescent literacy to NCLB legislation, as we have done here, suggests at least three areas where much more work is needed.

Forging Connections between work on Reform and Community.   More work needs to be done to understand and support adolescents in classroom, school, and community contexts—work that ties together what we know about adolescent literacy and school reform and drop-out prevention research. Connections between research on adolescent literacy and the NCLB legislation are very limited in these areas, despite the fact that teachers and schools deal with adolescents, drop-out prevention, and school reform programs on a daily basis. Many secondary teachers remain ill-equipped with strategies that could help them build bridges between adolescent, classroom, and community.

Providing an Authentic Role for Parents in Adolescent Literacy.   NCLB specifies a number of roles for parents in early literacy education, both in school and at home. Comparatively, parents are seldom seen in secondary schools, and very little research has been devoted in the area of adolescent literacy to parents and their role in schools.

Though many argue that it is critical to involve parents in their children's education, this is a tricky issue for parents of adolescents (Dauber & Epstein, 1993; Eccles, Wigfield, & Schiefele, 1998). Many adolescents work to discourage their parents' participation or, at a minimum, to delineate an existence apart from everything their parents imagine for them. Few studies have explored what it takes to involve parents in improving their adolescent's literacy or have documented the complexities or effect of such efforts. Teachers and other school professionals could benefit from more insights on what it takes to bring parents into secondary schools as partners in their adolescents' education.

Designing Interventions for Adolescents who Struggle with Reading.   NCLB acknowledges that much research has been conducted on interventions prior to grade 3. It also notes that much research has highlighted the inefficacy of interventions beyond grade 3 (Allington & Johnston, 1991).

Despite the lack of measurable gains from programs that likely "warehoused" students with packages of workbooks and isolated skills instruction (Allington & McGill-Franzen, 1989), one can imagine other kinds of interventions by which individuals through adulthood can be helped to improve literacy skills. However, more work also needs to be done to connect individual differences, individually appropriate reading instruction, and accountability for growth. There is little but anecdotal evidence for methods in this area (Curtis & Longo, 1999; Tovani, 2000).

Moreover, there continues to be a tension between raising standards and providing instructional opportunities and the various ways that students learn and grow in their literacy abilities. NCLB represents the world of higher standards and measuring growth. In contrast, the world of adolescent literacy has highlighted student diversity and multiple instructional approaches. Ways must be found to bridge these worlds so that policy, research, and practice are more congruent, particularly when it comes to measuring individual student growth and rewarding teachers and schools when it happens.

Research on adolescent literacy has explored factors such as multiple literacies; personal identity issues; the influence of race, gender, and ethnicity; teaching and learning beliefs and practices; and the roles of text and context. NCLB focuses on increasing accountability through expanded assessment, greater school choice, increased parental involvement, early intervention to promote reading success, and the promotion of greater English proficiency. One could conclude from this contrast that much of the adolescent literacy research has focused on identifying and explaining the conditions that promote or hinder adolescent literacy while U.S. government initiatives seek to create conditions for greater achievement. There is a paradox in that research suggests that accountability and assessment plans need to be applied with great care if they are to improve students' learning (Linn, 2000). What we don't have yet are empirically supported strategies for attending to both concerns at the same time.

In addition, there is emerging evidence that school choice and vouchers can lead to improved results on reading tests for African American students (Howell & Peterson, 2001). These results have been attributed to the combination of higher standards, smaller class sizes, and, in some cases, greater parental involvement when compared with public schools. Few studies have focused on the broad range of factors that influence adolescent literacy in school choice or voucher contexts or that consider that students from different backgrounds may need varying kinds of support.

Ongoing Crises

While considerable attention is currently applied within the research and policy communities to early literacy, there continue to be ongoing crises in adolescent literacy. In connecting the findings of adolescent literacy research to No Child Left Behind, this article creates the potential for including adolescent literacy in the renewed interest in promoting literacy for all students. This article poses some new directions for research in adolescent literacy. It connects adolescent literacy to initiatives for early literacy, thus making possible a broad dialogue about research and policies for building literacy from the preschool through the middle and secondary years.

References

Alexander, P. A., & Jetton, T. L. (2000). Learning from text: A multidimensional and developmental perspective. In M. L. Kamil, P. B. Mosenthal, P. D. Pearson, & R. Barr (Eds.), *Handbook of reading research* (Vol. 3, pp. 285–310). Mahwah, NJ: Erlbaum.

Allington, R., & Johnston, P. (1991). Remediation. In R. Barr, M. L. Kamil, P. B. Mosenthal, & P. D. Pearson (Eds.), *Handbook of reading research* (Vol. 2, pp. 984–1012). White Plains, NY: Longman.

Allington, R., & McGill-Franzen, A. (1989). School response to reading failure: Instruction for special education and Chapter 1 students in grades 2, 4, and 8. *Elementary School Journal, 89,* 529–542.

Alvermann, D. E. (2001). *Effective literacy instruction for adolescents.* Chicago: National Reading Conference.

Alvermann, D. E. (Ed.). (2002). *New literacies and digital technologies: A focus on adolescent learners.* New York: Peter Lang.

Alvermann, D. E., Hinchman, K., Moore, D., Phelps, S., & Waff, D. (1998). *Reconceptualizing the literacies in adolescents' lives.* Mahwah, NJ: Erlbaum.

Alvermann, D. E., & Moore, D. W. (1991). Secondary school reading. In R. Barr, M. L. Kamil, P. B. Mosenthal, & P. D. Pearson (Eds.), *Handbook of reading research* (Vol. 2, pp. 951–983). White Plains, NY: Longman.

Anderson, R. C., & Nagy, W. E. (1991). Word meanings. In R. Barr, M. L. Kamil, P. B. Mosenthal, & P. D. Pearson (Eds.), *Handbook of reading research* (Vol. 2, pp. 690–722). White Plains, NY: Longman.

Anderson, T. H., & Armbruster, B. B. (1984). Studying. In P. D. Pearson, & R. Barr, M. L. Kamil, & P. Mosenthal (Eds.), *Handbook of reading research* (pp. 657–679). New York: Longman.

Bean, T. (2000). Reading in the content areas: Social constructivist dimensions. In M. L. Kamil, P. B. Mosenthal, P. D. Pearson, & R. Barr (Eds.), *Handbook of reading research* (Vol. 3, pp. 629–644). Mahwah, NJ: Erlbaum.

Beck, M., & McKeown, I. (1991). Conditions of vocabulary acquisition. In R. Barr, M. L. Kamil, P. B. Mosenthal, & P. D. Pearson (Eds.), *Handbook of reading research* (Vol. 2, pp. 789–814). White Plains, NY: Longman.

Blachowicz, C. L. Z., & Fisher, P. (2000). Vocabulary instruction. In M. L. Kamil, P. B. Mosenthal, P. D. Pearson, & R. Barr (Eds.), *Handbook of reading research* (Vol. 3, pp. 503–523). Mahwah, NJ: Erlbaum.

Bush, G. W. (2001). *No child left behind: Executive summary.* Washington, DC: U.S. Department of Education.

Capella, E., & Weinstein, R. S. (2001). Turning around reading achievement: Predictors of high school students' academic resilience. *Journal of Educational Psychology, 93,* 758–771.

Carnegie Council on Adolescent Development. (1998). *Turning points: Preparing American youth for the 21st century.* Washington, DC: Carnegie Foundation.

Committee on Education and the Workforce. (2002). *President Bush signs landmark reforms into law* [Press release]. Washington, DC: White House Committee on Education and the Workforce.

Curtis, M., & Longo, A. M. (1999). *When adolescents can't read: Methods and materials that work.* Newton Upper Falls, MA: Brookline.

Daniels, H., Bizar, M., & Zemelman, S. (2001). *Rethinking high school: Best practice in teaching, learning, and leadership.* Portsmouth, NH: Heinemann.

Darling-Hammond, L., Ancess, J., & Falk, B. (1995). *Authentic assessment in action: Studies of schools and students at work.* New York: Teachers College Press.

Dauber, S., & Epstein, J. (1993). Parents' attitudes and practices of involvement in inner city elementary and middle schools. In N. F. Chavkin (Ed.), *Families and schools in a pluralistic society* (pp. 2–106). New York: State University of New York Press.

Eccles, J. S., Wigfield, A., & Schiefele, U. (1998). Motivation to succeed. In N. Eisenberg (Ed.), *Handbook of child psychology: Social, emotional and personality development* (5th ed., Vol. 3, pp. 1017–1095). New York: Wiley.

Freedman, S. W., Simons, E. R., Kalnin, J. S., Casareno, A., & the M-Class Teams. (1999). *Inside city schools: Investigating literacy in multicultural classrooms.* New York: Teachers College Press.

Fullan, M. (2001). *The new meaning of educational change.* New York: Teachers College Press.

Greenleaf, C., Schoenbach, R., & Cziko, C. (2001). Apprenticing adolescent readers to academic literacy. *Harvard Educational Review, 71,* 79–129.

Herber, H. L. (1970). *Teaching reading in content areas.* Englewood Cliffs, NJ: Prentice Hall.

Hinchman, K. A., & Moje, E. B. (1998). Locating the social and political in secondary school literacy research. *Reading Research Quarterly, 33,* 117–128. doi:10.1598/RRQ.33.1.6

Howell, W., & Peterson, P. (2001). *The education gap: Vouchers and urban schools.* Washington, DC: Brookings Institution Press.

Kos, R. (1991). Persistence of reading disabilities: The voices of four middle school students. *American Educational Research Journal, 28,* 875–895.

Linn, R. L. (2000). Assessments and accountability. *Educational Researcher, 29*(2), 4–16.

McCray, A. D., Vaughn, S., & Neal, L. I. (2001). Not all students learn to read by third grade: Middle school students speak out about their reading disabilities. *Journal of Special Education, 35,* 17–30.

Meier, D. (1995). *The power of their ideas: Lessons for America from a small school in Harlem.* Boston: Beacon Press.

Moje, E., & O'Brien, D. (2001). *Constructions of literacy: Studies of teaching and learning in and out of secondary schools.* Mahwah, NJ: Erlbaum.

Moore, D. W., Bean, T., Birdyshaw, D., & Rycik, J. (1999). *Summary of adolescent literacy: A position statement for the Commission on Adolescent Literacy of the International Reading Association.* Newark, DE: International Reading Association.

Moore, D. W., Readence, J. W., & Rickelman, R. (1983). An historical exploration of content area reading instruction. *Reading Research Quarterly, 18,* 419–438.

Nagy, W. E., & Scott, J. A. (2000). Vocabulary processes. In M. L. Kamil, P. B. Mosenthal, P. D. Pearson, & R. Barr (Eds.), *Handbook of reading research* (Vol. 3, pp. 269–284). Mahwah, NJ: Erlbaum.

National Institute of Child Health and Human Development. (2000). *Report of the National Reading Panel. Teaching children to read: An evidence-based assessment of the scientific research literature on reading and its implications for reading instruction* (NIH Publication No. 00-4769). Washington, DC: U.S. Government Printing Office.

Noblit, G. W., & Hare, R. D. (1988). Meta-ethnography: Synthesizing qualitative studies. Newbury Park, CA: Sage.

O'Brien, D., & Stewart, R. (1990). Preservice teachers' perspectives on why every teacher is not a teacher of reading: A qualitative analysis. *Journal of Reading Behavior, 22,* 101–129.

Pajares, F. (1996). Self-efficacy beliefs in academic settings. *Review of Educational Research, 66,* 543–578.

Palincsar, A. S., & Brown, A. (1986). Interactive teaching to promote independent learning from text. *The Reading Teacher, 39,* 771–777.

Paris, S. G., Wasik, B. A., & Turner, J. C. (1991). The development of strategic readers. In R. Barr, M. L. Kamil, P. B. Mosenthal, & P. D. Pearson (Eds.), *Handbook of reading research* (Vol. 2, pp. 609–640). White Plains, NY: Longman.

Pearson, P. D., & Fielding, L. (1991). Comprehension instruction. In R. Barr, M. L. Kamil, P. B. Mosenthal, & P. D. Pearson (Eds.), *Handbook of reading research* (Vol. 2, pp. 815–860). White Plains, NY: Longman.

Pressley, M. (2000). What should comprehension instruction be the instruction of? In M. L. Kamil, P. B. Mosenthal, P. D. Pearson, & R. Barr (Eds.), *Handbook of reading research* (Vol. 3, pp. 545–561). Mahwah, NJ: Erlbaum.

Readence, J., Bean, T., & Baldwin, S. (1981). *Content area reading: An integrated approach.* Dubuque, IA: Kendall Hunt.

Schunk, D. H., & Rice, J. M. (1993). Strategy fading and progress feedback: Effects on self-efficacy and comprehension among students receiving remedial reading services. *Journal of Special Education, 27,* 257–276.

Sizer, T. (1996). *Horace's hope: What works for the American high school.* Boston: Houghton Mifflin.

Snow, C. (2002). *Reading for understanding: Toward an R&D program in reading comprehension.* Santa Monica, CA: Rand Education.

Snow, C., Burns, S., & Griffin, P. (1998). *Preventing reading difficulties in young children.* Washington, DC: National Academy Press.

Tierney, R. J., & Cunningham, J. W. (1984). Research on teaching reading comprehension. In P. D. Pearson, R. Barr, M. L. Kamil, & P. Mosenthal (Eds.), *Handbook of reading research* (pp. 609–655). New York: Longman.

Tierney, R. J., & Shanahan, T. (1991). Research on the reading-writing relationship: Interactions, transactions, and outcomes. In R. Barr, M. L. Kamil, P. B. Mosenthal, & P. D. Pearson (Eds.), *Handbook of reading research* (Vol. 2, pp. 246–281). White Plains, NY: Longman.

Tovani, C. (2000). *I read it but I don't get it: Comprehension strategies for adolescent readers.* York, ME: Stenhouse.

U.S. Department of Education. (1997). *Dropout rates in the United States* (NCES 98-250). Washington, DC: National Center for Education Statistics.

U.S. Department of Education. (1999a). *The NAEP 1998 reading report card for the nation and the states* (NCES 1999-500). Retrieved August 21, 2001, from http://nces.ed.gov/nationsreportcard/pubs/main1998/1999500.asp

U.S. Department of Education. (1999b). *The NAEP 1998 writing report card for the nation and the states* (NCES 1999-462). Retrieved August 21, 2001, from http://nces.ed.gov/pubsearch/pubsinfo.asp?pubid=1999462

U.S. Department of Education. (2000). *NAEP 1999 trends in academic progress: Three decades of student performance* (NCES 2000-469). Retrieved August 21, 2001, from http://nces.ed.gov/pubsearch/pubsinfo.asp?pubid=2000469

Vacca, R., & Vacca, J. (1981). *Content area reading.* Boston: Little, Brown.

Wade, S. E., & Moje, E. B. (2000). The role of text in classroom learning. In M. L. Kamil, P. B. Mosenthal, P. D. Pearson, & R. Barr (Eds.), *Handbook of reading research* (Vol. 3, pp. 609–627). Mahwah, NJ: Erlbaum.

Implementing the No Child Left Behind Act: Using Student Engagement to Improve *Adolescent Literacy*

NCREL Quick Key 10 Action Guide

LEARNING POINT ASSOCIATES

• • • • •

The NCLB Act and Adolescent Literacy

The No Child Left Behind (NCLB) Act promotes significant changes in our nation's schools. This *Quick Key Action Guide* assists educators and administrators in understanding NCLB with a specific focus on the needs of adolescent learners who are building their literacy across content areas. Examples and suggestions are included to assist education stakeholders in the consideration of reform efforts at the school, district, and state levels.

Adolescent literacy—the reading and writing skills of middle and high school students—is critical to student success in all areas of the curriculum. Preparation for the worlds of work, college, and community involvement requires young people to be highly skilled in reading for understanding and in writing with clarity. Yet, while NCLB has fostered serious consideration of the literacy learning needs of young children, less attention was initially paid to supporting adolescent literacy development.

In 2003–04, that lack of attention began to be addressed with two ambitious federal efforts. The Bush administration proposed the Striving Readers Initiative to fund development and demonstration of research-based interventions that help improve the skills of teen students who read below grade level. In addition, the National Institute of Child Health and Human Development, the U.S. Department of Education's Office

Implementing the No Child Left Behind Act: Using student engagement to improve adolescent literacy. (2005). Naperville, Illinois: North Central Regional Education Laboratory.

of Vocational and Adult Education, and the Office of Special Education and Rehabili-
tative Services convened the Adolescent Literacy Research Network, which focuses on
multiyear investigations into the needs of adolescent learners and the teaching environments that support them most effectively.

Over the next few years, the results of these federal efforts and similar investigations
taking place in universities across the country will significantly advance our knowledge
of how to address adolescent learning needs. However, educators and administrators
need help now to implement the current best practices for the students in our middle
and high schools. This *Quick Key Action Guide* provides ideas and resources for practices
that have shown promise in the development of our adolescent readers and writers.

Adolescent Literacy Challenges

Literacy instruction does not end with reading success in early grades. As students move
to middle and high school, new challenges emerge that can affect literacy achievement.
Even for students who achieve early reading and writing success, the literacy demands
of middle and high school can pose substantial challenges. Older students must be able
to comprehend more complex texts; determine the meaning of obscure, unfamiliar,
and technical vocabulary; use higher-order thinking skills to analyze a wide variety of
literacy and expository texts and media; and develop skills for expressing their ideas by
writing informative, persuasive, and creative texts. For students who enter middle and
high school with compromised reading and writing skills, these challenges are even
more daunting.

In 2002, the reading and writing assessments of the National Assessment of
Educational Progress (NAEP) were administered to the nation's students in Grades 8
and 12. NAEP used the following achievement-level definitions (National Center for
Educational Statistics, 2003a, 2003b):

- Below Basic—Achievement that is less than partial mastery.
- Basic—Partial mastery of prerequisite knowledge and skills that are fundamental
  for proficient work at each grade.
- Proficient—Solid academic performance for each grade assessed. Students
  reaching this level have demonstrated competency over challenging subject matter, including subject-matter knowledge, application of such knowledge to real-
  world situations, and analytical skills appropriate to the subject matter.
- Advanced—Superior performance.

The 2002 NAEP data provide some provoking information about the challenges
facing our students and teachers in middle and high schools:

- Approximately 68 percent of Grade 8 students and 64 percent of Grade 12 students are reading below the proficient level.
- Approximately 69 percent of Grade 8 students and 77 percent of Grade 12 students are writing below the proficient level.

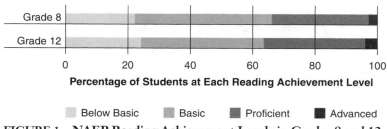

Percentage of Students at Each Reading Achievement Level

☐ Below Basic   ☐ Basic   ■ Proficient   ■ Advanced

FIGURE 1   NAEP Reading Achievement Levels in Grades 8 and 12

Source: National Center for Education Statistics (2003c, 2003d).

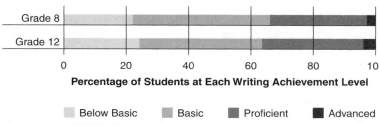

Percentage of Students at Each Writing Achievement Level

☐ Below Basic   ☐ Basic   ■ Proficient   ■ Advanced

FIGURE 2   NAEP Writing Achievement Levels in Grades 8 and 12

Source: National Center for Education Statistics (2003e).

- Less than 6 percent of students in Grades 8 and 12 performed at the advanced level in reading.
- Approximately 2 percent of students in Grades 8 and 12 performed at the advanced level in writing.

Given that colleges and work places both seek youth who are skilled readers and writers, these data do not bode well for the future success of the vast majority of our high school graduates.

Data are not the only source of information about the literacy challenges in our nation's schools. Interviews with educators and parents point to two factors affecting literacy achievement: student skills and student engagement. The two factors are fundamentally linked: Educators must work to build engagement levels if they hope to support students in meeting higher standards.

Why Focus on Student Engagement?

Middle and high school educators need both the skills required to teach adolescent literacy and the knowledge of the elements of student engagement. Educators who teach reading and writing skills without addressing student engagement are unlikely to yield substantial improvements. As anyone who has spent time with middle and high school students can attest, attempting to build the skills of disengaged adolescents is a futile enterprise. Whether expressed as defiant noncompliance or passive "checking out," the student who refuses to learn will succeed in that effort.

Students who are motivated to learn, on the other hand, can succeed even in less-than-optimal environments. Students who are engaged in learning are actively seeking meaningful information that makes sense in their lives—often because they see an immediate connection to real-life experiences. As defined by Blachowicz and Ogle (2001), engagement has multiple facets including motivation and purpose.

Student engagement and the literacy practices of adults can make a difference, as shown in recent research:

- Studies show that academic achievement is associated with engagement in reading and classroom-related activities. This association is found for various racial/ethnic groups (Asian Americans, Hispanic Americans, African Americans, non-Hispanic whites) and both gender groups alike (Finn, 1993).
- A recent international study of reading performance concluded that "15-year-olds whose parents have the lowest occupational status but who are highly engaged in reading achieve better reading scores than students whose parents have high or medium occupational status but who are poorly engaged in reading" (Kirsch, de Jong, LaFontaine, McQueen, Mendelovits, & Monseur, 2002, p. 106).

While educators might wish for classrooms full of students who arrive already motivated, there is in fact much that educators can do to help create student motivation and engagement. To make literacy instruction effective in the language arts classroom and across the curriculum, efforts must be made to engage adolescent learners.

What Are the Key Elements of Student Engagement?

The words "student engagement" might conjure up images of teachers using hip hop to deliver lessons on Shakespeare. The reality is less colorful and more difficult. Following are four key elements of student engagement:

- **Student confidence.**   Students with high self-efficacy—the belief that they can influence their own behavior—are more likely to engage in school-related reading than those with low self-efficacy (Alvermann, 2003). While this is true of many kinds of learners, it is especially important at the adolescent developmental stage, characterized as it is with a strong desire to avoid public failures and be seen as competent.
- **Teacher involvement.**   High school teachers contribute to adolescent self-confidence when they care about them as individuals and encourage them to learn (Dillon, 1989; Dillon & Moje, 1998). The caring teacher who believes that students can succeed can have a positive Pygmalion Effect—whereby believing in potential creates potential—on adolescents.
- **Relevant and interesting texts.**   Relevance of curricular materials and topics is essential to student success, requiring teachers to know about their students'

interests. While adolescents are developing the adult capacity to be motivated by extrinsic interests such as keeping a job, most require significant intrinsic interest in materials in order to persist in difficult tasks. In addition, developing literacy strategies and skills that are typically not of themselves interesting is made easier when students have a meaningful goal that requires those skills (Greenleaf, Jimenez, & Roller, 2002). For example, students may be highly motivated to learn about the characteristics of persuasive writing when engaged in an attempt to persuade school officials to relax a dress code. This type of connecting information is often not provided in classroom instruction but can make a world of difference in student engagement.

- **Choices of literacy activities.** Adolescent learners sometimes experience a world of rules and regulations imposed on them by adults who seem to not understand their world. The physical and emotional changes they experience are a further source of feelings that they have no control over in their lives. Teachers who create opportunities for students to choose among assignments and texts will find students less resistant to completing their work (Wigfield, 2004, p. 67). Students who also understand the goal of their chosen assignments and feel a sense of control over how they achieve that goal are more likely to work hard even in the face of difficulties. Teachers need to be skilled at developing a choice of assignments that balance student interests with effective research-based strategies for developing reading and writing skills.

References

Blachowicz, C., & Ogle, D. (2001). *Reading comprehension: Strategies for independent learners.* New York: Guilford Press.

Dillon, D. R. (1989). Showing them that I want them to learn and that I care about who they are: A microethnography of the social organization of a secondary low-track English-reading classroom. *American Educational Research Journal, 26,* 227–259.

Dillon, D. R., & Moje, E. B. (1998). Listening to the talk of adolescent girls: Lessons about literacy, school, and life. In D. E. Alvermann, K. A. Hinchman, D. W. Moore, S. F. Phelps, & D. R. Waff (Eds.), *Reconceptualizing the literacies in adolescents' lives* (pp. 193–223). Mahwah, NJ: Erlbaum.

Greenleaf, G. L., Jimenez, R. T., & Roller, C. M. (2002). Reclaiming secondary reading interventions: From limited to rich conceptions, from narrow to broad conversations. *Reading Research Quarterly, 37,* 484–496.

Kirsch, I., de Jong, J., LaFontaine, D., McQueen, J., Mendelovits, J., & Monsuer, C. (2002). *Reading for change: Performance and engagement across countries: Results from PISA 2000.* Paris, France: Organization for Economic Co-operation and Development. Retrieved June 7, 2005, from http://213.134.29/oecd/pdfs/browseit/9602071E.PDF

National Center For Educational Statistics. (2003a). The NAEP reading achievement levels. Retrieved June 7, 2005, from http:nces.edgov/nationsreportcard/reading/achieve.asp

National Center For Educational Statistics. (2003b). The NAEP writingachievement levels. Retrieved June 7, 2005, from http:nces.edgov/nationsreportcard/writing/achieve.asp

Wigfield, A. (2004). Motivation for reading during the early adolescent and adolescent years. In D. S. Strickland & D. E. Alvermann (Eds.), *Bridging the literacy achievement gap, grades 4–12.* (pp. 56–59). New York: Teachers College Press.

At Play in Fields of Ideas

ANDREW SCHOFIELD AND THERESA ROGERS

Teaching, curriculum, and the lives and multiple literacies of youth are all interrelated at a public alternative secondary school in British Columbia, Canada. After several years of collaborative work in a youth literacy program, we believe that developing the literacies of struggling youth requires a curricular playfulness with students' ideas, biographies, and imaginations across genres and media. We begin our description of the program with a student's poem. Introducing his anthology of poetry, this student wrote the following:

> My name is Scott Moloney. I live in B.C. Canada but hang out everywhere. I love the feeling of the street because only a few people know how it works—it has its own mind. I am trying to show everyone what it's like to be on the street and around it. I have my favorite poem at the end because it has no borders—it's what you want it to be—nothing more nothing less. (Moloney, 2002, p. 3)

The Girl

She dances
She spins
She jumps
She swirls around on the sidewalk
Showing her moves
The daughter of a father
The daughter of a mother
No one sees that
Because she stops dancing
For another hit
She eases it in her
> The needle goes into the skin
> Slumped against a wall
> She feels the warmth
> Of the one she loves
> The one thing that's never let her down
> The one thing she can trust

Schofield, A., & Rogers, T. (2004, November). At play in a field of ideas. *Journal of Adolescent & Adult Literacy, 48*(3), 251–257. Reprinted with permission of the International Reading Association.

134

She doesn't worry anymore
About friends
About family
All she needs is one more hit
That's all
Just one little needle is what she looks for
Such little needs
She does not need food
She does not need water
Just that last hit
As it goes through her blood
It hits her heart
She's lying on the ground now
Too much
Her heart slows
Lying there with a smile on her face
Life was fun she thinks
But now it leaves her
"Goodbye life I will love you," she said
Good-bye girl

Scott's poem illustrates the integration of biography—an adolescent's under-standings and experiences—and his imaginative retelling of life on the street: "I came from it, and it still interests me, of how it works, because you could be out there for years and years and you still have no idea of how it worked" (personal communication, March 13, 2002). Our view of multiple literacies, which includes cultural representa-tions across a variety of genres and media, rests on the intersections between our col-laborative work with the students and the writings on social literacies; multiliteracy theory and practice; and biography, identity, and imagination.

Social Literacies and Multiple Literacies

As social literacy theorists (e.g., Barton & Hamilton, 2000; Street, 1995) have pointed out, texts do not assume an autonomous life of their own but fit into the practices of the everyday lives of students; therefore, material practices of literacy—the uses to which the acts of reading and writing are put—are central. Just as practice occurs in differ-ent contexts, different literacies apply and assume importance in different contexts across homes, communities, and schools. This perspective opens up fruitful avenues of research (Barton, Hamilton, & Ivanic, 2000) and practice, and it reminds us that school literacies are different and unique, that literacy is learned not only inside the classroom, and that curricula focusing on a prescribed range of literacy practices are restrictive.

Multiliteracy theorists have added to this understanding of literacy practices by emphasizing the role of "multimodal" forms of representation and meaning making (Cope & Kalantzis, 2000) in students' lives. They argue that "literacy pedagogy must now account for the burgeoning variety of text forms associated with information and multimedia technologies" (New London Group, 2000, p. 9). They also argue that school curricula should be redesigned to mesh with different subjectivities or experiences of the students, with their attendant languages, discourses, and registers, using these as a resource for learning. In these ways, social literacy and multiliteracy theories are powerful and important reminders that literacy practices are varied and situated across different media and that school-based literacy practices need to be inclusive of a broad range of students, cultures, and text formats (Rogers, 2000). These ideas inform our practice of drawing on multiple literacies for struggling youth, who in turn bring their subjectivities in the forms of biography, imagination, hybrid and fluid identities, and playfulness.

As multiliteracy theorists hypothesize, and our experience confirms, emphasizing only print texts and "school literacies" with these and other students has the potential to push them further toward the margins of school. To overcome this marginalization and encourage various forms of literacy, we have come to rely increasingly on oral and written imaginative play, on rearticulating, transforming, and integrating the narratives and biographies (or the stories of the students' lives) into curricular texts. As O'Brien (1998) observed, for adolescents who struggle with literacy and have been alienated from traditional secondary schools, issues of biography, resistance, and school literacy practices intersect during curricular innovation and the teaching process.

(Auto)biography, Identity, and Imagination

To explore students' subjectivities in a multigenres and multimedia environment, we began to emphasize the dimensions of imagination (Egan, 1997; Greene, 2000; Searle, 1998) and biography (cf. Fine, 1994) that can transform practice, at times, and lessen or integrate student resistances to schooling. Cope and Kalantzis (2000) argued that transformed practice begins with the situated lives of learners and the multiple layers of their identities. We extend this idea by drawing on Harre's (1998) insight that an individual's life, in addition to a sequence of events and experiences, is "a story which I tell myself and which is forever being updated and revised" (p. 138). Because "one's life is lived and told with others, autobiographical story telling, like all forms of memory work, is essentially social, produced dialogically" (p. 146).

Therefore, we focus on (auto)biography, which we see as a rich and immediate source of literacy practice, because these are the stories youth tell to illustrate their shifting identities (Fine, 1994); these illustrations rely on imaginatively integrated readings and retellings of their material lives, as in Scott's poem quoted earlier. Our youth literacy practices, then, include the understanding of youth as engaging in a play of (auto)biography, resistance, and imagination within the context of curricular content and the institutional norms of schooling (c.f. Alvermann, 2001; Fine, 1994; Gee, 2000; McCarthey & Moje, 2002).

To capture the complexity of such youth literacy practices and to bring our argument to life, we draw on field notes and observations of ongoing teaching (since April 2001) with students designated at risk and enrolled in a youth literacy program, samples of student work, teacher and researcher journal entries, and student interviews.

The Learning Center's Youth Literacy Program

The youth literacy program accepts students ages 15 to 19 who are identified by educational administrations as at risk. The program is based at a learning center, one of

125 public schools in a school district with 61,000 students—the largest in British Columbia and one of the fastest growing in Canada. The learning center provides focused support to at-risk students within the school district, offering students the chance to earn their grade 12 graduation. District counselors and principals make the at-risk designations. Moderate (classified 323) and severe (classified 333) designations are made. Students with behavior difficulties are designated as 323s, and 333s are students with criminal records or substance abuse histories.

The students at the learning center face a number of additional problems. For example, over 7% of these students live independently (generally, on the street) at some point in the school year. On average, four students each month are entering or being discharged from a local youth detention center, and over half of the students experience violence as part of their daily lives, either at home or on the streets. Over 60% of the students indicated that a local train station was a focal point for their social interaction, a station replete with problems related to youth crime, drugs, and violence (Canadian Centre for Education Alternatives, 1999, p. 2). In a random survey, conducted by a literacy-class student, 64% of the learning center's morning student group had not eaten breakfast and had not eaten any food by 11:00 am.

Principals in the school district annually identify students who, in addition to their at-risk designation, have low literacy and numeracy scores on provincial standardized assessment tests. For example, at the center over 25% of all assessments in reading comprehension (Canadian Adult Achievement Test) scored at or below the fifth-grade level, and 30% of learning center students drop out because of literacy-based concerns. In addition, some students have moderate learning disabilities or attention deficit disorders. At-risk students such as these with low literacy levels throughout the school district are referred to the learning center's youth literacy program.

To address the literacy needs of these students, the learning center's youth literacy program accommodates 32 students, predominantly boys, who are divided into morning and afternoon class sessions. The students, with a range of literacy and numeracy levels, are enrolled and placed in the classroom on a full-time basis. They are free to leave the program and the learning center, at which point new students are accepted. Continuous entry and exit, therefore, require a flexible teaching and learning process. As the youth literacy teacher, Andrew Schofield (first author) provides individualized, group, and peer literacy support to participants. Building on curricula used in the school district, he orients his work toward meeting the province's specified learning outcomes by integrating the curriculum with student biographies, as revealed in the stories they tell.

Curricular Components of the Youth Literacy Program

The curriculum starts with the district's mandated set of course materials for alternative programs and is embellished with materials that range from Gothic fiction to poetry, from Internet sites on tattooing or medicine wheels to car magazines, from films such as *Pink Floyd: The Wall* (Parker, 1982) to rap lyrics, from cooking to drum making, as well as the students' own writing and multimedia projects. Any of these texts are the basis for student reflection and analysis. And any of these texts might engage a particular student, allowing reading skills to develop and writing to emerge in various forms or genres. They support a continual play between student biography and curricular materials and ideas.

Where appropriate, peer literacy activities and group learning are used; unplanned "break-out conversations" on a range of topics are encouraged interruptions as students work individually on curricular materials, serving to build community among students and teachers in the program. Topics include such diverse subject matter as plate tectonics and continental drift, the lives of sharks, safe sex, tattooing, and living on your own versus living with family or relatives.

At times, these breakout conversations also encourage students to think and imagine across disciplines in ways they have not necessarily been encouraged to do in other settings. They emphasize a playfulness that encourages students' imaginations while simultaneously reinforcing their connectivity to the diverse curricular areas and the life of the classroom. For example, the following breakout discussion took place between two students, Sam and Craig (pseudonyms), and their teacher, Andrew. Sam initiated the conversation.

Sam: Hey, can you imagine sitting in a car, getting away from the cops, and you speeeed up and speeeed up more an' more, an' you're just bookin' it down the road faster and faster 'til you are goin' at the speed of light. Can you imagine that, man? Bookin' it away from the cops at the speed of light?

[With an expression that is both quizzical and skeptical, Craig looks at Sam.]

Andrew: Craig, this is what's called a thought experiment. You can't do it really, but only in your mind . . . in your thoughts. What do you think you'd see going at the speed of light, getting away from the cops?

Craig: Dunno, man. Never done one of those.

Andrew: Can you imagine that?

Craig: Would you see anything?

Sam: You'd catch up with what you're seeing! You couldn't see 'cause you'd have to catch up with what you're seeing! Think about it, man; that's dope . . . man, that's like time travel . . . you'd catch up with time!

Craig: You can do that? You could pick your favorite day and catch up with it?

Sam: You could whip around the world, like, in 10 minutes. Maybe quicker.

Craig: You'd get away from the cops!

Andrew: There was this fellow Albert Einstein. He was the first person to do this thought experiment. Only he used a train. He figured about using light on a train, just like Sam figured using the cops. What do you think about these thought experiments?

Craig: They're trippy, man.

These breakout conversations can be a catalyst for thinking imaginatively in various disciplines, and they often lead to writing or other curricular products for which students receive credit as they work through their course units across subjects areas. Formal and informal evaluation of their work is ongoing as students progress through the curriculum requirements, and it includes observation, informal reading and writing inventories, and marks for completed work. Students with particularly low literacy or numeracy skills are supported with one-on-one tutoring from the teacher, researcher, youth-care worker, or a peer. Completed work is filed and constitutes a portfolio that is used to evaluate progress during teacher–student conferences.

Biography, Imagination, and Multiple Literacies

Photography, art and collage, and multimedia components have been introduced to engage students' multiple literacies. In the process of telling stories through conversation, photographs, artwork, video, and sound, the students construct narratives; these narratives then become the basis for further literacy-based activities within the structure offered by the specific curriculum choices made by students. We feel that this approach—integrating the grades 10 through 12 curriculum with the biographies, imaginations, and multiple literacies of adolescents designated at risk—grounds current notions of social and multiliteracy theory and provides a rich and sophisticated youth literacy program (Gee, 2000).

The student biographies are founded on the material contexts and events of students' lives and on their own readings and rereadings of these biographies. We have already illustrated how this reading plays itself out in Scott's life and storytelling. Another student, Kevin (pseudonym), draws on his biography to help us read his visual work, providing a different example but reiterating the importance of integrating biography, imagination, and curriculum.

In the spring of 2001, Kevin was 16 years old and in his first year of the program working on the grade 10 curriculum. He was unable to complete a standardized reading test that students are asked to take when entering the program. Kevin was living with his father (with whom he seemed to have many conflicts) and his sister, although he would sometimes leave home for several weeks. His mother left the family when he was 4 years old. Kevin wrote this biopoem with the help of a peer tutor:

Kevin

Honest, loving, caring, generous
Brother of Laura
Lover of seasons, the wind in my face when I bike,
the mist when I walk in the forest
I feel left behind, sad and unloved
. . . . I fear talking in crowds, working and not getting
anywhere in life. . . .

It became clear in conversations with Kevin that he was actively resistant to reading but had much confidence in his drawing and other visual representations. Kevin is a graphic artist whose work is largely inspired by popular cultural cartoon and video images. He describes his genesis as an artist as compensation for boredom and failure in school:

> The majority of people [in regular schools] don't really care about the students . . . they just pass you on. . . . Since grade 2 I've been told that I couldn't read. And I knew I couldn't read, and it just got stuck in my mind. I never used to write at all. Never. I used to get people to write for me . . . because I was so afraid of making mistakes. [Shows his journal now full of writing]

When asked how he got interested in art, Kevin said this:

> I didn't want to sit around and just do nothing at school so I started doodling . . . and it was pretty cool so I started teaching myself . . . tried out things . . . see if it made it look better, then I'd stick to it or not . . . until I found something better. . . . I draw things from ads like rock and roll . . . a video game . . . or from my imagination . . . a lot of my drawings go with my stories.

The two drawings in Figures 1 and 2 are representative of Kevin's work. The first one is what he calls "an abstract," and the second is the hero of an elaborate mythological story he wrote called "Rothgore." When we asked about his process of drawing pictures, Kevin replied as follows:

> Basically I get an idea or see something that I want to do, start drawing something, and then usually it doesn't turn out to be what I want. . . . It just—like creates something else, creates its own little thing.

Kevin later made a video of his work during the multimedia unit described below and called it "Artist's Portfolio" (see www.newtoniteracies.ca).

Kevin's interest in film has continued in the youth literacy program and is used to stimulate his reading and writing. For example, as part of a film course, Kevin was required to do a genre study and complete a series of film reviews. He was profoundly moved by *Schindler's List* (Spielberg, 1993) and asked if he could extend his review by creating his own film. Called "The Slaughter," Kevin's two-minute film integrates archival and documentary footage with digital photographs into a narrative that starkly reveals Adolf Hitler's "Final Solution." He drew on primary-source (Truszyuska-Frederick, 2003) and

FIGURE 1   Abstract

FIGURE 2   Rothgore

secondary-source (Berenbaum, 1993) material, conducting Internet searches for maps, tables of data, and images. He then created a voiceover narrative and, after listening to contemporary and classical musicians and composers, decided to use Felix Mendelssohn and Carl Orff to strengthen his film's message. Andrew's notes from his journal say that

> Kevin listened to Mendelssohn [and said] "for the first time . . . that's harsh [and] powerful with these [Holocaust] images." I haven't seen Kevin this engaged in schoolwork in a long time. He puts in a night at the chicken farm and still gets to school.

In this comment, Andrew is referring to the intersection of Kevin's work world and the rhythms of schooling. Kevin is now 19, living on his own, and working an eight-hour night shift at a chicken farm. Although exhausted, he still attends school, working with his math tutor and the youth-care worker to complete Math 11E and Film/TV *12*. He has also been "practicing reading" with a friend by reading short novels like *Hana's Suitcase* by Karen Levine (2002, Second Story Press) and advertisements whenever he sees them. His assessed reading scores have improved and helped him find a new job when his job was eliminated (after the recent collapse of the local poultry industry due to avian flu).

The work of Kevin and Scott illustrates how youth literacy pedagogy encourages students to develop a sense of the power of written and artistic expression through the conventions of various literary and popular genres and content knowledge; curriculum and biography anchor instruction. This process is never complete and is constantly fragile. Moment by moment, at-risk students may re-create and reinvent their own power. They display or withdraw literacy acts and discourses and even withdraw from school; but for some, and only some, of the time, literacy can momentarily be a "transformative act [that] begins to assume an active and decisive participation" (Freire & Macedo, 1987, p. 54). In this process,

> It is of tantamount importance that the incorporation of the student's language as the primary language of instruction in literacy be given top priority. It is through their own language that they will be able to reconstruct their history and culture . . . the student's language is the only means by which they can develop their own voice, a prerequisite to the development of a positive sense of self worth. (p. 151)

Earlier, we noted how youth literacy pedagogy integrates these elaborate(d) understandings of youth identity within a literacy framework that draws on available technologies to facilitate learning. Next, we describe the ways in which multimedia technology was integrated into this framework.

Multiliteracy Theory, Narrative, and Curriculum

As part of the collaboration, a multimedia technology (digital video, movies, CD compositions) and literacy unit was introduced to the youth literacy program. The unit, which took place at a university multimedia lab, provides a further example of the complex, sophisticated, and playful literacy practices that we use to address the needs of struggling adolescents. The unit integrated digital technology into the literacy program and encouraged the development of language and literacy skills through student multimedia projects: music CDs and short videos. Working from popular cultural artifacts, short stories, and student work, students developed storyboards and composed, acted, filmed, and edited their work. Finished projects included a video exploring peer pressure among girls, a video of an artist's portfolio of drawings that accompany an original mythological story, original poetry set to student-composed music, a video interview with a First Nation student exploring his culture and world view, a dance video, and a video showcasing snowboarding and skateboarding in an urban environment.

During the second year of our collaboration, we brought this technology to the school site to enable more students to participate and to more fully integrate the multimedia technology with the curriculum. Multimedia projects count toward the students' English, communication, or film and television course curricular goals, and the students are involved in evaluating their own uses of language and multimedia skills. As a result, we revised the portfolio guidelines for evaluating multimedia work in a way that is expansive enough to value the various accomplishments they represent. These guidelines include criteria that emphasize the *genesis* of the projects, including biographical, imaginative sources of storytelling; the integration and *transformations* of texts across media and genres; the *links* across students' out-of-school literacies (including cultural resources) and their in-school literacies; and their *reflections* on their work in the form of "artist statements," including a critique of their own "other" imaginative representations.

Digital video production also requires cooperative group work, negotiation and compromise, planning and coordination, and a critical reading of students' natural and social environments—skills that are less often employed in individualized, alternative programs such as this one. For example, during an interview with the university researcher, Theresa Rogers (second author), a student pointed out the importance of teamwork:

Theresa: What do you think you learned [from the digital video unit]?

Student: I learned teamwork . . . because, um, with this dance video D. and I were a team. It was basically guys versus girls 'cause D. and I would find some way to make the girls screw up, and the girls would find some way to make us screw up and everything. It was a fun experience, just generally working together and not somewhat more of an individual but as a team working as one, you know? . . . So I helped them do some dance and stuff like that, and then I watched the video and did the different angles and everything, like, and I was doing it more as the actor's point of view not the director or editor. But I still saw how stuff gets made as a whole. Sure, I wasn't sitting at my computer but I was sitting there watching other guys work. . . . I saw, yeah, I saw just how they fit stuff in and all, everything like that. It gave me a little bit of a feel to the whole video.

Integrating digital video and multiliteracies in this way encourages students to use their own cultural resources and to explore their own uses of literacy and media in new ways. Scott worked with a peer to turn "The Bullet," a poem about street life, into a CD—a rap version of his writing. Scott's poem was written in response to "Gregory," a short story (Ioannides, 1992). The story refers to the shooting of a prisoner during the 1950s liberation war in Cyprus, and it begins, "My hand was sweating as I held the pistol. The curve of the trigger was biting against my finger. Facing me, Gregory trembled. His whole body beseeching me, 'Don't'" (p. 153). Scott, integrating the execution theme into his biography, wrote from the perspective of the speeding bullet.

The Bullet

You thought you were safe
Walking down that dark wet ally
Then you see him
The dark figure
And then you see the shine
The shine of his gun
You panic and turn
And then you run
As fast as you can
BANG
I catch up to you
Blow through your back
You feel me burning in you
You feel my hate
You feel my power
You feel my anger
Then you fall
Hitting the wet cold cement
You lie there not feeling
Love, Hate, Power
You can't believe this is happening
You feel your heart slow down
I cool down in your cold body
You miss how much your mother loves you
You miss how much your father loves you
You miss how much your girlfriend loves you
Then you remember when you did the same thing
To the figure's brother
Made him fall
Made him hurt
Made him scared
Made him dead
You feel your gun strapped to you
You don't feel the power now
As you did when you were the dark figure
After you sending me through other people
And making me taste their blood
Now I get to taste your blood
Feel your heart pump
Feel your insides all around me
I love it
Finally you feel the hate
You feel the pain
You feel your life slowly slipping away
Then
It's gone
No more breathing
No more smiling
No more loving

You're lying there
Not moving
You are a memory
Goodbye

A richer sense of the texture and taste of the digital video component is captured in additional comments in the interview with Scott. The interview gives insights about the importance of using different approaches to teaching youth literacy and reveals the integral link between student biography, imagination, and multiple literacies.

Theresa: Tell me about the CD.

Scott: I sang into a microphone, a couple of times . . . so I was just reading it, and then he, P., the man that works up there, added in a beat when I was at break. And he asked me if I liked that, and I'm, like, "Yeah. Oh, that sounds good," and then I started getting some ideas and I put in a heartbeat because it's about a person dying. I put in a heartbeat and I put in . . . signs and I put in gunshots and stuff like that, and the finished product was, um, pretty neat, just and like the stuff he did and the way everything was set up and, I don't know, it just felt so cool to have my name on an actual CD.

Theresa: Have you been playing it?

Scott: Yeah, oh yeah, all my buddies hearing it and stuff like that, and that's pretty good for a weird guy from N.D. [a local area of the city]. It's the whole street hip-hop thing, oh, like, it's got feel to it, but. . . . It's too deep, like, too complex. . . . And I learned that, how technology is, like sitting there hearing my voice, you hear, there's nothing to beep, no nothing, and then the beat comes in, and then you get all these other things coming in, right, it's just whoa! I didn't even know you could do that, and then [it's] just the technology out there, even though it's not the greatest; but technology out there just blew me away, just the stuff that you could do.

Theresa: What were you trying to do in taking your poem and putting it to music?

Scott: I don't know. I would've liked it if I'd added in rhyming couplets to make it, like, actually rap, but I also just wanted to get a feel of it, see just how, see what you actually could do.

Theresa: You feel you're expressing yourself in a new way with the music?

Scott: Yeah, well, I think I was expressing myself through the poem because it's about a man getting shot in an alley for killing another guy's brother. And it had that beat, that evil, like, dark beat to it, and it just had the whole street sense to it.

Theresa: Right.

Scott: Right. So it's like, wow, that was pretty cool.

Theresa: And how did the music add to that?

Scott: It just, I don't know, just [gave] it more of a feel and like the deepness of it and everything like that, and then the more of that what kind of sounds you needed for stuff, and it just, I don't know, it was just me; I can just do that. It's just so many different things; and then you don't like it, just erase it. You just erased a sound. It's not very often you can erase a sound.

Scott's multiple literacy cycle included reading a story, writing a poem in response to the story, drawing on his biography and imagination, and then turning the poem into a rap CD. For Scott, the experience of erasing a sound occurred after engaging in reading and writing. Our approach to youth literacy pedagogy emphasizes student narratives and requires a respectful playfulness with those narratives and with texts and genres. It develops "pedagogical structures that provide students with the opportunity to use their own reality as a basis of literacy. This includes [using] the language they bring to the classroom" (Freire & Macedo, 1987, p. 151).

On the Playing Fields

The youth literacy program we describe incorporates recent reconceptualizations of adolescent literacy by integrating verbal and visual imagination, the material contexts and biographies of student lives, and traditional print-based literacies. It also provides opportunities for students to express themselves across multiple literacies. The curricular alternatives within the context of daily routines transform routine, the environment, and the school culture. We build on language and nonlanguage skills that may or may not be valued in many schools, and we scaffold literacy skills needed to augment student life skills and talents with student biographies and imagination. We attempt to identify, evaluate, and stimulate the specific literacy abilities of each student, but the complexities of student lives and the nature of their literacies also shape the structure of teaching, learning, and evaluation.

For us, supporting students' literacy in the alternative setting includes this playfulness with ideas, biography, and imagination. As we have attempted to illustrate, multiple literacy practices include, in addition to a conceptualization of broad pedagogical frameworks and attention to multiple text forms, sensitivity to the complex nexus of students' lives and the fields of ideas wherein teachers and students play. The students share their work with other students, staff, parents, and community members in a multimedia gallery at the end of the school year. The work includes their art, writings, photography, and a range of videos that provide rich "narrative tours" of their in-school and out-of-school lives and literacies (Rogers & Schofield, in press).

Literacy overlaps the lives and interests of these students. Teaching entails scaffolding their multiple literacies so that students can find voice as "public intellectuals in new times" (Dillon & O'Brien, 2001) by representing their ideas and attempting to address the complexity of their world through a variety of media texts as they strive to be heard and read.

Youth literacy pedagogies such as these move away from the emphasis on print literacy toward a braiding of narratives—stories constructed on the playing fields of curriculum—into multimedia texts that draw on adolescents' biographies, imaginations, and multiple and hybrid identities. This approach to youth literacy requires attention to new text forms, new technologies, and a new set of pedagogical practices, but it also draws attention to more important things: respect, passion, and playfulness.

References

Alvermann, D. (2001). Reading adolescents' reading identities: Looking back to see ahead. *Journal of Adolescent & Adult Literacy, 44,* 676–690.

Barton, D., & Hamilton, M. (2000). Literacy practices. In D. Barton, M. Hamilton, & R. Ivanic (Eds.), *Situated literacies: Reading and writing in context* (pp. 7–15). London: Routledge.

Barton, D., Hamilton, M., & Ivanic, R. (Eds.). (2000). *Situated literacies: Reading and writing in context.* London: Routledge.

Berenbaum, M. (1993). *The world must know.* London: Little, Brown.

Canadian Centre for Education Alternatives. (1999). *Peer to Peer Literacy Corps: Stage 3. Funding documentation prepared for Ministry of Advanced Education, Training and Technology. Province of British Columbia.* Vancouver: Author.

Cope, B., & Kalantzis, M. (Eds.). (2000). *Multiliteracies: Literacy learning and the design of social futures.* London: Routledge.

Dillon, D., & O'Brien, D. (2001, April). *Reconceptualizing "at risk" adolescent readers as literate intellectuals.* Paper presented at the meeting of the American Educational Research Association, Seattle, WA.

Egan, K. (1997). *The educated mind: How cognitive tools shape our understanding.* Chicago: University of Chicago Press.

Fine, M. (1994). Working the hyphens: Reinventing self and other in qualitative research. In N. K. Denzin & Y. S. Lincoln (Eds.), *Handbook of qualitative research* (pp. 70–82). Thousand Oaks, CA: Sage.

Freire, P., & Macedo, D. (1987). *Literacy: Reading the word and the world.* South Hadley, MA: Bergin & Garvey.

Gee, J. (2000). New people in new worlds: Networks, the new capitalism and schools. In B. Cope & M. Kalantzis (Eds.), *Multiliteracies: Literacy learning and the design of social futures* (pp. 43–68). London: Routledge.

Greene, M. (2000). *Releasing the imagination: Essays on education, the arts, and social change.* San Francisco: Jossey-Bass.

Harre, R. (1998). *The singular self.* London: Sage.

Ioannides, P. (1992). Gregory. In J. Barry & J. Griffin (Eds.), *The storyteller: Short stories from around the world* (pp. 153–157). Scarborough, ON: Nelson.

McCarthey, S. J., & Moje, E. (2002). Conversations: Identity matters. *Reading Research Quarterly, 27,* 228–238.

Moloney, S. (2002). *My thoughts.* Unpublished manuscript, Surrey, BC.

New London Group. (2000). A pedagogy of multiliteracies. In B. Cope & M. Kalantzis (Eds.), *Multiliteracies: Literacy learning and the design of social futures* (pp. 9–37). London: Routledge.

O'Brien, D. (1998). Multiple literacies in a high school program for "at risk" adolescents. In D. Alvermann, K. Hinchman, D. Moore, S. Phelps, & D. Waff (Eds.), *Reconceptualizing the literacies in adolescents' lives* (pp. 27–50). London: Erlbaum.

Parker, A. (Director). (1982). *Pink Floyd: The wall* [Motion picture]. United States: Columbia Pictures.

Rogers, T. (2000). What will be the social implications and interactions of schooling in the next millenium? *Reading Research Quarterly, 35,* 420–421. doi 10.1598/RRQ.35.3.5

Rogers, T., & Schofield, A. (in press). Things thicker than words: Portraits of multiple literacies in an alternative secondary program. In J. Anderson, M. Kendrick, T. Rogers, & S. Smythe (Eds.), *Portraits of literacy across family, community and schools: Tensions and intersections.* Mahwah, NJ: Erlbaum.

Searle, C. (1998). *None but our words. Critical literacy in classroom and community.* Philadelphia: Open University Press.

Spielberg. S. (Director). (1993). *Schindler's list* [Motion picture]. United States: Universal Studios.

Street, B. (1995). *Social literacies: Critical approaches to literacy in development, ethnography and education.* New York: Longman.

Truszyuska-Frederick, L. (2003). *Luba: The angel of Bergen-Belsen.* Toronto: Tricycle Press.

Classroom Implications

1. Based on your reading of the materials in this chapter, what do you believe are some specific ways classroom teachers can help adolescents with their reading, both in and out of the classroom?

2. What are some of the major problems related to adolescent literacy that must be faced and overcome before young people realistically consider reading to be an important part of their lives?

For Further Reading

Alvermann, D. (2004). Seeing and then seeing again. *Journal of Literacy Research, 36,* 289–302.

Challenging the achievement gap in a suburban high school: A multimethod analysis of an adolescent literacy initiative. (2004). Naperville, IL: North Central Regional Laboratory.

Conley, M., Kerner, M., & Reynolds, J. M. (2005). Not a question of "should" but a question of "how": Integrating literacy knowledge and practice into secondary teacher preparation through tutoring in urban middle schools. *Action in Teacher Education, 27,* 22–32.

Flood, J., & Anders, P. L. (Eds.). (2005). *Literacy development of students in urban schools: Research and policy.* Newark, DE: International Reading Association.

Henriquez, A. (2005). The evolution of an adolescent literacy program: A foundation's journey. *Reading Research Quarterly, 40,* 376–380.

Hopper, R. (2005). What are teenagers reading? Adolescent fiction reading habits and reading choices. *Literacy, 39,* 113–120.

Jetton, T. L., & Dole, J. A. (2004). *Adolescent literacy research and practice.* New York: Guilford.

Shanahan, C. (2005). *Adolescent literacy intervention programs: Chart and program review guide.* Naperville, IL: North Central Regional Laboratory.

Ten years of research on adolescent literacy, 1994–2004. (2005). Naperville, IL: North Central Regional Laboratory.

Online Resources

International Reading Association. (1999). *Adolescent literacy.* Position Statement.
www.reading.org/downloads/positions/ps1036_adolescent.pdf

Alvermann, D. E. (2001). *Effective literacy instruction for adolescents.* Paper commissioned by the National Reading Conference.
www.nrconline.org/publications/alverwhite2.pdf

· · · · ·

Chapter 5

Multicultural Literacy

The proper study of mankind is books.
—Aldous Huxley (1937)

[Reading] is a means whereby we may learn not only to understand ourselves and the world about us but whereby we may find out our place in the world.
—Elizabeth Neterer (1949)

The children attending our schools represent the diversity of our society, but too often our [reading] curriculum fails to mirror that diversity.
—Richard Allington & Patricia Cunningham (2007)

The students one finds in U.S. schools during the opening decade of the twenty-first century represent an unprecedented level of cultural and linguistic diversity—a diversity that, although often celebrated, poses daunting challenges to teachers. English language learners require differentiated strategies if they are to grow as readers and writers of English. Likewise, for those whose backgrounds represent cultural knowledge, customs, and values that differ from the traditional mainstream, comprehension can be threatened and identification with characters and content may be unlikely.

These trends raise crucial questions concerning how best to address the needs of these students. Some of these questions are matters of policy; others are matters of pedagogy. A few of these questions follow:

1. What language should be used for primary instruction, especially in the areas of reading and language arts?
2. For English language learners, what are the most appropriate teaching techniques and materials for language instruction?

3. What are the necessary modifications or changes in the traditional literacy curriculum to meet the educational needs of all students?
4. What types of literacy materials seem to work best to encourage multicultural understanding in all students, including those from the traditional mainstream?
5. How can a sense of mutual respect and tolerance be created for the diverse cultures represented both within and beyond the classroom setting?

There are many reasons for teachers to encourage mainstream students to read widely about other cultures and peoples. We live in a world society today that is dramatically impacted by events from many different locations. The advent of digital technologies has increased the interaction among countries and cultures. It affords endless opportunities to interact with people whose backgrounds differ from our own. While at one time many in the United States could feel comfortable in the relative isolation of their communities and schools, this option is no longer viable (if it ever was). Indeed, the makeup of many of today's classrooms calls for very different strategies. Teachers must find ways to address the fact that their classrooms in some cases represent patchwork quilts of languages and culture. Consider a "simple" example:

> It was the day of the big party. Mary wondered if Johnny would like a kite. She ran to her bedroom, picked up her piggy bank, and shook it. There was no sound. (Eskey, 2002, p. 6)

Think a moment about the assumptions this writer makes about the reader's cultural knowledge. How well would children comprehend if they represent cultures in which birthdays are celebrated differently? Clearly, it behooves the teacher to anticipate instances like this where prior knowledge must be bolstered. This is one characteristic of *culturally responsive teaching*, but another is to turn these differences into opportunities for mainstream children to grow as well by learning about their classmates' cultures (Radencich, 1998).

The Special Plight of English Language Learners

While cultural differences can limit reading comprehension of text written from unfamiliar perspectives, this problem is dwarfed (and compounded) by language differences that can make English-language literacy a frustrating goal. There are two major approaches to helping these children attain proficiency in English. Students of limited English proficiency (LEP) may be taught in a context of *bilingual education*, in which instruction in both English and the native language occurs in the same classrooms. During one period, instruction might be conducted in the native language while during another it might be conducted in English. In contrast, the *ESL approach* (English as a second language) is one in which intense instruction in basic English is conducted in separate classrooms so that students can become proficient as quickly as possible; for the remainder of the day, students are immersed in English-only classes.

The relative merits of these approaches have been hotly debated. Some research indicates that bilingual education can be effective in helping students evolve in their personal language acquisition to the point that they are capable of learning from written materials and oral presentations in English. However, many Hispanic parents object to instruction in Spanish because they believe that their children may be disadvantaged. In 1998, this sentiment led to passage of Proposition 227, the English for the Children Initiative, in California. This proposition called for an end to bilingual education and reliance instead on total immersion of California schoolchildren in English-speaking classrooms. Proponents of the proposition pointed to increases in the test scores of immigrant children as evidence that immersion works better than bilingual education. In 2005, on the other hand, the National Literacy Panel on Language Minority Children and Youth concluded that the available evidence casts doubt on the effectiveness of English-only instruction. The U.S. Department of Education, however, declined to publish the Panel's report, perhaps for political reasons (see *Reading Today*, October/November 2005, *23*(2), 1,3). The report was published privately in 2006 by Lawrence Erlbaum (Shanahan & August, 2006). The debate continues.

These major approaches do not resolve the more basic problem for many teachers—namely, that English language learners, representing various levels of proficiency, will continue to populate their classes. Although there is no magic bullet for responding to their needs, resources are beginning to appear that offer effective suggestions (e.g., Drucker, 2003; Echevarria & Graves, 2003; Echevarria, Vogt, & Short, 2004).

As You Read

The readings in this chapter were selected to help you carefully consider the many challenges and rewards of culturally responsive literacy instruction. The following articles were selected to provide an overview of current ideas. McCollin and O'Shea directly address many of the most important issues related to helping learners who represent a wide variety of cultural and linguistic backgrounds. Cummins and his colleagues expand this discussion, noting the importance of developing a learning atmosphere in the classroom that affirms the educational identities of all learners regardless of individual backgrounds or cultural identity. Forest then discusses the impact on multicultural literacy education of the No Child Left Behind Act of 2001. Issues such as teacher and school accountability, mandated assessments, and curriculum reforms are addressed in this article. In the final article, Glazier and Seo speak specifically about the experiences of one classroom as students read and then interact with a variety of multicultural text materials.

While reading, ask yourself these questions.

1. How do these different authors define *multiculturalism*?
2. In what ways is your personal definition of diversity similar or different from these stances?

3. What are some of the current multicultural issues that you believe educators need to be aware of, and how might they effectively deal with these concerns in their literacy instruction?

References

Allington, R. L., & Cunningham, P. M. (2007). *Schools that work: Where all children read and write* (3rd ed.). Boston: Allyn & Bacon.

Drucker, M. J. (2003). What reading teachers should know about ESL learners. *The Reading Teacher, 57,* 22–29.

Echevarria, J., & Graves, A. (2003). *Sheltered content instruction: Teaching English-language learners with diverse abilities* (2nd ed.). Boston: Allyn & Bacon.

Echevarria, J., Vogt, M., & Short, D. J. (2004). *Making content comprehensible for English learners: The SIOP model* (2nd ed.). Boston: Allyn & Bacon.

Eskey, D. E. (2002). Reading and the teaching of L2 reading. *TESOL Journal, 11*(1), 5–9.

Forest, S. (2004). Implications of No Child Left Behind on family literacy in a multicultural community. *Clearing House, 78,* 41–45.

Glazier, J., & Seo, J. (2005). Multicultural literature and discussion as mirror and window? *Journal of Adolescent & Adult Literacy, 48,* 686–700.

Huxley, A. (1937). *Chrome Yellow.* Garden City, NY: Sun Dial Press.

McCollin, M., & O'Shea, D. (2005). Increasing reading achievement of students from culturally and linguistically diverse backgrounds. *Preventing School Failure, 50,* 41–44.

Neterer, E. (1949). *This is reading.* Washington, DC: Association For Education International. 12.

Radencich, M. C. (1998). Multicultural education for literacy in the year 2000: Traversing comfort zones and transforming knowledge and action. *Peabody Journal of Education, 73*(3&4), 178–201.

Shanahan, T., & August, D. (Eds.). (2006). *Developing literacy in English language learners.* Mahwah, NJ: Lawrence Erlbaum.

Increasing Reading Achievement of Students from Culturally and Linguistically Diverse Backgrounds

MICHELLE McCOLLIN AND DORIS O'SHEA

Legislative language, mandated by the newly reauthorized *Individuals With Disabilities Education Improvement Act* (IDEIA) of 2004 and the *No Child Left Behind Act* (NCLB) of 2001, underscores a number of issues relevant to students from culturally and linguistically diverse backgrounds displaying reading-achievement difficulties. In this article, we offer strategies derived from scientific, research-based interventions to close the gaps in early literacy skills that are often observed for students from culturally and linguistically diverse backgrounds.

Addressing Phonological Awareness Gaps

Before learning to read, students need awareness of how sounds form words. Phonological awareness involves the "identification and manipulation of parts of spoken language" (Carnine, Silbert, Kame'enui, & Tarver, 2004). It includes, but is not limited to, an awareness of the various parts of spoken language (e.g., awareness of sounds, syllables, or words). Students from culturally and linguistically diverse backgrounds often experience difficulties with phonological awareness because of limited levels of literacy development in home settings, limited levels of literacy in students' native languages, cultural disparities, and/or cultural deprivation (Artiles & Zamora-Duran, 1997; Rueda, 1997; Zamora-Duran & Reyes, 1997).

Best practices point to a number of activities as the foundation for addressing phonological awareness gaps. As with other students displaying phonological awareness problems, students from culturally and linguistically diverse backgrounds require explicit instruction in skills to observe, think about, manipulate, and experience sounds in spoken language. For example, they need directed opportunities to listen for and discriminate letter sounds and sounds within words (Armbruster & Osborn, 2001).

McCollin, M., & O'Shea, D. (2005). Increasing reading achievement of students from culturally and linguistically diverse backgrounds. *Preventing School Failure, 50,* 41–44. Reprinted with permission.

153

When early reading opportunities are culturally and linguistically relevant, students can profit enormously from explicit instruction in awareness of the various parts of spoken language before proceeding to the meaning of the written word or text.

Using a Variety of Instructional Materials at Different Reading Levels Can Accommodate Individual Reading Acquisition Skills. Aiming for culturally and linguistically relevant materials that hold meaning to students (e.g., letter games based on home or community events, decoding activities based on family or ethnic traditions) can support linking of students' reading acquisition skills to functional reading motivation. Some examples of how to do this include using instructional materials from students' cultures, languages, or religious affiliations, and helping students to identify and manipulate spoken language through word games, alliteration activities, onset challenges, and rhyming intonations. Infusing culturally diverse materials and early reading opportunities can arouse students' interests, such as through the use of diverse dress themes as students acquire skills in making oral rhymes (e.g., "The sari is green, worn by the teen . . . The babushka is black and tied in the back"). Pairing a relevant cultural dress theme and an initial consonant of a syllable activity becomes meaningful as the onset receives attention (e.g., the onset of 'sari' is 's'; the onset of 'green' is 'gr'), followed by the rhyme or the part of the syllable containing the vowel and all that follows the vowel (e.g., the rhyme of 'green' is '-een').

Other examples to increase phonological awareness include playing clapping or skipping games with syllables in words focused on holidays or traditions ("I clap the word parts to 'Easter' (Christian), 'Bisakha Puja' (Buddhist), and 'Yom Hasho'ah' (Jewish)"). The key is to build students' phonological awareness directly using sociocultural materials and activities such that students notice, think about, and work with individual sounds in spoken words.

Encouraging Students to Compose Stories from Wordless Picture Books and to Respond Creatively to Phonemic Awareness, Alphabetic Knowledge, and Decoding Skills Based on Their Diverse Interests Can Help to Link Home, School, and Community Interests. For example, letter game activities based on students' skills in alphabet knowledge, beginning consonant awareness, words in the text, spelling using beginning and ending consonants, phonetic segmentation, and word recognition, or conceptual reading ability can help to develop early literacy skills. Home, school, and community interests can be used to explore alphabetic knowledge, letter–sound associations, letter–sound correspondences, sound–symbol correspondences, and sound spellings.

Some examples of how to do this include the use of word family activities linked to students' backgrounds. Building on parts of word families with which students are familiar, then, extending students' knowledge to unknown words that have similar parts can extend students' word awareness. For instance, asking students to respond creatively to phonics opportunities can include rhyming games using familiar, cultural, rhyming food words, such as "ham and jam," extended to less familiar food words, such as "yam and pam."

Providing wordless picture books can challenge students to expand rhyming words in sentences by blending sounds to form new words and sentences based on community or school activities. Such a challenge is illustrated in this Kwanzaa holiday example: "Who would like to create a Kwanzaa sentence using the rhyming words 'candle, handle, corn, morn'? Great job! You used our rhyming words when you said, 'Can the man with the candle handle the corn in the morn?' Our picture book shows the candle and corn."

Teaching Sounds and Words Systematically and Explicitly Always Makes a Difference.   Encourage sounds and word awareness through phonemic, letter sound, word-to-word matching, blending, phoneme segmentation, phoneme counting, and rhyming games (followed by word recognition, spelling, reading, and writing games) that are culturally and linguistically relevant (e.g., based on prominent home, community, or historical figures). An example of how to do this is stressing sociocultural experiences, such as "Community Awareness Week" or "Black History Month," with systematic practice in sounds and words ("As we study Black History Month, how many phonemes do we hear in the name *Martin Luther King* or *George Washington Carver*?").

Explicitly Teaching Students to Use Key Steps in Decoding Unfamiliar Words Improves Achievement   (e.g., using context clues, sounding out initial consonant or vowel blends, checking for structure clues, using phonics, consulting a dictionary). By planning reading lessons based on family traditions, favorite community sporting events, or school traditions, educators can emphasize students' reading readiness and relevant socio-cultural experiences in fun, achievement-oriented activities. Explicitly teaching students prerequisite skills requires that they decode unfamiliar words, target knowledge of letter–sound correspondences, blend a series of sounds, and then translate a series of connected sounds into meaningful words. For example, achievement gains may increase as students move from simple passage reading of stories composed of words taught in word-list exercises (such as the words tamale, tacos, and fajitas) to use of word skills that gradually increase in length and difficulty (such as when the words are now embedded in a sentence: "What are words we need to look up in the dictionary as we read this sentence: 'My grandmother cooked my favorite menu of hot tamales, beef and cheddar tacos, and chicken fajitas'?"). By infusing decoding and culturally relevant activities based on family or community traditions, students' literacy readiness and relevant life experiences come together in developmentally appropriate activities.

Addressing Fluency Gaps

Fluency involves students reading faster and with fewer errors. Fluency is important because it leads to gains in comprehension—it is the bridge between word recognition and comprehension (Carnine et al., 2004). Explicit fluency opportunities infused with culturally relevant themes can close the gaps in early literacy skills that are often observed for students from culturally and linguistically diverse backgrounds.

Securing Reading Materials Can Support Fluency Gains by Providing the Opportunity to Experience Written Text or Visual Media   (e.g., books, magazines, newspapers, television, computers). Students increase culturally relevant opportunities and reading gains as they observe models of fluent reading. Adults should preread orally relevant sections related to cultural themes, mores, values, traditions, history, or customs so that students listen to fluent readers using culturally responsive reading materials. For example, asking students to listen to and discuss a passage from *I Know Why the Caged Bird Sings* by Maya Angelou, can encourage them to hear and recognize unfamiliar words and key phrases and themes before they read the passage independently. At the same time, this helps students increase awareness of culturally diverse poets.

Embedding Culturally Relevant Themes When Students Reread Passages Can Help Them Gain Fluency Meaning from What They Read.   Asking students to reread passages aloud several times and to receive feedback from adults as they read aloud builds fluency (O'Shea, Sindelar, & O'Shea, 1987). For example, repeated reading of passages infused with story characters from African American, Asian, or Hispanic backgrounds provides students with cues to read faster and with fewer errors in opportunities that highlight students' understandings of meaningful, diverse characters.

Implementing Choral Reading and Using Responsive Passages Can Influence Fluency.   In choral reading, entire groups of students repeat passages after listening to adults model appropriate reading. In responsive passages, students use a listening device, such as a tape recorder, mp3 player, or iPod, to increase fluency (Rasinski & Padak, 2004). By integrating relevant topics corresponding to interests in art, culture, dance, values, traditions, history, language, or music, students can focus attention on making connections among ideas in text and between these ideas and students' background knowledge (i.e., text-to-self connections). An example of how to do this includes planning choral reading and responsive passages to correspond to affluent literary genres and poetry readings from several of the cultures present in the United States (e.g., Native American, Asian, African, Korean, Mexican, Hispanic, African American, Irish, and Japanese). This gives students exposure to various cultures, and their thoughts and worldviews, so that they can simultaneously immerse themselves in developmentally appropriate literature.

Teaching Vocabulary before Starting the Lesson Can Build Meanings Based on Students' Prior Backgrounds and Experiences.   When reading opportunities tie in dance, music, dress, or food activities and materials from students' sociocultural or linguistic backgrounds, reading experiences can be meaningful and motivating. Students become more familiar with vocabulary meaning, relating new vocabulary words to their prior experiences. Students receive key vocabulary prior to initial reading, followed by repeated reading opportunities. An example of how to do this is implementing vocabulary-building activities with ethnic dance opportunities (e.g., "before rereading the passage, let's do a salsa or hip-hop dance to the new vocabulary words we just read"). Such activities can enhance fluency opportunities such that students use language in fun ways and for a variety of purposes.

Selecting Reading Materials That Offer Multicultural Story Settings and Diverse Story Characters Can Make Repeated Reading Opportunities More Meaningful.   Shortening length of reading tasks, then gradually increasing these tasks as students demonstrate reading gains, can help to gauge students' readiness to move on to new stories or to repeat stories read previously. For example, observing students' motivation to reread stories can be based on the amount of discussion generated after each repeated reading, choral reading, and responsive passage or on speed and accuracy of words, phrases, sentences, and stories reread. Culturally enhanced materials for diverse students can access a variety of themes, genres, and formats. And because we read for many purposes, reference books, lists, written directions, menus, and catalogs are valid classroom materials to target students' cultural interests and fluency experiences. The key in doing this is to target reading materials with relevant sociocultural themes (e.g., characters from ethnic backgrounds, historical themes relevant to community events, language experiences unique to students' heritages) to support diverse readers' fluency gains.

Addressing Comprehension Gaps

Reading comprehension is the ability to process and understand information (Kuder & Hasit, 2002). Promoting a variety of culturally relevant experiences at different reading levels can facilitate individual text comprehension skills. Focusing on culturally and linguistically relevant materials and activities support students' understanding of what they are reading. Some examples of how to do this include having a variety of multinational reading materials available so students engage in varied experiences (e.g., modeled, shared, interactive, guided, and independent reading on their own cultural or ethnic backgrounds). These materials may include picture books, books on tape, comic strips, trade books, basal reader textbooks, content-area books, and/or self-selected books.

Modifying Content with Reading Aids Can Support Comprehension.   To activate background knowledge and build motivation, purposefully select stories relevant to the experiences and backgrounds of culturally and linguistically diverse students, then help them target relevant themes by stressing story titles, illustrations, themes, headings and subheadings, characters, setting, plots, and so forth. Use graphic organizers and story maps to support students' focus on relevant details, story sequences, or logical conclusions. Adapt or modify with culturally or linguistically relevant changes. For example, select or modify reading materials that offer multicultural story settings and diverse story characters. For example, *Romeo and Juliet* by Shakespeare is set in Las Vegas, instead of England, and Romeo is a Native American Indian, whereas Juliet is an Asian American teenager. Use a semantic web to identify important interrelationships in the passage to help students to diagram the plot. When students from different backgrounds receive multicultural story settings and diverse story characters, data can surface on what students do and do not understand. Students support their own comprehension skills when they self-monitor reading opportunities using graphic organizers or story maps. You can generate questions, answer students' questions, and help students to review the content and relate what they have learned to what they already know in the context of the diverse story setting.

Creating Opportunities to Paraphrase in Students' Own Words Can Support Understanding after Reading.   Encourage students to summarize short passages and longer passages in familiar words after oral or silent reading experiences. By asking students to draw pictures to represent their understanding of the written text, many sociocultural themes relevant to students' life experiences may develop in classroom discussions. As oral classroom discussions and written reactions to stories read become more elaborate, so too can problem solving on in-depth story themes, details, predictions, hypothesis, and conclusions. For example, after reading a selected passage from Mark Twain's *The Adventures of Huckleberry Finn*, encourage students to tell the story in their own words and in their own time frame. Ask students to draw pictures of Huckleberry's problems, as if he were alive today. Ask them to repeat their understanding of the written text using a different sociocultural theme, such as an urban setting, instead of a river environment.

Selecting Reading Assignments That Are Culturally and Linguistically Diverse Fosters Comprehension.   Encourage and model effective daily reading, writing, speaking, and listening skills by directly and explicitly teaching students to process meaningful connections within and between sentences. Cue students to link text to self and prior experiences/information. By using questioning techniques (e.g., why, when, where) and providing immediate feedback on students' answers, guide students to practice comprehension skills. To encourage increased independent-reading comprehension skills, ask students to follow up with meaningful and independent reading, writing, speaking, or listening activities to generalize comprehension from text to their own lives and experiences. Use story maps, mnemonics, or sentence organizers to over learn reading material and to differentiate main ideas and supporting ideas as students process meaningful connections within and between sentences and make inferences about what is comprehended. For example, assign reading passages on the ecology status of neighborhoods. Assign students tasks to create memory aids by representing beginning letters of story slogans evolving from major events in neighborhood ecology passages. Also, ask students to summarize succinctly important passage ideas using other mnemonics. Remind students that mnemonics represent what is important in what they are reading. Ask students to remember in their own words what they read. Encourage more advanced comprehension skills by asking students to present the story plot as theatrical skits.

Providing Explicit Opportunities for Students to Apply Their Experiences and Knowledge.   Seek out opportunities to increase students' content and situational vocabularies by helping diverse students become familiar with written language from various literary genres and by increasing access to information outside of students' own experiences. Inviting prominent community role models, motivational speakers, or citizens who promote reading success in the classroom is one way to do this. Encourage students to become proficient in newspaper or journal reading and computer usage and technology. Arrange for school and community experiences to expand students' local and global horizons. Seek out creative, novel, fun activities, such as drama, poetry, and music experiences, to stress additional readings on topics or to extend periods of longer reading comprehension tasks, and writing or speaking follow-up activities. Encourage culturally and linguistically relevant reading materials by stressing readers' systematic opportunities for self-monitoring and checking of reading comprehension skills.

Planning, Recording, and Monitoring Increased Time on Task Help to Improve All Reading Opportunities.   Be cognizant of the actual time allotted to reading comprehension opportunities in the classroom. In order to channel readers' motivation to acceptable avenues, allow students to work with partners, in small groups, or in centers with reading models and tutors. By alternating high- and low-interest reading comprehension tasks, allow struggling readers to have closer proximity to the teacher and effective reading peers who may model appropriate reading behaviors. The most appropriate way to maintain time on task for reading is to increase the time to actually read and model the reading act. Finally, explicitly reinforce students' self-esteem, motivation, and reading success by praising them often for their reading attempts.

Closing the Achievement Gap

Legislative language, mandated by the IDEIA of 2004 and the NCLB of 2001, stresses issues relative to students from culturally and linguistically diverse backgrounds who may be displaying reading achievement difficulties. The educational challenge that remains is being able to differentiate readers with actual learning problems who require special education from those with limited reading opportunities. Closing the achievement gap means providing opportunities so students acquire early literacy skills. Educators can encourage the reading achievement of students from culturally and linguistically diverse backgrounds by directly and explicitly attending to research-based components of early literacy. By actively using effective reading strategies, educators may help to differentiate readers with actual learning problems who require special education from those with limited reading opportunities. Concurrently, educators may help to lessen the overidentification of minority representation in special education by understanding and supporting students from culturally and linguistically diverse backgrounds. By doing so, students can realize achievement gains and school success.

References

Armbruster, B. B., & Osborn, J. (2001). *Put reading first. The research building blocks for teaching children to read.* Washington, DC: U.S. Department of Education.

Artiles, A. J., & Zamora-Duran, G. (Eds.). (1997). *Reducing disproportionate representation of culturally diverse students in special and gifted education.* Reston, VA: The Council for Exceptional Children.

Carnine, D. W., Silbert, J., Kame'enui, E. J., & Tarver, S. G. (2004). *Direct instruction reading.* Upper Saddle River, NJ: Pearson.

Kuder, S. J., & Hasit, C. (2002). *Enhancing literacy for all students.* Upper Saddle River, NJ: Pearson.

O'Shea, L. J., Sindelar, P. T., & O'Shea, D. J. (1987). The effects of repeated reading and attentional cues on the reading fluency and comprehension of learning disabled readers. *Learning Disabilities Research, 2,* 103–109.

Rasinski, T., & Padak, N. (2004). *Effective reading strategies: Teaching children who find reading difficult.* Upper Saddle River, NJ: Pearson.

Rueda, R. (1997). Changing the context of assessment: The move to portfolios and authentic assessment. In A. J. Artiles & G. Zamora-Duran (Eds.), *Reducing disproportionate representation of culturally diverse students in special and gifted education* (pp. 7–26). Reston, VA: The Council for Exceptional Children.

Zamora-Duran, G., & Reyes, E. I. (1997). From tests to talking in the classroom: Assessing communicative competence. In A. J. Artiles & G. Zamora-Duran (Eds.), *Reducing disproportionate representation of culturally diverse students in special and gifted education* (pp. 47–58). Reston, VA: The Council for Exceptional Children.

Affirming Identity in Multilingual Classrooms

JIM CUMMINS, VICKI BISMILLA, PATRICIA CHOW, SARAH COHEN, FRANCES GIAMPAPA, LISA LEONI, PERMINDER SANDHU, AND PADMA SASTRI

In *How People Learn*, Bransford, Brown, and Cocking (2000) synthesized research regarding the optimal conditions that foster learning; a follow-up volume edited by Donovan and Bransford (2005) examines the application of these learning principles to teaching history, mathematics, and science. Bransford and colleagues emphasize the following three conditions for effective learning: engaging prior understandings and background knowledge, integrating factual knowledge with conceptual frameworks by encouraging deep understanding, and supporting students in taking active control over the learning process.

Any instructional intervention that claims scientific credibility should reflect these principles, which are particularly important when it comes to English language learners. Prior knowledge refers not only to information or skills previously acquired in formal instruction but also to the totality of the experiences that have shaped the learner's identity and cognitive functioning. In classrooms with students from linguistically diverse backgrounds, instruction should explicitly activate this knowledge.

Knowledge is more than just the ability to remember. Deeper levels of understanding enable students to transfer knowledge from one context to another. Moreover, when students take ownership of their learning—when they invest their identities in learning outcomes—active learning takes place. Numerous research studies have shown that scripted, transmission-oriented pedagogy, which tends to be both superficial and passive, fails to build on English language learners' pre-existing cultural and linguistic knowledge (Warschauer, Knobel, & Stone, 2004).

Pre-existing knowledge for English language learners is encoded in their home languages. Consequently, educators should explicitly teach in a way that fosters transfer

Cummins, J. et al. (2005) Affirming identy in multicultural classrooms. *Educational Leadership, 63*, 38–43. Reprinted with permission. The Association for Supervision and Curriculum Development is a worldwide community of educators advocating sound policies and sharing best practices to achieve the success of each learner. To learn more, visit ASCD at www.ascd.org.

of concepts and skills from the student's home language to English. Research clearly shows the potential for this kind of cross-language transfer in school contexts that support biliteracy development (Cummins, 2001; Reyes, 2001). It is hard to argue that we are teaching the whole child when school policy dictates that students leave their language and culture at the schoolhouse door.

Embracing Differences

Sidra's experiences as an English language learner illustrate some of these concerns. Two years after she emigrated from Pakistan with her family, she described her early days as a 5th grader in a Canadian school:

> I was new, and I didn't know English. I could only say little sentences. I wore cultural clothes, and people usually judge a new person by their looks. If they see the clothes that I am wearing are not like their clothes, they will just think that I'm not one of them. If we had any partner activities, no one will pick me as their partner. I felt really, really left out. Kids also made fun of me because I looked different, and I couldn't speak English properly.

Sidra highlights themes that are notably absent from the "scientifically proven" prescriptions of No Child Left Behind (NCLB). She talks about the struggle to express herself, not just linguistically, but also culturally. Her "cultural clothes" are an expression of an identity that her peers have rejected, causing her to feel "really, really left out." But Sidra also had caring teachers who welcomed her into school. As she explained,

> I was the only person in grade 5 who wore cultural clothes. The teachers liked what I wore. They tried to talk to me and ask me questions. I liked telling teachers about my culture and religion. It made me feel more comfortable and welcome.

Sidra's experiences show that human relationships are important in children's adjustment to schooling; engagement in learning, particularly for English language learners, is fueled as much by affect as by cognition. Despite her still-limited access to academic English, she writes extensively because she has a lot to share, and she knows that her teacher, Lisa Leoni, is genuinely interested in her experiences and insights. Sidra's account also illustrates the opportunity—and the responsibility—that teachers have to create environments that affirm the identities of English language learners, thereby increasing the confidence with which these students engage in language and literacy activities.

One Size Does Not Fit All

Affect, identity, respect, and human relationships: These constructs have not been evident in the radical education reforms ushered in by NCLB, which supposedly are based on scientific research. Numerous commentators have critiqued the scientific basis and instructional consequences of these policies (Allington, 2004; Garan, 2001; Krashen, 2004). Several false assumptions underlying these reforms apply specifically to English language learners:

- Students' home language is, at best, irrelevant. At worst, it is an impediment to literacy development and academic success.
- The cultural knowledge and linguistic abilities that English language learners bring to school have little instructional relevance.
- Instruction to develop English literacy should focus only on English literacy.
- Students can learn only what teachers explicitly teach.
- Culturally and linguistically diverse parents, whose English may be limited, do not have the language skills to contribute to their children's literacy development.

These assumptions, common before NCLB, have now become entrenched as a result of the ubiquity of high-stakes testing and the mandate for systematic and explicit phonics instruction from kindergarten through 6th grade (Lyon & Chhabra, 2004). Yet they violate the scientific consensus about how people learn (Bransford et al., 2000). They also reduce the opportunities for literacy engagement within the classroom (Guthrie, 2004). Finally, they are refuted by empirical data on literacy development among English language learners, which show that students' home language proficiency at time of arrival in an English-speaking country is the strongest predictor of English academic development (Thomas & Collier, 2002).

We present an alternative set of principles for promoting academic engagement among English language learners, which we draw from Early and colleagues' research project in Canada (2002). Central to our argument are two interrelated propositions:

- English language learners' cultural knowledge and language abilities in their home language are important resources in enabling academic engagement; and
- English language learners will engage academically to the extent that instruction affirms their identities and enables them to invest their identities in learning.

The Dual Language Identity Text

Teaching for cross-language transfer and literacy engagement can be problematic for teachers when multiple languages are represented in the classroom, none of which the teacher may know. One approach that we have been exploring in several schools in Canada's Greater Toronto area involves *identity texts*. These products, which can be written, spoken, visual, musical, dramatic, or multimodal combinations, are positive statements that students make about themselves.

Identity texts differ from more standard school assignments in both the process and the product. The assignment is cognitively challenging, but students can choose their topics. They decide how they will carry out the project and are encouraged to use the full repertoire of their talents in doing so.

For example, when she was in 7th grade—and less than a year after arriving in Canada—Madiha coauthored a 20-page English-Urdu dual language book titled *The New Country*. . . . Together with her friends, Kanta and Sulmana, also originally from Pakistan, she wrote about "how hard it was to leave our country and come to a new country." Kanta and Sulmana were reasonably fluent in English because they had arrived in Toronto several years before, in 4th grade. Madiha, however, was in the early stages of English language acquisition.

The students collaborated on this project in the context of a unit on migration that integrated social studies, language, and ESL curriculum expectations. They researched and wrote the story over the course of several weeks, sharing their experiences and language skills. Madiha spoke little English but was fluent in Urdu; Sulmana was fluent and literate in both Urdu and English; Kanta, who was fluent in Punjabi and English, had mostly learned Urdu in Toronto. The girls discussed their ideas primarily in Urdu but wrote the initial draft of their story in English. Sulmana served as scribe for both languages.

In a "normal" classroom, Madiha's minimal knowledge of English would have severely limited her ability to participate in a 7th grade social studies unit. She certainly would not have been in a position to communicate extensively in English about her experiences, ideas, and insights. When the social structure of the classroom changed in simple ways, however, Madiha could express herself in ways that few English language learners experience in school. Her home language, in which all her experience prior to immigration was encoded, became once again a tool for learning. She contributed her ideas and experiences to the story, participated in discussions about how to translate vocabulary and expressions from Urdu to English and from English to Urdu, and shared in the affirmation that all three students experienced when they published their story.

Students can create identity texts on any topic relevant to their lives or of interest to them. Sometimes teachers will suggest topics or ways of carrying out the project; in other cases, students will generate topics themselves and decide what form the projects will take. Because these projects require substantial time to complete, it is useful to aim for cross-curricular integration. That way, the project can meet standards in several different content areas. For example, students might research the social history of their communities through document analysis and interviews with community members. Such a project would integrate curricular standards in language arts, social studies, and technology.

Because students *want* to do the work in the first place, they generally treasure the product they have created and wish to share it with those they care about. This usually doesn't happen with worksheets, regardless of how accurately the student completes them. The worksheet has no life beyond its immediate function, whereas the identity text lives on for a considerable time, either in tangible form, as in a book, or as a digital text on the Web.

Language in the Classroom

Thornwood Public School, a K–5 school in the Peel District School Board in Toronto, Canada, pioneered the process of the dual language identity text (Chow & Cummins,

2003; Schecter & Cummins, 2003). As is common in many urban public schools in Canada, students in Thornwood speak more than 40 different home languages, with no one language dominating. Patricia Chow's 1st and 2nd grade students created stories initially in English, the language of school instruction, because most of the primary students had not yet learned to read or write in their home languages. Students illustrated their stories and then worked with various people—parents, older students literate in their home languages, or teachers who spoke their languages—to translate these stories into the students' home languages. The school created the Dual Language Showcase Web site (http://thornwood.peelschools.org/Dual) to enable students to share their bilingual stories over the Internet with parents, relatives, and friends, both in Canada and in the students' countries of origin. With identity texts, audience becomes a powerful source of validation for the student.

As the Thornwood Dual Language Showcase project has evolved, dual language books have become a potent tool to support the integration of newcomers and English language learners. Students write initial drafts of stories in whichever language they choose, usually in their stronger language. Thus, newcomer students can write in their home language and demonstrate not only their literacy skills but also their ideas and feelings, giving full play to their imaginations. The image of newcomer students, in both their own eyes and in the eyes of others, changes dramatically when these students express themselves in this way within the school curriculum.

When none of the teachers or class members speaks the language of a particular newcomer student, the school explores contacts with community members or board-employed community liaison personnel or involves older students from the same language background whose English is more fluent. High school students from various language backgrounds receive credit for their involvement as community service work. Consequently, dual language texts have become a catalyst for fruitful forms of school-community engagement.

At Floradale Public School, another highly multilingual school in the Peel District School Board, teacher-librarian Padma Sastri has integrated both student-created and commercial dual language books into all aspects of library functioning. She prominently displays student-created dual language books near the library entrance, welcomes parents into the library to read books to students in their native languages, and encourages students to check out dual language books to take home to read with their families.

When students gather around her for the day's lesson in the library, Sastri enlists students to read a given story out loud in English. She also encourages various students to retell the story afterward in their home language. Said one observer,

> I listen amazed as one by one the students retell the story in Urdu, Turkish, Vietnamese, Chinese, Gujerati, Tamil, Korean, and Arabic. The other students in the class appear to be equally entranced, although neither I nor they understand most of the languages being used. It is captivating to hear the same story repeated in different languages with new or sometimes the same gestures to express a change in action.

By welcoming a student's home language, schools facilitate the flow of knowledge, ideas, and feelings between home and school and across languages.

Elementary school teacher Perminder Sandhu integrated discussions about students' language and culture into the curriculum of her 4th grade class in Coppard Glen Public School of Toronto's York Region District School Board. Students wrote about their languages, discussed the importance of continuing to speak their languages, and worked in pairs to create dual language or multilingual books, often with the help of their parents. One of Sandhu's students writes about his engagement with literacy and popular culture outside the school. Jagdeep, who is fluent in Punjabi, Hindi, and English, illustrates the importance of connecting, both cognitively and affectively, with students' prior experience:

> I love Punjabi stories. They're so exciting. When it comes to Hindi movies, I just can't stop watching them! They are very funny, and the problems are very sophisticated. It makes me proud of my cultural background.

For Sandhu, acknowledging and actively promoting students' linguistic and cultural capital is not simply a matter of activating students' prior knowledge—she fuses these practices in a pedagogy of respect. Sandhu explains,

> It informs my practice through and through. It runs in the bloodstream of my classroom. It's all about relationships, how we validate students' identities, how they accept their own identities. That ethos is fundamentally important—it's not an add-on. It takes less than two extra minutes of my time to get students to see the humanity of another human being at a most basic level. Because once they begin to see their own and one another's vulnerabilities, inhibitions, and realities, they connect.

The pedagogical orientation illustrated in the examples above differs from many schools' current policies and practice in two major respects. First, the teacher acknowledges that the language in which English language learners' prior experience is encoded is an important resource for learning. Consequently, instruction explicitly aims for transfer of knowledge and skills across languages. Second, instruction communicates respect for students' languages and cultures and encourages students to engage with literacy and invest their identities in the learning process.

The Heart of Schooling

Educators, individually and collectively, always have choices. They can choose to go beyond curricular guidelines and mandates. They can meet curricular expectations and standards in ways that acknowledge and respect students' prior knowledge. They can engage English language learners in powerful literacy practices, such as creating identity texts. Identity texts also encourage collaboration among teachers, parents, and students. By including parents in the process, these practices affirm the funds of knowledge available in the community.

When we talk about the *whole child*, let us not forget the *whole teacher*. The process of identity negotiation is reciprocal. As teachers open up identity options for students, they also define their own identities. The teachers who supported and appreciated Sidra in her struggles to express herself and belong in her new school were also expressing what being educators meant to them. They saw Sidra not as a "limited-English-proficient" student but as a young person with intelligence, emotions, aspirations, and talents. They created classrooms that enabled her to express her identity.

Although NCLB has reinforced the bleak pedagogical landscapes that exist in many urban school systems, it *has* reinserted the achievement of English language learners and low-income students into policy discussions. Schools cannot meet adequate yearly progress goals without improving these students' achievement. Schools can achieve this goal much more effectively when they take into account identity investment as a core component of learning.

Many teachers understand intuitively that human relationships are at the heart of schooling. Student achievement will increase significantly only when this insight permeates all levels of education policymaking.

References

Allington, R. L. (2004). Setting the record straight. *Educational Leadership, 61*(6), 22–25.

Bransford, J. D., Brown, A. L., & Cocking, R. R. (2000). *How people learn: Brain, mind, experience, and school.* Washington, DC: National Academy Press.

Chow, P., & Cummins, J. (2003). Valuing multilingual and multicultural approaches to learning. In S. R. Schecter & J. Cummins (Eds.), *Multilingual education in practice: Using diversity as a resource* (pp. 32–61). Portsmouth, NH: Heinemann.

Cummins, J. (2001). *Negotiating identities: Education for empowerment in a diverse society* (2nd ed.). Los Angeles: California Association for Bilingual Education.

Donovan, M. S., & Bransford, J. D. (Eds.). (2005). *How students learn: History, mathematics, and science in the classroom.* Washington, DC: National Academy Press.

Early, M. et al. (2002). *From literacy to multiliteracies: Designing learning environments for knowledge generation within the new economy.* Proposal funded by the Social Sciences and Humanities Research Council of Canada.

Garan, E. M. (2001). What does the report of the National Reading Panel really tell us about teaching phonics? *Language Arts, 79*(1), 61–70.

Guthrie, J. T. (2004). Teaching for literacy engagement. *Journal of Literacy Research, 36,* 1–30.

Krashen, S. D. (2004). False claims about literacy development. *Educational Leadership, 61*(6), 18–21.

Lyon, G. R., & Chhabra, V. (2004). The science of reading research. *Educational Leadership, 61*(6), 12–17.

Reyes, M. L. (2001). Unleashing possibilities: Biliteracy in the primary grades. In M. L. Reyes & J. Halcón (Eds.), *The best for our children: Critical perspectives on literacy for Latino students* (pp. 96–121). New York: Teachers College Press.

Schecter, S., & Cummins, J. (Eds.). (2003). *Multilingual education in practice: Using diversity as a resource.* Portsmouth, NH: Heinemann.

Thomas, W. P., & Collier, V. P. (2002). *A national study of school effectiveness for language minority students' long-term academic achievement.* Santa Cruz, CA: Center for Research on Education, Diversity and Excellence, University of California–Santa Cruz.

Warschauer, M., Knobel, M., & Stone, L. (2004). Technology and equity in schooling: Deconstructing the digital divide. *Educational Policy, 18*(4), 562–588.

Implications of No Child Left Behind on Family Literacy in a Multicultural Community

SCOTT N. FORREST

According to Paulo Freire (1999), humans are not prescriptions of life; they are the actions and reflections of life. Life cannot be controlled with prescribed established formulas. So, members of life will succeed only when they are able to collaboratively consider and use individuals' ideas, skills, talents, and expertise to face life's countless challenges. Similarly, this article, in response to the No Child Left Behind Act of 2001 (NCLB), is based in the belief that members of an educational community must collaboratively reflect and act on issues to develop a truly effective program.

Implications

NCLB calls for sweeping reforms in education. The main focus of the reform plan is on creating "stronger accountability for results, expanded options for parents, and an emphasis on teaching methods that have been proven to work" (NCLB 2002b). As with many reforms, this act has both positive and negative implications on policy and curricula. This discussion focuses on the implications of the NCLB Act as it relates to ethno- and linguistically diverse communities.

Positive Implications

A predominant theme throughout NCLB is promoting reading and literacy skills. The act calls for the implementation of scientific-based programs to encourage reading. For ethno- and linguistically diverse communities, it specifically requires the

Forrest, S. (2004). Implications of No Child Left Behind on family literacy in a multicultural community. *Clearing House, 78*, 41–45. Reprinted with permission.

implementation of scientifically based programs that help English language learners (ELLs) meet the same high academic standards as other students (NCLB 2002b). This view that ELLs need a different type of program supports fair and equal access (Darder 1991). Thus, in theory, NCLB takes into consideration that just providing the same quantity and quality of programs to ELLs as to other students is unfair and unequal. As a result, NCLB allocates extra funds to support program development aimed at effectively educating ELLs (NCLB 2002b).

Another theme throughout NCLB is allowing more parental choice concerning their children's education. First, parents are given information about their children's needs and the overall performance of the schools that their children attend. Finally, the parents are given opportunities to make choices related to the education of their children (NCLB 2002b). This freedom takes into account the importance of stakeholder involvement in making decisions. However, there also are negative implications that affect ethno- and linguistically diverse families.

Negative Implications

Although NCLB provides for the implementation of research-based programs to help ELLs meet high academic standards, any mention of biliteracy, bicultural, and bilingual programs is excluded. In fact, NCLB mentions that the act "will focus support on enabling all limited English proficient (LEP) students to learn English as quickly and effectively as possible" (NCLB 2002b). However, the transfer approach to bilingual and biliterate education is ignored. That is, the act discourages the development of first language literacy as a means of transferring content and literacy skills into a second language. The transfer of literacy skills and strategies from the first language to the second language (Baker 1996) is a widely used, effective technique that the act overlooks.

Another area of contention concerns parental involvement. Under this act, parents choose to keep their children in the school or to transfer the children to another school (NCLB 2002b). However, this is not an authentic choice because other solutions exist, and they should be considered carefully. Parents should be encouraged and allowed to play a larger role in curriculum and program development, especially in the restructuring of underperforming schools. Their participation would promote more stakeholder input and elicit a greater variety of perspectives, both of which allow for better informed decision making. Then a qualitative approach of researching, evaluating, and developing programs should be used. The school's ELL programs should be studied in depth for a period of time to better understand them from the participants' points of view (Leedy and Ormrod 2001). In addition, parental involvement should promote programs for ELLs that are more collaborative and adaptive to specific circumstances (Anthony et al. 1991). Furthermore, minority parents should be encouraged to contribute to the school curriculum. Cummins (1986) suggests that minority language students are empowered or disabled to "the extent to which minority communities are encouraged to participate in their children's education (ctd. in Baker 1996, 346).

Problematic Issues

Title III, Section 3115, "Subgrants to eligible entities," states:

> Activities by agencies experiencing substantial increases in immigrant children and youth (1) . . . [S]hall use the funds to pay for activities that provide enhanced instructional opportunities for immigrant children and youth, which may include (A) family literacy, parent outreach, and training activities designed to assist parents to become active participants in the education of their children. (NCLB 2002a)

This section is valuable in that it promotes parental involvement in the literacy development of children both at school and at home. Studies show that the amount of print in a student's environment, at home and at school, correlates with the amount of free voluntary reading that is accomplished (Lee and Krashen 1996; Rodrigo, McQuillan, and Krashen 1996). Consequently, the more time students spend reading, the more their reading comprehension scores will improve (Kim and Krashen 1998; Rodrigo, McQuillan, and Krashen 1996). However, this section of the act also is problematic in relation to issues of teaching and equity.

Problems Related to Teaching

The problem related to teaching concerns the omission of the importance of the family heritage language to family literacy. The importance of the levels of family literacy in the heritage language is seen again in the transfer view of learning (Baker 1996). A student's level of literacy in his or her native language affects the transferability of literacy to a second language. Within the context of the school setting, this lack of consideration of each family's literacy level is problematic. Many of the parents of ELLs do not speak English because they are immigrants from other countries. These parents may be unable to effectively promote English literacy, but most are able to promote literacy in their native language at home. The use of native language texts in the home promotes literacy through transfer skills from one language to another. A student's second language competence is partially dependent on the level of competency already achieved in his or her first language (Baker 1996).

Problems Related to Equity

NCLB's undervaluation of the importance of biliteracy also is evident in the area of equity. Failing to take into account students' literacy levels in their first language is not fair and equitable in developing a family literacy plan. It ignores the individual needs, viewpoints, and learning styles of each student and family. Students need resources that address their individual needs to have a fair and equal opportunity to succeed at the same level as other students (Darder 1991). Some students and their families may need literacy development in their first language to facilitate literacy development in English.

Program Recommendations

Biliteracy is critical to the development of both English literacy and family literacy (Baker 1996). The following program recommendations outline the foundations, development, and successful implementations of a school-based family literacy program.

Foundations

Educational reform through literacy programs will not occur as long as educators and policymakers remain comfortable with the conservative norm (Levine 1995). As a result, a more multicultural and constructivist approach should be used to develop a family literacy program. The important tenets of authentic program development are represented in table 1.

Effective program development lies in placing family participation and individual perspectives at the center of the development process. To create an optimal content learning environment, topics must be meaningful and purposeful to the learners and relate to their prior knowledge (Peregoy and Boyle 2001). In addition, the family's heritage cultures and languages must be considered and utilized. A family's level of literacy in its native language affects the transferability of literacy to the second language (Baker 1996).

Development of a Family Literacy Program

Parental groups, such as the English Learner Advisory Council (ELAC) found in California school districts, should form committees to develop family literacy programs. This program development and implementation process could be done based on Moses' (2001) model. The first step should be a trip for the family literacy committee

TABLE 1   Do's and Don'ts of Authentic Program Development

DO'S	DON'TS
Focus on the students' learning and meeting the objectives in authentic contexts in school and at home	Focus on meeting only the objectives as outlined in NCLB.
Lead the families to success and mastery of objectives before moving to the next.	Get through the whole program guide before the end of the year.
Observe model programs which are having learner-centered successes.	Compare program time frames with other families and schools.
Discuss with the families the skills they are developing, why they are developing them, and how they can best achieve those goals.	Simply display, read, and repeat the program objectives, assuming the families fully understand them.

to observe established and active family literacy programs. This field trip will provide a common knowledge base from which the stakeholders may draw upon in future steps.

Second, the stakeholders should each draw a picture or construct a model of their experience. These pictorial representations serve as impressions of the various family literacy programs the stakeholders observed. They also represent the participants' values and beliefs.

Third, the participants should discuss and write their impressions of the physical event. Moses (2001) points out that it is important to allow the participants to speak and write in the language of their daily lives. This point remains consistent with the focus on the importance of heritage language in the transfer of knowledge (Baker 1996). Those ideas and impressions generated should be recorded. This ensures that all the participants' perspectives are valued. These perspectives and ideas also may be analyzed for predominant themes, indicating topics about which the group feels strongly.

Fourth, administrators should share their expertise of the law as it relates to the program's development. The group should read sections of the act concerning expectations of student achievement and parental involvement. At that time, the participants should relate their experiences and impressions of family literacy programs to NCLB's nebulous rhetoric.

And last, the whole group should create a collaborative flowchart of the ideal family literacy program that meets the needs of community. From this flowchart, a family literacy program should be developed to also include components mentioned in NCLB (2002a).

Research and Evaluation

As a family literacy program solidifies and becomes institutionalized, an assessment of its overall effectiveness is necessary. An evaluation system must be set up to validate or invalidate the program's success as it relates to the needs of the learners, families, schools, and government requirements.

Type of Research

Qualitative research is used to "answer questions about the complex nature of phenomena, often with the purpose of describing and understanding the phenomena from the participants' point of view" (Leedy and Ormrod 2001, 101). The phenomenon in this case is the development of reading comprehension skills among ELLs who participate in a family literacy program. The participants are the ELLs, their families, and teachers. Their points of view should be analyzed to guide questions about improved reading comprehension, effective reading strategies, and successful components of the family literacy program.

But the overall guiding question of the research assessment should be, "Does the family literacy program have a general effect on ELLs' reading comprehension of English?" Two secondary questions also should be explored. First, what components of the family literacy program do ELLs find most effective in learning to read English?

Second, what components of the family literacy program have positive effects on the reading comprehension of ELLs? These questions are important because NCLB requires ELLs to show growth, to include "passing rates" on English standardized tests, within two years (NCLB 2002b).

Methodology

The evaluation system's design is qualitative in nature and organized within the working model of a data analysis quad (Anthony et al. 1991). Collecting a balanced amount of data within the four sections of the quad produces more reliable results. Table 2 is a representation of a data analysis quad. The four sections include data from observations of students' processes, analysis of students' products, classroom measures of reading comprehension, and decontextualized measures of reading comprehension. Observations, interviews, documents, and records supplement that data.

The first quad, observations of process, includes observations, surveys, and anecdotal accounts of the teachers and family members. The second quad, observation of products, contains student reading logs, comprehension strategy surveys, and reading assignments in the students' portfolios. The reading assignments are generated from both classroom and family literacy activities. The third quad, classroom measures, consists of a formal classroom reading assessment in the form of book summaries. The fourth quad includes pre- and posttest scores from the *Gates-MacGinitie Reading Tests* (MacGinitie et al. 2000). The data should be analyzed with respect to the effects of the family literacy program. Validity is increased through the use of triangulation between teachers' and parents' observations, students' products, and reading assessment scores. In addition, the validity of reading measures is increased through pre- and postcomprehension assessments.

Three main criteria should be used to determine the effects of the family literacy program. First, the results of the data should identify the most effective reading

---

TABLE 2   Data Analysis Quad

Quadrant 1	**Quadrant 2**
Student Processes	Student Products
• Observations	• Student reading logs
• Surveys from parents and teachers	• Comprehension strategy surveys
• Anecdotal accounts from teachers	• Student portfolios
Quadrant 3	**Quadrant 4**
Classroom Measures	Decontextualized Measures
• Formal reading assessments	• Pre- and post-Gates-MacGinitie reading tests
• Pre- and post-book summaries	• California English Language Development Test (CELDT)
	• State achievement tests
	• Audit/evaluation from an outside source

Note: Adapted from Anthony et al. (1991).

strategies of the students. These results should come primarily from the teachers, family members, and student surveys. Once the strategies are identified, they should be evaluated by whether or not they are taught and promoted through the family literacy program. The family literacy program is successful if it provides families and students with the necessary training to effectively use these strategies. Second, the results should be analyzed for growth in the reading comprehension scores of both classroom assessments and decontextualized measures. The program is successful in this regard if significant improvement is evident. Third, the success of the family literacy program also should be determined by the evaluation and recommendations of an audit by an outside source. The program is successful in this respect if the goals and outcomes of the family literacy program positively contribute to the goals outlined in the comprehensive school plan.

Conclusions

NCLB is problematic to issues of teaching and equity. The undervaluation of the importance of the family heritage language to family literacy and biliteracy greatly hinders the act's potential effectiveness. A student's literacy level in his or her native language absolutely must be considered when focusing on the development of a student's literacy in English. Not accounting for the literacy levels of students in their native language hampers the development of family literacy plans, because it fails to recognize the needs, viewpoints, and learning styles of each student and family. Therefore, the learning styles and literacy heritage of each family must be valued throughout the development of family literacy programs.

Educators must not return to the tenets of systems management styles, standardized tests, and viewing children as products (Levine 1995). If literacy programs are to be successful, the collaboration and perspectives of all stakeholders are necessary. All involved must invest energy, time, and money into the education of human students rather than student products.

References

Anthony, R., T. D. Johnson, N. I. Mickelson, & A. Preece. 1991. *Evaluating literacy: A perspective for change*. Portsmouth, NH: Heinemann.

Baker, C. 1996. *Foundations of bilingual education and bilingualism*. 2nd ed. Philadelphia: Multilingual Matters.

Cummins, J. 1986. Empowering minority students: A framework for intervention. *Harvard Educational Review* 56(1): 18–36.

Darder, A. 1991. *Culture and power in the classroom: A critical foundation for bicultural education*. Westport, CT: Bergin and Garvey.

Freire, P. 1999. *Pedagogy of the oppressed*. New York: Continuum.

Kim, H., and S. Krashen. 1998. The author recognition and magazine recognition tests, and free voluntary reading as predictors of vocabulary development in English as a foreign language for Korean high school students. *System* 26(4): 515–23. http://elservier.lib.sjtu.edu.cn/cgi-bin/sciserv.pl?collection=journals&journal=0346251x&issue=v26i0004.

Lee, S., and S. Krashen. 1996. Free voluntary reading and writing competence in Taiwanese high school students. *Perceptual and Motor Skills 83*(2): 687–94.

Leedy, P. D., and J. E. Ormrod. 2001. *Practical research: Planning and design.* 7th ed. New Jersey: Prentice-Hall.

Levine, D. 1995. Building a vision of curriculum reform. In *Rethinking schools: An agenda for change,* ed. D. Levine, R. Lowe, B. Peterson, and R. Tenorio, 52–60. New York: New York Press.

MacGinitie, W. H., R. K. MacGinitie, K. Maria, and L. G. Dreyer. 2000. *Gates-MacGinitie reading tests.* 4th ed.; forms S and T. Itasca, IL: Riverside.

Moses, R. P. 2001. *Radical equations: Civil rights from Mississippi to the Algebra Project.* Boston: Beacon Press.

No Child Left Behind Act of 2001. 2002a. Public law 107-110. 107th Cong. (January 8, 2002). Title III: Language instruction for limited English proficient and immigrant students.

No Child Left Behind Act of 2001. 2002b. Summary and overview. http://www.ed.gov/nclb/overview/intro/index.html (accessed March 8, 2004).

Peregoy, S. F., and O. F. Boyle. 2001. *Reading, writing, and learning in ESL: A resource book for K–12 teachers.* 3rd ed. New York: Longman.

Rodrigo, V., J. McQuillan, and S. Krashen. 1996. Free voluntary reading and vocabulary knowledge in native speakers of Spanish. *Perceptual and Motor Skills 83*(2): 648–50.

Multicultural Literature and Discussion as Mirror and Window?

JOCELYN GLAZIER AND JUNG-A SEO

In the United States, multicultural literature (here defined as literature that represents voices typically omitted from the traditional canon) and texts have made their way into language arts education-reform documents, onto classroom shelves, and ultimately into the hands of a diverse student body. The use of multicultural literature—coupled with dialogic instruction within a safe classroom context—can provide students with both a window to other cultures and a mirror reflecting their own (Galda, 1998). However, if practitioners (particularly white-majority teachers) assume a monoculture in which there are those like "us" and "others," the use of multicultural literature may also reinforce notions of "culturelessness" among white European American student populations. This article documents the experiences of a group of high school students as they read and responded to N. Scott Momaday's *The Way to Rainy Mountain* (1996, University of New Mexico Press)—a multigenre text focusing on the Kiowa nation—and related texts. While the experience allowed minority students to find their voices in the classroom, in some ways it simultaneously stifled the voices of majority students.

Multicultural literature is often touted as a tool that "helps children to identify with their own culture, exposes children to other cultures, and opens the dialogue on issues regarding diversity" (Colby & Lyon, 2004, p. 24); it is viewed as a resource for "promoting students' inter/intra-cultural understanding and appreciation" (Fang, Fu, & Lamme, 1999, p. 259). However, similar to broader critiques of multicultural education, discussions of multicultural literature often omit explorations of "whiteness" within the larger discussion of culture. And yet "to read books by and about people of color does not exclude Whites from the discussion of multiculturalism" (Cai, 1998, p. 315). Studies in multicultural education tend to examine those in the minority, in many ways avoiding a close interrogation of the white majority. This avoidance further perpetuates a notion of "them" (those perceived as having culture) and "us" (those perceived to be without culture). Because whiteness—often along with the notion of what

Glazier, J., & Seo, J.-A. (2005, May). Multicultural literature and discussion as mirror and window? *Journal of Adolescent & Adult Literacy, 48*(8), 686–700. Reprinted by permission of the International Reading Association.

it means to be an American—has been largely unexplored territory in U.S. school contexts in particular, majority students often feel "cultureless." (See related examples in Frankenberg, 1993; McIntyre, 1997.) In describing her work with pre-service teachers, Florio-Ruane (2001) wrote,

> When I ask my [European American] students to write vignettes of their cultural experience as literacy learners, they are usually nonplussed. "I don't have a story," they say. "I'm not anything." Responses like these lack a sense of history or place. The normal or "unmarked" form is the bland, commonsense one. It is the water the fish would be the last to discover. (p. 24)

As a result, majority readers of multicultural literature are left "mostly looking in from outside" (Singer & Smith, 2001, p. 13). Thus, while we vigorously applaud the use of multicultural literature in the classroom setting as both a way to encourage students who are most often voiceless in schools to find voice and a means by which multiple cultural experiences can be explored, we also encourage teachers, more than 80% of whom in the United States are part of the majority population (National Center for Education Statistics, 2004), and teacher educators alike to consider ways to bring all students to examine their cultural voices—a necessary goal if we are to ever view cultural diversity as a resource rather than a deficit.

Canonical Curricula and Silent Spaces

Curricula in schools are far from neutral. Rather, the curriculum is always part of a selective tradition: someone's selection or some group's vision of legitimate knowledge. School knowledge most often manifests itself as a particular representation of the dominant (read as white, middle class) culture (Giroux, 1989). Accordingly, the languages and texts that support and perpetuate dominant ideals and practices continue to be valued in a majority of schools. School curricula confirm and privilege students from the dominant culture while excluding and often disconfirming the experiences of subordinate groups. Ultimately, "school knowledge disables to the extent that it silences students" (Sleeter & Grant, 1991, p. 52), particularly those who are not part of the culture of power (Delpit, 1988). In the case of the literature curriculum, canonical literatures and stories representative of white, male, middle class perspectives are privileged still (Applebee, 1993). Left on the margins—silenced—are the stories of other cultures.

Just as curricular choices often privilege majority students, a teacher's discourse—indeed, what he or she says and does not say and what he or she allows students to say—may lead to further marginalization of minority students. Talk is central to the work of teaching and learning in U.S. classrooms (e.g., Cazden 1988; Nystrand, 1997). Indeed, discourse is the means by which we come to acquire and create knowledge of the world and of our lives (Bakhtin, 1986). And yet, for all the talk resounding in classrooms, much remains unsaid. Silence about certain issues is often a salient characteristic of schools and classrooms. Silencing most often occurs around stories that conflict with the grand narrative of school curriculum. Official knowledge in schools practically necessitates silence because "silencing removes any documentation that all is not well with the workings of the U.S. economy, race and gender relations, and public schooling as the route to class mobility" (Fine, 1992, p. 153). It is most often those students who are silenced for whom these topics and stories are most critical and central; silence renders "irrelevant the lived experiences, passions, concerns, communities, and biographies of low-income, minority students" (Fine & Weis, 2003, p. 155).

Silenced topics in U.S. classrooms are usually "hot lava" topics (Glazier, 2003), including social class, culture, and race, that are generally avoided rather than explored (Fine & Weis, 1993; Frankenberg, 1993; Landsman, 2001; McIntyre, 1997; Morrison, 1992). Other silenced topics include politics and religion (Black, 2003; Haynes & Thomas, 2001), particularly post–September 11, 2001. These topics are too often omitted, at least in part, to avoid the difficult dialogues and "dangerous discourses" (Bigler & Collins, 1995, p. 10) that might accompany them. As a result, "smoothed over or ignored [are] the social contradictions [and complexities] that students' daily lives present" (Fine, as cited in Bigler & Collins, 1995, pp. 20–21). What emerges is not only a silencing around certain topics but also a silencing of certain individuals. The questions remain of (a) how to provide voices for all within the classroom; (b) how to allow the "discursive undergrounds of students" (Fine & Weis, 1993, p. 2) to move above ground; and (c) how to "fill baffling silences" (Morrison, 1993) about racism, inequality, difference, and culture, thus validating the lives and stories of all students.

If we are to move to a more culturally affirming reality, teachers need to develop a curriculum and pedagogy for transformation, one that is characterized by an ongoing effort to create new space for dialogic discourse, to rewrite cultural narratives, and to allow for discussion of multiple literatures and perspectives.

Transforming Curriculum and Pedagogy

> Multicultural literature . . . can provide opportunities for meeting many goals of multicultural education, where voices interact and students reflect, think creatively and critically, increase cultural awareness, decrease ethnocentrism, and create a global perspective. (Cliff & Miller, 1997, p. 1)

"Multicultural curricula have the potential to challenge the 'silences' that exist in schools around issues such as race and class" (Bigler & Collins, 1995, p. 3). Much research in the area of multicultural language arts curriculum has focused on "the importance of using multicultural literature for understanding cultural differences, building community, and preparing students for the twenty-first century" (Willis, 1997, p. 139). The hope persists that this inclusion of oft-marginalized voices will "positively affirm student identities, empower students, and challenge popular stereotypes in the larger society" (Bigler, 1996, p. 4). Indeed, the Standards for the English Language Arts (International Reading Association & National Council of Teachers of English, 1996) require the incorporation of diverse texts representing a variety of cultural experiences into the language arts curriculum. A common reading of these standards is that the inclusion of multicultural literature in one's curriculum provides the means through which language arts teachers can help students achieve understanding of and respect for their own culture and those of others.

> While it seems apparent that literature has the power to open eyes and change lives, it is also apparent that this does not happen merely by reading a piece of culturally diverse literature in a classroom. The multiple voices brought to our interpretive communities make the use of literature as a vehicle for cultural understanding quite complex. (Desai, 1997, p. 175)

Clearly, the text cannot stand alone to achieve desired ends. Adding multicultural texts to the curriculum will not by itself create respect for cultural differences or an understanding across cultures. The reason for this is in part because

> readers resist texts and readings . . . because of their cultural memberships and various identity positions: as female, as African American, as homosexual, as white students who resist challenges to their own privilege, or as Americans who cannot grasp the cultural meanings and values in stories of other countries. (Rogers & Soter, 1997, p. 3)

The text must instead be interrogated from multiple perspectives and act as a comparison point for students' own lives in order for it to be transformative, or life—and culture—affirming. As a result, it must act as both mirror—allowing students to reflect on their own experiences—and as window, providing the opportunity to view the experiences of others. Thus, the text becomes central to a conversation *across* cultures. This requires changing the nature of instruction from monologic to dialogic, thereby opening a way for student voices to be heard in the classroom. "Dialogically organized instruction provides public space for student responses, accommodating and promoting the refraction of voices representing differing values, beliefs, and perspectives, and ideally including the voices of different classes, races, ages, and genders" (Christoph & Nystrand, 2001, p. 4). Dialogic instruction requires a teacher to assume a stance other than the "all-knowing" one that, too often, teachers believe they need to assume. Certainly the teacher's role in encouraging dialogue around text is critical. Moller and Allen (2000) commented on their study of multicultural texts, "Although the text was an important catalyst, so was the space that was created . . . [and] the teacher's role in encouraging and supporting students as they engage[d] in open dialogue on difficult and uncomfortable issues" (p. 177).

The following question inevitably arises. What might make the dialogue productive—and capable of "promoting students' inter/intra-cultural understanding and appreciation" (Fang et al., 1999, p. 259), ultimately allowing "voices [to] interact and students to reflect, . . . [leading to] increase[d] cultural awareness, decrease[d] ethnocentrism" (Cliff & Miller, 1997, p. 1)? According to literacy researchers, students need to make multiple connections to the text being studied, exploring it as a piece in and of itself (making text-to-text connections) and as a connection to self. Of particular importance, given the goals associated with the use of multicultural literature, is the students' "need to be able to connect text to self in order to promote greater meaning" of the text (Colby & Lyon, 2004, p. 24). This concept dates back to Rosenblatt's (1938/1983) work on reader response and the notion that the individual creates his or her own meaning through a "transaction" with the text based on personal associations. Because all readers bring their own emotions, concerns, life experiences, and knowledge to their reading, each interpretation is subjective and unique. Rather than relying on a teacher or critic to provide a single, standard interpretation of a text, students learn to construct their own meaning(s) by connecting the textual material to issues in their lives, describing what they experience as they read. As Sleeter and Grant (1991) reminded us, "no matter who the students are, their power to learn and act begins with knowledge generated within their own lived experience" (p. 66).

Reader response encourages students to become aware of what they bring to texts as readers; it has the potential to help them recognize the specificity of their own cultural backgrounds and strive to understand the cultural backgrounds of others. Often students read and respond to texts with an eye toward the first goal *or* toward the second, but not toward both. However, multicultural literature is capable of doing both simultaneously, promoting intercultural *and* intracultural understanding. Bakhtin (1990) advised us that the only way to truly know ourselves is with and through the "other"; wholeness emerges in and through that dialogue, that interaction. Therefore, one might argue that multicultural literature must work to serve as both mirror and window; one without the other is simply not sufficient.

> Changes in value stance are unlikely to occur merely from responding to multicultural literature alone, or only from discussion with diverse peers, or only in responding to challenges from a teacher or peer, but rather from a combination of all three factors. (Beach, Parks, Thein, & Lensmire, 1991, p. 19)

In the remainder of this article we explore what happens when text and talk come together in a ninth-grade language arts classroom, which leads us to consider further roadblocks to the use of multicultural literature as a bridge across cultures. While the use of multicultural literature raises multiple voices, in this case it creates different sorts of silences at the same time.

Context and Methodology

Julie (all names are pseudonyms) was a teacher in a school we'll call Curie High School, which is in a suburb of a major metropolitan area. Curie's student body comprises diverse demographic groups: 41% white, 19.2% black, 21.6% Hispanic, 15.2% Asian/Pacific Islander, and 3% other. The demographics of this particular institution resemble those of many other high schools within the school district and elsewhere. During the 2001–2002 school year, Julie's classroom was typical of the diverse classrooms encountered throughout the United States (American Association of Colleges for Teacher Education, 1999; Latham, 1999; Yasin & Albert, 1999). Of the 16 ninth graders in her secondary language arts class, 5 hailed from Central America, 1 from the Philippines, 2 from Afghanistan, 1 from Iran, 1 from West Africa, and 1 from the former Soviet Union; the remaining 5 were European American. These students ranged in age from 14 to 18, as a number of them had only recently been mainstreamed, having previously been assigned to "sheltered" English as a second language classes.

Two researchers (including one of the authors) observed Julie's class 27 times, each consisting of a full class session, over three months. Observations were most intense as Julie taught a six-week unit based on Momaday's *The Way to Rainy Mountain*, which contains mythical, historical, and personal accounts of the Kiowa. The latter section consists of Momaday's autobiographical description of his family's Kiowa ancestry. The focus of the research on this segment of the course arose from Julie's involvement in a yearlong professional development project in which she and other language arts teachers read and discussed multicultural literature that they would subsequently present to their students. *The Way to Rainy Mountain* was one of the multicultural texts the teachers chose to read together. Data collected in Julie's classroom included audiotapes and videotapes of classroom events, audiotapes of teacher and student interviews, artifacts of student work, and researcher fieldnotes. Audiotapes were then transcribed.

Ethnographic and sociolinguistic methods of analysis were used to analyze the data in an effort to determine what unfolded during the process as students—in conjunction with their teacher—engaged in conversations prompted by multicultural texts. The research questions framing this detailed review of Julie's class included these three: What happens when students from diverse backgrounds talk about texts that include discussions of cultural differences? What or who "impacts" these discussions and how? Does multicultural literature and discussion of that literature lead to "inter/intra-cultural understanding" (Fang et al., 1999, p. 259)?

Julie and Her Teaching

During the study, Julie was in her fourth year of teaching and her first year at Curie, where she arrived in her mid-20s with a master's degree in creative writing. Earlier, she had taught at an all African American high school, and she often reflected on her experience working as a white teacher in that context. Identity, culture, and faith were topics of deep concern and interest to Julie and clearly had an impact on her teaching. Most likely—and perhaps inevitably—"the assumptions that teachers bring to the classroom are shaped by their own cultural, biographical, and institutional experiences" (Bigler, 1996, p. 34). Julie herself commented, "As teachers, you always bring what's important to you into the room. And for me . . . that's . . . a lot of faith and spirituality. So I tend to feed that into my room" (transcript, November 2002). Julie often asked her students to assume a critical stance, particularly when issues of culture were involved. This pattern is evidenced, among other factors, by comments she made in the classroom, such as "We see things in particular ways because of how we're raised. That's what's dangerous, because we then judge these characters [in texts] for being a certain way" (transcript, March 14, 2002). Thus, she often asked students to examine their own ideas and opinions in light of those of others.

Julie's classroom accurately reflected her philosophy. The following describes what one researcher noticed upon first entering her room.

The walls of Julie's classroom are covered with students' work. On the back wall are posters titled "The American Dream." "What does it mean to be an American?" is written atop one poster. The students did this activity in groups earlier in the semester. Along the same wall are smaller posters—"My Name" posters—typed neatly and then adhered to colored construction paper. The names identify the diversity in the school more broadly, in this classroom in particular Mada, Jose, Abdallah, Danielle, Nancy, John. On the wall to the right . . . are more "My Name" posters, underneath which are collages with images from all sorts of magazines representing how students illustrate who they are. On the front wall, covering the chalkboard, are long sheets of paper on which *modernism* is defined in green marker. Next to these posters are sayings including "Fear is what yields hate." . . . Atop other pieces of paper are the questions "Who am I?" "Where am I going?" Over the board is the quote "Your mind is like a parachute. It works best when it's open." The room is colorful and busy. Students' work is evident and displayed. An easel at the front of the room lists the day's agenda. (Fieldnotes)

Evidence of the importance of culture and identity appeared not only on the classroom walls but also in and through Julie's curriculum and pedagogy. During the course, she introduced students to a variety of texts representing several genres and authors, both canonical and multicultural. She also used a number of different pedagogical approaches in her classroom, ranging from whole-class discussion to small-group work to individual journal writing.

A Roundabout Way to *Rainy Mountain*

In setting out to teach *The Way to Rainy Mountain*, Julie created an environment that enabled each student to share his or her interpretation of the text with the other students in the class. She taught the text as part of a larger unit that she described as follows:

> [Before teaching *Rainy Mountain*], I took a good three and a half weeks to let my students get to know one another, get to know their cultures. They gave presentations about their backgrounds . . . they would bring in stuff from their culture [and talk about it]. Then I started bringing in multicultural pieces, pieces from Sandra Cisneros, pieces from Langston Hughes, and I let students discuss how they were split in their own identities. And they learned what it meant to be us versus them, how the selves are split essentially.
>
> And then we did kind of a long process with myths. And I thought it was important for them to study myths and learn about myths, to recognize that the truth is perspective, that when we say "This is real, this is my experience," that it is just your experience. What's your religion may not be someone else's religion; what's your truth or history may not be somebody else's. . . . And then we sort of felt safe, and that's when I started teaching *The Way to Rainy Mountain*.

In teaching *The Way to Rainy Mountain*, Julie used a number of diverse pedagogical approaches and resources. For example, students often worked in small groups to gain an understanding of various chapters of the book. Students presented their interpretations to their peers in a large-group forum, pointing out important quotations and a rationale for their interpretation. Another of Julie's approaches was to provide opportunities for whole-class discussion of the text and related topics. Finally, she often asked students to state their personal connections to the text, ending the unit by encouraging class members to tell their own stories in three voices, similar to Momaday's approach. Like Rosenblatt (1938/1983) and others, Julie believed that establishing text-to-self connections was critical in enabling students to cross boundaries not only between themselves and the text but also among themselves as members of diverse cultures. To achieve this goal, she often supplemented students' reading of the Momaday text with related textual materials and encouraged students to make connections across these texts and the texts of their lives.

Students Finding Authentic Voices in the Classroom

Conversations in Julie's class took two basic forms: small-group talk (generally emerging as students worked together on a project) and whole-class talk. Julie played a significant part in whole-class conversations, asking students questions designed to encourage responses. In many ways, the conversations were typical of traditional classrooms, in which the teacher initiates the questions, students respond, and the teacher evaluates the responses. Close analysis of a whole-class conversation under her guidance helps to establish how and when students participated, as well as Julie's impact on their participation. Dialogic episodes stood out as worthy of particular scrutiny because they were less common across the transcripts.

The conversation analyzed below occurred midsemester, after students had become familiar with one another and with the patterns of Julie's class. This conversation arose from a discussion of text, although not specifically *The Way to Rainy Mountain*. Although we analyzed other conversations across the unit, we have included a close description of this particular discussion to give readers a more vivid picture of the conversational events that occurred in Julie's classroom. The patterns here are similar to those in other whole-class conversations across the dataset. Furthermore, Julie identified this exchange as one that interested her and that she subsequently chose to discuss in the company of her teaching colleagues in their professional development seminar. The following analysis highlights the topics of the conversation, the amount of time spent on topics, and student participation patterns. Finally, it focuses on the points at which students made text-to-other and text-to-self connections—allowing students the opportunity to form both intercultural and intracultural understanding and empathy.

April 5, 2002, Conversation Analysis

On April 5, Julie showed her students a documentary that highlighted the Battle of Wounded Knee and the Ghost Dance. The battle occurred in December 1890 when members of the Sioux nation, camped on the banks of Wounded Knee Creek, were surrounded by U.S. troops. Refusing to relinquish their weapons, the Sioux donned "ghost shirts" they believed would protect them from the troops' bullets. More than 150 Sioux were killed. One motive for the massacre was the military's fear of the Native Americans' religious fervor, manifested in the Ghost Dance (Public Broadcasting Service, 2002; Robertson, 1996).

The students had watched part of the documentary the day before. They had also read through chapter 12 of the Momaday text and had begun to discuss related experiences and struggles of the Kiowa, including concepts such as death and spiritual beliefs. Julie's expressed goal in presenting the film was to enable her students to learn more about Native Americans, the Ghost Dance, and prayer and, through that, to better connect to *The Way to Rainy Mountain.* The timeline in Table 1 illustrates the pattern of the day's events and conversations.

During the first segment of the conversation, Julie informed her students about an upcoming project. Class participation during this segment consisted primarily of students asking questions in order to clarify and confirm information. In the second segment, students responded to factual questions about the film section they had observed a day earlier. The film itself occupied the third segment, while the fourth consisted of general comments on the film, the fifth of talk directly related to the Ghost Dance material (which Julie describes as the "heart of the film"), and the sixth of discussion built on the fifth segment but framing the discussion more specifically. Julie initiated the conversation in this sixth segment by asking students, "Has anyone in here ever felt like their own faith was shaken?" Students responded by sharing their personal narratives. The final segment of talk, segment seven, consisted of students and Julie sharing their closing comments about the film.

Although all segments of talk were interesting in some respects, the data suggest that the degree of students' participation reached its highest points in segments five and six, with 51 and 45 utterances respectively, even though segment four, for example, was longer in length. What was it, we wondered, that prompted students to speak so often in these segments? It became evident that in segments five and six, students were making the highest numbers of text-to-self connections. Close analysis allowed us to discern who participated in these conversational segments, how the various students contributed, and the length of their turns.

In segment five, Julie initiated conversation about the film, specifically the Ghost Dance. The following excerpt from the transcript illustrates how the conversation began.

TABLE 1   April 5, 2002, Timeline

SEGMENT	MINUTES IN SEGMENT	STUDENT UTTERANCES	TOPIC
One	6:36	24	Organizational component
Two	2:00	7	Review of yesterday's film viewing
Three	35:20	0 (film watching)	Viewing part two of the film
Four	14:00	37	General remarks on film
Five	13:24	51	"The heart of the film": The Ghost Dance discussion
Six	10:20	45	Shaken faith discussion
Seven	9:00	15	Closing points

Julie: The heart of the film was clearly what?

Citana: The Ghost Dance.

Julie: The Ghost Dance. And what do you think was the most interesting *feeling* for you? Can you talk to me about what you *felt* when you saw what you saw today?

Alita: The way that they were treated—how they treated the Kiowa—for example, when they were doing the—I *felt* sad.

Julie: You *felt* sad? For the people?

Alita: Yeah—for the people.

Julie: What else? Anybody else *feel* something? I mean, I was watching your expressions—I know you were *feeling* something because some of you had different expressions on your face so. . . .

Siham: It reminded me of a time in my country.

Julie: So you've seen it yourself?

Siham: Well, when I was watching it, it reminded me of my government and a time in my country.

Julie's use of the term *feel* was one of the ways she invited students to make sense of their own lives in comparison to the text—in this case, the text of the film. Students—beginning here with Siham—drew parallels between the text and their own lives, making text-to-self connections, using text as mirror. Simultaneously, in this segment Julie asked the students to attempt some basic analysis of the text they watched, asking such questions as "Sitting Bull was going to be part of the Ghost Dance—and what was he?" "What were they fighting for?" and "What's the deal with the shirt?" She also urged them to engage in another level of analysis, one that asked them to think beyond—but not *too* far beyond—the specific texts to the lives of the Kiowa more generally, making text-to-other connections. She asked questions such as these:

What did the Ghost Dance teach the people?

Were they supposed to be violent?

What do you think happened to some of the Native Americans' faith at a massacre like this when they were dancing and believing that the ancestors were coming back and . . . that the new earth would regenerate and then this kind of a tragedy happens?

Do you think that this would shake a people's faith?

This multiple-level questioning allows Julie to involve more students in the conversation than otherwise might participate. Indeed, in this segment of talk, many students expressed their ideas and feelings.

In segment six, Julie began by asking "Has anyone in here ever felt like their own faith was shaken?" She invited students to make additional text-to-self connections. Students responded by sharing their personal experiences with faith. Whereas Julie's participation in segment five consisted primarily of asking questions, her role here was that of extender; she posed clarifying questions and reframed students' responses in order to extend and expand their personal narratives. In contrast to earlier segments, Julie's participation was less prominent; the students themselves asked each other for clarification and stepped in to challenge one another. This segment is more dialogic than previous segments. Julie appeared to establish the conversational floor, and then the students took it over. Julie reentered at various times, for various reasons, including to ensure that students felt safe within the conversation. (See her comment "That's OK—you don't have to" below.) The following transcript excerpt illustrates this type of student exchange:

> **Noya:** So what's your belief?
>
> **Ciro:** I mean, I believe in God, but it's different now. Like I—it's a bit different. It's different. I mean it's really complicated.
>
> **Noya:** What do you feel like—you say that you don't believe that the world was made in seven days, so now what do you believe in?
>
> **Ciro:** I don't want to say it now.
>
> **Julie:** That's OK—you don't have to.
>
> **Ciro:** I would like to, but it's going to take me a lot of time.
>
> **Citana:** Is it something in science?
>
> **Ciro:** Yeah, it's science. I mean, they teach you how to apply it to—science.

Students like Ciro (above) and Alita later in the conversation took this opportunity to connect their personal experiences to their work and texts in English class and did so in extended narrative form. For example, Alita subsequently explained, "I was going to share something that happened. I was—before two years ago—I was a Christian. I always went to church . . . but some day, a temptation came to my life." She went on to describe her personal experience of "losing faith" (across seven speaking turns—interspersed with the turns of other participants who asked her for clarification), which was similar to Ciro's and to the characters in the text. Another example of a student's text-to-self connection was Citana's comment later in the segment,

> Like when you were little, you were really religious because somebody told you to be, or they taught you to be. Then when you grow, you find out you're not really that religious. Like I used to wear a cross and I don't anymore. Like I found out that I'm not really religious. It was my grandmother—I was following her.

The length of Citana's turn here—61 words—was similar in length to turns taken by Alita (examples of turn lengths include 51, 146, and 41), Siham (e.g., 71 and 107), and Ciro (e.g., 43 and 57) during this segment.

Other participation during the same segment appears to be significantly different. Whereas Alita, Ciro, and Citana shared personal narratives as a way to connect to the text, Nancy, for instance, shared an example that did not emphasize a personal experience. She commented, "And then the priests go on and tell you how to act, and they go molest little children. Have you heard about that?" Nancy's contribution, although connected to her own Catholic religion, was removed from Nancy herself.

This was in essence a text-to-other connection. Furthermore, although Nancy participated frequently in this segment (9 times), none of her turns were longer than 31 words. Still other contributions were presented in entirely different forms. Twice during this segment of discussion, another participant, Mark, made it clear that he would prefer to talk about something other than "loss of faith." After Ciro's participation (noted above), he observed, "I thought we were talking about [the Kiowa]." Later, he commented, "Are we still on [this topic]?"

Close analysis across these two highly involved segments of conversation (segments five and six) suggests that those sharing personal narratives—making text-to-self connections, using text as mirror—were the minority students in the class. Furthermore, these were the turns that were longer than others and appeared to invite more dialogic involvement with other students. Although all students participated in conversation to clarify textual understanding as well as to make text-to-text connections, the European American members of the class did not make the text-to-self connections.

If one goal of multicultural literature and texts is to enable students to draw connections between self and other, for text to act as both window and mirror, one has to explore whether or not that process is actually occurring in the classroom. It was clearly happening in this classroom for the minority students who reflected on their own experiences and those of others, doing the latter by asking one another questions, for example. However, it did not appear to be happening for the European American students. An indepth look at the participation of two class members—Mark, a European American student, and Alita, a Latina student—further illustrates this pattern.

Case Studies of Mark and Alita

Mark, one of five European American, monolingual students in Julie's class, was among the most talkative members of the classroom community, regularly participating in small-group and large-group discussion. Mark consistently scored well on class assessments, understood the material, and raised thought-provoking questions. In small-group presentations, he was generally the most talkative member of his group. During the conversation described above, Mark took 23 turns, the third highest in the class. However, nearly half of his contributions occurred in segment four as the students attempted to make sense of the text of the film, making text-to-text connections. When given the opportunity to connect personal (inner) text to the text the students were reading or watching (text-to-self), Mark refrained from doing so. His turns during these segments of talk were brief, offering few clarifying or extending ideas (e.g., "A majority isn't"; "Well, I don't know"), or they were text-to-text contributions (e.g., "She was shot. She lost her faith"). Mark seemed eager to move away from these text-to-self conversations, asking such questions as "Are we still on [this topic]?" His contributions provide a contrast with those made by Alita.

Alita, from Central America, was one of the more talkative members among the minority students in Julie's classroom. Even though this was her first mainstreamed English class, she contributed consistently. On April 5 she delivered 32 utterances, compared to 28 from the next most prolific student and then 23 from Mark. More than two thirds of her utterances occurred in segments five and six and were focused on text-to-self connection (text-to-self = 25 turns; text-to-other/text = 7 turns). Specifically, Alita provided the class with a personal account of the time that her faith was shaken. The following excerpt illustrates her personal connection to the text (i.e., the film the students are watching in segment five):

> I was going to share something that happened. I was—before two years ago—I was a Christian. I always went to church . . . I always wear skirts, not pants or shorts. I was so deeply in the religion. But . . . some day, a temptation came to my life. . . . And so at this point, I don't go to church. I believe in that and the Bible and all that but I don't follow the religion. I think that I am not able to.

In segment six, Alita continued to make personal connections to the text. For example, later in the discussion she said,

> I—my mom has told me. She always tells me, "Why don't you go to church? Why have [you] changed?" And I say, "Mom—I feel like I cannot do it anymore. I feel like I cannot stand up again." I don't know.

Religion, a topic generally silenced in the typical U.S. classroom, is central to the discussion in which Alita played a major role, making text-to-self connections throughout.

In addition to providing her students with opportunities to share their personal narratives in conjunction and connection with texts, Julie also gave them multiple openings to explore aspects of their lives via other activities. During the unit on *The Way to Rainy Mountain*, Julie invited students to share an aspect of their culture by bringing to class a symbolic representation or artifact and discussing its significance with their peers. In response to this request, Mark presented three pins: a U.S. flag pin, a U.S. Navy pin belonging to a relative, and a third one commemorating the September 11 destruction of the World Trade Center twin towers. During the presentation, when a classmate asked Mark about his culture, the following conversation ensued.

Malaya: How is this your culture?

Mark: I don't know . . . it's American. That's all I have—that's all the culture I know . . . I don't know what my culture is.

Julie: Do you feel like you don't have one? You said you're American.

Mark: I'm American, but I don't. . . .

Julie: Does that mean there's no American culture?

Mark: A melting pot—anybody that believes in freedom and believes in the right of free speech and the right of anything you can do that Americans do.

Malaya: Do you have a special kind of food or something?

Mark had significant difficulty here identifying his culture. A similar theme appeared in his closing interview. When he was asked how he defines himself, he said simply "I'm me—that's it." Mark's analysis of what he had learned in the class, according to his self-report during the closing interview, was that he "learned things that I didn't know about [my peers'] cultures"; thus the text was a useful window for him to

Native American culture and the cultures of his peers. He did *not* reveal learning anything about his own culture, a culture he had difficulty naming. Mark instead identified himself as wanting to "hear what other people were doing in their lives." When asked whether or not the book and related activities helped him to learn about himself, Mark had nothing to say.

On the other hand, Alita stated that, through reading and discussing *The Way to Rainy Mountain*, she had a chance to share her culture and express her thoughts. In her closing interview, she said that she felt very comfortable sharing her culture with classmates and that this classroom setting provided a very warm, receptive environment compared to her other classes, due in part to the inclusion of multicultural texts. She mentioned too that she had learned a great deal about her classmates. Moreover, she felt that

> it is important for everybody to know about their cultures, where they come from, and it's good to research . . . everybody's cultures so we can respect their beliefs and acts. Even though we don't need to practice the other person's religion, still it is important to respect all of that.

Thus, while Alita could use text as window and mirror, Mark could only look out through the window; he was unable to bring himself to the text, and Julie (also a member of the European majority, similar to many of the teachers in the United States) did not press him to do so. We believe that teachers such as Julie should encourage students such as Mark to see themselves in the mirror of multicultural literature.

On the One Hand . . .

By including multicultural texts in her curriculum, talk about text, talk about others in relation to the text, and opportunities for students to make text-to-self connections, Julie helped students learn to respect and understand the cultures represented in the text and those of classmates from various cultural communities. *The Way to Rainy Mountain* is a good example of literature that provides the opportunity to develop respect for and understanding of cultural diversity. The use of different voices in this book offered students the chance to observe different interpretations of the same topic, resulting in part from the students' own diverse cultural knowledge and experience. All students in Julie's ninth-grade English class could interpret the meaning of text as perceived through the eyes of their own culture, their own experiences. The unit on *The Way to Rainy Mountain* enabled students to share their cultures and express their thoughts. Julie commented about this phenomenon: "In my classroom, I felt like so many walls were completely dissolved that I could not imagine ever happening" (transcript, November 2002).

Julie's minority students were identified as being accustomed to passivity in traditional classrooms dominated by teacher interpretations and silence around topics such as race and religion. In Julie's class, however, those who were formerly silenced were "not afraid to talk out" (student interview) in the class discussions. Julie fostered for some what one student called the "right atmosphere for discussion" (student interview) in her verbal and nonverbal behaviors by creating a space where texts were open to multiple interpretations and ways of knowing. In addition, she "modeled the process of making connections between lived-world experiences and the texts" (Beach et al., 1991, p. 15) by sharing some of her own experiences with students. She explained, "My students feel safe talking about things that normally, I think, we're not supposed to [talk about]" (transcript, November 2002). This was particularly true for students like Alita, Ciro, and Citana. Julie went on to say this:

> You need to break silences. When you have a classroom full of students that, especially some that have always had power, always had the say-so, and then you've got a group of students that have never had the voice and have never, their stories have never been valid or have never been looked at as being important—you need to make a safe place, you need to create a community, essentially where your students want to walk into that class- room and feel like, I now can take off the mask, I can be who I am, I can speak safely.

Indeed Alita, for example, was able to "speak safely."

Nelson-Barber and Meier (1990) stressed the need for teachers to create classroom environments that "grant voice and legitimacy to the perspectives and experiences of those who are different from themselves—communities that do not require students to surrender personal and cultural identity in exchange for academic achievement" (p. 5). Julie created this environment for her minority students, using multicultural literature as the catalyst. Her classroom became a third space (Guitierrez, Baquedano-Lopez, & Tejeda, 1999), a place where questions appeared to be easily asked, and where concepts and difficult ideas are explored rather than ignored. It was a place where it was not uncommon to hear students speak Spanish or Urdu. It was a place where, to cite an example, a Muslim student in a post–September 11 classroom could sing an Islamic hymn to demonstrate what music is like in her culture. And in this classroom space, students were asked to "link this myth to your cultures" (Julie, transcript, March 21, 2002). The students demonstrated an implicit understanding—apparent in their com- ments during class as well as in their interviews—that "in this class, we are trying to get to know one another" (Carlos, transcript, March 19, 2002). However, what does it mean to experience the context of this class when you consider yourself cultureless, or when your culture is hidden, not as apparent as the cultures of your peers? How might Julie further complicate the experience for someone like Mark?

On the Other Hand . . .

As literature teachers begin to incorporate more multicultural literature into the cur- riculum, they are encountering some resistance from majority students (Jordan & Purves, 1993). When asked to explain their resistance, students cite their difficul- ties in understanding the linguistic and cultural practices portrayed in the text. They also feel uneasy discussing issues such as racism, particularly when these discussions challenge certain students' privileged perspectives on the world. These students may respond negatively to literary texts perceived as challenges to their privileged stance, leading them to apply negative stereotypical portrayals of cultural differences and avoid thoughtful discussion of cultural issues. As in the case of Mark and his European American peers, majority students simply may not readily see themselves written into the pages of a text. They may view the text as being about the "other," far removed from themselves, and dismiss it.

To counter such problems, teachers like Julie need to create opportunities for all students to "read, write, and talk about themselves, their family and peers, and their communities and cultures" (Moller & Allen, 2000, p. 149). Students like Mark must learn, with a teacher's help, to perceive themselves as an integral part of the conversation rather than as apart from it. Julie and other teachers need to openly explore with their students such previously unexplored cultural territory as whiteness and to invite majority students—along with minority students—to consider not only different cultures but also their own. Others have argued similarly (e.g., Kincheloe, Steinberg, Rodriguez, & Chennault, 1998). As it was, Julie's own stance, her discourse, in some ways "othered" Mark. Her questions at times privileged the cultures of her minority students. For example, in a March conversation, Julie asked, "Is anybody else here from any other cultures that are represented in the room?" and "Does anybody else here represent other cultures in this room. . . . [have] anything else to add?" Despite efforts to be inclusive, to encourage conversation across cultural borders, Julie's comments made visible the cultures of her minority students but made invisible in some respects her own culture and that of Mark.

What could Julie have done differently? Rather than ask, "Is anybody else here from any other cultures?" she needed to ask, "How does your culture connect to or differ from the text?" and thus help her students realize that they all have culture and can make cultural connections to the text. She needs to help her students understand that culture is multifaceted. She needs to help them mark the majority culture(s) that too often remain unmarked (Florio-Ruane, 2001). Rather than looking at culture only when reading and responding to multicultural literature, thus perpetuating the notion that culture exists only outside canonical literature and the so-called mainstream, Julie must invite her students to read all texts multiculturally. This will bring discussions of culture to conversations not only about *The Way to Rainy Mountain* but also about other works of literature. "The multicultural stance provides the reader with an instrument, a magnifier if you will, to expose assumptions about race, class, and gender hidden in a story" (Cai, 1998, p. 321). If students can explore these assumptions in a text, perhaps they can do the same in their own lives and the world in which they live.

We caution, however, that it is imperative to not simply maintain the same canonical bookshelves, simply reading these works multiculturally. While one can both look through the window of canonical literature and use it as a mirror, the mirror image may at times be distorted. What is in the reflection is highly dependent on the text. Multicultural literature can reflect back to majority readers a picture of themselves as part of a larger system of oppression. This literature, in many cases, sheds light on minorities whose lives have often been affected by racism and other forms of discrimination. Multiple opportunities to view others and oneself across a set of different mirrors—by reading multiple texts—might ultimately increase cultural awareness, decrease ethnocentrism, and create a global perspective (Cliff & Miller, 1997).

Finally, Julie needs to be aware of how and whether students participate in particular conversations. A close analysis of her students' discourse may help her to discern patterns, particularly patterns of silence, that she might not have noticed otherwise, recognizing perhaps her own complicity in creating those silenced spaces.

For multicultural literature to be an effective tool that helps young people learn about cultural diversity and improves intercultural and intracultural understanding, teachers must use it skillfully. And if multicultural literature is to realize its full potential as mirror and window for all students, teachers must conceive of culture more broadly so as to include talk about whiteness, an unaddressed topic in many U.S. schools today.

References

American Association of Colleges for Teacher Education. (1999). *Teacher education pipeline IV: Schools, colleges and departments of education enrollments by race, ethnicity and gender.* Washington, DC: Author.

Applebee, A. (1993). *Beyond the lesson: Reconstructing curriculum as a domain for culturally significant conversations* (Report No. 1.7). Albany: National Research Center on Literature Teaching and Learning, State University of New York, University at Albany.

Bakhtin, M. M. (1986). *Speech genres and other late essays.* Austin: University of Texas Press.

Bakhtin, M. M. (1990). *Art and answerability: Early philosophical essays.* Austin: University of Texas.

Beach, R., Parks, D., Thein, A., & Lensmire, T. (1991). *High school students' responses to alternative value stances associated with the study of multicultural literature.* Paper presented at the annual meeting of the American Educational Research Associations, Chicago.

Bigler, E. (1996). *On exclusion and inclusion in classroom texts and talk* (Report Series 7.5). Albany: National Research Center on Literature Teaching and Learning, State University of New York, University at Albany.

Bigler, E., & Collins, J. (1995). *Dangerous discourses: The politics of multicultural literature in community and classroom* (Report Series 7.4). Albany: National Research Center on Literature Teaching and Learning, State University of New York, University at Albany.

Black, S. (2003). Teaching about religion. *American School Board Journal, 190*(4), 50. Retrieved November 8, 2004, from http://www.asbj.com/2003/04/0403research.html

Cai, M. (1998). Multiple definitions of multicultural literature: Is the debate really just "ivory tower" bickering? *The New Advocate, 11,* 311–324.

Cazden, C. (1988). *Classroom discourse: The language of teaching and learning.* Portsmouth, NH: Heinemann.

Christoph, J., & Nystrand, M. (2001). *Taking risks, negotiating relationships: One teacher's transition towards a dialogic classroom* (CELA Research Rep. 14003). Albany: The National Research Center on English Learning & Achievement, State University of New York, University at Albany.

Cliff, C., & Miller, S. (1997). *Multicultural dialogue in literature-history classes: The dance of creative and critical thinking* (Report Series 7.9). Albany: National Research Center on Literature Teaching and Learning, State University of New York, University at Albany.

Colby, S., & Lyon, A. (2004). Heightening awareness about the importance of using multicultural literature. *Multicultural Education, 11*(3), 24–28.

Delpit, L. (1988). The silenced dialogue: Power and pedagogy in educating other people's children. *Harvard Educational Review, 58,* 280–298.

Desai, L. (1997). Reflections on cultural diversity in literature and in the classroom. In T. Rogers & A. Soter (Eds.), *Reading across cultures* (pp. 161–177). New York: Teachers College Press.

Fang, Z., Fu, D., & Lamme, L. (1999). Rethinking the role of multicultural literature in literacy instruction: Problems, paradox, and possibilities. *The New Advocate, 12,* 259–275.

Fine, M. (1992). Silencing and nurturing voice in an improbable context: Urban adolescents in public school. In M. Fine (Ed.), *Disruptive voices: The possibilities of feminist research* (pp. 115–138). Ann Arbor: University of Michigan Press.

Fine, M., & Weis, L. (1993). *Beyond silenced voices: Class, race, and gender in U.S. schools.* Albany: State University of New York Press.

Fine, M., & Weis, L. (2003). *Silenced voices and extraordinary conversations: Reimagining schools.* New York: Teachers College Press.

Florio-Ruane, S. (2001). *Teacher education and the cultural imagination.* Mahwah, NJ: Erlbaum.

Frankenberg, R. (1993). *White women race matters: The social construction of whiteness.* Minneapolis: University of Minnesota Press.

Galda, L. (1998). Mirrors and windows: Reading as transformation. In T. E. Raphael & K. H. Au (Eds.), *Literature-based instruction: Reshaping the curriculum* (pp. 1–11). Norwood, MA: Christopher-Gordon.

Giroux, H. A. (1989). *Schooling for democracy: Critical pedagogy in the modern age.* London: Routledge.

Glazier, J. (2003). Moving closer to speaking the unspeakable: White teachers talking about race. *Teacher Education Quarterly, 30*(1), 73–94.

Guitierrez, K., Baquedano-Lopez, P., & Tejeda, C. (1999). Rethinking diversity: Hybridity and hybrid language practices in the third space. *Mind, Culture and Activity, 6,* 286–303.

Haynes, C., & Thomas, O. (2001). *Finding common ground: A guide to religious liberty in public schools.* Nashville, TN: First Amendment Center.

International Reading Association & National Council of Teachers of English. (1996). *Standards for the English language arts.* Retrieved January 19, 2005, from http://www.reading.org/advocacy/ elastandards/standards.html

Jordan, S., & Purves, A. (1993). *Issues in the responses of students to culturally diverse texts: A preliminary study.* Albany, NY: National Research Center on Literature Teaching and Learning.

Kincheloe, J., Steinberg, S., Rodriguez, N., & Chennault, R. (1998). *White reign: Deploying whiteness in America.* New York: St. Martin's Press.

Landsman, J. (2001). *A white teacher talks about race.* Lanham, MD: Scarecrow Press.

Latham, A. (1999). The teacher–student mismatch. *Educational Leadership, 56*(7), 84–85.

McIntyre, A. (1997). *Making meaning of whiteness: Exploring racial identity with white teachers.* Albany: State University of New York Press.

Moller, K., & Allen, J. (2000). Connecting, resisting, and searching for safer places: Students respond to Mildred Taylor's *The Friendship. Journal of Literacy Research, 32,* 145–186.

Morrison, T. (1992). *Playing in the dark: Whiteness and the literary imagination.* Cambridge, MA: Harvard University Press.

Morrison, T. (1993). *Nobel lecture.* Retrieved July 21, 2004, from http://www.nobelprize.org/literature/ laureates/1993/Morrison-lecture.html

National Center for Education Statistics. (2004). *Mini-digest of education statistics 2003.* Washington, DC: U.S. Department of Education.

Nelson-Barber, S., & Meier, T. (1990, Spring). Multicultural context: A key factor in teaching. *Academic Connections, 1*–5, 9–11.

Nystrand, M. (with Gamoran, A., Kachuer, R., & Prendergast, C.). (1997). *Opening dialogue: Understanding the dynamics of language and learning in the English classroom.* New York: Teachers College Press.

Public Broadcasting System (2002). *Freedom: A history of us.* Retrieved July 20, 2004, from http://www. pbs.org/wnet/historyofus

Robertson, P. (1996). Wounded Knee massacre, 1890. In F. Hoxie (Ed.), *Encyclopedia of North American Indians* (p. 437). New York: Houghton Mifflin.

Rogers, T., & Soter, A. (1997). Introduction. In T. Rogers & A. Soter (Eds.), *Reading across cultures* (pp. 1–9). New York: Teachers College Press.

Rosenblatt, L. (1983). *Literature as exploration.* New York: The Modern Language Association of America. (Original work published 1938.)

Singer, J., & Smith, S. (2001). *Text and context: Using multi-cultural literature to help teacher education students develop understanding of self and world.* Paper presented at the annual meeting of the American Educational Research Association, Seattle, WA.

Sleeter, C., & Grant, C. (1991). Race, class, gender, and disability in current textbooks. In M. Apple & L. Christian-Smith (Eds.), *The politics of the textbook* (pp. 78–101). New York: Routledge.

Willis, A. I. (1997). Exploring multicultural literature as cultural production. In T. Rogers & A. Soter (Eds.), *Reading across cultures* (pp. 135–160). New York: Teachers College Press.

Yasin, S., & Albert, B. (1999). *Minority teacher recruitment and retention: A national imperative.* Washington, DC: National Partnership for Excellence and Accountability in Teaching.

Classroom Implications

1. Reexamine your personal views of multicultural education, particularly as related to your current teaching of the classroom literacy curriculum.

2. Interview the ESL teacher(s) in your school and district, noting what they consider to be the most important issues related to multicultural education. What are some of their suggestions as to how these various problems might be solved?

3. To what extent are you helping prepare your students for life in the future as it relates to multicultural interaction? What are the primary problems in accomplishing these goals?

For Further Reading

Hammond, B., Hoover, M. E., & Pressley, I. (2005). *Teaching African American learners to read: Perspectives and practices.* Newark, DE: International Reading Association.

Jimenez, R. T. (2005). *Moving beyond the obvious: Examining our thinking about linguistically diverse students.* Naperville, IL: Learning Point Associates.

Landt, S. M. (2006). Multicultural literature and young adolescents: A kaleidoscope of opportunity. *Journal of Adolescent & Adult Literacy, 49,* 690–697.

Louie, B. (2005). Development of empathetic responses with multicultural literature. *Journal of Adolescent & Adult Literacy, 48,* 566–578.

Moore-Hart. P. (2004). Creating learning environments that invite all students to learn through multicultural literature and information technology: The intermingling of cultures, religions, and languages across the United States enriches classrooms, while presenting new challenges to teaching and learning. *Childhood Education, 81,* 87–92.

Smith, S. A., & Singer, J. Y. (2006). Reading "The Friendship" and talking about race. *Urban Education, 41,* 321–342.

Stallworth, B. J., Gibbons, L., & Fauber. L. (2006). It's not on the list: An exploration of teachers' perspectives on using multicultural literature. *Journal of Adolescent & Adult Literacy, 49,* 478–489.

Sutherland, L. M. (2005). Black adolescent girls' use of literacy practices to negotiate boundaries of ascribed identity. *Literacy Research, 37,* 365–406.

Zuidema, L. A. (2005). Myth education: Rational and strategies for teaching against linguistic prejudice. *Journal of Adolescent & Adult Literacy, 48,* 666–675.

Online Resources

International Reading Association. (2001). *Second-language literacy instruction.* Position Statement. **www.reading.org/downloads/positions/ps1046_second_language.pdf**

Internet TESL Journal. This well-designed forum offers materials that one can download as well as articles, teaching techniques, lesson plans, and links to issues of interest to ESL teachers. It includes electronic discussion lists and news groups. **http://iteslj.org**

it's Online Network. Hub of six sites for English learners and their teachers. **www.its-online.com/**

Barahona Center. This project of California State University San Marcos "promotes literacy in English and Spanish. The Center endeavors to inform current and future educational decision-makers about books centered around Latino people and culture and about books in Spanish and their value in education of English-speaking and Spanish-speaking children and adolescents." **www.csusm.edu/csb**

Assessment-Driven Instruction

*Let him now take liberty to exercise himself in an English book till he can
perfectly read in any place of a book that is offered to him; and when he can do this
I adjudge him fit to enter into a Grammar School, but not before.*

—C. H. (1659)

*Misused, [literacy tests] can be a source of inestimable harm, not only to the pupils
whom they should benefit primarily, but to teachers and entire schools as well.*

—George A. Prescott (1952)

*[Reading] Assessment is not grading—although assessment can
help you determine and support the grades you give. Assessment is
collecting and analyzing data to make decisions about how children are
performing and growing.*

—Patricia Cunningham & Richard Allington (2007)

What role should assessment play in the reading program? Should it be used to compare the collective progress of all students in a school or district with their national age peers? Should it be a yardstick used to determine the attainment of curriculum standards and adequate yearly progress? Should it be used to determine whether a child qualifies for special services? To these questions, we might respond "all of the above," but are quick to acknowledge that opinions differ widely, making assessment a contentious issue across the United States. This chapter is actually designed to address another question, one that has reemerged in recent years: How should assessment inform instructional planning? First, however, let's situate this question in the context of assessment's other uses.

Assessment-Driven Instruction versus High-Stakes Assessment

Assessment presently serves multiple purposes in a reading program. Some assessments are designed to monitor how effectively students are, on average, improving their proficiency. Not only educators but other stakeholders, such as the general public, lawmakers, and parents, have a right to know. Assessments of this kind are often based on standardized measures (both norm-referenced and criterion-referenced), and the pressure to perform well can be a major source of stress in a particular school. Because so much can ride on the outcomes, these group achievement measures are frequently called "high-stakes tests."

The results of these assessments do not go very far toward helping teachers plan instruction, however. For this purpose, different measures are called for. Some of them, such as the unit test provided by the commercial materials a teacher may be using, are routinely given because of their close alignment with the instructional program. Other measures, such as screening and diagnostic tests, might be used to detect and define problems and to identify students for special services. Complicating matters is the fact that special educators must use a separate battery of individually administered norm-referenced tests in conducting their diagnoses. In addition to these measures, an array of informal classroom assessments, such as the information collected in portfolios, is often used by classroom teachers to inform instructional planning.

Clearly, the assessment arm of the reading program is quite complex, and it is always a challenge to those responsible for directing and coordinating the program. A few of the principal issues might be summarized as follows.

With respect to mandated group achievement testing, it is tempting to conclude that this component of the assessment system requires few choices. However, such testing must be carefully scheduled, teachers must be adequately prepared, a policy must be developed for best utilizing the results within the school, and a decision must be made as to whether a commercial test preparation program will be used with the students.

With respect to testing used within the school, school policies must be developed that address the questions of which test will be given and how much latitude will be afforded to individual teachers. What kind of information will be useful at year's end for deciding issues such as retention and fall classroom assignments? Should grade-level teams be given the authority to determine, to a meaningful degree, the assessment system that will be most useful to them? And should an outside, Web-based agency be used to gather test data electronically so that reports can be periodically generated at the level of the individual child, the classroom, the grade level, and the school?

A Brief History of Assessment-Driven Instruction

How exactly can assessment inform instruction? Decades ago, this question was addressed in terms of a diagnostic-prescriptive model, borrowed (terminology and all) from medicine. Tests were used to diagnose a reading deficit and materials (often in the form of worksheets) were prescribed to remedy the deficit. This model is still alive and well, especially in present-day computerized integrated learning systems. In domains like mathematics, in which skills are rigorously sequenced, the diagnostic-prescriptive model can work fairly well. In reading, it is more difficult to implement, though hardly impossible. One requirement is the use of watchful follow-up assessments to determine whether what is prescribed is truly working to address the deficit.

Current ideas about assessment-driven instruction can be summarized as follows: A screening test is administered individually in a fairly broad area (let's say phonics). Results are compared against a benchmark or criterion predictive of future success. If a child is found to be at risk, a diagnostic test is administered. This test delineates the area into specific skills (consonant sounds, for instance), revealing more clearly where instruction should be focused. Once the teacher decides on materials and strategies to address the deficits, follow-up measures are administered periodically, as often as every week, to determine whether the instruction is having the desired effect.

As You Read

Invernizzi and her colleagues discuss the fit between assessment-driven instruction and the other roles assessment might play in a reading program. They address the role test publishers play and how all parties must be aware of differing agendas. Decide whether their calls for "peaceful coexistence" are justified and realistic. McKenna and Walpole then describe in detail one model of assessment-driven instruction. In their system, which is now popular in Reading First schools, assessment begins at the level of screening, then proceeds to diagnostic assessments and finally to progress monitoring. Consider whether you would you find such a system useful in your setting. What would be the costs in time and effort? Can such costs be justified?

References

C. H. (1659). *The Petty-School shewing a way to teach little children to read English with delight and profit. Especially according to the New Primer.* London: Printed by J. T. for Andrew Crook, at the Green Dragon in Pauls Church Yard.

Cunningham, P. M., & Allington, R. L. (2007). *Classrooms that work: They can all read and write* (4th ed.). Boston: Allyn & Bacon.

Prescott, G. A. (1952). Use reading tests carefully—They can be dangerous tools. *The Reading Teacher, 5*, 3–5.

Toward the Peaceful Coexistence of Test Developers, Policymakers, and Teachers in an Era of Accountability

MARCIA A. INVERNIZZI, TIMOTHY J. LANDRUM,
JENNIFER L. HOWELL, AND HEATHER P. WARLEY

● ● ● ● ●

In the past five years U.S. teachers have witnessed unprecedented political insistence on the use of research-based, scientifically proven assessments and instructional techniques. Pressure to apply scientific methodology to the day-to-day work of teaching children to read and write is perhaps even stronger today than it was during the days of Sputnik and the Cold War. Then, the press for science was propelled by competition against the Soviet Union to maintain the United States's academic edge in the rush to the moon and beyond. Today, the press for science is from within, driven by the desire to preserve and extend the effectiveness of public education to all segments of our democratic society—so that "no child will be left behind." This is indeed a valiant goal, and to reach it the federal government has made money available through grants such as Reading First, designed to support states' efforts to implement scientifically based reading instruction driven by valid and reliable assessments. But there may be a disconnect between what is required to meet external demands for scientifically based reading assessment and the type of assessment information teachers need on a day-to-day basis to provide appropriately designed and targeted reading instruction for all students. In other words, there may be significant challenges associated with selecting assessment tools and implementing a comprehensive yet efficient assessment program that (a) meets high standards of scientific rigor and (b) provides teachers with instructionally useful information.

In this article we focus on the potential disconnect between research and practice in reading assessment and instruction that may be an unfortunate byproduct of increased accountability and growing emphasis on scientifically based reading

Invernizzi, M., Landrum, T., Howell, J., & Warley, H. P. (2005, April). Toward the peaceful coexistence of test developers, policymakers, and teachers in an era of accountability. *The Reading Teacher*, *58*(7), 610–618. Reprinted with permission.

research. It is important to clarify that a focus on the empirical base in designing literacy assessment and instruction is long overdue and is clearly an essential foundational step toward improved literacy—to ignore the empirical base is little short of nonsensical. Moreover, a focus on science finds generally widespread support among those concerned with enhancing the literacy development of U.S. schoolchildren. But an unintended side effect of a headlong rush toward science and accountability in assessment that does not take into account the practicalities of everyday teaching may create a disconnect between what assessments tell us about students' performance and what teachers need to know to instruct them.

We discuss specifically eight standards for the evaluation of educational assessments and assessment practices, recommended by the American Educational Research Association, the American Psychological Association, and the National Council on Measurement in Education, as applied to reading assessments typically used in Reading First schools across the country. These eight standards constitute the basic obligations of test developers and research professionals to provide technically sound assessment tools to teachers. For each standard, we briefly define the constructs it entails, provide examples, and explain its importance. Next, we describe the tension that may develop in implementing each construct within classrooms, especially in the context of existing curricula and teachers' current knowledge, skill sets, and beliefs about reading. Finally, we offer solutions to these tensions by describing some examples of instructionally transparent assessments that also meet scientific requirements for technical adequacy.

Standard 1: Validity

A well-constructed assessment must first and foremost be valid. In simple terms, a measure is valid to the extent to which it measures what it is intended to measure. There are several forms of validity: content validity, construct validity, and criterion-related validity (predictive and concurrent). Relative to this discussion, predictive validity is probably the most critical focus for test developers because they must ensure that their assessments accurately predict real reading outcomes. To establish the predictive validity of an instrument, test developers compare student performance on their assessment with some external measure obtained at a later point in time. While predictive validity is critical for test developers and policymakers, teachers want assessments that are instructionally useful in the here and now.

The disconnect between scientifically based standards for assessment and the information teachers need for instruction becomes apparent in examining specific assessments that do have a high degree of predictive validity. Consider the example of tasks involving nonsense word reading. Measures of nonsense word reading are highly predictive of overall reading achievement at future points in time (Good, Wallin, Simmons, Kame'enui, & Kaminksi, 2002; Speece, Mills, Ritchey, & Hillman, 2003), and these measures appear in several reading assessments commonly used in Reading First projects across the country such as the Test of Word Reading Efficiency (TOWRE; Torgesen, Wagner, & Rashotte, 1999) and Dynamic Indicators of Basic Early Literacy Skills (DIBELS; Good & Kaminski, 2002). The developers of such tests meet rigorous standards for predictive validity by including a nonsense word task on an assessment, and from an accountability or research standpoint, such tasks provide quite valuable information. Indeed, teachers do want to know which students are at risk for reading difficulties and in need of extra help. But a student's performance on a nonsense word task is not instructionally transparent to most teachers. For the purposes of planning and guiding instruction, teachers need specific information about a student's performance at that moment in time, such as which phonics features a first-grade student already knows and which features he or she needs to know next.

The best assessments provide tasks with a high degree of predictive validity while simultaneously providing instructionally relevant information. An example of such a task is a simple spelling assessment organized by phonics features or orthographic patterns. Spelling-by-stage inventories tell teachers where their students are along a developmental continuum of phonics and spelling achievement and exactly which phonics and spelling features a student has mastered and not mastered (Bear, Invernizzi, Templeton, & Johnston, 2004; Ganske, 2000; Viise, 1994). Grade-level spelling inventories yield instructional levels of spelling achievement and also indicate which phonics and spelling features are not yet fully developed (Henderson, 1990; Schlagal, 1986). Quantitative scores from qualitative spelling and phonics inventories have been shown to be excellent predictors of future reading achievement (Ehri, 2000; Ellis & Cataldo, 1992; Morris & Perney, 1984; Zutell & Rasinski, 1989), and they also provide information to the teacher about what phonics and spelling elements the student has already learned and which elements should be taught next. Teachers need this information for individual students as well as for the entire class to group for appropriate phonics and spelling instruction.

Standard 2: Reliability

Reliability refers to the consistency with which a test measures a construct, or the extent to which an obtained score can be trusted to represent a "true" score. Just as there are many forms of validity, there are also many forms of reliability: test-retest, equivalent forms, split-half, and interrater. Interrater reliability is especially critical when item scoring involves a subjective judgment, such as rating the fluency of a child's oral reading on a scale of one to four, as does the National Assessment of Educational Progress (NAEP; Pinnell et al., 1995).

Reliability is important because it ensures that teachers receive accurate, trustworthy information. Because of the importance of having reliable measures, test developers sometimes may limit or avoid the use of more authentic, qualitative, or subjective measures, the reliability of which is difficult to establish, in favor of more contrived, quantitative, objective measures that can be more easily constructed to be reliable.

The measurement of reading comprehension, for example, is exceedingly complex and the currently available measures have been criticized on a number of grounds, including their inability to represent the abstract nature of the comprehension process, lack of standardized assessment strategies, and inadequate evidence of reliability and validity (Rathvon, 2004). Adequate assessment of comprehension would require multiple measures to address all of the variables in play: attention and engagement, interest, readability, vocabulary, background knowledge, oral language comprehension, written word recognition, and knowledge of genre, to name only a few (Sweet & Snow, 2003). Because administering a reliable battery of this many measures is not generally feasible for a classroom teacher or even a reading specialist, test developers usually opt for multiple choice formats that are quick and easy and that can be constructed reliably, even if narrowly. In this case, content validity (an indicator of the extent to which the questions actually measure reading comprehension) may be sacrificed for internal consistency (a measure of the reliability of the items).

Comprehension is the ultimate goal of reading, so it is a skill that teachers want to assess accurately and quickly. As a result, teachers have become dependent on the practice of asking students a few open-ended questions after the student reads a passage, or asking students to provide an oral retelling of what was just read to measure comprehension. For example, the Qualitative Reading Inventory–3 (QRI–3; Leslie & Caldwell, 2001) offers story retelling as well as open-ended explicit and implicit comprehension questions following each passage. Although nonstandardized procedures for story retelling and open-ended comprehension questions have scant evidence of validity and reliability (Rathvon, 2004), the QRI–3 and the Developmental Reading Assessment (DRA; Beaver, 1997) suggest moving students back to a reading level at which they answer most of the questions or retell most of the story correctly. Despite the unreliable nature of constructed responses, these assessments use story retelling and open-ended comprehension questions to determine a student's overall reading level, potentially limiting a student's further growth by holding them back in easier text levels even if they can read accurately and fluently at higher levels. In these instances, a technically questionable measure (i.e., open-ended comprehension questions) appears to trump more reliable measures (e.g., oral reading accuracy) in the designation of overall reading levels (Beaver; Leslie & Caldwell, 2001).

While there are other issues to consider in terms of establishing instructional reading levels, in terms of reliability, it may make more sense to focus on the more technically sound procedures available. It may be surprising to many teachers that some of the most valid and reliable measures of a student's overall reading level include simple measures of word-recognition accuracy and speed, in and out of context (Rasinki, 2000; Torgesen, Wagner, Rashotte, Burgess, & Hecht, 1997). Automatic word recognition makes reading comprehension possible. As decoding and word-recognition skills become automated, the mental capacity available for comprehension increases (LaBerge & Samuels, 1974). Once a student's reading level has been determined based on reliable measures (e.g., word recognition, oral reading accuracy, and reading rate), the student can be instructed at that level with an emphasis on comprehension instruction through building vocabulary, activating prior knowledge, scaffolding the use of comprehension strategies, and discussing what has been read.

Standard 3: Test Development

Test developers are obligated to state the purpose of a given assessment tool, provide the theoretical framework, and demonstrate the technical adequacy of their instrument through a description of the test development procedures, item analyses, field tests of revisions, and the validity of their scoring procedures. These aspects of test development may be easily overlooked because they seem obvious; however, it is important for teachers to be aware of the criteria by which test developers define an instrument. Guidelines include stating the purpose(s) of the test; defining a framework for the test; developing test specifications; and describing the process involved in developing and evaluating the items and their associated scoring procedures, assembly, and revisions.

Educators are on shaky ground when a test is used in a way or for a purpose other than that for which it was intended. If a test has been developed specifically for a certain population (e.g., preschool students, native English speakers), then it is imperative that the test be used solely for those it was designed to assess. Teachers should be careful not to use assessments designed for specific groups of students on other, more diverse, groups of students. When reviewing an instrument, decision makers should look for information about the population sampled in item development and field tests, pilot testing, and the establishment of norms. Several of the assessments that appeared on the initial Reading First list of acceptable assessment instruments, for example, were designed for students with language impairments and have questionable applicability to more diverse groups of students. Conversely, some assessments have been normed on typically achieving students and few if any special education students may have been included in the sample. This may be especially troublesome when assessing students with disabilities (e.g., learning disabilities or speech or language disorders); teachers would be wise to carefully consult test manuals to determine whether a given test is appropriate for a certain subpopulation of students.

A disconnect also may be seen when assessments are used for purposes other than those for which they were designed. A screening tool is not intended to provide diagnostic information, for example, and outcomes should not be assessed using tools not intended to measure outcomes. Reading First in fact requires that states use measures that address four purposes of assessment: screening, diagnosis, progress monitoring, and outcome assessment. However, it is not necessary that separate assessment tools be used for each purpose. For example, both the Phonological Awareness Literacy Screening (PALS; Invernizzi, Meier, & Juel, 2003; Invernizzi, Swank, Juel, & Meier, 2003) and the Texas Primary Reading Inventory (TPRI; 2003–2004) can be used for screening and then for obtaining more detailed diagnostic information. Decision makers at the district and state levels must carefully map out the various purposes of assessment in the process of selecting assessment tools.

Standard 4: Fairness in Testing

Test developers are also obligated to demonstrate that their test is fair and free of bias. Fairness in testing demands the equitable treatment of all test takers. This means that tests should be free of bias in content, materials, and administration procedures that might differentially affect the performance of subgroups of test takers. Proof of this lack of bias is that students of similar levels of achievement should earn similar scores regardless of group status (i.e., gender, disability, race, ethnicity, socioeconomic status). Test developers test their measures and procedures for bias through their sampling procedures and through item analyses across different demographic segments of the population. Thus, samples used for field-testing and pilot studies should include students from all segments of the population. PALS (Invernizzi et al., 2003), for example, describes how pilot samples used in item development and field-testing mirrored the demographics of state enrollment in kindergarten through third grade.

Test developers address other elements of bias by standardizing administration procedures to prevent the subjectivity of a test administrator from unfairly swaying test results. For example, a teacher who believes a child is reading on Guided Reading level G (Fountas & Pinnell, 1999) may decide to take a running record of the child's oral reading at a level corresponding only to level G, despite the fact that the child may be able to read equally well on level H, I, or J. In this case, the absence of an objective, standardized procedure for selecting which level passage to administer for the running record may simply confirm the teacher's initial bias. While teacher knowledge of student performance provides valuable information for instruction, this prior knowledge can also result in a failure to fully explore all possibilities in an assessment context. This type of bias, called confirmation bias (Evans, 1989), has been well documented and leads to the type of measurement selection problem described above.

A fairer way to select passages for running records would be to use an objective, standardized procedure. For example, teachers using the QRI–3 (Leslie & Caldwell, 2001) administer the passage corresponding to the highest grade-level word list on which the student achieved a score of 90% or greater. In a similar manner, teachers using the TPRI (2003–2004) first administer screening word lists that direct them to the appropriate level passage. PALS (Invernizzi et al., 2003), using a similar procedure, reported that 97% of students who read 15 or more words on a grade-level word list read the corresponding grade-level passage with 90% accuracy or greater. By providing an objective procedure for administering the passages, PALS, the QRI–3, and the TPRI avoid this common type of confirmation bias.

Standard 5: Scales, Norms, and Score Comparability

The interpretation of test scores can be a complex task, and a full description of the different types of scores and their uses is beyond the scope of this article. Perhaps what is more important is that teachers should be familiar with basic distinctions between the most common types of tests: norm referenced and criterion referenced. Put simply, a norm-referenced test uses the results from a large and representative sample of other similar students who also took the test to establish a student's relative standing compared to his or her age- or grade-level peers. Norm-referenced scores are often expressed as percentiles; for example, a student obtained a score of 13 on a word-recognition test, which puts him or her at the 70th percentile. This means that the student's score of 13 was equal to or better than that of 70% of children the same age who took this test. It is important that teachers and other decision makers understand that norms are established by test developers who draw their normative samples from the larger population. The extent to which a given normative sample is representative of the nation as a whole, a particular state, or an individual school varies. When decisions are made based on norm-referenced testing, close attention to how norms were established is essential. Some proponents of curriculum-based measurement, for example, advocate the development and use of local norms, so that students' performances are compared to other students like them from the same school district or even the same school (e.g., Marston & Magnusson, 1988).

Tests may also be criterion referenced, which means that students' performances are measured against some established criterion, rather than against other students' performances. In the previous example, the student's score of 13 on a word list (which put that student at the 70th percentile) may still be below the criterion of 15 (out of 20) for on-grade-level reading determined by the theoretical construct of instructional level.

Researchers, administrators, and policymakers often prefer norm-referenced tests because these results indicate the standing of a student within a population of students at specific age or grade levels. Teachers, however, usually prefer the more specific instructional information provided by criterion-referenced tests. The disconnect between research-based standards for assessment practices and the culture of teaching and learning is perhaps most dramatic in the administration and scoring of norm-referenced curriculum-based measures. For example, DIBELS (Good & Kaminski, 2002) directs a teacher to discontinue students from further administration of their curriculum-based, one-minute oral reading fluency task if they read fewer than 10 words correctly on the first of three grade-level passages. While the rule for discontinuing the student informs the administrator that the student is well below expectations, it tells the teacher very little beyond what he or she already knew—that the student was struggling. Student reading of frustration-level text affords little instructional information for teachers who want to determine the student's instructional level. In this situation, a criterion-referenced test that provides multiple gradations of easy oral reading passages would allow the teacher the leeway to move up or down in passage difficulty to find the highest difficulty level at which the student can read.

It is important to note that curriculum-based measurement (CBM; Deno, 1985) presents a unique case in terms of the assessment information it provides. By definition, CBM involves regular, brief assessments of a student's achievement within the curriculum in use. Measurement items (typically passages in the case of reading) are drawn directly from instructional materials. As such, CBM can provide useful instructional information about the effects of instruction on student performance and progress over time toward a specific criterion or goal, such as grade-level reading (e.g., Deno, 1985). An additional benefit of CBM can be derived from the establishment of local norms (Deno, 2003; Marston & Magnusson, 1988), which allow comparison of an individual child's performance with similar peers in the same class, school, or district. In this application, CBM addresses the key element of norm-referenced assessment. Thus, while they do not provide a full diagnostic picture, CBM procedures can provide teachers with tools for monitoring progress toward a criterion within a normative context.

Standard 6: Standardized Administration, Scoring, and Reporting

Standardized procedures for administering and scoring a test and for reporting its results are also essential for ensuring the accuracy and integrity of the assessment outcomes. How scores are reported clearly influences their usefulness to teachers. Some assessments report scores in terms or in formats that are intended more for statisticians than for teachers (e.g., stanines). Other assessments report results in categorical terms such as "High risk—Danger!" (Torgesen, 2003). Reports that label children in such terms might be useful for administrators, but they do not provide teachers with specific information to guide their teaching. Often raw scores from reading assessments are reported in massive data files or complicated charts intended for technical specialists or researchers who can use these files to answer specific questions of interest, often for an entire school district. Classroom teachers and reading specialists usually do not have the time and resources to interpret such massive amounts of data. Fortunately, many tests provide interpretive reports via the Internet (e.g., DIBELS, Good & Kaminski, 2002; PALS, Invernizzi et al., 2003) while also providing the option of downloading raw data files. These reports are usually in a standard format and "based on a combination of empirical data and expert judgment and experience" (American Educational Research Association, American Psychological Association, & National Council on Measurement in Education, 1999, p. 62). Rigorous computer-generated reports provide an efficient way for educators to review test scores. The PALS Internet database, for example, provides a number of interpretive reports, including class or school groupings of students by common reading levels and phonics features (Partridge, Invernizzi, Meier, & Sullivan, 2003).

Standard 7: Testing Individuals of Diverse Linguistic Backgrounds

Students whose native language is not English present a particular challenge for test developers and educators alike. According to the *Standards for Educational and Psychological Testing* (American Educational Research Association et al., 1999), test developers should pay special attention to "issues related to language and culture when developing, administering, scoring, and interpreting test scores and making decisions based on test scores" (p. 91). This means that norms that are based on native English speakers' performances should not be used as a comparison group for nonnative speakers. In terms of reading, most researchers agree that it is important to establish which language is dominant for a particular student, and then to establish a student's proficiency level with literacy fundamentals in that language (American Educational Research Association et al.). Although a student may not be able to read or even name the letters of the alphabet in English, he or she may be quite knowledgeable about phonetics in his or her native language. Ideally, reading assessments for individuals of diverse linguistic backgrounds should be conducted in the dominant language first, and in English as soon as English proficiency allows. Several reading assessments used in Reading First projects in the United States offer assessment in both Spanish and English. For example, Texas offers reading assessment through the TPRI (2003–2004) and a Spanish language assessment through El Inventorio de Lectura en Espanol de Tejas (Tejas LEE, 2003–2004). The problems schools face in assessing the reading development of students of diverse linguistic backgrounds are (a) the huge number of different languages now represented in the United States and the lack of corresponding assessment tools in those languages, and (b) lack of a standardized procedure for when to include English language learners in English-literacy assessments.

One possible solution is to use a continuum of English proficiency and designate an agreed-upon level above which students are assessed in English. In Virginia, for example, students are designated along a continuum from emergent to proficient with respect to oral language, reading, and writing. The student's English-language proficiency level dictates whether he or she is included in the statewide English reading assessment.

Standard 8: Responsibilities of Policy Decision Makers

The *Standards for Educational and Psychological Testing* (American Educational Research Association et al., 1999) stated that test results are used for multiple purposes: to evaluate student achievement and growth in a domain, diagnose student strengths and weaknesses, plan educational interventions, design individual instructional plans, and place students in appropriate educational programs. To accomplish these purposes, policymakers sometimes require multiple tests to be administered. Often the tasks on tests administered to the same students overlap, causing a redundancy of testing. For example, school divisions may administer the DRA (Beaver, 1997), the Developmental Spelling Assessment (DSA; Ganske, 2000), and PALS (Invernizzi et al., 2003). When students take all three assessments, they are taking multiple oral reading in context tasks and two different qualitative spelling inventories. Furthermore, a school receiving a Reading First grant may administer a screening test (e.g., Essential Skills Screener; Erford, Vitali, Haas, & Boykin, 1995), a diagnostic test (e.g., Gray Diagnostic Reading Test; Bryant, Wiederholt, & Bryant, 2004), an additional test to monitor progress (e.g., TOWRE; Torgesen et al., 1999), and yet another test to assess outcomes (e.g., Stanford–10 Achievement Test). In addition, many schools have district- or state-imposed assessments or may be tied to earlier investments in other assessment routines. Schools may have selected several different instruments to assess the five core areas that must be assessed under Reading First (i.e., phonological awareness, phonics, fluency, vocabulary, and comprehension), in addition to meeting the four areas of assessment required (i.e., screening, diagnosis, progress monitoring, and outcomes assessment).

To decrease testing time and increase instruction time, a comprehensive, flexible assessment could be selected that evaluates all of the components of reading and serves multiple purposes. Such an assessment would ideally serve as a general screening tool yet provide an opportunity for further diagnosis on a case-need basis. PALS 1–3 (Invernizzi et al., 2003), for example, begins with a brief screening battery consisting of graded word lists and a phonics and spelling inventory. Students meeting the entry-level benchmarks established for their grade level need not be assessed further. Students who do not meet the entry-level or screening benchmarks are further diagnosed with regard to more basic skills. (Graded reading passages are also available for teachers to take running records of students' oral reading accuracy, rate their oral expression, obtain an overall reading speed, and probe comprehension.) Assessment tools that allow teachers to match students to the proper level of texts for instruction and to plan appropriate phonics instruction would serve children best.

Information Teachers Can Use

Does the increased focus on accountability and scientific rigor mean that teachers will not get the instructionally useful information they need from newly designed assessment protocols? It certainly does not have to. Teachers have been making their own formative assessments for teaching for years. Running records of students' oral reading accuracy, miscue analyses, qualitative analyses of students' uncorrected writing samples, and the like have traditionally provided the link between assessment and instruction. While these teacher-made assessments have not always had their technical adequacy established, teachers have relied on them because they make sense, are closely tied to instruction, and reflect their beliefs about reading. They trust that these classroom-based reading assessments are valid—that they measure what they are supposed to measure. But as researchers have frequently pointed out, there is a trade-off between validity and reliability because the most reliable measures are often the narrowest, and the narrowest measures are often the least valid. The tension that exists between scientifically based research standards for assessment versus more grass-roots utilitarian practices of teachers may be summed up by this "validity dilemma" (Mac-Ginitie, 1993, p. 558). As valid as running records appear to be, are all teachers in the school counting the same things as errors? Are they all administering comprehension questions the same way (e.g., look back versus no look back)? Given the same array of student data such as oral reading accuracy, words per minute, and comprehension scores based on eight open-ended questions, would more than one teacher come to the same conclusion about a student's instructional reading level? Would two different teachers in the same school rate and interpret the same writing sample the same way? Research suggests that the answer to these questions is often no, and, as a result, external assessments with scientifically established validity and reliability have recently been imposed.

The result is too often a loss of instructional time and more student testing than ever before. Rather than give up what they consider to be valid, instructionally useful assessment practices such as running records of students' oral reading, most teachers have continued with their own procedures while "adding on" what is externally imposed. The resulting redundancy is staggering. It is common practice for schools with Reading First grants, for example, to administer to all students a complete informal reading inventory, a qualitative writing or spelling assessment, the assessment that comes with their new core reading program, plus externally imposed assessments required for screening, diagnosis, and progress monitoring for Reading First. In some grades, students are additionally required to take the end-of-year state standards tests in reading and math.

Some middle ground may be found in assessments that provide teachers the information they can use to teach tomorrow yet that have scientifically established evidence of technical adequacy. Such assessments must be steeped in familiar classroom practices and reflect the theoretical integrity of how children learn to read. They must be instructionally transparent and logically lead to specific instructional recommendations (Justice, Invernizzi, & Meier, 2002). In addition, ideal assessments are flexible, allowing movement within the assessment procedures to accommodate individual differences in performance. Such an assessment for grades 1 through 3 might have different levels such that not *all* students are thoroughly diagnosed. Such an assessment may have an entry level for general screening and additional deeper levels for more diagnostic information for those who did not meet the screening criteria. The information yielded from all levels should provide practical and reliable information that teachers can use: specific reading levels, phonics and spelling features, specific letter-recognition needs, letter sounds, and the like. Assessments associated with core reading programs should be carefully considered with respect to their instructional value. Components selected should be interspersed in brief intervals across time as quick probes for curricular congruency. It makes sense, for example, for teachers to periodically check students' oral reading accuracy in instructional materials to make sure they are properly placed in the right level text, or to give unannounced "spell checks" to see if certain phonics features or spelling patterns are generalizing to unstudied words. The effectiveness of all of this, however, hinges on relentless communication of purpose and procedure so that the information gleaned will be trustworthy and valid. At the same time, our current concern with policy compliance and the identification of at-risk students must be tempered with a more wholesome attempt to illustrate opportunities to help children in specific areas of literacy need.

References

American Educational Research Association, American Psychological Association, & National Council on Measurement in Education. (1999). *Standards for educational and psychological testing.* Washington, DC: American Educational Research Association.

Bear, D. R., Invernizzi, M., Templeton, S., & Johnston, F. (2004). *Words their way: Word study for phonics, vocabulary, and spelling instruction* (3rd ed.). Upper Saddle River, NJ: Prentice Hall.

Beaver, J. (1997). *Developmental reading assessment.* New York: Celebration Press.

Bryant, B. R., Wiederholt, J. L., & Bryant, D. P. (2004). *Gray diagnostic reading test* (2nd ed.). Austin, TX: PRO-ED.

Deno, S. L. (1985). Curriculum-based measurement: The emerging alternative. *Exceptional Children, 52,* 219–232.

Deno, S. L. (2003). Developments in curriculum-based measurement. *Journal of Special Education, 37,* 184–192.

Ehri, L. C. (2000). Learning to read and learning to spell: Two sides of a coin. *Topics in Language Disorders, 20,* 19–36.

Ellis, N., & Cataldo, S. (1992). Spelling is integral to learning to read. In C. M. Sterling & C. Robson (Eds.), *Psychology, spelling, and education* (pp. 122–142). Clevedon, UK: Multilingual Matters.

Erford, B., Vitali, G., Haas, R., & Boykin, R. (1995). *Essential skills screener.* East Aurora, NY: Slosson.

Evans, J. (1989). *Bias in human reasoning: Causes and consequences.* Hillsdale, NJ: Erlbaum.

Fountas, I. C., & Pinnell, G. S. (1999). *Matching books to readers.* Portsmouth, NH: Heinemann.

Ganske, K. (2000). *Word journeys: Assessment-guided phonics, spelling, and vocabulary instruction.* New York: Guilford.

Good, R. H., & Kaminski, R. A. (Eds.). (2002). *Dynamic indicators of basic early literacy skills* (6th ed.). Retrieved November, 30, 2004, from http://dibels.uoregon.edu

Good, R. H., Wallin, J. U., Simmons, D. C., Kame'enui, E. J., & Kaminski, R. A. (2002). *System-wide percentile ranks for DIBELS benchmark assessment* (Tech. Rep. No. 9). Eugene, OR: University of Oregon.

Henderson, E. H. (1990). *Teaching spelling* (2nd ed.). Boston: Houghton Mifflin.

El Inventorio de Lectura en Espanol de Tejas (Tejas LEE). (2003–2004). Austin: Texas Education Agency and the University of Texas System.

Invernizzi, M., Meier, J. D., & Juel, C. (2003). *Phonological awareness literacy screening* (PALS 1-3). Charlottesville: University of Virginia Press.

Invernizzi, M., Swank, L., Juel, C., & Meier, J. D. (2003). *Phonological awareness literacy screening* (PALS-K). Charlottesville: University of Virginia Press.

Justice, L., Invernizzi, M., & Meier, J. (2002). Designing and implementing an early literacy screening protocol: Suggestions for the speech-language pathologist. *Language, Speech, and Hearing Services in Schools, 33*, 84–101.

Laberge, D., & Samuels, S. J. (1974). Toward a theory of automatic information processing in reading. *Cognitive Psychology, 6*, 293–323.

Leslie, L., & Caldwell, J. (2001). *Qualitative reading inventory–3*. New York: Addison Wesley Longman.

MacGinitie, W. H. (1993). Some limits of assessment. *Journal of Reading, 36*, 556–560.

Marston, D. B., & Magnusson, D. (1988). Curriculum-based assessment: District-level implementation. In J. Graden, J. Zins, & M. Curtis (Eds.), *Alternative educational delivery systems: Enhancing instructional options for all students* (pp. 137–172). Washington, DC: National Association of School Psychologists.

Morris, D., & Perney, J. (1984). Developmental spelling as a predictor of first-grade reading achievement. *Elementary School Journal, 84*, 441–457.

Partridge, H., Invernizzi, M., Meier, J., & Sullivan, A. (2003, November/December). Linking assessment and instruction via Web-based technology: A case study of a statewide early literacy initiative. *Reading Online, 7*(3). Retrieved November 17, 2004, from http://www.readingonline. org/articles/art_index.asp?HREF=partridge/index.html

Pinnell, G. S., Pikulski, J. J., Wixson, K. K., Campbell, J. R., Gough, P. B., & Beatty, A. S. (1995). *Listening to children read aloud*. Washington, DC: U.S. Department of Education, National Center for Education Statistics.

Rasinski, T. V. (2000). Speed does matter in reading. *The Reading Teacher, 54*, 146–151.

Rathvon, N. (2004). *Early reading assessment: A practitioner's handbook*. New York: Guilford.

Schlagal, R. (1986). Informal and qualitative assessment of spelling. *Pointer, 30*(2), 37–41.

Speece, D., Mills, C., Ritchey, K., & Hillman, E. (2003). Initial evidence that letter fluency tasks are valid indicators of early reading skill. *Journal of Special Education, 36*, 223–233.

Sweet, A. P., & Snow, C. E. (Eds.). (2003). *Rethinking reading comprehension*. New York: Guilford.

Texas Primary Reading Inventory. (2003–2004). Austin: Texas Education Agency and the University of Texas System.

Torgesen, J. K. (2003). *Establishing a firm foundation: Phonemic awareness and phonics*. Retrieved June 3, 2004, from http://www.justreadflorida.org/conf-03-lead/ppt-torgesen.pdf

Torgesen, J. K., Wagner, R. K., & Rashotte, C. A. (1999). *Test of word reading efficiency*. Austin, TX: PRO-ED.

Torgesen, J. K., Wagner, R. K., Rashotte, C. A., Burgess, S., & Hecht, S. (1997). Contributions of phonological awareness and rapid naming ability to growth of word-reading skills in second to fifth grade. *Scientific Studies of Reading, 12*, 161–185.

Viise, N. M. (1994). *Feature word spelling list: A diagnosis of progressing word knowledge through an assessment of spelling errors*. Unpublished doctoral dissertation, University of Virginia, Charlottesville.

Zutell, J., & Rasinski, T. (1989). Reading and spelling connections in third and fifth grade students. *Reading Psychology, 10*, 137–155.

How Well Does Assessment Inform Our Reading Instruction?

MICHAEL C. MCKENNA AND SHARON WALPOLE

Nowadays the word *assessment* is apt to conjure up unpleasant thoughts of the often acrimonious controversy involving high-stakes testing (e.g., Allington, 2002). As important as we know that debate to be, in our view there is an issue of far greater consequence facing reading educators. To what extent is the instruction they provide informed by the results of assessments? In this column, we will contrast what we believe has long been the norm for assessments with a promising trend spurred by recent U.S. federal initiatives such as Reading First. Like our colleagues in a recent article in this journal (Invernizzi, Landrum, Howell, & Warley, 2005), we see great potential for "peaceful coexistence" between policymakers and teachers when assessments are chosen and used to plan effective instruction.

Consider Ms. Henderson (pseudonym), a conscientious teacher who has taught second grade for many years. Her school has always provided her with a program that offers a variety of materials and resources. This core program includes various assessment tools that help her place students in the series and monitor their progress through unit tests. This teacher does not administer all of the assessments because she feels she lacks the time to conduct them and the expertise to interpret them accurately; nor does her school provide time for her to work with her colleagues to consider these issues. Ms. Henderson's students progress through the core materials all year, though some of them fall further behind despite her efforts.

At issue is how Ms. Henderson recognizes and addresses the specific needs of each of these students during this pivotal time in their development. Her core materials include supplemental strands, but she is uncertain about which students would profit from them, how to schedule such activities, and how to tell when the strands have accomplished their purpose. To complicate matters, she has collected over the years a hodgepodge of specialized materials—workbooks, kits, software, and the like. She sometimes uses these on a trial-and-error basis with her struggling students but has been largely disappointed with the results. Sometimes these materials appear to

McKenna, M. C., & Walpole, S. (2005). How well does assessment inform our reading instruction? *The Reading Teacher (59)*, 84–86.

work, however, and she keeps them as a last-resort measure that might assist some of her children. If they don't seem to work, she abdicates her instructional responsibility to the Title I or special education teachers. (Title I is a U.S. federally funded program for at-risk students.) Ms. Henderson is, we suspect, typical of teachers trying to make the best of the materials they have in the limited time available to them.

An Alternative

Now let's contrast this teacher's approach with the more structured alternative emerging from initiatives like Reading First. We believe that the model of assessment-driven instruction embraced by this reform effort has much to recommend it. It assumes that elementary teachers will be using a core reading program and that additional materials have been purchased, both to supplement weaknesses in the core and to offer intensive intervention in key areas. This is no different from the programs we have seen in most U.S. schools and classrooms. An expectation, however, is that these materials do not amount to a hodgepodge collected over time but have been carefully selected by school and district representatives to constitute a coherent reading program. The Reading First model further assumes that valid and reliable assessments of various types are in use. These include (a) screening measures to alert classroom teachers to troublesome areas of reading development; (b) diagnostic assessments to aid teachers as they attempt to address the problems identified through screening; (c) progress-monitoring tests to gauge whether instruction and intervention efforts are working; and (d) outcome measures, which include not only those inescapable high-stakes tests but also other indicators as well. These assessments may be part of the commercial materials used, or they may operate independently of materials. Phonological Awareness Literacy Screening (Invernizzi, Meier, & Juel, 2003) and Dynamic Indicators of Basic Early Literacy Skills (Good & Kaminski, 2002) are two such measures; for other examples, see Web-based summary documents prepared by the Florida Center for Reading Research (2002–2003) or the Reading First Assessment Committee (Kame'enui, 2002).

The First Step

Choosing assessments is only the first step toward using assessments. In Figure 1, we have tried to capture the assessment-driven instruction model in a decision-making chart. It illustrates how students who do not progress adequately within the core program are identified early through quick, periodic screening measures given at least three times a year. These students are grouped flexibly to receive extra assistance that is planned on the basis of diagnostic assessments that may accompany the program materials. When regular progress-monitoring assessments indicate that their needs have been met, these students return to the mainstream core activities.

We have worked with many elementary school administrators and teachers who are struggling to improve the reading achievement of their students. Some of them "must" use the assessment-driven instruction model because the legislation, in a sense, requires it.

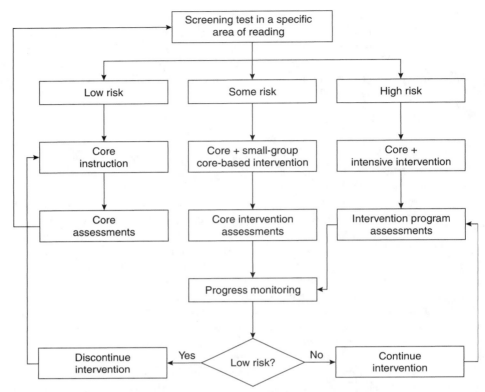

FIGURE 1   A Model of Assessment-Driven Reading Instruction

However, collecting and reporting the data are a far cry from actually using data to inform instruction for every student. That takes continual support in the form of professional development and collegial collaboration, again mandated but not always realized in Reading First (Walpole & McKenna, 2004). When we work in schools not constrained by Reading First mandates, we still conceptualize assessment in this way, and we still must provide and participate in extensive professional development and collegial collaboration. We suspect that expert teachers of reading have always conceptualized assessment in this manner, and there is compelling evidence that schools successful in meeting the needs of struggling readers gather and use data in structured and systematic ways (Taylor, Pearson, Clark, & Walpole, 2000). The assessment model in Reading First may focus our collective attention on issues that have always been part of our work to support student achievement: how best to understand and accelerate the progress of our students.

References

Allington, R. L. (Ed.). (2002). *Big brother and the national reading curriculum: How ideology trumped evidence*. Portsmouth, NH: Heinemann.

Florida Center for Reading Research. (2002–2003). *Pre-kindergarten and kindergarten emergent literacy skills assessments.* Retrieved March 3, 2005, from http:// www.fcrr.org/assessment/index.htm

Good, R. H., & Kaminski, R. A. (2002). *Dynamic indicators of basic early literacy skills* (6th ed.). Retrieved March 3, 2005, from http://dibels.uoregon.edu

Invernizzi, M. A., Landrum, T. J., Howell, J. L., & Warley, H. P. (2005). Toward the peaceful coexistence of test developers, policymakers, and teachers in an era of accountability. *The Reading Teacher, 58,* 610–618.

Invernizzi, M., Meier, J., & Juel, C. (2003). *Phonological awareness literacy screening (PALS 1-3).* Charlottesville, VA: University of Virginia Press.

Kame'enui, E. J. (2002). *Analysis of reading assessment instruments for K–3.* Retrieved March 3, 2005, from http://idea.uoregon.edu/assessment/index.html

Taylor, B. M., Pearson, P. D., Clark, K. F., & Walpole, S. (2000). Effective schools and accomplished teachers: Lessons about primary-grade reading instruction in low-income schools. *Elementary School Journal, 101,* 121–165.

Walpole, S., & McKenna, M. C. (2004). *The literacy coach's handbook.* New York: Guilford.

Classroom Implications

1. What barriers do you anticipate in implementing assessment-driven instruction in your setting? How might you overcome such barriers?

2. What are some specific reading assessments that might be useful in informing your instructional planning?

For Further Reading

Diamond, L. (2005). Assessment-driven instruction: A systems approach. *Perspectives, 31*(4), 33–37.

Popham, W. J. (2003). *Test better, teach better: The instructional role of assessment.* Alexandria, VA: ASCD.

Online Resources

Boston, C. (2001). The Debate over National Testing. ERIC Digest.
www.eric.ed.gov/ERICDocs/data/ericdocs2/content_storage_01/0000000b/80/2a/34/28.pdf

International Reading Association. (1999). High-Stakes Assessments in Reading. Position Statement.
www.reading.org/positions/high_stakes.html

La Marca, P. M. (2001). Alignment of Standards and Assessments as an Accountability Criterion. ERIC Digest.
www.eric.ed.gov/ERICDocs/data/ericdocs2/content_storage_01/0000000b/80/2a/34/3c.pdf

National Council of Teachers of English. (1999). Resolution on High-Stakes Testing.
www.ncte.org/about/over/positions/category/assess/118588.htm

American Educational Research Association. (2000). High-stakes testing in PreK–12 education. (Position Statement).
www.aera.net/policyandprograms/?id=378

Phonemic Awareness Literacy Screening (PALS). Free screening system developed at the University of Virginia.
http://pals.virginia.edu

Dynamic Indicators of Basic Early Literacy Skills (DIBELS). Free screening system developed at the University of Oregon.
http://dibels.uoregon.edu

Chapter 7

Literacy Coaching

In schools where teachers work with [literacy] coaches regularly, teachers, coaches and administrators report a growth of collaborative teacher culture marked by increased teacher willingness and ability to collaborate, peer accountability, and individual teacher knowledge about other teachers classrooms.

—Kiley Reynolds (2003)

Because the primary role of reading coaches is to provide support to classroom teachers for classroom reading instruction, it is essential that they be excellent classroom teachers themselves.

—International Reading Association (2004)

The coach's major job is to provide professional development and support to teachers to improve [literacy] instruction.

—Camile Blachowicz et al. (2005)

Leaders are made, not born. They are made by hard effort, which is the price which all of us must pay to achieve any goal that is worthwhile.

—Vince Lombardi

What exactly is a literacy coach? While consensus standards are emerging (e.g., the joint standards for middle school coaches developed by the International Reading Association (IRA), the National Council of Teachers of English (NCTE), the National Council of Teachers of Mathematics (NCTM), the National Science Teachers Association (NSTA), and the National Council for the Social Studies (NCSS), the most appropriate job descriptions are still evolving and the current dialogue is rich and varied. However, there seems to be complete agreement on one matter: The primary function of a coach is to facilitate professional development. Most educators would agree that the minimal course requirements at the preservice level fail to adequately prepare beginning teachers for the challenges of effective reading instruction. This means that their continued growth must be fostered once they enter the profession, and it is not enough to assume that the "on-the-job training" involved in running a classroom will be sufficient. An effective program of professional development can play an important role, and the literacy coach is well situated to make it happen.

Just what can a coach do, specifically, to facilitate the professional growth of teachers in a school? Although no exhaustive list exists, a literacy coach can enhance the expertise and practice of classroom teachers in *at least* the following ways:

- observing and conducting follow-up conferences with individual teachers
- modeling a particular instructional approach while a teacher observes
- organizing book study groups
- interpreting achievement data and meeting with grade-level groups and individual teachers to discuss patterns
- learning as much as possible about commercial programs in use
- arranging for sales representatives to visit the school to address implementation issues
- conducting professional development surveys
- establishing, monitoring, and contributing to teacher blogs
- researching the answers to questions posed by teachers
- arranging for consultants to visit the school to address focused topics identified through surveys or achievement patterns
- following up such presentations by observing individuals or meeting with groups of teachers.

These last two points lead to an important caveat. By far the worst approach to professional development begins with a presentation by a consultant or some other expert and ends with teachers being left to their own devices as to how the ideas presented will be implemented in their classrooms. Typically, they listen politely and then return to business as usual. This system is sometimes disparagingly referred to as "drive-by" professional development or "the seagull approach," in which an expert flies in, drops his load, and flies out again. Such derogatory characterizations capture a long history of dismal research. One-shot presentations, without follow-up, usually do not have the intended effect. The coach, however, is positioned to make such presentations more effective by making follow-up visits to classrooms, meeting with grade-level groups, and so forth.

A coach might also facilitate degree or endorsement programs. These are costly and time-consuming, but they meet the needs of recertification and help to build a working community of literacy educators. We make this latter point not just because it sounds good or because the interests of our institutions are served. When a school is populated by teachers knowledgeable about reading, a climate conducive to growth is created. A good example involves an elementary school in Kansas. All of the teachers attained their state reading endorsement through a district-paid project. Subsequent reading achievement scores rose significantly (Miller & Ellsworth, 1985). Of course, not all degree programs and endorsements are the same. Regrettably, some include fluff and theory while minimizing practical applications. Nevertheless, this route to professional development can be a very effective one, and a literacy coach can organize and promote such a program.

As You Read

Coaching entails a host of practical questions, and these two articles address many of them. Walpole takes a general approach reflecting her extensive experiences as an elementary literacy coach, while Buly and her colleagues focus specifically on the middle school. Among the questions they address, sometimes fully and sometimes in passing, are these: What exactly should a coach be doing? How will the cost of a coach be budgeted? (Reading First grants have paved the way, but what about other contexts in which outside funding is not available?) And just what credentials should a coach possess? Should a person serving in this position be a reading specialist, for example? If so, should the coach be expected to assume part-time teaching duties? What relationship works best between the coach and the principal? How far should a coach be expected to go in contending with resistant teachers? Don't expect definitive answers to these questions. Do expect to see them addressed extensively in the professional literature over the next few years.

References

Blachowicz, C. L., Obrochta, C., & Fogelberg, E. (2005). Literacy coaching for change. *Educational Leadership, 62,* 55–58.

International Reading Association. (2004). *The role and qualifications of the reading coach in the United States.* Newark, DE: International Reading Association.

Miller, J. W., & Ellsworth, R. E. (1985). Evaluation of a two-year program to improve teacher effectiveness in reading instruction. *Elementary School Journal, 85,* 485–496.

Reynolds, K. (2003). *Literacy coaching: How school districts can support a long-term strategy in a short-term world.* San Francisco: Bay Area School Reform Collaborative.

Standards for middle and high school literacy coaches. (2005). Joint publication of the Carnegie Corporation, IRA, NCTE, NCTM, NSTA, and NCSS. Available online at www.reading.org/resources/issues/reports/coaching.html

Coaching in Context: Crafting a Site-Based Staff Development System

SHARON WALPOLE

School-wide instructional change may look easy on paper—examine current achievement and instructional practice, identify areas for change, and provide materials and support to initiate and sustain the change. What is not so easy in practice is making the change truly school-wide; providing the type and amount of support necessary for every teacher to internalize and manage the instructional change in the complicated everyday world of teaching and learning. With increasing frequency, professional development initiatives are including site-based coaches to provide that support. Federally-funded school-wide change efforts have created an instant demand for such coaches. In fact, Reading First initiatives in almost every state require (and provide funding for) a literacy coach to spearhead school-level staff development. In many states, school-based coaches are supported by regional coaches. And in all of these instances, the pressure on the coaches to produce increased achievement is very real.

Few individuals have professional training as coaches—of necessity, many coaches are learning on the job. The International Reading Association (2004) produced a position statement to address the role and qualifications of the reading coach. Ideally, the IRA Board of Directors indicated that a coach is an excellent reading teacher, with extensive knowledge of reading research, specialized training in working with adult learners, and experience in providing a cycle of modeling, observing, and providing feedback. A coach with these qualifications would be in a powerful position to support teaching and learning.

I have worked as a coach in a federally-funded initiative and currently work to provide support to building-level and regional coaches. What I have learned about coaching is that it can be either an effective or an ineffective strategy for improving teaching and learning. One key to effectiveness may be clarity in the building's goal and the match of the coach's knowledge, skills, and activities with those goals. Below I provide discussion of the context for coaching and also lessons that might guide an instructional leadership team in setting and supporting the stage for coaching. Finally, I provide a challenge to coaches to provide ongoing, non-evaluative, differentiated support for teachers.

Reprinted with permission from the International Dyslexia Association Quarterly periodical, *Perspectives, 41*, Fall 2005, by Sharon Walpole.

220

Why Use Coaching?

There are strong themes in the professional development literature about the characteristics of efforts that are effective in promoting changes in instruction and in achievement, and coaching is emerging as a strategy to capitalize on those themes. First, professional development must be situated within the knowledge and skills of the adult learners who are targeted—what they believe about teaching and learning matters (Richardson, 1990). Second, theory-only, stand-and-deliver sessions are rarely effective; specific, active initiatives, with teachers reviewing student work, are more likely to produce change (Anders, Hoffman, & Duffy 2000; Birman, Desimone, Porter, & Garet, 2000). Systematic, long-term, sustained efforts hold promise. Such efforts do involve theory, but also include demonstration, practice, observation and feedback. They are designed to be sensitive to the district- and school-level context, and they are supported by the school's leadership (Joyce & Showers, 1988) In this way the staff development is sensitive to issues of content, context, and process. It is directly aimed at increasing teacher and administrator knowledge, influencing the practices of both. If both knowledge and practice are changed, school policies improve (Guskey & Sparks, 1996). That combined emphasis on building knowledge, improving practice, and changing school policy has real potential to influence student achievement—realizing the power of a thoughtful coaching program.

What Is Coaching?

For districts and schools who say they are using coaching as a form of professional development, the first question that I ask is what do *you* mean by coaching? Many models for coaching may be effective, especially if they are adopted deliberately. When people ask me what coaching is, I always answer that coaching is doing whatever it takes to support a teacher's growth within his or her own classroom and school. There are many models, and no research documents which is best. In fact, I imagine that best is relative—the best coaching model for a given setting is the one that is most directly responsive to the needs of the learners in that setting. Three very different models described below give some indication of the diversity in approaches.

One early form of coaching is called collaborative consultation. Collaborative consultation has a long history in the special education community (Friend, 1988), and it has been proposed as a role for reading specialists (Jaeger, 1996). In both instances, a specialist spends part of his or her day working with children and part working with adults who are seeking support. This type of coaching involves a voluntary relationship between a classroom teacher and a specialist with the general aim of providing more effective instruction for a child or group of children who are struggling in the classroom. It is the classroom teacher who identifies the goals of the consultation and the specialist responds to those goals. Ostensibly, then, a planned system for collaborative consultation would demand that the specialist has some time set aside to provide the service and that teachers can access the service in an organized way.

Another coaching model with broad support and applicability is the peer coaching model developed and tested by Beverly Showers and Bruce Joyce. In this coaching model, once a new practice is identified and introduced, all teachers in a school are organized into small peer coaching teams who plan together and model for one another (Showers & Joyce, 1996). The coaching occurs primary through modeling. When a teacher is being observed, he or she is coaching the colleagues who are observing. Peer coaching, then, demands time for shared planning and classroom observations among the members of each team. This model might be most useful for an effort focused on one specific instructional change that could be integrated into all classrooms; it might allow school leadership teams to design long-term follow-up strategies to augment the introduction of new theories, avoiding the pitfalls of theory-only sessions. One strength of this model is that it does not demand that a new staff member be added; that may also be a weakness if the needs of teachers are great.

Mike McKenna and I have proposed a different model for coaching, one nested within massive school-wide instructional change (Walpole & McKenna, 2004). Our model assumes that a coach is a full-time member of the staff whose only focus is working with adults—at first blush, a costly stance. However, we also see the responsibilities of a coach as extensive and inconsistent with the daily responsibilities of teaching children. Our coach works as a partner with the principal and with the teachers to set school-wide goals, design an assessment system, evaluate the instructional schedule, select curriculum resources, provide theory-based presentations, analyze data, and model, observe, and provide feedback in classrooms. It is within that definition of coaching which I frame some general themes to consider in the design of a coaching program.

Understanding the Context

A coach who does not work to understand the context of the school in which he or she is serving is like a soccer coach who only knows football rules. Everyone (players, parents, referees) would revolt, and no positive outcomes would be realized. Successful coaching is specific. It is nested within a particular school and district. It is sensitive to the community served by the school, the state curriculum and testing requirements, the state and district textbook adoption calendar, and the state and district regulations for special services (e.g., Title I and special education). In short, successful coaching is unique. That is not to say that outsiders cannot coach; in fact, outsiders who respectfully and thoroughly investigate the context may be especially well suited to support change.

Whether a coach is an insider or an outsider, there are some specific strategies that can help him or her to understand the context. First, a series of walk-throughs can provide a very good sense of how the curriculum in the school is enacted in classrooms. Coaches can notice the extent to which instruction is consistent between and across the grade levels, what grouping configurations are currently used, what curriculum materials are actually used by individual teachers, how classrooms are configured. They can notice strong classroom managers and teachers who struggle. A week of classroom walk-throughs can sensitize a coach to many, many strengths and issues in a particular school, especially if the coach helps the teachers to understand that he or she is walking through to learn about the school's strengths.

Walk-throughs are necessary but not sufficient to understanding the context of a school. Another important piece of any school's puzzle is the culture of planning. How and when do you typically plan your day is a very important question to ask. Why do you plan individually or at the grade level? What does the principal require in terms of evidence of planning? What are the strengths and weaknesses that teachers see in the current culture of planning? The answers given by individual teachers and by groups of teachers illustrate the existing collaborative structures and also where and why some teachers will be reluctant to collaborate.

And finally, understanding the context means understanding the history of student achievement in the building. Most teachers will say that their students made substantial progress last year, and that is important. However, a coach must actively confront the data that answer questions about grade-level goals; that data is part of the school's story. How many students achieved at district and state benchmarks? What percentage of students passed criterion-referenced tests at each grade level? Was success influenced by student demographics, or did all groups achieve equally? Was data collected systematically during the school year to make instructional decisions? What data were collected but not used? Coaches that I work with tend to begin their tenure afraid of summarizing school-level data, but, once they do it, they realize the power of that process to provide a focus for instructional change.

Organizing for Teaching and Learning

Once a coach understands the context, he or she can begin to address structural characteristics that either help or hinder teaching and learning. It is in this area more than any other that collaboration with the principal is essential. A coach without the support of the principal may be able to support change, but not quickly. The biggest obstacle to school-wide change that I have seen over and over is a fragmented school schedule. In many schools, the schedule seems to be divinely ordained and immutable. In fact, the schedule is made by people and it can be remade by people.

In making school-level schedules, I have learned that there are a set of decisions that must be made before the hands-on work begins.

1. How much uninterrupted time is needed in each area of the curriculum?
2. When will teachers have shared planning time?
3. Will differentiation be accomplished by grouping children within their heterogeneous classrooms or across classrooms?
4. When will additional instruction take place? What will it replace in the curriculum?

If the initial conceptual commitments are made, some of the scheduling options become more obvious. Ideally, coaches will work with teachers and administrators to weigh these questions, and they will be ready for implementation at the start of a new school year.

In the area of time, for example, if 2.5 hours are needed to teach reading and writing, 1 hour to teach math, and 1 hour to teach either science or social studies, teacher schedules are much less free. The school schedule, especially for the "specials" (music, physical education, art, technology, library, group counseling) must be manipulated to preserve teaching time and provide transitions for children between (rather than during) instructional blocks. It is easiest to conceptualize this by considering that the teachers at each grade level might have all of their specials at the same time each day. In fact, in many schools, specials teachers negotiate their own schedules with classroom teachers rather than working together as a specials team to protect chunks of instructional time in all classrooms. Coaches can help re-envision instructional time so that teachers have time to teach and children have time to learn.

It might be easier to commit to such a schedule if the teachers earn shared planning time through their sacrifice of independent choices. Planning time during the regular work day is often more productive than after-school meetings. If all teachers at a given grade level or on a specific instructional team have their children at specials at the same time, then they can meet together to collaborate. If that is not possible (usually because the number of specials are too few) the schedule might be constructed so that a team of regular substitutes is used to move across the school, giving specific teams one or two hours of shared planning time. That shared planning time is essential to the coach's role of providing professional support during the school day, scheduling study groups to read professional literature, to review student data, to learn about new curriculum materials, or to group or regroup students as their achievement changes.

Grouping decisions put additional constraints on the schedule. Planned and flexible groups are at the heart of a well-structured differentiation plan. When teachers realize that students' needs are different, they should provide them with different types and amounts of instruction. Some instruction is best provided to all children in the class, but other instruction is best provided to needs-based groups. Managing groups is no small task. Mike McKenna and I have worked with schools using different grouping plans: parallel-block schedules (where teachers from two classes each send half of their class to a special and keep the rest), within-class groupings (where a teacher groups and regroups his or her heterogeneous homeroom class into several groups more homogeneous by achievement) and between-class groupings (where several teachers group and regroup among more than one homeroom class). There are costs and benefits to each grouping decision, especially in terms of scheduling. Parallel block schedules tend to minimize teacher planning time, within-class groupings are easy to schedule, but tend to minimize the instructional time for each group and put pressure on teachers to integrate many independent activities into their routines; between-class groupings tend to focus teacher preparation time for fewer groups who meet for longer periods, but they are more complicated to schedule into the master schedule. Again, each of these grouping configurations can be both manageable and successful. For a coach, having a school-wide commitment to a specific grouping configuration is essential to providing organized and consistent professional support.

Whatever grouping decisions are made, needs-based instruction will not be sufficient to support achievement for all students. In the area of additional instruction, teachers and administrators must face the fact that they cannot *make* time (unless they extend the school day). They must *take* time from other activities. Moving such instruction into the classroom, in the form of "push-in" Title I and special education services, allows the school to take time away from individual practice or choice time and replace it with more specialized instruction. In order to do that, though, teachers must make the commitment to organized, consistent instructional routines so that when specialists are scheduled to provide additional instruction, the children they are to work with have already had instruction and are able to get additional help. A classic rotation of small-group instruction, seatwork, and centers time is a good model. If specialists are to provide specialized instruction during the rotation, their children's rotation must be well orchestrated so that centers and seatwork time is predictable. And, to use specialists efficiently, teachers must coordinate their schedules across classrooms so that the specialists can move quickly. A coach can provide the leadership and support to make that possible.

Using Data for Decisions

Grouping plans and thoughtful master calendars provide the organizational structure for improving teaching and learning in a school-wide reform, but the driving force in the instructional change must be data. I have begun to think that two types of data are equally useful to the coach who is helping teachers to understand and address students' needs: student achievement data, especially targeted, curriculum-specific progress-monitoring data, and data on teacher instruction. The real question that faces all coaches is a correlational question about teaching and learning: what type, amount, and intensity of classroom instruction is associated with the student achievement that the building is targeting? Once the coach answers that question, the next step he or she must take is to learn from the teachers who are successful in the reform and then provide support to those who are not yet successful.

Nurturing Honest Relationships

Again, this is no easy task. Coaches watch teachers work, on good days and on challenging days. Coaches evaluate data that indicate progress and problems. Coaches are entering teachers' classrooms, sometimes for the first time. However, this is the heart of coaching. Coaching is happening when a coach and a teacher can have an honest and confidential conversation about teaching and learning. Coaching is happening when a teacher admits a struggle, and a coach responds with a slate of supportive options (co-planning, modeling, observation and feedback) to allow the teacher to select the type of help that is most comfortable.

Some of the novice coaches that I have worked with tend to avoid uncomfortable conversations about teaching` and learning. That is a coaching mistake. Others tend to respond to teachers with overly-positive feedback. Again, a mistake. I have learned that the heart of coaching is honesty, compassion, and a positive outlook. Once a problem is identified, coaches and teachers can go about addressing it together. Coaches must know that teachers have always struggled and worked diligently, especially in times of instructional change. Few, though, have had support, especially not compassionate, immediate, differentiated, non-evaluative support.

The Need for Relentlessness

Within the school-wide change model, coaches have enormous responsibility and enormous potential to support teacher growth. They work with the building's leadership to gain deep understanding of the context, to provide options for better organizing it for teaching and learning, they guide the use of data for instructional decision-making, and they build and nurture relationships with teachers. A good coach, facing a struggling teacher or a disappointing data set, decides to try something new. A good coach is a relentless support for the adult who works every day to provide relentless support for children.

As I think about the need for relentlessness among coaches themselves, I also think about the need for relentless research studies to define and describe many successful approaches to coaching. The key will be choosing the one that is right for your school.

Resources for Coaches

Several recent books provide practical suggestions for coaches:

Block, C. C., & Israel, S. E. (2005). *Reading First and beyond: The complete guide for teachers and literacy coaches.* Thousand Oaks, CA: Corwin Press.

Guskey, T. R., & Sparks, D. (1996). Exploring the relationship between staff development and improvements in student learning. *Journal of Staff Development 17*, 34–38.

Toll, C. A. (2005). *The literacy coach's survival guide: Essential questions and practical answers.* Newark, DE: International Reading Association.

Walpole, S., & McKenna, M. C. (2004). *The literacy coach's handbook: A guide to research-based practice.* New York: Guilford Press.

Additional Helpful Web-Based Resources

Hall, B. (2004, Fall). *Literacy coaches: An evolving role.* Retrieved August 30, 2005 from http://www.carnegie.org/reporter/09/literacy

Russo, A. (2004, July/August). *School-based coaching: A revolution in professional development—or just the latest fad.* Retrieved August 30, 2005 from http://www.edletter.org/past/issues/2004-ja/coaching.shtml

Learning Point Associates. (2004*). Reading First coaching: A guide for coaches and Reading First Leaders.* Retrieved August 30, 2005 from http://www.ncrel.org/litweb/coaching

References

Anders, P. A., Hoffman, J. V., & Duffy, G. G. (2000). Teaching teachers to teach reading: Paradigm shifts, persistent problems, and challenges. In M. Kamil, P. Mosenthal, P. D. Pearson, & R. Barr (Eds.), *Handbook of reading research: Vol 3* (pp. 721–744). Mahwah, NJ: Lawrence Erlbaum.

Birman, B. F., Desimone, L., Porter, A. C., & Garet, M. S. (2000, May). Designing professional development that works. *Educational Leadership*, 28–33.

Friend, M. (1988). Putting consultation into context: Historical and contemporary perspectives. *Remedial and Special Education, 9*, 7–13.

International Reading Association. (2004). *The role and qualifications of the reading coach in the United States.* Newark, DE: Author.

Jaeger, E. J. (1996). The reading specialist as collaborative consultant. *Reading Teacher, 49*, 622–629.

Joyce, B., & Showers, B. (1988). *Student achievement through staff development.* White Plains, NY: Longman Inc.

Richardson, V. (1990). Significant and worthwhile change in teaching practice. *Educational Researcher, 19*, 10–18.

Showers, B., & Joyce, B. (1996, March). The evolution of peer coaching. *Educational Leadership, 56*, 12–17.

Literacy Coaching: Coming Out of the Corner

MARSHA RIDDLE BULY, TRACY COSKIE, LEANNE ROBINSON, AND KATHY EGAWA

• • • • •

. . . [T]wo years ago, the idea of literacy coaching was just beginning to gain popularity. It is now red-hot. Reading coaches, literacy coaches, and instructional coaches are being hired in almost all schools across the nation.

The roles of coaches, the support they receive, and the rapport they are able to gain with teachers during instructional sessions, however, varies dramatically. The multiple definitions, descriptions, and support relating to coaching concern us, especially as coaching continues to move from elementary into middle and high schools. We fear that coaching will go the way of whole language, multiage classrooms, and developmentally appropriate practice where misunderstandings and a lack of systematically reported data on student impact prevented their widespread implementation.

Over the past two years, we have talked with many coaches and administrators, reviewed the literature that is available about coaching, begun to collect data on student outcomes, and visited coaching sessions—some effective, some less effective. . . .

Effective Coaches Have Clearly Defined Job Descriptions

As the notion of literacy coaches has increased in popularity, districts are hiring for a job that often hasn't before existed in a school. In the best situations, a carefully considered job description has been conveyed, understood, and accepted by both administrators and teachers in a district. The description must include what we believe to be the absolute essential for success—the non-evaluative role of the coach. Effective instructional coaching requires a collegial relationship built around trust and mutual goals.

Coaches are not simply reading teachers redefined. Where a reading teacher might model strategies and skills for teachers, a coach truly works with a teacher to shift understandings. NCTE and the International Reading Association (IRA) in collaboration with the National Council of Teachers of Mathematics, the National Science Teachers Association, and the National Council for the Social Studies devised Standards for Middle and High School Literacy Coaches (2006). The document "outlines the ideal of what a literacy coach should know and be able to do in delivering both leadership and support in individual content areas. It is offered as a blueprint not only for literacy coaches themselves, but for policymakers, school and district administrators, and teacher educators, in the hope that it will help support and develop coaching in ways that will most benefit adolescent learners." This document is available at http://www.reading.org/resources/issues/reports/coaching.html.

Effective Coaches Have Support over Time

If coaches are to be successful, they must have support over time and it must be part of the design before they are hired. They must have support in developing their own skills as coaches. One model for coaching offered through The Learning Network (Richard C. Owen Publishers) includes a carefully structured support system. This is the system that Bellingham School District first used and then adapted to be their own. The first year, a newly selected coach is coached in his or her classroom as he or she deepens personal instructional reflection. The second year, the coach begins to coach others and is coached, in a transparent manner, in front of the teachers he or she is coaching, by a more experienced coach. The more experienced coach helps administrators to clearly understand the role of the new coaches in the school. The district and the coaches recognized that coaches continue to do best when they have support even after the second year, so a mechanism for that continued support has been developed.

Essential Components of an Effective Coaching Session Can Be Identified and Defined

Effective instructional coaching is really a structured conversation with a focus on mutual goals. The conversation consists of a dialogue focused on areas and questions identified by the person receiving the coaching. That conversation revolves around instruction, with the purpose of improving student learning. The coach offers insights, but does not overtly direct a teacher. Coaches listen carefully and talk little. Coaches then nudge, similar to what happens in effective writing conferences, helping the teacher think critically about his or her instructional practice. When this reflective dialogue is free of judgment, teachers are more likely to make real and lasting changes in their practice, which should ultimately benefit their students.

As the coach talks with the teacher, the coach skillfully prompts the teacher to continually ask "why"; this is accomplished by helping the teacher to clarify understandings and objectives while considering assessments and mandated state outcomes.

The instructional dialogue ends when the teacher has stated one next teaching and learning point—not three teaching points, not five teaching points, but *one* clear point. At that juncture, the teacher knows where he or she will focus, and the coach knows what to watch for in the next observation and where the teacher may need support.

Developing reflection comes as a result of the structured conversation focused on mutual goals. The conversation provides a teacher (or person being coached) with feedback and assistance in such a way that he or she is able to state clearly, "This is *what* I am doing, *why* I am doing it, and *how* I can change my practice to make instruction more effective." This is instructional dialogue.

In her book on conducting effective instructional dialogue, *Developing Effective Teachers through Instructional Dialogue* (Richard C. Owen, in press), author and coach of coaches, Marilyn Duncan, reminds us that our educational culture has often been one where teachers are told what to do and how to do it, but not necessarily with the understanding of why it's important. It can, therefore, be disconcerting to be asked about the why. It takes skill, which can be learned, to know how to ask a teacher "why?" without it sounding like an accusation.

The way in which the conversation begins is critical. A good way for a coach to open such a conversation might be to ask a question similar to that suggested by Cathy Toll (2005, p. 59): "When you think about your goals for teaching—the kind of readers and writers you want your students to be, the kind of classroom you want to have, and the kind of work you want to do—what gets in your way?" This question allows the teacher (or coach being coached) to begin to think about *why* without feeling defensive. This question also shows the teacher that he or she is setting the agenda. Once set by the person being coached, the coach is then able to help the teacher become reflective about what needs to happen.

Coaching May Look Different in Middle and High Schools

As coaching moves into middle and high schools, one challenge often comes when a model that has been effective in elementary schools is implemented in middle or high

---

Questions for Guiding More Research

1. What are effective ways to prepare and support literacy coaches?
2. How do various models of coaching influence the culture of the school?
3. How can we compare literacy coaching across contexts when schools are enacting different coaching models?
4. What are the characteristics of highly effective coaches? What professional qualifications, prior experiences, and training are related to success in the coaching role?
5. How is coaching enacted differently in settings with different accountability statuses? (See Teachers' College Record for a discussion of how assessment looks different in schools on watch lists than those making AYP: http://www.tcrecord.org/Content.asp?ContentID=11569.)

schools without appropriate consideration or adaptation to the world of secondary schools. High schools are not elementary schools. The teachers are trained differently and they are often assigned to very different teaching situations—usually focusing on one or two content areas with many students throughout the day.

Middle and high school teachers are usually hired for a position because they have focused on the specific content of a particular area of the curriculum. The perception is usually that middle and high school teaching, therefore, is all about the content of a specific discipline. While that is true, how the knowledge is imparted is equally important. In that respect, elementary teachers may have an advantage about delivery. Their preparation tends to emphasize teaching methodology across several subjects for a range of students, whereas secondary preparation programs often have a heavier emphasis on content with less emphasis on individualization of instruction. As a result, middle and high school teachers may need extra help thinking about the *why* behind their instructional practices and assistance in identifying alternative methods of instruction for students who are not successfully accessing content. Classrooms in the upper grades are often filled with students who are several years behind grade-level standards as well as students who are ready for more than what is offered. Simply teaching the content isn't going to work for a large portion of the students.

We believe that an appropriate model for coaching at middle and high school levels involves a focus on developing a thorough understanding of the teaching and learning cycle: this means helping teachers to learn to assess all students in a classroom in every content area taught; to use that assessment data to evaluate the different needs of students; and to then appropriately plan instruction, and select materials for that instruction, based on the assessed needs of each and every student. This daunting task has been accomplished over and over in schools with truly reflective, and effective, coaching models. These are schools that understand that if teachers have been hired with depth of content knowledge, then a coach can provide support in considering a teaching and learning cycle regardless of the content area of the teacher. There's a learning process that undergirds everything—how a scientist reads, how a mathematician considers problems, how a basketball player considers a play. For example, a coach with expertise in reading can coach a teacher who has questions about how to set up a math classroom in a workshop format that will allow the teacher to meet the math needs (and often content literacy needs) of a diverse group of students. This opens up what coaching at middle and high school can and should look like. It's not necessarily about a math teacher coaching a math teacher about math—though it might be; it's also about providing support as teachers work to understand how to assess and instruct each student in a classroom.

Concerns about Coaching

As we move to our concerns about coaching, we focus on two key areas: the need for support and the need for documentation of results. Michael Fullan, well known in the world of educational change, once said, "The greatest single problem in contemporary professional development is the absence of follow-up" (as cited in Leggett & Hoyle, 1987, p. 16). We wonder if the second greatest problem, and in fact a problem that contributes to that identified by Fullan, is the absence of support for those who are expected to provide professional development. In many districts, we find good teachers who are simply removed from the classroom or reading specialist positions and labeled as "coach" and left without the support they need to be an effective coach.

We believe that coaching is effective—when all the pieces of support are in place and when the right people receive appropriate scaffolds within this important work. This brings us to our second major point of concern: the scarcity of published studies focused on the outcomes of coaching. As this work is done, it will be critical to carefully evaluate what is working and adjust what isn't. There is much to learn about coaching.

Most of us are aware of the research in professional development that shows that fewer than 10% of teachers actually implement instructional innovations following workshops or inservice experiences. Researchers Beverly Showers and Bruce Joyce found, however, that when coaching was included as a follow-up, most teachers incorporated the innovations into their instruction (1996). However, we can't make the same assertions about student change.

Coaches, administrators, and students express a belief that coaching is making a difference, and our observations support that assertion. In addition, there is even trend data in districts to indicate that something is changing in schools and districts that have fully embraced reflective coaching approaches. The Learning Network has been able to document substantial changes in elementary schools located in Michigan, Indiana, and Tennessee; these schools attribute the positive changes to implementation of their approach to coaching (see http://www.rcowen.com/rcoprfdv.htm), and we are in the process of collecting data focused on student outcomes in middle schools. At the

---

Critical Points about Literacy Coaching

1. Teachers' understandings, skills, and knowledge have a definite impact on student achievement. (Peisner-Feinberg, Ellen S. et al. 2000. *The Children of Cost, Quality, and Outcomes Study Go to School: Technical Report.* Chapel Hill, NC: University of North Carolina at Chapel Hill, Frank Porter Graham Child Development Center.

2. Literacy coaching should be effective because it provides professional development which is "ongoing, deeply embedded in teachers' classroom work with students, specific to grade levels or academic content, and focused on research-based approaches." (Russo, Alexander. 2004, July/August. School-Based Coaching: A Revolution in Professional Development—or Just the Latest Fad? *Harvard Education Letter* [Online])

3. Literacy coaching, or sustained, job-embedded professional learning, maximizes the likelihood that teachers will translate newly learned skills and strategies into practice. (Neufeld, Barbara, & Roper, Dana. 2003. *Coaching: A Strategy for Developing Instructional Capacity—Promises and Practicalities.* Prepared for the Aspen Institute Program on Education and The Annenberg Institute for School Reform. Cambridge, MA: Education Matters.)

4. Different models of literacy coaching reflect different beliefs, values, and perspectives about teachers, teaching, and teacher change, and therefore the choice of a model of literacy coaching is political. (Toll, Cathy A. 2005, December. *Models of Literacy Coaching and Their Political Implications.* Paper presented at the National Research Conference, Miami, Florida.)

same time, schools and classrooms are not collecting or analyzing all the rich assessment data they have in a way that allows us to definitively make assertions about the effectiveness of coaching on student achievement. While we recognize that systematically collecting data on individual students seems to add another layer to an already full teaching, coaching, and administering plate, it is essential if coaching is going to receive the funding and support needed to continue. The more data we collectively compile, the more we'll know and be able to say about the possibilities of coaching.

Where Do We Go from Here?

Coaching is an exciting step forward for middle and high school classrooms. One coach who moved from elementary to middle school reports that it is easier to coach in middle schools than it was to coach in elementary schools because middle school teachers have not had much support and, therefore, are eager to learn. Of course, this is not always true, but as with all good things in education, when we truly understand what it is we are trying to do, when the focus is on improving instruction for the benefits of students, and when appropriate support is provided, we see great things happen. Coaching appears to be a means to improving schooling in middle and high schools.

We recognize that there are coaches of all different types and with varying support in middle and high schools. We also recognize the critical importance of connecting with each other, providing support to one another, and observing each other. Some districts have been at this a long time and have very developed approaches. Others are just starting on what should be an exciting journey. We encourage all coaches and administrators to remain connected through the NCTE-sponsored listserv available through http://www.ncte.org/listsubscribe/subscribe.aspx?list_=literacy-coach.

References

Duncan, M. (in press). *Developing effective teachers through instructional dialogue*. Katonah, NY: Richard C. Owen.

Leggett, D., & Hoyle, S. (1987). Peer coaching: One district's experience in using teachers as staff developers. *Journal of Staff Development*, 8(1), 16–20.

Showers, B., & Joyce, B. (1996). The evolution of peer coaching. *Educational Leadership*, 53(6), 12–16.

Toll, C. (2005). *The literacy coach's survival guide: Essential questions and practical answers*. Newark, DE: The International Reading Association.

Classroom Implications

1. What qualities do you think are important for a coach to possess? Are these characteristics likely to vary from one school to another? In what ways?

2. What factors will affect the success or failure of the coaching movement? What is your own prediction concerning this movement? Will we find coaches in schools a decade from now?

For Further Reading

Bean, R. M. (2003). *The reading specialist: Leadership for the classroom, school, and community.* New York: Guilford.

Toll, C. A. (2005). *The literacy coach's survival guide: Essential questions and practical answers.* Newark, DE: International Reading Association.

Walpole, S., & McKenna, M. C. (2004). *The literacy coach's handbook.* New York: Guilford.

Online Resources

The Literacy Coaching Clearinghouse, a site jointly sponsored by IRA and NCTE.
www.literacycoachingonline.org

Collected online articles about coaching, compiled at the University of Virginia and presented in reverse chronology.
http://curry.edschool.virginia.edu/reading/projects/garf/CoachingArticles.htm

International Reading Association. (Posted 2000). Roles of the Reading Specialist. Position Statement.
www.reading.org/resources/issues/positions_specialist.html

International Reading Association. (Posted 2004). Roles and Qualifications of the Reading Coach in the United States. Position Statement.
www.reading.org/resources/issues/positions_coach.html

Clair, N., & Adger, C. T. (1999). Professional Development for Teachers in Culturally Diverse Schools. ERIC Digest.
www.eric.ed.gov/ERICDocs/data/ericdocs2/content_storage_01/0000000b/80/2a/2e/fb.pdf

Ferraro, J. (2000). Reflective Practice and Professional Development. ERIC Digest.
www.eric.ed.gov/ERICDocs/data/ericdocs2/content_storage_01/0000000b/80/2a/32/84.pdf

Fillmore, L. W., & Snow, C. (2000). What Elementary Teachers Need To Know about Language. ERIC Digest.
www.eric.ed.gov/ERICDocs/data/ericdocs2/content_storage_01/0000000b/80/2a/31/f0.pdf

Grisham, D. L., Albright, L., Berger, S., Kozub, R., Loughman, P., Sanchez, C., & Sullivan, A. (Posted August 2000). Teacher Voices: Research as Professional Development. [Editorial].
www.readingonline.org/editorial/edit_index.asp?HREF=/editorial/august2000/index.html

Huling, L. (2001). Teacher Mentoring as Professional Development. ERIC Digest.
www.eric.ed.gov/ERICDocs/data/ericdocs2/content_storage_01/0000000b/80/2a/34/e4.pdf

International Reading Association. (Posted 2000). Excellent Reading Teachers. Position Statement.
www.reading.org/resources/issues/positions_excellent.html

National Staff Development Council.
www.nsdc.org

Weiss, E. M., & Weiss, S. G. (1999). Beginning Teacher Induction. ERIC Digest.
www.eric.ed.gov/ERICDocs/data/ericdocs2/content_storage_01/0000000b/80/2a/2f/a7.pdf

Chapter 8

Technology

I believe that the motion picture is destined to revolutionize our education system and that in a few years it will supplant largely, if not entirely, the use of textbooks.

—Thomas Edison (1922)

Computers in the future may weigh no more than 1.5 tons.

—*Popular Mechanics* (1949)

As intuitively appealing as technology may appear, it will be little more than a sophisticated novelty unless teachers are equipped with the skills needed to use it effectively in support of literacy instruction.

—Linda Gambrell (2006)

Change is good. You go first.

—Scott Adams, *Dilbert* cartoon

Technology in schools is here to stay. At least two powerful arguments suggest that literacy teachers must find effective means of integrating computers into their instruction. The first argument is that the world itself, and particularly the business world, is increasingly driven by technology. Educators at all levels must contend with the question of what sort of future they are preparing their students for. A wired world outside of school necessitates, to some degree, technology-based literacy instruction. The second argument is that computer technology has created reading and writing skills that do not have print counterparts. That is, students must now be able to navigate hypermedia and to compose using not only word processing software, but desktop publishing systems capable of integrating multimedia. The times, they are a changin'.

Schools, however, are often resistant to embracing technology. Seymour Papert (1994), in his book, *The Children's Machine*, compares a school's reaction to computers to the body's reaction to an invading virus. Computers are often relegated to labs or ignored and isolated by classroom teachers. Some teachers are obviously more enthusiastic about technology applications than others, and these technophilic teachers sometimes form a subcommunity within the school or district.

Technology applications raise practical financial questions, such as the turnover of obsolete hardware and the funds needed to purchase quality software. But there are also important pedagogical questions to be addressed by anyone responsible for overseeing a comprehensive reading program.

Perhaps the biggest question is whether to invest time and resources in an integrated learning system (ILS). Like a basal reading program, an ILS embodies a scope and sequence of activities and assessments. Children make their way through a sequence of activities, usually constructed with appealing art and self-competition formats. All the while, their progress is monitored automatically and reports are generated for use by teachers. Objective studies on particular commercial ILSs are hard to come by. One exception is IBM's Writing to Read, an expensive ILS that was effectively killed by the lack of positive research findings (Slavin, 1990). Another is the Waterford Early Reading Program. A recent study showed that it offered no advantages over traditional instruction (Patterson et al., 2003). Coiro and her colleagues (2003) concluded that an ILS typically offers early gains, perhaps due to novelty, but that the advantage rapidly disappears.

Another important question is what stand-alone software to purchase. Once again, publishers' in-house studies may be all the research available, which is why it is essential to have a working knowledge of effective non-technology-based reading instruction. The degree to which software can embody such techniques is likely to be a good indicator of its effectiveness. In our view, two good sources for exploring new software are the Center for Applied Special Technology (www.cast.org) and the Florida Center for Reading Research (www.fcrr.org). These two websites are well worth a visit.

Studies conducted at the National Reading Research Center (NRRC) have repeatedly validated the value of "e-books". These are electronic versions of print trade books, equipped with digitized pronunciations accessible on a point-and-click basis. When young children read such books, they can independently tackle material near their frustration level and they also acquire new sight words incidentally in the process. For middle schoolers, teachers can use software such as Write Out Loud (Don Johnston) to make digitized pronunciations available with materials for students who still struggle with decoding.

Perhaps the most notable success story involving technology applications to literacy instruction is word processing. Numerous studies confirm that the use of word processing software to teach writing leads to better results (both affective and cognitive) than conventional "paper-and-pencil" approaches. The engaging qualities of computers can probably be thanked for this, together with the ease with which children can form words and letters and revise and edit their work. Of course, as David Reinking (1995) points out, the fact that word processing leads to better writers and writing is almost beside the point. The fact is, students will enter a world of work in which word processing is the expectation. The questions that should concern educators are not whether to embrace word processing but which software best meets our instructional goals.

Internet access in schools, together with its host of ethical issues (ranging from equity of access to plagiarism to child safeguards) has now taken center stage. The primary challenge is to find ways to successfully integrate these technology applications with the instructional objectives that make up the curriculum. This task is more difficult than it sounds and teachers find it tempting to use computer stations as a means of motivating students or occupying them so that they can work with other children without giving adequate thought to the alignment of computer activities with the literacy curriculum.

As You Read

The two selections that follow were chosen to provide a foundation of knowledge for making informed decisions about technology applications in literacy education. This foundation has two parts. The first involves the rapidly changing notion of what counts as literacy. Renee Hobbs explores the significant and perplexing expansion of this concept into the realm of multimedia. Conventional notions of reading and writing, she maintains, must be revised. The second part concerns research into what constitutes best practice as it pertains to technology use. McKenna and his colleagues describe evidence-based applications for younger and older students and offer suggestions for instructional planning.

References

Coiro, J., Leu, D. J., Jr., Kinzer, C. K., Labbo, L., Teale, W., Bergman, L., Sulzen, J., & Sheng, D. (2003, December). *A review of research on literacy and technology: Replicating and extending the NRP subcommittee report on computer technology and reading instruction.* Paper presented at the 53rd annual meeting of the National Reading Conference, Scottsdale, AZ.

Gambrell, L. (2006). Technology and the engaged literacy learner. In M. C. McKenna, L. D. Labbo, R. Kieffer, & D. Reinking (Eds.), *International handbook of literacy and technology* (Vol. 2, pp. 289–294). Mahwah, NJ: Lawrence Erlbaum.

Papert, S. (1994). *The children's machine: Rethinking school in the age of the computer.* New York: Basic Books.

Paterson, W. A., Henry, J. J., O'Quin, K., Ceprano, M. A., & Blue, E. V. (2003). Investigating the effectiveness of an integrated learning system on early emergent readers. *Reading Research Quarterly, 38,* 172–207.

Reinking, D. (1995). Reading and writing with computers: Literacy research in a post-typographic world. In K. A. Hinchman, D. J. Leu, & C. K. Kinzer (Eds.), *Perspectives on literacy research and practice: Forty-fourth yearbook of the National Reading Conference* (pp. 17–33). Chicago: NRC.

Slavin, R. E. (1990). IBM's Writing to Read: Is it right for reading? *Phi Delta Kappan, 72,* 214–216.

Multiple Visions of Multimedia Literacy: Emerging Areas of Synthesis

RENEE HOBBS

Screen activity is a central fact of life for American children and teens, with children ages 8 to 18 spending an average of eight hours per day using media, including television, videogames, the Internet, newspapers, magazines, films, radio, recorded music, and books (Kaiser Family Foundation, 2001). Even American babies and toddlers spend two or more hours per day using media (Kaiser Family Foundation, 2003a). In contemporary society, with rapid changes taking place in the way that information is created and distributed, children and young people need to be able to find, select, comprehend, and evaluate information and entertainment messages. While educators rightly emphasize the development of language competencies, it is also valuable for students to learn to use symbol systems, including images, sound and music as a means of self-expression and communication, as these are now an integral part of contemporary life. While educational technologists have privileged interactive computing, online synchronous and asynchronous communication as focal issues (Fouts, 2000; Oppenheimer, 2003), consumption of popular culture and mass media messages is still the central leisure activity for Americans, Europeans, and an increasingly large number of people around the world. Mass media messages provide most people with their primary source of information about the world (Kubey & Csikszentmihalyi, 1990) and the use of media messages—particularly popular music, film and television—continues to be a primary component of adolescent social interaction (Lenhart, Rainie & Lewis, 2001) and socialization (Calvert, 1998). Adolescents' interest in mass media and popular culture may drive much of their electronic reading and writing (using Web sites and interactive online communication experiences), particularly for youth from high-poverty communities (Bussiere & Gluszynski, 2004; Chandler-Olcott & Mahar, 2003; Monroe, 2004). As a result, literacy educators are recognizing the need to respond to the changing array of media technologies and resources used in the world outside the classroom in order to make education more responsive to the needs of learners in the 21st century.

Hobbs, Renee, Multiple Visions of Multimedia Literacy: Emerging Areas of Synthesis. From the *International handbook of literacy and technology* (Vol. 2). Mahwah, NJ: Lawrence Erlbaum Associate Publishers. Reprinted with permission.

As a result, more and more scholars and educators are using terms such as *visual literacy, media literacy, critical literacy, information literacy*, and *technology literacy* to expand the concept of literacy so that visual, electronic, and digital forms of expression and communication are included as objects of study and analysis. Academic scholars in the fields of literary theory, cultural studies, history, psychology, library and information science, medicine and public health, linguistics, rhetoric, communication and media studies have become increasingly interested in how people comprehend, interpret, critically analyze and compose texts of various kinds. Literacy educators no longer "own" the concept of literacy. Questions about the processes of literacy are being interrogated by many different scholars using a variety of theoretical and disciplinary lenses. Each year, a growing number of K–12 educators are using technologies to bring students access to online newspapers, magazine articles, audio programs, narrative films and television documentaries, blogs, and other multimedia resources to help students build critical thinking, communication, creativity and collaborative problem-solving skills (Hobbs, 2004). They are involving students in creating their own messages using visual, electronic and digital media tools. Stakeholders also include business leaders, youth development specialists, federal and state education officials, parents, community activists and artists who have voiced their ideas about issues related to the uses of media and technology in literacy education. Like the parable of the blind men and the elephant, each stakeholder group approaches the topic of *multiliteracy* from different perspectives, and as a result, there are numerous, differentially nuanced visions of what these skills encompass (Hobbs, 1998a; Tyner, 1998).

This paper reviews the disciplinary traditions and key concepts of some of the new literacies and examines the consensus (and disjunctures) that are beginning to emerge among diverse stakeholders and scholars as some key ideas are beginning to circulate in a range of disciplines. A model that synthesizes this literature is created in order to support the work of scholars interested in investigating how teachers translate the "big ideas" of multiliteracies into classroom practice and to support the development of measures to assess students' learning. This paper then reviews the small, but growing body of evidence about the uses of film, video, newspapers, and computers as tools for literacy learning and identifies research opportunities for future interdisciplinary scholarship focused on understanding how multimedia and popular culture texts can be used as tools to support literacy development among K–12 learners.

Disciplinary Frameworks Shape Priorities for the New Literacies

Throughout the 20th century, calls to expand the concept of literacy have arisen from a number of scholars from different disciplinary and intellectual backgrounds, including media studies, technology education, literary studies, library and information sciences, education, cultural studies, and the visual arts. By and large, the discourse between these scholarly fields has been limited and only a few scholars have served as intermediaries and translators, framing ideas across multiple fields (Flood, Heath & Lapp, 1997; Kellner, 1995). Increased access to scholarship online has probably been a contributing factor in the growth of border crossing and cross-disciplinary or inter-disciplinary work in literacy education.

Visual Literacy. Based on nearly 100 years of work by cognitive psychologists, artists, literary scholars, graphic designers, art historians, and philosophers on the psychology of vision, aesthetics, and spatial intelligence (see reviews in Gregory, 1970), academics and K–12 classroom teachers in both arts and humanities fields have long incorporated visual materials into the classroom in order to demonstrate how factors like selection, framing, composition, sequence, and aesthetic dimensions of images influence viewers' interpretations and emotional responses. While critics identify long-standing questions about the coherence and viability of assertions about the value of visual literacy made by practitioners and scholars (Avgirinou & Ericson, 1997), visual literacy education aims to demonstrate how genres, codes, conventions and formats shape perceptual and interpretive processes. Scholars with interests in visual literacy have examined how images are comprehended and interpreted, how language and images interact in the meaning-making process (Worth & Gross, 1981), how exposure to visual images affects general cognitive and intellectual development (Messaris, 1994), and how semiotic and aesthetic dimensions of images can be examined and appreciated (Eco, 1979; Natharius, 2004). In comparing the differences in emphasis among various multiliteracies, it is clear that visual literacy privileges the "reading" process of "viewing and interpreting" images more than the "composing" process of creating and constructing images (Tyner, 1998).

Learning about the visual conventions of images gives viewers a foundation for heightened conscious appreciation of artistry and the ability to recognize the manipulative uses and ideological implications of visual images (Messaris, 1994). A fundamental dimension of teaching visual literacy is the emphasis on distinguishing between pictures and reality, as naïve viewers imagine that images produced by photographic media are simple mechanical records of actuality with high levels of correspondence and fidelity (Griffin & Schwartz, 1997). The problem of "representation" has been articulated by film scholars throughout the 20th century (see Nichols, 1991 for review). Texts are only representations of reality but scholars have been intrigued by the ways in which people process visual texts as if they were veridical experience (Messaris, 1994). While in elementary and secondary educational practice, a focus on the aesthetics of images has its locus in visual arts education, there is a tradition of exploring visual literacy in language arts, particularly in film (or film and literature) courses often offered as electives in U.S. and European high schools. Concepts including realism, truthfulness, accuracy, bias, objectivity, and stereotyping have shaped classroom activity not only in English language arts, but also in social studies, science, and even health education (Aufderheide, 1993).

Information Literacy. Information literacy has been defined as a set of abilities requiring individuals to recognize when information is needed and have the ability to locate, evaluate, and use it (American Library Association, 2000). At the heart of it, information literacy emphasizes the need for careful selection, retrieval and choice-making in response to the abundant information available in the workplace, at school, and in all aspects of personal decision-making, especially in the areas of citizenship and health. Deriving from the influential *A Nation at Risk* report in 1983, a coalition of 65 national organizations founded the National Forum on Information Literacy which was highly influential in outlining the role of the library and information resources in the development of K–12 and higher education (Plotnick, 1999).

Information literacy education emphasizes the critical thinking, meta-cognitive, and procedural knowledge used to locate information in specific domains, fields, and contexts. A prime emphasis is placed on recognizing message quality, authenticity and credibility. Personal and contextual factors activate or suppress people's evaluative stance towards information, and scholars have examined the conditions under which people are likely to critically assess information or accept information at face value (see Fitzgerald, 1999 for review).

Critics have claimed that information literacy does not emphasize the ways in which meaning is constructed through interpretation (Lankshear, Snyder & Green, 2000). Among some K–12 practitioners, information literacy may be defined more narrowly as mere skills, as in the process of locating information using library classification systems and Boolean search strategies, using checklist-type criteria to evaluate Web-based source materials, and avoiding plagiarism through correct citation of source materials (Dibble, 2004). Critics perceive that information literacy appears to emphasize the simple acquisition of "facts" to be sought and used to make a case for an argument, without the recognition that information and knowledge are the products of cultural practices that exist within the context of economic and political relations (Kapitzke, 2003; Vandergrift, 1987). But since the process of finding, using and handling information is always context-specific, it is never only just a routine application of a particular set of operations. In line with this perspective, some scholars see information literacy as more broadly and more closely akin to processes involved in reading. Dissatisfied with the focus on information and eager to connect the critical thinking tradition of information literacy with newer forms of online communication, Gilster (1998) has coined the term *digital literacy* as the ability to understand, evaluate, and integrate information in multiple formats. Even more broadly, Lloyd (2003, 90) has rejected information as a set of skills, describing it instead as a meta-competency, where individuals are able to "recognize the nature of their need for information, actively navigating cognitive and environmental barriers, and accommodating and assimilating information as they create new knowledge."

Media Literacy. Media literacy education in the United States has been deeply influenced by the work of British, Canadian and Australian educators and scholars who have developed a significant body of writing about instructional practices that engage children and young people in critically analyzing mass media messages and popular culture (see Alvarado & Boyd-Barrett, 1991 for review). This approach is theoretically aligned with communication scholarship in audience reception studies, which emerged from mid-20th century research in the fields of literary studies, cultural studies, and media effects. Scholars have used concepts including uses and gratifications, spectatorship, resistant and oppositional reading of media texts, conceptualizations of active and passive audiences, fan culture and interpretive communities, and screen theory (see Brooker & Jermyn, 2003 for an identification of central texts and scholars). Positioned in the 1970s as a response to television's supposed deleterious impact on childhood socialization, and originally labeled "critical viewing skills" (Brown, 1991), educators and scholars have broadened the focus to emphasize an expanded conceptualization of literacy as the ability to access, analyze, evaluate, and communicate messages in a wide variety of forms (Aufderheide, 1993). As used here, the term *critical* refers to the recognition that visual and electronic messages are constructed texts that present particular, distinctive points of view as a result of the economic, political and social contexts in which they circulate. In this view, critical readers and viewers are aware of the "constructedness" of media messages and explore who produces texts, their motives and purposes for communication and expression, and the role of media institutions, economics, and ideology in the construction and dissemination of cultural messages (Brunner & Tally, 1998; Buckingham & Sefton-Green, 1994). A "generic" focus is evident among media literacy educators, as media literacy educators emphasize specific ways of reading messages in the genres of print and television news media, advertising, non-fiction television, and narrative film. Issues including advertising and materialism, media violence, the First Amendment and freedom of expression, and the representation of gender and race in the media are also featured in curriculum for secondary students. This reflects the enduring traditions of media literacy which have been associated with questions whether to conceptualize the audience as innocent victim, active text reader, hedonistic pleasure-seeker, or political dupe (McLuhan, 1964).

Media literacy education is often defined by its emphasis on pedagogy: it stresses a more active, student-centered, participatory style that emphasizes inquiry and learning by doing (Buckingham, 2003; Kist, 2000). Rather than emphasize teachers as providers of knowledge, media literacy pedagogy stresses 1) the process of inquiry, with critical questions guiding the process of message analysis and 2) situated action learning, based on the work of Freire and Macedo (1987) which emphasizes the cycle of awareness, analysis, reflection, action and experience in a community context that is responsive to the needs of individuals, particularly as they relate to social inequalities and political injustices. Media literacy educators emphasize the centrality of "composition" using media tools and technologies and advocate for moving media production away from its historically vocational track in secondary education to align it more closely within English education. Media literacy practices involve students in actively creating messages using publishing software, digital cameras, video, and other media. Recently, the National Council of Teachers of English (NCTE) approved a resolution stating that they will 1) encourage preservice, in-service, and staff development programs that will focus on new literacies, multimedia composition, and a broadened concept of literacy, 2) encourage research and develop models of district, school, and classroom policies that would promote multimedia composition, and 3) encourage integrating multimedia composition in English language arts curriculum and teacher education, and in refining related standards at local, state, and national levels (NCTE, 2003). As yet, however, there is little evidence to know the extent to which increasing access to low-cost, home video, editing software, and Web publication tools have affected instructional practices in secondary English education. But more than 40 states in the U.S. have included media literacy outcomes in their state education frameworks (Kubey & Baker, 1999), which reflects the gradual perceptual changes among educational leaders concerning the value of these skills for life in a media-rich and technology-saturated society.

Critical Literacy. Arising from traditions established by work in semiotics and cultural studies, literacy scholars have begun to define reading as not just extracting meaning from text, but the process of constructing meaning through interaction and involvement. "Meaning," in this view, is understood in the context of social, historic and power relations, not just the product of the author's intentions (Kellner, 1995; Cervetti, Pardales, & Damico, 2001). For these scholars and practitioners, "texts" are any form of symbolic expression used in the communication of meaning (Barthes, 1972). As used by critical literacy scholars, the term *critical* refers to the recognition of oppression and exploitation as embedded in texts and textual activity; critical literacy is a component of the struggle for a better society, with an explicit ideological focus on issues of inequity as related to race, gender, class, and sexual orientation (Kellner, 1995). Critical literacy education emphasizes that identity and power relations are always part of the process of composing and interpreting texts, and that these processes occur in a socio-culturally and historically-bound framework.

Connected to Freire and Macedo's (1987) exploration of reading within a socio-cultural context, critical literacy scholars and educators examine and understand how various texts, including pictures, icons, and electronic messages (as forms of symbolic expression) are used to influence, persuade, and control people. Critical literacy emphasizes that literacy cannot be understood as just "cracking the code" or "analyzing the author's intentions" but must be understood as an embodiment of social and political relationships. This perspective foregrounds sociocultural factors within a framework of power relations, incorporating within literacy practices an understanding of the identity of the participants, how the activity is defined or executed, the timing of the activity, where it occurs, and why participants are motivated to perform the activity (Rand Reading Study Group, 2004). At the same time, these scholars emphasize the importance of not just reading texts critically, but understanding how people can control their experience of the world through constructing messages as part of transforming society (Gee, 1996). A central component of critical literacy pedagogy is its focus on examining multiple perspectives and points of view, often through juxtaposing diverse materials, including photos, videos and artifacts of popular culture (Luke, 1997; McLaughlin & DeVogel, 2004) and exploring themes related to power, identity, pleasure, and transgression (Alvermann, Moon & Hagood, 1999).

A Model for Synthesizing Emerging Consensus in Multiliteracies

Led by the rapidly changing communications media in contemporary society, scholars and practitioners are working as fast as possible to re-conceptualize literacy in ways that reflect emerging perspectives on the communicative competencies required for life in the 21st century. As Tyner (2004, 373) notes, each of the new literacies described above is "provisional, speculative and distinguished by the subtle ideological and professional differences of its various constituents." At the present time, it is unclear whether various terms for new literacies will continue to multiply as a result of increased attention from diverse interest groups, or whether they will slowly decline as consensus gradually emerges among scholars, educators, and policy makers. But an array of similar terms for distinctive concepts and ideas has real-world implications for educational practice, as Cervetti, Pardales and Damico (2001) pointed out in explaining how the distinctions between *critical reading* and *critical literacy* were confusing to practitioners and policy makers. There is a risk that misunderstandings of the multiple formulations of these new literacies could twist and warp how these concepts are understood by the public and by policy makers.

Fortunately, the emerging consensus among these different perspectives is obvious and considerable: all of the proponents reflect an appreciation that visual, electronic, and digital media are reshaping the knowledge, skills and competencies required for full participation in contemporary society, and all view these abilities as fundamentally tied to the intellectual and social practices known as literacy (New London Group, 1996). Multiliteracies proponents recognize that the acquisition and development of these competencies will require changes to the K–12 learning environment, including significant changes in teacher preservice and in-service education, design of learning experiences, access to tools, resources and materials, and techniques of classroom management (Buckingham, 2003; Film Education Working Group, 1999). And one can find scholars and practitioners in each of these new literacies who frame these concepts within a social, political, and economic context, a stance which recognizes literacy as a form of social power which enables fuller control over the circulation of messages and meanings in society (Giroux & Simon, 1989; Luke, 1997).

What tenets or principles do the practitioners and scholars advocating new literacies share? A typology developed by the Film Education Working Group (1999) identified broad categories of inquiry focusing on authors, audiences, messages, language, values, and representation. Table 1 presents a synthesis of the key conceptual tenets or working principles that are emphasized in the work of media literacy, visual literacy, critical literacy, and information literacy scholars and practitioners from the United Kingdom, Canada, and the United States, whose work has been briefly described above. Tenets from all four multiliteracies are collapsed into three broad categories: AA (authors and audiences), MM (messages and meanings), and RR (representations and reality). These three categories cut across print, visual, electronic and digital forms and genres and represent a simplified way to express the key dimensions of multiliteracies education in a framework that may be resonant and useful to K–12 classroom practitioners.

This model may also support research on staff development and the development of new methods and tools for assessing student learning. In my work with practitioners of information literacy, media literacy, visual literacy and critical literacy in elementary and secondary schools, I have found teachers' perceptions of their own goals and aims to be critically implicated in the shape of the curricular choices they make in the classroom (Hobbs, 1998b; 1994). Among teachers, there are a wide range of motivations and beliefs concerning multiliteracies that leads to a proliferation of instructional methods and approaches to classroom practice. As a result, it is difficult to recognize "best practices" in new literacies. By synthesizing the key ideas of multiliteracies into three broad categories, it may be easier to describe instructors' objectives and goals with more precision and identify the types of overt and covert instructional aims and priorities now extant among practitioners in K–12 settings. For example, use of this model may enable researchers to observe and document differences between teachers' stated aims and their instructional practices, a phenomenon described as ubiquitous by Hart and Suss (2002) in their cross-national case studies of teachers of adolescents. Future research might explore how these three broad conceptual tenets may help char-

TABLE 1   A Model for Integrating the Conceptual Tenets of Multimedia Literacies

THEMES	TENETS	SOURCES
AA AUTHORS AND AUDIENCES	AA1. Consumers of texts make selections and choices of texts to meet various needs and gratify different desires.	M, I
	AA2. Consumers of texts are defined, targeted and conceptualized by producers of texts.	M, C, V, I
	AA3. Texts are consciously created by authors and involve the coordination of different types of labor.	M, C, V, I
	AA4. Texts are often produced and distributed for power, gain and profit; economic and political factors shape the content and format of texts.	M, C, V, I
MM MESSAGES AND MEANINGS	MM1. Texts use a variety of combinations of symbol systems (language, image, sound, music) and delivery systems (print, visual, electronic) and employ genres, codes and conventions that can be identified and classified.	M, C, V, I
	MM2. Individuals and social groups select, use, interpret and respond to texts by using their unique life experiences, prior knowledge, and social positions.	M, C, V
	MM3. People's interpretation of texts influence aspects of decision-making, attitude formation, world view and behavior.	M, C, V, I
RR REPRESENTATIONS AND REALITY	RR1. Texts reflect the ideologies and world views of their authors, and as a result, they selectively omit information and have distinctive points of view.	M, C, V, I
	RR2. Texts use techniques that affect people's perceptions of social reality.	M, C, V, I
	RR3. Texts can be examined in relationship to people's different understandings about social reality within various political, social and economic contexts.	M, C, V

Support for this tenet found in Visual literacy (V), Media literacy (M), Information literacy (I), and Critical literacy (C).

acterize the changes in students' growth that may result from learning opportunities with print, visual, electronic, and digital media in (and out of) the classroom.

What do the new literacies have in common? How are they different? These new literacies have as a central focus the development of students' engagement with texts and their concern for the meaning-making process, the constructed process of authorship, and questions about how texts represent social realities. They differ in their relative emphasis on the reader, the text, and the socio-historical and political contexts in which interpretations take place. For example, media literacy emphasizes an understanding of the processes involved in "constructing texts" and conceptualizes the audience as a construction designed within a particular economic framework. Information literacy emphasizes the process of "selection and choice" of texts as a component of the meaning-making process. By contrast, critical literacy emphasizes the constructed nature of "meaning," recognizing that meaning-making occurs as individuals interact with texts and make sense of other readers' interpretations in relation to their own social positions and lived experiences of the world. Visual literacy emphasizes the "aesthetic and rhetorical" functions of images, examining how people make connections between the visual texts they encounter and their own experience of reality, examining media texts for their plausibility and correspondence with other media representations.

The disjunctures among these new literacies reflect important differences in emphasis, pedagogy, and ideology. While media literacy, critical literacy and technology literacy emphasize the connection between reading and writing, this is less emphasized in visual literacy and information literacy, which are both primarily centered on the process of accessing, reading, and using texts. There is a disjuncture between multiliteracies regarding the appropriate message genres deserving attention, from those [which] include or emphasize popular culture (media literacy, visual literacy, cultural literacy) and those which focus primarily on informational messages (information literacy). This disjuncture reflects well-entrenched arguments in English language arts education, as Robert Scholes (1998) articulates when he proposes replacing the canon of literary texts with a canon of methods of critical analysis (including theory, history, production, and consumption) that enable a reader to read all kinds of texts in all kinds of media, including entertainment and popular culture, while opposite arguments are made by E. D. Hirsch (1987), who calls for a focus on core literacy and historical texts so that students can acquire the world knowledge they need to be culturally literate.

Another disjuncture concerns fundamental conceptualizations of teaching and learning, as some practitioners and scholars in all the new literacies described in this paper emphasize participation and peer-interaction, inquiry-based learning, and constructivist learning principles, while others tend to view learning as a form of skills and content delivery from experts who guide instruction. The teacher-centered transmission model of instruction is common to most classrooms in the United States, and this model tends to emphasize textbooks as the *de facto* curriculum, whereas in participatory classrooms, a wider range of textual materials (including visual, multimedia and popular culture texts) is used (Wade & Moje, 2000). As yet, there is little consensus among K–12 practitioners about how visual texts, digital media, and technology tools are best infused into learning environments. Even though this debate will continue to create divisions among scholars and practitioners, it is likely that a hybrid of teacher-centered and participatory approaches will be used in most K–12 settings by selectively structuring learning experiences to match students' needs (Tyner, 2004).

Examining Multimedia Literacy Practices in Schools

Much research in the past 20 years has examined the impact of television on the development of children's reading skills (Newman, 1991), but relatively little is known about the ways that visual media (including film and television programs) or mass media (like newspapers, magazines, radio or audio resources) may be useful in the context of literacy instruction in primary or secondary education. By contrast, there is a substantial literature that examines how computers, online, and digital information technologies are used (or not used) in schools (Fouts, 2000; Norris, Sullivan, Poirot & Soloway, 2003). Historians of education should investigate the factors that led to shift towards conceptualizing educational technology as focused exclusively on computers, thus marginalizing film and video forms as technologies.

Although neither "fish nor fowl" in its status as non-print media, film and video use is ubiquitous among secondary educators, with at least 90% of teachers using video, film or documentaries, and 1 in 4 teachers using video once a week or more often (PBS, 2004). No one is startled to learn that English teachers use films like *To Kill a Mockingbird* and *Hamlet*, but a survey of English teachers in Minnesota found that a wide variety of genres and types of films are in use (from Hollywood classics to low-budget independent films). More than 200 unique titles were described among the 161 teachers who participated in the study (Larsson, 2001). Researchers know much less about why and how teachers use video in the classroom as a learning tool, but based on field observations, it appears that the content transmission model is dominant, along with a pervasive attitude that video is a form of entertainment and useful primarily for non-academic students, and only rarely used to support literacy learning or the development of critical thinking skills (Hobbs, in press; Hobbs, 1994). Future research should explore how teachers' current uses of film and video in the classroom may be more meaningfully connected to students' literacy development in elementary- and secondary-education contexts, as well as in home-school and family literacy initiatives.

Another under-researched mass media form that is highly relevant to the work of literacy educators is newspapers and magazines. Newspaper use has been a common feature of instruction in many schools since the 1960s, with more than 950 U.S. daily newspapers sponsoring year-round programs providing newspapers to 106,000 schools at reduced rates. Used by 381,000 teachers as a text for learning in the classroom, newspaper-in-education programs reach almost 14.5 million students each year (NAA Foundation, 2004). A study of home literacy practices has shown that newspapers are a valuable resource for family communication, particularly with boys (Sullivan, 2004). One wonders why there is such a dearth of scholarly research on how newspapers (and their new online variants) are used in schools. The newspaper industry has produced some evidence that newspaper use in the classroom influences newspaper reading in later life. Researchers interviewed a large representative sample of 18 to 34 year olds, finding that 64% of those who had had a class where newspapers were part of the curriculum were regular readers of newspapers; by contrast, only 38% of those who didn't have exposure to newspapers in the classroom were regular newspaper readers (Saba, 2004). Further research should investigate the how comparing and contrasting online newspapers and television news media might support literacy development.

Emerging Evidence from Research on Multimedia Literacies

How have the new literacies been shown to affect student learning? Most examinations of multimedia literacy look at very small numbers of students, usually a single classroom (Alvermann, Moon, & Hagood, 2001; Anderson, 1983). Studies have explored whether students learned the facts, vocabulary, and information provided as part of the instruction (Baron, 1985; Kelley, Gunter, & Kelley, 1985) or whether a video broadcast about media literacy affects cognitive or critical analysis skills (Vooijs & Van der Voort, 1993). In addition, case studies from a number of countries have documented teachers' instructional strategies in implementing media literacy in classrooms (Hart & Suss, 2002; Hart, 1998; Hurrell, 2001; Kist, 2000), and a further body of research has examined media literacy as an intervention tool for prevention and public health (see Kaiser Family Foundation, 2003b for review).

There is emerging evidence that media literacy instruction affects the development of reading comprehension and writing. In a quasi-experimental study, eleventh grade students who participated in a year-long English language arts/media literacy curriculum were compared to students from a demographically matched group who received no instruction in critically analyzing media messages. Critical message analysis skills were measured by examining students' ability to identify the purpose, point of view, and construction techniques used in print newsmagazines, TV news segments, print advertising, and radio news segments. Statistically significant differences were found in students' reading comprehension, writing skills, critical reading, critical listening, critical viewing, and knowledge of media production, media history, media economics, and understanding of media terminology (Hobbs & Frost, 2003).

Information literacy skills have been measured among students in middle school and high school. A large-scale study of New Zealand students showed students have only limited understanding of the information literacy skills involved in using library-related resources, specifically libraries, parts of a book, and reference sources (Brown, 2001). Instructional models intended to foster the acquisition of research, problem-solving, and metacognitive skills were found to be effective with a class of eighth-grade students who were asked to research and write about events surrounding the African-American Civil Rights Movement (Wolf, 2003). Students were provided support in the activities required to solve information-based problems through six processes: task definition, information seeking strategies, location and access, use of information, synthesis, and evaluation. Such models, maps, and organizers should continue to be tested among many groups of learners to determine the full range of their value for increasing metacognitive awareness of the processes involved in using information for problem solving.

While numerous teacher staff development programs are available to preservice and in-service teachers to learn to integrate multiliteracies into instruction, few have been evaluated. Begoray and Morin (2002) investigated a teacher summer institute that brought English teachers from Manitoba, Canada together to explore music, visual arts, media, and drama, finding that even after one year, teachers believed they increased their use of technology, art, music, drama, and media in their classrooms. Begoray (2002) videotaped and interviewed teachers in a Canadian city who were learning to use visual literacy concepts over a period of two years. Teachers implemented lessons involving the use of cameras and photography, made active use of videotaping to document students' learning progress, and involved students in mental visualization as a means to promote reading comprehension. Further research should continue to explore why and how teachers decide to implement new literacies instruction, the role of staff development in supporting teachers' growth and change, and outcomes including student motivation, literal and inferential comprehension, listening skills, and collaboration.

Conclusion

There is no shortage of theories about the promise of media, technology, and popular culture in education. However, as Bazalgette, Bevort and Savino (1992, 3) point out, "the realities of teaching and learning are harder to define and share." In reviewing accounts of practice of media education in more than a dozen countries, they emphasize that what is institutionally appropriate in one setting may not be so in another. The conceptual model which presents tenets of the four new literacies represents an effort to synthesize some key themes in a rich and varied literature now emerging from many academic disciplines and fields. Such synthesis may support the development of new research which examines teachers' and students' engagement with popular culture and mass media texts in the context of learning in English language arts. The current range and diversity of philosophies and approaches to new literacies, like Solomon's beard, may be a prime source of strength for the future of the field. But the diverse perspectives and areas of emphasis may also lead to academic sniping, divisiveness, and sheer exhaustion. Models that support cross-disciplinary dialogue and continued border crossing, now routinely appreciated as an essential component of postmodern scholarship, should move forward the development of this emerging field of inquiry.

The growing band of literacy educators now interested in popular culture, mass media, and online and digital technologies must be responsive to what Masterman (1990, 24) has identified as a central objective for media education: the ability to apply knowledge and skills learned in the classroom to the world of everyday life. In reflecting on the appropriate learning outcomes for teaching information literacy, media literacy, visual literacy, and critical literacy, teachers must design learning experiences that help students, as quickly as possible, to stand on their own two feet and apply critical thinking skills to the media and technology experiences they have at home. Future research must more systematically begin to explore the student learning outcomes that result from instruction that emphasizes information literacy, visual literacy, media literacy, and critical literacy and to find better ways to help teachers assess when and how such learning occurs.

In contrast to the idealistic visions of education scholars and academics, the institutional nature of schooling demands that teachers adapt and modify their work to fit with the normative values of school culture. As a result, teachers often encounter situations and experiences in using media, technology, and popular culture in the classroom that are not described in the scholarly academic literature, whose voices "demand that the repertoire of acceptable cultural objects be expanded" (Aronowitz & Giroux, 1993, 182). The dynamism and complexity of contemporary life in a media-saturated and information-rich culture remind us that the use of media, technology, and popular culture in the classroom is not for the faint of heart. Such work vitally depends on the initiative and perseverance of individual teachers, who are inspired and motivated by a wide range of different understandings about the role of the mass media, technology, and popular culture in society. These individuals need to have courage, imagination, and creativity to enable students to develop the competencies they need to be citizens of an information age.

References

Alvarado, M., & Boyd-Barrett, O. (1991). *Media education: An introduction.* London: British Film Institute.

Alvermann, D., Moon, J., & Hagood, M. (1999). *Popular culture in the classroom: Teaching and researching critical media literacy.* Newark, DE: International Reading Association.

American Library Association (2000). Information literacy competency standards for higher education. Accessed September 1, 2004 online at http://www.ala.org/ala/acrl/acrlstandards/informationliteracycompetency.htm.

Anderson, J. A. (1983). The theoretical lineage of critical viewing curricula. *Journal of Communication, 30*(3), 64–70.

Aronowitz, S., & Giroux, H. (1993). *Education still under siege.* Westport, CT: Bergin & Garvey.

Aufderheide, P. (1993). *Media literacy: A report of the national leadership conference on media literacy.* Queenstown, MD: Aspen Institute.

Avgirinou, M., & Ericson, J. (1997). A review of the concept of visual literacy. *British Journal of Educational Technology, 28*(4), 280–291.

Baron, L. (1985). Television literacy curriculum in action. *Journal of Education Television, 11*(1), 49–55.

Barthes, R. (1972). *Mythologies.* New York: Hill and Wang.

Bazalgette, C., Bevort, E., & Savino, J. (1992). *New directions: Media education worldwide.* London: British Film Institute.

Begoray, D. (2002). Visual literacy across the middle school curriculum: A Canadian perspective. Paper presented at the American Educational Research Association, New Orleans, LA, April 1. ERIC ED467283.

Begoray, D. L., & Morin, F. (2002, November). Multiple literacies in language arts: Sustainable teacher change through a summer institute. *Reading Online, 6*(4). Available: http://www.readingonline.org/article/art_index.asp?HREF=begoray/index.html

Brooker, W., & Jermyn, D. (2003). *The audience studies reader.* New York: Routledge.

Brown, J. A. (1991). *Television "critical viewing skills" education: Major media literacy.* Hillsdale, N.J.: L. Erlbaum Associates.

Brown, G. (2001). Locating categories and sources of information: How skilled are New Zealand children? *School Library Media Research, 4.* Accessed November 2, 2004 at http://www.ala.org/ala/aasl/aaslpubsandjournals/slmrb/slmrcontents/volume42001/brown.htm

Brunner, C., & Tally, W. (1998). *The new media literacy handbook.* New York: Anchor.

Buckingham, D. (2003). *Media education.* London: Polity Press.

Buckingham, D., & Sefton-Green, J. (1994). *Cultural studies goes to school: Reading and teaching popular media.* London: Taylor & Francis.

Bussiere, P., & Gluszynski, T. (2004, May). The impact of computer use on reading achievement of 15-year olds. SP-599-05-04E. Learning Policy Directorate, Human Resources and Skills Development, Government of Canada. Accessed November 28, 2004 online at http://www11.hrsdc.gc.ca/en/cs/sp/lp/publications/2004-002625/page01.shtml

Calvert, S. (1998). *Children's journeys through the information age.* New York: McGraw Hill.

Cervetti, G., Pardales, M., & Damico, J. (2001, April). A tale of differences: Comparing the traditions, perspectives and educational goals of critical reading and critical literacy. *Reading Online, 4*(9). Available: http://readingonline.org/articles/art_index.asp?HREF=/articles/cervetti/index.html

Chandler-Olcott, K., & Mahar, D. (2003). Tech-savviness meets multiliteracies: Exploring adolescent girls' technology mediated literacy practices. *Reading Research Quarterly, 38*(3), 356–386.

Dibble, M. (2004). Directory of online resources for information literacy: The information literacy process. University of South Florida, Tampa Library. Accessed online September 1, 2004 at http://www.lib.usf.edu/ref/doril/

Eco, U. (1979). *A theory of semiotics.* Bloomington: Indiana University Press, Midland Book Edition.

Film Education Working Group (1999). *Making movies matter.* London: British Film Institute.

Fitzgerald, M. (1999). Evaluating information: An information literacy challenge. *School Library Media Research 2.* Accessed online December 1, 2004 at http://oldweb.ala.org/aasl/SLMR/vol2/evaluating.html

Flood, J., Heath, S. B., & Lapp, D. (1997). *Handbook of research on teaching literacy through the communicative and visual arts.* International Reading Association. New York: Macmillan.

Fouts, J. (2000). Research on computers and education: Past, present and future. A report prepared for the Bill and Melinda Gates Foundation. Seattle Pacific University, Seattle, WA. Accessed online November 28, 2004 at http://www.esd189.org/tlp/images/TotalReport3.pdf

Freire, P., & Macedo, D. (1987). *Literacy: Reading the word and the world.* South Hadley, MA: Bergin & Garvey Publishers.

Gee, J. P. (1996). *Social linguistics and literacies: Ideology in discourses* (2nd ed.). London: Taylor & Francis.

Gilster, P. (1998). *Digital literacy.* New York: Wiley.

Giroux, H., & Simon, R. (1989). *Popular culture, schooling and everyday life.* New York: Bergin & Garvey.

Gregory, R. (1970). *The intelligent eye.* New York: McGraw-Hill.

Griffin, M., & Schwartz, D. (1997). Visual communication skills and media literacy. In J. Flood, S. B. Heath, & D. Lapp (Eds). *Handbook of research on teaching literacy through the communicative and visual arts.* International Reading Association. New York: Macmillan.

Hart, A. (1998). *Teaching the media: International perspectives.* Mahwah, N.J.: Erlbaum.

Hart, A., & Suss, J. (2002). Media Education in 12 European Countries. Research report from the Euromedia Project. E-collection of the Swiss Federation Institute of Technology. Zurich. Accessed December 3, 2004 at: http://e-collection.ethbib.ethz.ch/ecol-pool/bericht/bericht_246.pdf

Hirsch, E. D. (1987). *Cultural literacy.* Boston: Houghton Mifflin.

Hobbs, R. (in press). Non-optimal uses of media in the classroom. *Learning Media and Technology.*

Hobbs, R. (2004). A review of school-based initiatives in media literacy. *American Behavioral Scientist, 48*(1), 48–59.

Hobbs, R., & Frost, R. (2003). The acquisition of media-literacy skills. *Reading Research Quarterly, 38*(3), 330–355.

Hobbs, R. (1998a). The seven great debates in media literacy education. *Journal of Communication, 48*(2), 9–29.

Hobbs, R. (1998b). Media literacy in Massachusetts. In A. Hart (Ed.), *Teaching the media: International perspectives.* Mahwah, NJ: Lawrence Erlbaum Associates, (pp. 127–144).

Hobbs, R. (1994). Pedagogical issues in U.S. media education. In S. Deetz (Ed.), *Communication Yearbook 17.* Newbury Park: Sage Publications (pp. 453–466).

Hurrell, G. (2001). Intertextuality, media convergence and multiliteracies: Using *The Matrix* to bridge popular and classroom cultures. *Journal of Adolescent and Adult Literacy, 44*(5), 481–483.

Kaiser Family Foundation (2003a). Zero to six: Children and electronic media. Accessed November 1, 2004 at http://www.kff.org/entmedia/entmedia102803pkg.cfm

Kaiser Family Foundation (2003b). Key facts: Media literacy. Accessed November 1, 2004 at http://kff.org/entmedia/Media-Literacy.cfm

Kaiser Family Foundation (2001). *Kids and media @ the new millennium.* Accessed online October 27, 2003 at: http://www.kff.org/content/1999/1535/

Kapitzke, C. (2003). Information literacy: A positivist epistemology and a politics of outformation. *Educational Theory, 53*(1), 37–53.

Kelley, P., Gunter, B., & Kelley, C. (1985). Teaching television in the classroom: Results of a preliminary study. *Journal of Educational Television, 11*(1), 57–63.

Kellner, D. (1995). *Media culture: Cultural studies, identity and politics between the modern and postmodern.* New York: Routledge.

Kist, W. (2000). Finding "new literacy" in action: An interdisciplinary high school Western civilization class. *Journal of Adolescent and Adult Literacy, 45*(5), 368–377.

Kubey, R., & Baker, F. (1999). Has media literacy found a curricular foothold? *Education Week, 19*(9).

Kubey, R., & Csikszentmihalyi, M. (1990). *Television and the quality of life: How viewing shapes everyday experience.* Hillside, NJ: Lawrence Erlbaum Associates.

Lankshear, C., Snyder, I., & Green, B. (2000). *Teachers and technoliteracy: Managing literacy, technology and learning in schools.* St. Leonards, New South Wales: Allen and Unwin.

Larsson, D. (2001). Use of film in Minnesota high schools. Unpublished manuscript, Minnesota State University. Accessed online November 1, 2004 at: http://www.english.mnsu.edu/larsson/SCS/MNSurvey.html

Lenhart, A., Rainie, L., & Lewis, O. (2001, June 20). *Teenage life online.* A report of the Pew International American Life Project. Accessed November 28, 2004 at http://pewinternet.org/reports/oc.asp?Report=36

Lloyd, A. (2003). Information literacy: The meta-competency of the knowledge economy? An exploratory paper. *Journal of Librarianship and Information Science, 35*(2), 87–92.

Luke, C. (1997). Media literacy and cultural studies. In S. Muspratt, A. Luke, & P. Freebody (Eds.), *Constructing critical literacies: Teaching and learning textual practice.* Cresskill, NJ: Hampton, (pp. 19–49).

Masterman, L. (1990). *Teaching the media.* London: Routledge.

McLaughlin, M., & DeVogel, G. (2004). Critical literacy as comprehension: Expanding reader response. *Journal of Adolescent and Adult Literacy, 48*(1), 52–62.

McLuhan, M. (1964). *Understanding media: The extensions of man.* New York: McGraw-Hill.

Messaris, P. (1994). *Visual "literacy": Image, mind, and reality.* Boulder, CO: Westview.

Monroe, B. (2004). *Crossing the digital divide: Race, writing, and technology in the classroom.* New York: Teachers College Press.

NAA Foundation. (2004). *Measuring up! The scope, quality and focus of newspaper in education programs in the United States.* Vienna, VA: Newspaper Association of America Foundation.

Natharius, D. (2004). The more we know, the more we see: The role of visuality in media literacy. *American Behavioral Scientist, 48*(2), 238–247.

National Council of Teachers of English. (2003). On Composing with Non-Print Media. Resolution passed December 2003. Accessed November 1, 2004 at: http://www.ncte.org/about/over/nty/resol/115073.htm

Neuman, S. (1991). *Literacy in the television age: The myth of the TV effect.* Norwood, NJ: Ablex.

New London Group. (1996). A pedagogy of multiliteracies: Designing social futures. *Harvard Educational Review, 661,* 60–92.

Norris, C., Sullivan, T., Poirot, J., & Soloway, E. (2003). No access, no use, no impact: Snapshot surveys of educational technology in K–12. *Journal of Research on Technology in Education, 36*(1), 15–28.

Nichols, B. (1991). *Representing reality: Issues and concepts in documentary.* Bloomington: Indiana University Press.

Oppenheimer, P. (2003). *The flickering mind.* New York: Random House.

Plotnick, E. (1999). Information literacy. ERIC Clearinghouse on Information and Technology, Syracuse University. ED-427777. Accesses online September 1, 2004 at http://www.ericfacility.net/ericdigests/ed427777.html

Public Broadcasting Service (2004, August 25). PBS programming tops the list of teacher favorites for second consecutive year. Accessed November 29, 2004 at http://www.pbs.org/aboutpbs/news/20040825_teacherfavorite.html

Rand Reading Study Group. (2004). Reading for Understanding: Toward a R&D Program in Reading Comprehension. Accessed September 24, 2004 at http://www.rand.org/multi/achievementforall/reading/readreport.html

Saba, J. (2004, September 26). NAAF study bolsters newspapers-in-school notion. *Editor and Publisher.* Accessed November 29, 2004 at http://www.editorandpublisher.com/eandp/search/article_display.jsp?schema=&vnu_content_id=1000642391

Scholes, R. (1998). *The rise and fall of English.* New Haven, CT: Yale University Press.

Sullivan, M. (2004). Why Johnny won't read. *School Library Journal, 50*(8), 36–40.

Tyner, K. (2004). Beyond boxes and wires: Literacy in transition. *Television and New Media, 4*(4), 371–388.

Tyner, K. (1998). *Literacy in the digital age.* Mahwah, NJ: Lawrence Erlbaum Associates.

Vandergrift, K. (1987). Critical thinking misfired: Implications of student responses to *The Shooting Gallery. School Library Media Quarterly, 15*(2), 86–91.

Vooijs, M., & Van der Voort, T. (1993). Teaching children to evaluate television violence critically: The impact of a Dutch schools television project. *Journal of Educational Television, 19*(3), 139–152.

Wade, S., & Moje, E. (2000). The role of text in classroom learning. In M. Kamil, P. Mosenthal, P. Pearson, & R. Barr (Eds.), *Handbook of reading research* (Vol. 3, pp. 609–627). Mahwah, NJ: Lawrence Erlbaum Associates.

Wolf, S. (2003). The Big Six information skills as a metacognitive scaffold: A case study. *School Library Media Research, 6.* Accessed November 1, 2004 at http://www.ala.org/ala/aasl/aaslpubsandjournals/slmrb/slmrcontents/volume62003/bigsixinformation.htm

Worth, S., & Gross, L. (1981). *Studying visual communication.* Philadelphia: University of Pennsylvania Press.

Digitally Innovative Teaching: Effective Uses of Technology in Literacy Instruction

**MICHAEL C. MCKENNA, LINDA D. LABBO,
DAVID REINKING, AND TRICIA A. ZUCKER**

The Evolving Concept of Literacy

Traditional notions of literacy, based squarely on the printed word, are rapidly giving way to multiple ideas of what constitutes literate activity. It is now common to use the plural of the term, *literacies,* to refer to a range of concepts, including visual, digital, and others (see Richards & McKenna, 2003). Digital literacy has been defined as being skillfully prepared to use, comprehend, and manipulate computer-related content and processes to meet communicative, personal, academic, social, and cultural goals (Labbo, 2004). But even digital literacy is no longer viewed as singular, and we now speak of the "new literacies" of the Internet and other digital environments (Lankshear & Knobel, 2003).

Where technology is concerned, these are far more than theoretical musings. Literacy use in digital environments varies considerably from its print origins (Reinking, 1995, 1998; Leu, 2000, 2002; Gambrell, 2005; Valmont, 2003). Moreover, because digital applications are increasingly represented both in the workplace and at home, the curricular imperative to prepare children for such applications is clear. We believe that it is essential for schools to assist students in developing the technological skills that will be required of literate citizens in the future. After all, as Brandt (2001) argues, literacy is the energy supply of the information age. Modern-day demands for literacy increasingly require us to be adept users of digital literacies.

A second reason for integrating technology into literacy instruction, even with the youngest children, is its efficacy. Research has shown that digital environments, when properly structured, have extraordinary potential to engage and scaffold students. The advantages of multimedia are considerable and include new and powerful ways of communicating, ways that better reflect developmental realities than a strict diet of print.

For both of these reasons, we explore in this chapter some of the major technology-based classroom applications shown to be effective to date, applications that we believe to offer promise to literacy teachers. First we examine overarching principles for successfully integrating technology. Then, while space prevents our describing all possibilities, we hope to exemplify best practices through descriptions of innovative teaching.

Successfully Integrating Computers into the Literacy Curriculum

We begin by drawing on relevant research and underlying sociocognitive theory (Vygotsky, 1978) to offer suggestions for establishing a classroom environment that promotes demonstration, collaboration, and other forms of social interaction. The evidence is clear that the social environment of the classroom will always play a central role in determining how a computer is used by children in schools (see Kamil, Intrator, & Kim, 2000; Leu, 2000). It is our belief that if computers are to adequately support both the conventional and electronic literacy development of children, the computer-related activities must be woven into the fabric of daily classroom routines through planned activities in areas such as (1) teacher-interactive demonstration, (2) diverse collaboration among students and teachers, and (3) attention to special needs.

Interactive Demonstration and Discussion

Our research (Labbo, Phillips, & Murray, 1995–96) suggests that teachers can effectively integrate technology by employing interactive demonstrations of classroom computer applications during whole- and small-group lessons. For example, an LCD projector allows a teacher to demonstrate specific features, such as how to navigate through software. However, the makeup of the demonstration should include more than just a teacher explaining or modeling. Rather, demonstrations should combine teacher modeling with opportunities for child involvement. Teachers might solicit children's input during demonstrations of using the computer for maintaining a class calendar of events, setting alarm reminders for special class appointments, composing and printing notes to parents, writing the morning message, making class lists of things to do, and creating signs for classroom events. In the middle grades, teachers might demonstrate using PowerPoint to craft multimedia reports and presentations. Likewise, a high school math teacher might use a digital tablet to project notes and examples, storing them after class for students to retrieve if they wish.

By socially negotiating the form, content, and context of the demonstration, teachers can help children create a rich schema for employing technology in ways that quite naturally involve many literacy-related activities. Moreover, this schema will, over time, become more sophisticated as teachers present new applications that students assimilate. Thus, the perspective we advocate implies much more than perfunctory uses of technology. Computers should be placed as seamlessly as possible into the mainstream of the literacy activities in the classroom. The first step in doing so is an interactive, shared viewing of the computer application using an LCD projector or large monitor. The following steps prepare students to use the software or website effectively:

- First, introduce the title and general purpose of the computer application and demonstrate procedures to open the application. Then, state a specific purpose for interacting with the program. Comparing the objectives of different software reveals distinct software functions such as, reading for pleasure, practicing decoding, or playing a game to learn a stated objective.
- Next, model how to navigate through the program. For example, when modeling how to use an electronic text, guide students in how and when to click on words to hear the pronunciation.
- During this modeling, children may be invited to take turns operating the software as a check for understanding. This provides an opportunity for students to offer opinions about the software and develop strategies for making decisions when using the software independently.
- Add procedural reminders-during the demonstration such as how to take turns with computer partners. This helps avoid "mouse wars" that can detract from cooperative learning at the computer (see Labbo, 2000).
- After a shared viewing, encourage the children to critically discuss the information, presentation of the content, and the operation of the program itself. This activity helps students develop the ability to critically analyze software and digital material, just as we hope they will critically examine conventional printed materials.

Adult modeling of literacy activities is a major factor in children's acquisition of conventional literacy. Such modeling is no less powerful in the acquisition of digital literacy. As Papert (1980) suggested during the infancy of technology applications, children will use a computer in ways they see the adults in their lives use computers. When children dictate personal news to the morning message and watch their words typed on the screen, they have an opportunity to become aware of letter–sound relationships, to be sure, but they also gain a new perspective on what it means to write. Likewise, when children receive an individual printout of the morning message and are invited to circle words, letters, or letter-sounds they recognize, not only an opportunity to enrich or refine their conventional literacy knowledge, but also the interconnectedness of print and digital literacies. Similar benefits of social, interactive digital processes are evident for older children as well. For example, when adults model how to compose emails with proper Internet etiquette (netiquette) or how to practically evaluate the veracity of a website, students' digital literacy knowledge may increase. But through such modeling, teachers also afford their students platforms for productive social interaction within the literate community they are joining.

Diverse Opportunities for Collaboration

Weaving computer-related activities into the classroom culture requires collaboration among students and teachers. From a sociocognitive perspective, we believe that children who observe and interact with teachers and peers during technology demonstrations will internalize relevant vocabulary, develop approaches to problem solving, and encounter action schemes—all of which enable them to use the computer as a tool for thinking, learning, and communicating. Collaborative computer activities are also beneficial because children who collaborate at the computer can simultaneously construct both conventional and digital literacy knowledge. In this section we examine various worthwhile collaborative computer-based applications.

Collaborative writing processes employing paper-and-pencil tools are enhanced by the malleability possible on a computer screen (e.g., cut and paste). Other effective collaborations involve digital pen pals, now called keypals. Garner and Gillingham (1998) explain how students use e-mail to communicate effectively with students in various geographic regions. Beach and Lundell (1998) report that shy students become more interactive and even develop online personalities when they exchange messages through digital communication systems.

Another computer-based collaboration is paired keyboarding. This occurs when a child with knowledge about computer operations and the Internet is paired with another, who is less knowledgeable about accessing information from the internet. Peters (1996) suggests that such interaction can extend the less-knowledgeable partner's zone of proximal development, enabling the child to internalize strategies for successful explorations. Lewis and Fabos (2005) suggest using instant messaging and other socially mediated technologies, such as blogging, to heighten students' analytical thinking skills, which are crucial for critically navigating the vast assortment of online materials. Leu and Leu (2000) argued for a project approach to Internet use, because . . . it is collaborative and because students can share their expertise. In the middle grades teachers can use projects with highly motivating possibilities (Miller, 2003), and linking projects to technology appears especially promising.

Teachers should be aware that empowering students to use technology cooperatively can be a demanding task that requires persistence. Yang and Liu (2005) found that it took considerable time and effort for collaborative learning to move beyond simpler skills of technological proficiency to higher-level skills such as synthesizing information. We suggest that teachers remain diligent in training their students to work cooperatively with technology by modeling strategies and cooperative learning procedures, mentoring children's use of strategies, and managing strategy use and computer procedures (see Labbo, 2000, for a detailed description). Purposeful and goal-directed computer tasks encourage better collaboration. This approach helps minimize interpersonal struggles such as "mouse wars" (see Labbo, Sprague, & Montero, 2000 for computer center management tips). Carroll (2004) describes how concluding computer projects by asking students to rate their collaborative efforts with a "Collaboration Rubric" helped students work more effectively (p. 119).

Digital Applications for Special Populations

Technology can support the learning needs of diverse learners. Students at all grade levels who struggle with reading and writing may benefit from particular computer applications. We define special populations broadly to include readers who are not fluent in decoding, reluctant readers, children for whom English is a second language, or students who struggle with a particular area of reading and writing. Software applications can make age-appropriate text comprehensible to these learners through a system of built-in supports. Dalton and Strangman (2006) describe this notion in terms of "universal access," the architectural concept that has led to barrier-free construction to permit easy access by the handicapped.

Children who struggle with learning to read may benefit from various types of support available in electronic texts, supports that make the texts accessible. Rather than a traditional instructional or tutorial approach for struggling readers, one that may slow down the pace of instruction (Walmsley & Allington, 1995), supported texts can allow these readers to maintain a pace similar to that of the regular classroom. How readers use supported text will vary with their developmental level. Struggling emergent readers can access the full listening version of a text, whereas readers at later developmental levels who are learning to decode may gain more from resources such as digitized pronunciations of difficult words. More advanced readers who are approaching fluency will have greater recourse to glossary entries, prose simplifications, digitized video clips, and the like as they endeavor to acquire content from expository text (Anderson-Inman & Horney, 1998). At this stage, their comprehension will also benefit from accessing linked resources, such as graphic organizers, databases, or electronic encyclopedias. Because the efficacy of these resources is based on aligning software with a child's stage of reading development, it is essential that assessment be aimed at precisely determining that stage. This alignment allows teachers to guide the child to the most appropriate use of electronic resources (McKenna, Reinking, Labbo, & Kieffer, 1999; Reinking, Labbo, & McKenna, 2000).

Technology for struggling readers must offer resources that meet the needs of the individual learner. Dalton and Strangman (2006) argue that technology should not be approached from the standpoint of one size fits all. They review promising research on hypertext enhanced with learning supports to create a "scaffolded learning environment." Dalton and Strangman's work with a program called *Thinking Reader* supports a range of learners by offering a text-to-speech function, a multimedia glossary, background knowledge links, and embedded strategy instruction. The software aims to develop metacognitive strategies and increase comprehension by prompting children to "stop and think" or to use a comprehension strategy such as predicting, clarifying, questioning, summarizing, making connections, or visualizing. Their research with middle-school students reading at or below the 25th percentile rank showed significantly better gains in reading achievement when using *Thinking Reader* and reciprocal teaching as compared with the control group. Dalton and Strangman's (2006) work suggests that digitized, flexible, leveled supports in a hypertext environment can improve students' comprehension skills.

Many young readers and a small percentage of middle-grade readers require extensive decoding support to read successfully. When using electronic texts, children find they can "read" material that far exceeds their decoding ability because of the support the computer offers. When beginning readers click on unfamiliar words and hear them pronounced, they make substantial gains in sight word acquisition, provided they can already name letters and recognize word boundaries (Reinking, Labbo, & McKenna, 2000). We have obtained the same results with older, struggling readers (McKenna, Cowart, & Watkins, 1997; McKenna & Shaffield, 2002). Hasselbring

(1999) provided *Start-to-Finish* (Don Johnston, Inc.) electronic books to struggling middle-grade readers and reported significantly improved comprehension and motivation. Similarly, McKenna and Shaffield (2002) used *WriteOutLoud* to create tailored texts (including scanned textbook passages) for a similar sample of students, and observed increased confidence and success as a result of the support received. Another example of effective electronic decoding instruction is the work of Hanlon and Cantrell (1999), who used software called *WordSort* to compare and contrast spelling patterns in conjunction with additional tutoring to help a 31-year-old male experiencing severe problems learning to read make notable strides in learning to read and spell.

A future abundance of supported text will mean both advantages and drawbacks for the struggling reader. Surely, one of the challenges of electronic literacy is the need to develop the ability to navigate strategically through hypermedia environments. Even when these environments are limited to a few helpful sources, the appearance of so many choices can seem . . . labyrinthine to a struggling reader. On the positive side, students will be able to read text independently that would have frustrated them without the built-in support that McKenna (1998) has called "electronic scaffolding" (p. 47). Indeed, the notion of the instructional reading level will have to be reexamined in electronic environments, because many struggling readers will be able to read at or near their listening levels (McKenna, Reinking, & Labbo, 1997).

Burns (1996) and Kamil, Intrator, and Kim (2000) note that multimedia technology can be used to facilitate the English language acquisition of non-native speakers. Multimedia resources accommodate the needs of English-language learners as they progress in second-language proficiency and gain content area knowledge. Some electronic books have the option of listening to the story in Spanish or another language. After using CD-ROM storybooks with children who were inexperienced with the mainstream school language, Bus, de Jong, and Verhallen (2006) reported promising results for scaffolding these children's understanding of the story through supportive animations. They concluded that hearing the text in combination with animations bolsters children's ability to derive the meaning of unknown words and sentences. They describe this as an "interactive cycle." Specifically, "when children understand more of the story, they will understand more of the text. When language is better understood this will stimulate their understanding of the story" (Bus, de Jong, & Verhallen, 2006, p. 137). More research about the effectiveness of such programs on children's acquisition of a second language, and their understanding of specific reading passage content, is needed.

Notably, speech-synthesizer software offers some promising directions for supporting spelling development of English language learners and native-speaking nonfluent writers. Shilling (1997) introduced the use of a basic word-processing program and an external speech synthesis unit that gave children a choice of listening to a word they had attempted to spell on the screen, listening to the entire text they had typed on the screen, or not using speech synthesis at all. Findings suggest that before children consistently benefit from synthesizer software, they need to have acquired some basic concepts about print, phonemic awareness, and a notion of the alphabetic principle. As the capabilities of speech-synthesizer software improve, continued research is warranted.

For struggling and proficient readers alike, technology often increases student motivation and can boost confidence when children use technology successfully. Our work with Digital Language Experience Approach activities (D-LEA, Labbo et al.,

2002) provided a unique opportunity for a struggling reader to envision herself as a literate being, capable of writing and reading. When adding text to a digital photograph of her writing, she exclaimed, "Say, I'm writing! I'm [verbal emphasis and a pause] writing! I'm a writer!" (Labbo et al., 2002). It is worth noting that this new self-awareness appeared to foster an elevated level of confidence that resulted in her willingness to participate more actively in literacy activities in the classroom. Kamil et al. (2000) also described consistent findings that computer use in classrooms leads to increased intrinsic motivation especially when technology gives opportunities to "customize one's work and increase the control, curiosity, and challenge of a task" (p. 778). Gambrell (2006) noted that the Internet in particular holds great capabilities for motivating and engaging students because students can self-select their reading materials and explore others' opinions about texts.

Research-Based Practices for Integrating Technology

In the following sections we describe the classroom applications of actual teachers who recognize the potential of technology to enhance their literacy instruction. We turn first to effective computer applications with children in primary classrooms. These students are all learning to read and can be classified as emergent or beginning readers. Several of the scenarios occur at the classroom computer center, which is centrally located and adjoins other areas of high activity thereby making the computer part of the classroom culture (Haughland, 1992). We will use a series of vignettes from Ms. Martin's kindergarten unit, "Creatures that Fly in the Night Sky," to demonstrate how this teacher puts the classroom computer to good use. Then we will consider an array of other computer applications useful with beginning readers.

Thematic Integration and Innovation: Ms. Martin's Kindergarten Class

It is 9:20 a.m. on a cold October morning in Ms. Martin's kindergarten class, and the room is filled with the sounds of children working at various centers. Ms. Martin provides her students with choices (within limits) at the computer center so that children learn how to select an activity that they find interesting and meaningful. Patrick and Dartrell chose a software application called *My First Incredible Amazing Dictionary* (1995). Because Ms. Martin already introduced the class to this software with an interactive demonstration, Patrick and Dartrell are equipped to seek out new information about bats and other nocturnal creatures using the electronic dictionary. They adeptly locate a definition of *bat* and hear the text on the color monitor read aloud to them. . . . Next, they decide to click on the illustration that produces the sound of a feeding bat.

Digitally innovative teachers, like Ms. Martin, often discover natural connections between curricular themes, learning objectives, and innovative uses of technology. Ms. Martin's unit, "Creatures that Fly in the Night Sky," brings together a variety of children's books and software related to the theme, computer-based learning center activities connected to the theme, and occasions for celebrating children's computer experiences and products. Collecting, displaying and demonstrating themed books and software is the first step to a successful technology-related unit. After reading aloud a favorite children's book, *Stella Luna* (Cannon, 1993), and discussing the plot, characters, and author's purpose, Ms. Martin extends the learning at the classroom computer center with activities like the ones Patrick and Dartell chose. She carefully introduces additional software applications related to the theme such as an electronic book version of *Stella Luna*.

At 9:50 a.m., Aerial and Jasmine sit side-by-side at the computer center and compare a storybook version to the electronic book version of *Stella Luna*—a technique we have called a "screen and book read-along" (Labbo & Ash, 1998). The children connect the audio, text, and animation on the screen with the print and illustrations of the book by turning the virtual pages on the screen and the real pages in the book simultaneously. Children can point to the words in the book as they are read on the screen. Our research suggests that listening to an electronic book, echo reading, or chorally reading all can help children develop a sense of story, extend their vocabulary, increase knowledge of words, and enrich concepts about print (McKenna, 1998).

Aerial and Jasmine delight in clicking on screen illustrations and watching animation of the mother bat flying over trees, calling, and looking for her baby, who is lost but safely snuggled in a nest of baby birds. Soon after, the girls move to the sociodramatic play center and use a *Stella Luna* bat puppet and a bird puppet to retell the story they just read in the electronic book. They invite three peers to serve as an audience to their innovative retelling which is filled with plot twists, melancholy dialogue, humorous events, and voices that sound a great deal like the characters from the electronic book.

Notice how Aerial and Jasmine's sociodramatic or dramatic play is related to the unit theme and to the use of technology. In Ms. Martin's classroom, the sociodramatic play center was transformed into a puppet theater equipped with puppets related to the characters in the books and the software. Reenacting and often extending the story through dramatic puppet play gives children additional occasions for trying out characterizations, reinforcing story structure, and reliving story plots.

Later in the day, JaMaris has decided to contribute to the class book of collected stories on nocturnal creatures by drawing and writing something about bats using *KidPix*. When JaMaris visits the computer during afternoon center time, he brings an informational book about bats and the *Stella Luna* puppet from Ms. Martin's unit display area with him. He props the book up beside the computer monitor and holds the puppet in his lap as he prepares to begin his composition. When children bring objects with them to the computer center, they may use the objects to inspire stories and illustrations, to focus them on the topic, and to help them acquire information from a different source. As Schwartz (1985) has pointed out, three-dimensional objects such as stuffed animals or books may help children connect to a similar, two-dimensional object they see on the computer screen.

As JaMaris begins he is joined for a few minutes by his teacher, who crouches by his side and offers gentle scaffolding.

Ms. Martin: So, what's your story going to be about?

JaMaris: It's going to be a story about a really cool bat named Spidey and his super powers.

Ms. Martin: Okay. So how do you want to begin? With "Once upon a time?"

JaMaris: No . . . my name first *(selects the keyboard function and types in the letters of his name using the hunt-and-peck method)* . . . and I want to draw Spidey.

Ms. Martin: That's not a bad idea. If you draw that bat, you might get some good story ideas. So, what does this old bat look like—like Stella Luna?

JaMaris: Sorta like this one but with big green eyes *(pointing to the photograph of a bat on the book cover)*. How do I get green?

Ms. Martin: Remember how I showed you the other day, during rug time? *(Ms. Martin demonstrates how to access the color option from the program's menu before leaving the computer center.)*

JaMaris uses electronic artist tools to draw a bat with big green eyes, large fangs, and a crooked "B" on his chest. . . . He then writes a two-line story that consists of strings of letters and a word copied from the book cover. He makes two printouts. One is placed in a folder of children's stories that will be bound into a class book, and the other goes into his backpack, so he can show his mother.

These scenarios provide concrete instances of four guidelines that have proved to be instrumental in designing technology-related units, such as Ms. Martin's "Creatures that Fly in the Night Sky":

1. Collect, display, and demonstrate how to use themed children's books and software related to the unit.
2. Design computer-based learning center activities connected to the theme.
3. Enhance socio-dramatic play that connects the theme and computer-based activities.
4. Provide occasions for celebrating children's computer experiences and products.

The fourth step, celebrating children's computer experiences and work, is crucial in making technology a central element of the classroom culture and in increasing student motivation. Collections of students' computer-related work may be bound into a class book, exhibited as artwork, or displayed in a computer presentation, such as an electronic slide show. When children learn how to use a computer to accomplish their communicative tasks, teachers can invite them to demonstrate and explain their newfound knowledge to their classmates.

A useful technique for supporting and celebrating children's development of conventional and digital literacy is to provide a physical space to share and discuss computer activities at the Author's Computer Chair (Labbo, 2004). Our research suggests that that, although many of the goals and procedures of the Author's Computer Chair are similar to the traditional Author's Chair that was conceived in the 1980s (see, Calkins, 1983; Graves, 1983; Graves & Hansen, 1983), the key difference is that children discuss computer-mediated meaning making. The Author's Computer Chair is a time of social, peer collaboration in which children request feedback and support from peers and teachers during any phase of a computer task. This routine, sanctioned time benefits students as they ask for advice, share knowledge and pointers, and celebrate the completion of a computer activity (see Labbo, 2004 for guidelines to successfully implement Author's Computer Chair).

A classroom visitor, witnessing the children's computer work in Ms. Martin's room, might assume that they are all remarkably gifted or that they come from affluent homes, where they have daily access to computers. However, quite the reverse is true. None of the five children mentioned in these vignettes has a computer at home; all qualify for free or reduced-price lunches and have average or below-average literacy ability. The primary reason the children are adept at using technology is because their teacher consistently plans inviting, enriching, and appropriate computer-related experiences. In Ms. Martin's classroom, computer-related learning is meaningful and purposeful.

Exploring Other Computer Applications with Beginning Readers

Thematic integration and innovation is a powerful tool for promoting digital literacies with young readers. We now turn to other effective computer applications for beginning readers. For instance, we used case studies to explore the use of D-LEA in Ms. Maggie's kindergarten classroom (see Labbo, Eakle, & Montero, 2002). Like the traditional Language Experience Approach, this digital version utilizes the same powerful strategy of providing students a unique, contextualized occasion for literacy development through dictation of a story that is usually related to a specific, stimulating experience (Stauffer, 1970). However, it is enhanced by digital photography and creativity software. Ms. Maggie created partnerships with her local community to bring in adults who could work one-on-one with children of different ability levels to take digital photos of an experience and record students' D-LEA stories on the computer. The adult and child collaborate to create a digital presentation enhanced with multimedia features of word-processing and creativity software such as *KidPix*. D-LEA allows students to compose stories with drawing tools, imported video animations, sounds, speech synthesis, and writing (see also Turbill, 2003; Turbill & Murray, 2006).

D-LEAs offer endless possibilities for Ms. Maggie's students to see their oral words transformed into digital texts. Each child utilized their D-LEA compositions to distinguish themselves as readers and writers. For example, after reading an ABC book with her adult facilitator, one of Ms. Maggie's students created her own digital version of an alphabet book. She used the creativity software to embellish a close-up picture of herself as a clown to represent the letter *c*. Another student used the voice recording feature on the *KidPix* software to create an interactive text for her peers to explore. Authoring digital LEA stories is an authentic literacy experience because they are shared with admiring peers. Purcell-Gates (2004) suggests that technology is best used to facilitate authentic literacy tasks, or tasks that replicate or reflect reading and writing events that occur in the world outside of a schooling context.

Recall how Ms. Martin enhanced sociodramatic play connected to the theme and computer-based activities. This is an effective use of technology because when sociodramatic play centers are enriched with literacy props, including a computer center or even a cardboard model of a computer, children gain insights into the role of technology and literacy in various cultural and workplace settings (see Labbo & Ash, 1998; Neuman & Roskos, 1992). For example, if a unit theme focuses on various ways to travel, the sociodramatic play center may be transformed into an imaginary travel agency. After the teacher demonstrates ways to plan travel online and learn about possible destinations using the Internet, children can transfer this knowledge to the computer center where they make tickets, time tables, maps, travel posters, destination booklets, and passports to use in their dramatic play scenarios. As an extension, a field trip or a virtual field trip (using videoconferencing) to a travel agency will help children understand how the office works, the role of print and digital literacies at the workplace, and what types of conversational discourse are appropriate in that setting. By creating and playing at the computer and dramatic play centers, children have opportunities to enrich their schemata about the forms and functions of workplace literacy.

Another digitally innovative teacher, Mr. Saunders, uses software and electronic texts effectively in his first-grade computer centers. He makes use of well-designed decoding software, such as *Reading Mansion*, that embodies research underlying effective instructional practice (see Fox & Mitchell, 2000; Kuhn & Stahl, 2006; McKenna, 2002).

Computer centers are an ideal location for engaging students with electronic texts. Electronic texts include commercially available electronic texts such as the *Living Books* software developed by Broderbund and Internet texts such as the electronic books available at websites such as, www.Starfall.com, free of charge. Students can click on words to hear them read aloud, and they can interact with hidden seek-and-find features within the illustrations. Caution is suggested because these hidden animations or sound effects can be both engaging and distracting for children (see Labbo & Kuhn, 2000). Mr. Saunders managed this by allowing students to first explore the book in a spirit of play and later return to the book in a "read only" manner. Teachers recognize that they cannot rely on the computer to produce positive literacy results. Therefore, clear expectations must be communicated, and careful monitoring must follow (Labbo, Sprague, Montero, & Font, 2000). Brief post-reading discussions and comprehension checks lead children to critical and inferential questioning.

Another promising technology for beginning readers is teacher-created electronic texts, which have become simple to produce. Teachers can compose passages and use a text-to-speech program such as *WriteOutLoud*, produced by Don Johnston, Inc. The software automatically provides pronunciations for any of the words typed into program. Even programs with widespread use such as Microsoft's PowerPoint contain tools to record voice narration of text. Teachers can tailor texts to focus on specific words or word study features.

In a meta-analysis of 42 computer-assisted instruction (CAI) studies with children in first through third grade, Blok, Oostdam, Otter, and Overman (2002) concluded that these programs have a small, but positive effect size ($d = 0.19$) on beginning readers. Their analysis included a range of CAI programs in six categories: phonological awareness, word reading with speech feedback, flashed word reading, text reading with speech feedback, reading/listening, and mixed-methods software. Their review also noted an interesting finding—that English-speaking students benefited more from CAI programs than speakers of other languages. Blok et al. (2002) suggested that this finding could be explained by the fact that English orthographic rules require more practice to master than those of the other languages employed in their sample. They caution that the poor quality of many studies may have negatively influenced their findings for effect size and that more research with better research designs are needed.

These applications by resourceful teachers are representative of a wide variety of effective strategies for integrating technology in classroom-based literacy centers (for others, see Labbo, 2000). For a list of additional ideas for integrating technology into beginning readers' literacy curricula, see Figure 1.

FIGURE 1 Suggested Applications That Integrate Technology into Literacy Instruction: Presents Examples, Organized by Instructional Area.

INSTRUCTIONAL AREA	SUGGESTED APPLICATION
Phonological Awareness	• Use well-designed phonological awareness software such as *DaisyQuest* or *Daisy's Castle* by Blue Wave Software (Pressley, 2006) at the computer center. • Students can use talking electronic books for phonological awareness tasks such as identifying rhyming words and checking by clicking the computer pronunciation (see Labbo, 2000).
Phonics and Spelling	• Teachers can type daily Morning Message or student stories using an LCD projector (see Labbo, 2005a) and smart boards to highlight word features and spelling patterns. • Well-designed decoding software such as *Reading Mansion* can supplement students developing phonics skills (see McKenna, 2002 for guidelines to select phonics software aligned with research-based practices). • Tutors, paraprofessionals, volunteers, or teachers can create individual student word banks for beginning readers (Bear, Invernizzi, Templeton, & Johnston, 2004), but store the words electronically using Microsoft PowerPoint. This is a growing bank of words the child can read automatically in isolation. • Students dictate digital language-experience stories (D-LEA). Print individual copies for isolating words and phonics lessons (see Labbo, Eakle, & Montero, 2002; Turbill, 2003).
Vocabulary	• Extend themes and concepts with Internet, electronic encyclopedias, video streaming, and other multimedia (see Labbo, 2005c for ideas to support young learners). • Virtual field trips can build vocabulary (Blachowicz & Obrochta, 2005) related to units of study. Use the Internet, electronic encyclopedias, and other media to build prior knowledge and vocabulary that can be saved digitally (see Doe, 2003 for more on virtual field trips). • Use digital photography combined with text to document class field trips and build rich vocabulary in class authored books (Turbill & Murray, 2006). • Build a collection of useful and important vocabulary in a class database. This resource can include a reference to the text or place where the vocabulary word was first encountered (see Doe, 2003). • Students can build their vocabulary and prior knowledge by going on a virtual scavenger hunt. See Valmont (2003) for a step-by-step guide to creating an HTML document to guide your students to specific websites during a virtual scavenger hunt.
Fluency	• Students can build fluency using electronic texts with computer pronunciations of speech as a model for fluent reading. Speech recognition software can record and track students' fluency progress (see Adams, 2006). • Repeated readings and echo readings of electronics texts are beneficial for students who need practice reading aloud in a risk-free environment (see Labbo, 2000).

FIGURE 1 **Continued**

INSTRUCTIONAL AREA	SUGGESTED APPLICATION
Fluency *(continued)*	• Students can use talking books for Readers Theatre practice (see Labbo, 2000) and then share their performance with an online webcast or podcast of their dramatic reading.
	• Students can practice repeated readings of literature, record themselves reading the book on tape, then donate the books and student-authored tapes to kids in hospitals. Using a class webpage to spread the word about this community service brings in an authentic audience (see Sangiuliano, 2005).
Comprehension	• Electronic texts at the computer learning center can include response activities or retellings at the sociodramatic play center to foster comprehension (see Labbo, 2000).
	• Children can benefit from the meaning making that occurs when they respond to read alouds or literature using desktop publishing software such as *KidPix* or *Inspiration* (see Labbo, 1996).
	• Internet links to author websites (see Valmont, 2000) can enhance author studies by learning more about the author and their writing process or to communicate via email with the author.
	• Students evaluate and take a critical stance toward digital material including considerations of credibility of source and potential bias (see Leu, 2000; Morrell, 2002).
	• Internet, instant messaging, and email provide opportunities for socially constructed learning (see Lewis & Fabos, 2005).
Writing	• Written responses to stories or process writing techniques such as Writing Workshop can include computer-based work that constructs knowledge through a variety of symbols systems (Labbo, 1996, 2003).
	• Student's poetry creations using the computer can be enriched with symbols including unique: font type, colors, stamps/clipart, layout templates, animated graphics, and embedded music (see Carroll, 2004).
	• A variety of open-ended tools for digital publishing facilitate process writing. See Wood (2004, p. 23) for a description of publishing tools including: PowerPoint (Microsoft), Microsoft Publisher (Microsoft), EasyBook Deluxe (Sunburst Communications), HyperStudio (Knowledge Adventure), Inspiration (Inspiration, Inc.), Amazing Writing Machine (Broderbund, The Learning Company).
	• Electronic pen pals via email or instant messaging can link students and classrooms around the globe. Topics can include literature discussions or common units of study (see Leu, 2002; Wood, 2004).
	• Teacher and student authored classroom websites or blogs (an electronic journal) can display student work and communicate classroom events (see Chamberlain, 2005; Leu, 2002).
	• Students conduct research projects using the Internet and present their findings in a multimedia PowerPoint presentation (see Kinzer, 2005). See Morrell (2002) for ideas on critically evaluating pop culture using the Internet and other sources.
	• Collaborative Internet projects based on traveling stuffed animals (see Leu, 2002) or the Flat Stanley Project which generate online reading and writing experiences (see Hubert, 2005).

Recommended Practices with Older Children

More sophisticated applications are possible as children's print literacy improves. Collaborations now result in products that reflect higher-order decision making. These students are now reading to learn and can be described as skilled or independent readers who have a firm grasp of decoding and recognize many words automatically. We will discuss how creating multimedia book reviews can increase the amount and diversity of students' independent reading. We then consider a variety of other potentially effective computer practices with skilled readers. Together these examples provide insights into classroom communities where students are as comfortable with reading and writing on a computer screen as they are with reading and writing on paper. As with younger students, teachers must aim for applications in which the technology becomes transparent, merely a platform for communicating.

Multimedia Book Reviews.   It is 1:45 p.m. and the computer lab is bustling with the noise of Ms. Broward's fourth-graders developing their multimedia·book reviews by means of PowerPoint. One student is adding a digital movie to a slide, capturing the thoughts of a classmate. Another student links a slide to an audio file containing her best voice impressions of celebrities speaking about books. The slide contains pictures of those celebrities captured from the Internet. Another student is coaching a peer who is preparing to submit her book review to the school database of Power-Points so others can access it. They discover a misspelled word and quickly address it because they know others will be using these reviews. You would hardly know that many of these students struggle with reading because they exude confidence as they enter sophisticated critiques of books they read during independent reading time into a school database. In our work with students and teachers in upper elementary school grades, creating multimedia book reviews on the computer benefited students' reading and writing in ways unlikely to be achieved with conventional book reports and produced results that exceeded the widely used Accelerated Reader program (Reinking & Watkins, 2000).

Students were much more engaged in creating the multimedia book reviews, and we found their use of technology to respond to independent reading provided them a much richer socially interactive process (Reinking & Watkins, 1996). These benefits were derived partly from the fact that, unlike conventional book reports, the multimedia book reviews were stored in a searchable database that was easily accessible to other student looking for books to read and to parents who visited the school at various times (including a technology fair). Students' interactions about the books they were reading often took place incidentally outside of the classroom because they were celebrating their accomplishments in mastering the technology. For example, when one student eagerly explained to another, who was avidly listening, how he had added sound effects to his book review, the latter student incidentally discovered an interest in the book that was the subject of the sound-enhanced review. Note that this example illustrates how celebrating accomplishments in one medium can enhance involvement in another medium. Likewise, we found that some teachers' outlooks, approaches to instruction, and patterns of social interaction in the classroom changed through the process of creating and celebrating multimedia book reviews with their students.

Additional Computer Applications with Skilled Readers. Technology supplies skilled readers with a myriad of tools to conceptualize the knowledge they gain from reading and to chronicle their developing understandings of reading and writing. Jonassen (2006) suggests the best way to use computers is to use technology-based modeling tools, which he calls "Mindtools" (p. 12). Modeling tools help learners build alternative representations of ideas or experiences. For instance, Jonassen describes how using semantic organizers, concept mapping, or databases helps students construct representations of processes and relationships. After reading an expository text, a student could use the computer to develop a concept map to reconstruct the most important concepts from the text. Alternatively, students could collect an index of texts read in a database. Then, students can use this as a reference for solving problems and answering questions based on ideas they have documented. As these examples illustrate, technology provides enriching methods for students to acquire and manage ideas gained in content area reading.

A process-writing approach to composition, such as Writing Workshop, can be enhanced by computer-based collaborations. When children brainstorm, write drafts, revise, edit, and publish with a word-processing program, they can focus more on managing and organizing ideas and less on tedious or mechanical aspects of writing (Jones, 1994). Creating high-quality final drafts is also facilitated by desktop publishing capabilities such as formatting text, incorporating graphics, and selecting fonts. Wild and Braid (1996) noted that collaborative or cooperative computer-related word-processing experiences foster children's cognitively oriented talk related to the task of writing.

We believe that it is important for teachers to provide enough time for children to be able to compose on the computer, and not just retype a handwritten draft to be printed. To reap the benefits of technology, and, indeed, to prepare children to use the tools of contemporary writing, word processing must be integrated into all phases of the writing process. The computer can function as a digital writing folder or portfolio by storing text files such as reflective journals, topic ideas, responses to books, works in the early draft stage, works to be edited or spell-checked, or works to be read by and responded to by peers. However, unlike a conventional portfolio, the digital version reinforces the idea that electronic writing is never a final product. Each electronic file awaits future modification. Valmont (2003) described teachers who have successfully used technology to encourage older students to write. He illustrates how e-cards (electronic greeting cards) and e-zines (electronic magazines) are motivating opportunities for students to compose. Guzzetti and Gamboa (2004) also studied how adolescent girls use e-zine writing to develop and express their individual identities.

For teachers who are interested in improving their students' fluency, and thereby enhancing comprehension, Adams' (2006) work sheds light on a new technology that has the potential to boost reading while tracking fluency progress: a speech recognition program called *Reading Assistant*. This promising technology best supports novice and intermediate readers. These levels of readers already know how to decode but lack automaticity, vocabulary, or comprehension skills. When the child mispronounces a word, the *Reading Assistant* pronounces it correctly and marks the difficult word. When using the read-and-record feature, the speech-recognition layer of the software listens to the student as she or he reads aloud. If the computer detects that the student has stumbled or gotten stuck on a word, it provides assistance. Simultaneously, the computer records the reading and builds an ongoing record of what the student has read and reread, the difficulties the student had, and the progress made. A teacher can access fluency reports and various data that parallel the type of notes taken during a traditional running record. Adams' (2006) initial findings suggested that students who used the speech recognition program made fluency gains that were significantly greater than children who did not. Furthermore, many students were motivated to use the program because it kept them engaged during rereadings and they could chart their improvements.

Like the research with beginning readers, how to use technology appropriately with skilled readers is an area where more research is needed. Unfortunately, much of the research in this area is broad but shallow (Labbo & Reinking, 1999). For additional suggestions and strategies for integrating technology and literacy with skilled readers, see Figure 1.

Educator Collaboration to Envision New Digital Realities

How do you envision the model classroom that successfully integrates technology into literacy instruction? McKenna (2006) described a model primary-level classroom as including "computer-guided word study, electronic storybooks with decoding scaffolds, social interaction guided by software applications, graphics packages to assist children as they illustrate their work, and software designed to reinforce concepts about print" (p. xi). How many of these model classrooms have you visited recently? Despite what is known about effective uses of technology in literacy instruction, it appears that schools are slow to change and model classrooms are hard to come by. For instance, Turbill and Murray (2006) observe the disinclination of many Australian teachers to integrate technology and commented, "It is our belief that currently most teachers of early literacy view technology as something that their students can 'play' with during 'free time' or as a 'reward' after the real 'work' has been completed" (p. 93). Further, many websites claim to be technological resources for educators, but only contribute to the problem by offering little more than drill-and-skill activities or printable blackline images (Turbill & Murray, 2006).

How do you achieve your vision of new digital realities? When integrating technology into the reading curriculum, there is no prescription for how it should occur. Each classroom and school must negotiate the multiple realities that shape their own practice (Labbo & Reinking, 1999). An initial step in the change process may be locating or creating assessments like Turbill and Murray's (2006) "Concepts of Screen" that measures children's basic skill level in using the computer (e.g., use of the mouse, matching cursor and mouse, understanding the function of icons, etc.). Assessment data can guide starting points for instruction.

Safe first steps might include adding digital innovations that emulate established, effective literacy practices that lend themselves to computer innovation (see Labbo, 2005a, for ideas on Digital Morning Message or Digital K-W-L charts). Generally, teachers who succeed at making the cutting edge a comfortable place to be are constantly becoming technologically literate and keeping up with technological innovations through activities such as taking educational technology courses, participating in professional development either online or in real time, attending professional conferences, and reading professional articles (Labbo, 2005b, pp. 167–168). These professional development activities can be a starting point for conceiving new digital realities in one's classroom.

Yet, new digital technologies will not transform classrooms if teachers are not interested in and comfortable using them. Coiro (2005) describes teachers' lack of enthusiasm for large-group, workshop-style presentations about technology, in part because this format does not allow teachers to voice their own needs and their agendas for professional development. In contrast, she reports teachers' active engagement when they direct literacy learning Internet projects that are supported by various constituents including the library media specialist, the principal, and a university researcher. Small group or online professional development is adaptable to teachers' specific needs and to technological realities. Collaboration can enhance technology-based professional development (see Kinzer, Cammack, Labbo, Teale, & Sanny, 2006), just as collaboration can enrich the process of reflecting on one's practice.

Engagement Activities

Before reflecting on your next steps to implement technology in your classroom, school, or district, consider these overarching goals for integrating technology into literacy curricula:

1. New digital technologies should be available for literacy instruction.
2. New digital technologies should be used to enhance the goals of conventional literacy instruction.
3. New technologies should be used to positively transform literacy instruction.
4. New technologies should be used to prepare students for the literacy of the future.
5. New technologies should be used to empower students. (Labbo & Reinking, 1999, p. 481)

Your school or district may have similar technology goals and standards in place. With these general goals in mind, narrow your focus to your particular role and educational context as you address the following reflection questions.

Teachers

- What resources can I take advantage of to integrate literacy and technology? Consider computers and digital tools available, professional development opportunities, and people with high backgrounds in technology (e.g., reading specialists, technology coordinators, older students, parent volunteers, university partnerships).

- What tools (hardware or software) do I need to achieve my literacy and technology goals, how can I get these things, and how much time will be needed?
  - Hardware/Software: digital cameras, LCD projectors, flash drives, literacy software, etc.
  - Time: time to explore software and available resources, time to plan, and time to collaborate with others
- Do I need to seek additional funding through grant writing or donations from local businesses?
- How will I celebrate and showcase your students' digital work (e.g., organizing technology open houses, writing articles for professional journals, creating classroom websites, blogs or podcasts)?
- What is my action plan for implementing technology this year? What steps will I take first? What is my big goal and how do I need to collaborate to achieve this goal? How will I expand these goals next year?

Reading Coaches and Administrators

- How can I support teachers as they explore new technologies, trade ideas, and gain mastery of digital innovations?
- How can I create environments where teachers can experiment with technology together, collaborate, and develop action plans for implementing technology?

References

Adams, M. J. (2006). The promise of automatic speech recognition for fostering literacy growth in children and adults. In M. C. McKenna, L. D. Labbo, R. D. Kieffer, & D. Reinking (Eds.), *International handbook of literacy and technology* (Vol. 2, pp. 109–128). Mahwah, NJ: Erlbaum.

Anderson-Inman, L., & Horney, M. A. (1998). Transforming text for at-risk readers. In D. Reinking, M. C. McKenna, L. D. Labbo, & R. D. Kieffer (Eds.), *Handbook of literacy and technology: Transformations in a post-typographic world* (pp. 15–43). Mahwah, NJ: Erlbaum.

Beach, R., & Lundell, D. (1998). Early adolescents' use of computer-mediated communication in writing and reading. In D. Reinking, M. C. McKenna, L. D. Labbo, & R. D. Kieffer (Eds.), *Handbook of literacy and technology: Transformations in a post-typographic world* (pp. 93–112). Mahwah, NJ: Erlbaum.

Bear, D. R., Invernizzi, M., Templeton, S., & Johnston, F. (2004). *Words their way: Word study for phonics, vocabulary, and spelling instruction.* Upper Saddle River, NJ: Pearson Education, Inc.

Blok, H., Oostdam, R., Otter, M. E., & Overmaat, M. (2002). Computer-assisted instruction in support of beginning reading instruction: A review. *Review of Educational Research, 72,* 101–130.

Brandt, D. (2001). *Literacy in American lives.* Cambridge, UK: Cambridge University Press.

Burns, D. (1996, March). Technology in the ESL classroom. *Technology and Learning,* pp. 50–52.

Bus, A. G., de Jong, M. T., & Verhallen, M. (2006). CD-ROM talking books: A way to enhance early literacy? In M. C. McKenna, L. D. Labbo, R. D. Kieffer, & D. Reinking, (Eds.), *International handbook of literacy and technology* (Vol. 2, pp. 129–142). Mahwah, NJ: Erlbaum.

Calkins, L. (1983). *Lessons from a child: On the teaching and learning of writing.* Exter, N.H.: Heinmann Educational Books, Inc.

Calkins, L. M. (1983). *Lessons from a child.* Portsmouth, NH: Heinemann.

Carroll, M. (2004). *Cartwheels on the keyboard.* Newark, DE: International Reading Association.

Chamberlain, C. J. (2005). Literacy and technology: A world of ideas. In R. A. Karchmar, M. H. Mallette, J. Kara-Soteriou, & D. J. Leu (Eds.), *Innovative approaches to literacy education: Using the Internet to support new literacies* (pp. 44–64). Newark, DE: International Reading Association.

Coiro, J. (2005). Every teacher a Mrs. Rumphius: Empowering teachers with effective professional development. In R. A. Karchmar, M. H. Mallette, J. Kara-Soteriou, & D. J. Leu (Eds.), *Innovative approaches to literacy education: Using the Internet to support new literacies* (pp. 199–219). Newark, DE: International Reading Association.

Dalton, B., & Strangman, N. (2006). Improving struggling readers' comprehension through scaffolded hypertexts and other computer-based literacy programs. In M. C. McKenna, L. D. Labbo, R. D. Kieffer, & D. Reinking (Eds.), *International Handbook of Literacy and Technology* (Vol. 2, pp. 75–92). Mahwah, NJ: Erlbaum.

Doe, H. M. (2003). *Technology through children's literature: Grades K–5.* Portsmouth, NH: Teacher Ideas Press.

Flood, J., Heath, S. B., & Lapp, D. (Eds.). (1997). *Handbook of research on teaching literacy through the communicative and visual arts.* New York: Macmillan.

Fox, B. J., & Mitchell, M. J. (2000). Using technology to support word recognition, spelling, and vocabulary acquisition. In S. B. Wepner, W. J. Valmont, & R. Thurlow (Eds.), *Linking literacy and technology: A guide for K–8 classrooms* (pp. 42–75). Newark, DE: International Reading Association.

Gambrell, L. B. (2005). Reading literature, reading text, reading the Internet: The times are a' changing. *The Reading Teacher, 58,* 588–591.

Gambrell, L. B. (2006). Technology and the engaged literacy learner. In M. C. McKenna, L. D. Labbo, R. D. Kieffer, & D. Reinking (Eds.), *International Handbook of Literacy and Technology* (Vol. 2, pp. 289–294). Mahwah, NJ: Erlbaum.

Garner, R., & Gillingham, M. G. (1998). The Internet in the classroom: Is it the end of transmission-oriented pedagogy? In D. Reinking, M. C. McKenna, L. D. Labbo, & R. D. Kieffer (Eds.), *Handbook of literacy and technology: Transformations in a post-typographic world* (pp. 221–231). Mahwah, NJ: Erlbaum.

Graves, D. (1983). *Writing: Teachers and children at work.* Exeter, NH: Heinemann.

Graves, D., & Hansen, J. (1983). The Author's Chair. *Language Arts, 60,* 176–183.

Guzzetti, B. J., & Gamboa, M. (2004). Zines for social justice: Adolescent girls writing on their own. *Reading Research Quarterly, 39,* 406–436.

Hanlon, M. M., & Cantrell, J. (1999). Teaching a learning disabled adult to spell: Is it ever too late? *Journal of Adolescent and Adult Literacy, 43,* 4–11.

Hasselbring, T. (1999, May). *The computer doesn't embarrass me.* Paper presented at the meeting of the International Reading Association, San Diego, CA.

Haughland, S. W. (1992). The effect of computer software on preschool children's developmental gains. *Journal of Computing in Childhood Education, 3,* 15–29.

Hickman, C. (1994). *KidPix, Version 2.* Novato, CA: Broderbund Software.

Hubert, D. (2005). The Flat Stanley Project and other authentic applications of technology in the classroom. In R. A. Karchmar, M. H. Mallette, J. Kara-Soteriou, & D. J. Leu (Eds.), *Innovative approaches to literacy education: Using the Internet to support new literacies* (pp. 121–137). Newark, DE: International Reading Association.

Jonassen, D. H. (2006). *Modeling with technology: Mindtools for conceptual change.* Upper Saddle River, NJ: Pearson Education, Inc.

Jones, I. (1994). The effect of a word processor on the written composition of second-grade pupils. *Computers in Schools, 11*(2), 43–54.

Kamil, M. L., Intrator, S., & Kim, H. S. (2000). Effects of other technologies on literacy and learning. In M. L. Kamil, P. B. Mosenthal, P. D. Pearson, & R. Barr (Eds.), *Handbook of reading research* (Vol. 3, pp. 771–788). Mahwah, NJ: Erlbaum.

Kinzer, C. K. (2005). The intersection of schools, communities, and technology: Recognizing children's use of new literacies. In R. A. Karchmar, M. H. Mallette, J. Kara-Soteriou, & D. J. Leu (Eds.), *Innovative approaches to literacy education: Using the Internet to support new literacies* (pp. 65–82). Newark, DE: International Reading Association.

Kinzer, C. K., Cammack, D. W., Labbo, L. D., Teale, W. H., & Sanny, R. (2006). Using technology to (re)conceptualize pre-service literacy teacher education: Considerations of design, pedagogy, and research. In M. C. McKenna, L. D. Labbo, R. D. Kieffer, & D. Reinking (Eds.), *International Handbook of Literacy and Technology* (Vol. 2, pp. 211–233). Mahwah, NJ: Erlbaum.

Labbo, L. D. (1996). A semiotic analysis of young children's symbol making in a classroom computer center. *Reading Research Quarterly, 31*, 356–385.

Labbo, L. D. (2000). 12 things young children can do with a talking book in a classroom computer center. *The Reading Teacher, 53*(7), 542–546.

Labbo, L. D. (2003). The symbol-making machine: Examining the role of electronic symbol making in children's literacy development. In J. C. Richards & M. C. McKenna (Eds.), *Integrating multiple literacies in K–8 classrooms: Cases, commentaries, and practical applications* (pp. 10–17) Mahwah, NJ: Erlbaum.

Labbo, L. D. (2004, April). Author's computer chair [Technology in Literacy department]. *The Reading Teacher, 57*(7), 688–691. Available at www.readingonline.org/electronic/elec_index.asp?HREF=/electronic/RT/4-04_column/index.html

Labbo, L. D. (2005a). Moving from the tried and true to the new: Digital Morning Message. *The Reading Teacher, 58*(8), 782–785.

Labbo, L. D. (2005b). Fundamental qualities of effective Internet literacy instruction: An exploration of worthwhile classroom practices. In R. A. Karchmar, M. H. Mallette, J. Kara-Soteriou, & D. J. Leu (Eds.), *Innovative approaches to literacy education: Using the Internet to support new literacies* (pp. 165–179). Newark, DE: International Reading Association.

Labbo, L. D. (2005c). Books and computer response activities that support literacy development. *The Reading Teacher, 59*(3), 288–292.

Labbo, L. D., & Ash, G. E. (1998). Supporting young children's computer-related literacy development in classroom centers. In S. Neuman & K. Roskos (Eds.), *Children achieving: Instructional practices in early literacy* (pp. 180–197). Newark, DE: International Reading Association.

Labbo, L. D., Eakle, A. J., & Montero, K. M. (2002, May). Digital language experience approach: Using digital photographs and creativity software as a language experience approach innovation. *Reading Online, 5*(8). Available at www.readingonline.org/electronic/elec_index.asp?HREF=labbo2/index.html

Labbo, L. D., & Kuhn, M. R. (2000). Weaving chains of affect and cognition: A young child's understanding of CD-ROM talking books. *Journal of Literacy Research, 32*, 187–210.

Labbo, L. D., Montero, M. K., & Eakle, A. J. (2001, October). Learning how to read what's displayed on school hallways walls—and what's not. *Reading Online, 5*(3). Available at www.readingonline.org/newliteracies/lit_index.asp?HREF=labbo/index.html

Labbo, L. D., Phillips, M., & Murray, B. (1995–1996). "Writing to read": From inheritance to innovation and invitation. *The Reading Teacher, 49*(4), 314–321.

Labbo, L. D., & Reinking, D. (1999). Negotiating the multiple realities of technology in literacy research and instruction. *Reading Research Quarterly, 34*, 478–492.

Labbo, L. D., Sprague, L., with Montero, M. K., & Font, G. (2000, July). Connecting a computer center to themes, literature and kindergarteners' literacy needs. *Reading Online, 4*(1). Available at http://www.readingonline.org/electronic/elec_index.asp?HREF=labbo/index.html

Lankshear, C., & Knobel, M. (2003). *New literacies: Changing knowledge and classroom learning.* Philadelphia: Open University Press.

Leu, D. J. (2000). Literacy and technology: Deictic consequences for literacy education in an information age. In M. L. Kamil, P. B. Mosenthal, P. D. Pearson, & R. Barr (Eds.), *Handbook of reading research* (Vol. 3, pp. 745–772). Mahwah, NJ: Erlbaum.

Leu, D. J. (2002). The new literacies: Research on reading instruction with the Internet. In A. E. Farstrup & S. J. Samuels (Eds.), *What research has to say about reading instruction* (pp. 310–336). Newark, DE: International Reading Association.

Leu, D. J., & Leu, D. D. (2000). *Teaching with the Internet: Lessons from the classroom* (3rd ed.). Norwood, MA: Christopher-Gordon.

Lewis, C., & Fabos, B. (2005). Instant messaging, literacies, and social identities. *Reading Research Quarterly, 40*, 470–501.

McKenna, M. C. (1998). Electronic texts and the transformation of beginning reading. In D. Reinking, M. C. McKenna, L. D. Labbo, & R. D. Kieffer (Eds.), *Handbook of literacy and technology: Transformations in a post-typographic world* (pp. 45–59). Mahwah, NJ: Erlbaum.

McKenna, M. C. (2002). Phonics software for a new millennium. *Reading and Writing Quarterly, 18*, 93–96.

McKenna, M. C. (2006). Introduction: Trends and trajectories of literacy and technology in the new millennium. In M. C. McKenna, L. D. Labbo, R. D. Kieffer, & D. Reinking (Eds.), *International Handbook of Literacy and Technology* (Vol. 2, pp. 1–18). Mahwah, NJ: Erlbaum.

McKenna, M. C., Cowart, E., & Watkins, J. W. (1997, December). *Effects of talking books on the reading growth of problem readers in second grade.* Paper presented at the meeting of the National Reading Conference, Scottsdale, AZ.

McKenna, M. C., Reinking, D., & Labbo, L. D. (1997). Using talking books with reading-disabled students. *Reading and Writing Quarterly, 13,* 185–190.

McKenna, M. C., Reinking, D., Labbo, L. D., & Kieffer, R. D. (1999). The electronic transformation of literacy and its implications for the struggling reader. *Reading and Writing Quarterly, 15,* 111–126.

McKenna, M. C., & Shaffield, M. L. (2002, May). *Creating electronic books and documents for poor decoders.* Paper presented at the meeting of the International Reading Association, San Francisco, CA.

Miller, S. D. (2003). How high- and low-challenge tasks affect motivation and learning: Implications for struggling learners. *Reading and Writing Quarterly, 19,* 39–57.

Morrell, E. (2002). Toward a critical pedagogy of popular culture: Literacy development among urban youth. *Journal of Adolescent and Adult Literacy, 46,* 72–77.

My first incredible amazing dictionary (CD-ROM). (1995). New York: Dorling Kindersley Multimedia.

Neuman, S. B., & Roskos, K. (1992). Literacy objects as cultural tools: Effects on children's literacy behaviors in play. *Reading Research Quarterly, 27,* 202–225.

Papert, S. (1980). *Mindstorms.* New York: Basic Books.

Peters, J. M. (1996). Paired keyboards as a tool of Internet exploration of 3rd grade students. *Journal of Educational Computing Research, 14,* 229–242.

Pressley, M. (2006). *Reading instruction that works: The case for balanced teaching.* New York: Guilford Press.

Purcell-Gates, V. (2004). Foreword. In J. M. Wood *Literacy online: New tools for struggling readers and writers.* (pp. v–viii). Portsmouth, NH: Heinemann.

Reading Mansion [Computer software]. (1998). Scotts Valley, CA: Great Wave Software.

Reinking, D. (1995). Reading and writing with computers: Literacy research in a post-typographic world. In K. A. Hinchman, D. J. Leu, & C. K. Kinzer (Eds.), *Perspectives on literacy research and practice, 44th yearbook of the National Reading Conference* (pp. 17–33). Chicago: National Reading Conference.

Reinking, D. (1998). Technology and literacy education in the next century: Exploring the connection between work and schooling. *Peabody Journal of Education, 73,* 273–289.

Reinking, D. (1994). *Electronic literacy.* (Perspectives in Reading Research No. 4, National Reading Research Center). Athens: University of Georgia Press.

Reinking D., Labbo, L. D., & McKenna, M. C. (2000). From assimilation to accommodation: A developmental framework for integrating digital technologies into literacy research and instruction. *Journal of Reading Research, 23,* 110–122.

Reinking, D., & Watkins, J. (2000). A formative experiment investigating the use of multimedia book reviews to increase elementary students' independent reading. *Reading Research Quarterly, 35,* 384–419.

Reinking, D., & Watkins, J. (1996). A formative experiment investigating the use of multimedia book reviews to increase elementary students' independent reading. *Reading Research Report No. 56.* Athens, GA: National Reading Research Center, College Park, MD.

Richards, J. C., & McKenna, M. C. (Eds.). (2003). *Teaching for multiple literacies: Cases and commentaries from K–6 classrooms.* Hillsdale, NJ: Erlbaum.

Sangiuliano, G. (2005). Books on tapes for kids: A language arts-based service-learning project. In R. A. Karchmar, M. H. Mallette, J. Kara-Soteriou, & D. J. Leu (Eds.), *Innovative approaches to literacy education: Using the Internet to support new literacies* (pp. 13–27). Newark, DE: International Reading Association.

Schwartz, S. (1985). Microcomputers and young children: An exploratory study. In *Issues for educators: A monograph series.* Flushing, NY: School of Education, Queens College, City College of New York.

Shilling, W. (1997). Young children using computers to make discoveries about written language. *Early Childhood Education Journal, 24*, 253–259.

Stauffer, R. G. (1970). *The language-experience approach to the teaching of reading.* New York: Harper & Row.

Turbill, J. (2003, March). Exploring the potential of the digital language experience approach in Australian classrooms, *Reading Online, 6*(7). Available at http://www.readingonline.org/international/inter_index.asp?HREF=turbill7

Turbill, J., & Murray, J. (2006). Early literacy and new technologies in Australian schools: Policy, research, and practice. In M. C. McKenna, L. D. Labbo, R. D. Kieffer, & D. Reinking (Eds.), *International Handbook of Literacy and Technology* (Vol. 2, pp. 93–108). Mahwah, NJ: Erlbaum.

Valmont, W. J. (2000). What do teachers do in technology-rich classrooms? In S. B. Wepner, W. J. Valmont, & R. Thurlow (Eds.), *Linking Literacy and Technology.* Newark, DE: International Reading Association.

Valmont, W. J. (2003). *Technology for literacy teaching and learning.* Boston: Houghton Mifflin Company.

Vygotsky, L. (1978). *Mind in society: The development of higher psychological processes.* Cambridge, MA: Harvard University Press.

Walmsley, S. A., & Allington, R. L. (1995). Redefining and reforming instructional support programs for at-risk students. In R. L. Allington & S. A. Walmsley (Eds.), *No quick fix: Rethinking literacy programs in America's elementary schools* (pp. 19–44). Newark: DE/New York: International Reading Association and Teachers College Press.

Wild, M., & Braid, P. (1996). Children's talk in cooperative groups. *Journal of Computer Assisted Learning, 12*, 216–321.

Wood, J. M. (2004). *Literacy online: New tools for struggling readers and writers.* Portsmouth, NH: Heinemann.

Yang, S. C., & Liu, S. F. (2005). The study of interactions and attitudes of third-grade students learning information technology via a cooperative approach. *Computers in Human Behavior, 21*, 45–72.

Children's Literature

Cannon, J. (1993). *Stella Luna.* New York: Harcourt Brace.

Classroom Implications

1. To what extent do you agree or disagree with Hobbs' arguments about the evolution of literacy? What are the implications of her expanded notion for the literacy curriculum?

2. To what extent have you observed the applications described by McKenna and colleagues in your school setting? How practical are such applications? Can you suggest changes you might make in your instruction in order to implement some of their ideas?

For Further Reading

Eagleton, M. B., Dobler, E., & Leu, D. J. (2006). *Reading the Web: Strategies for Internet inquiry.* New York: Guilford.

McKenna, M. C. (2002). Hypertext. In B. J. Guzzetti (Ed.), *Literacy in America: An encyclopedia of history, theory, and practice* (pp. 233–237). Santa Barbara, CA: ABC-CLIO.

McKenna, M. C., Labbo, L. D., Kieffer, R., & Reinking, D. (Eds.). (2006). *International handbook of literacy and technology* (Vol. 2). Mahwah, NJ: Lawrence Erlbaum.

Online Resources

Bruce, B. (Posted May 2001). Constructing a Once-and-Future History of Learning Technologies. *Journal of Adolescent and Adult Literacy*
www.readingonline.org/electronic/elec_index.asp?HREF=/electronic/jaal/5-01_Column/index.html

Dalton, B., & Grisham, D. L. (Posted March 2002). Taking a position on integrating literacy and technology in the curriculum
www.readingonline.org/editorial/edit_index.asp?HREF=/editorial/march2002/index.html

International Reading Association. (Posted December 2001). Integrating literacy and technology in the curriculum. Position Statement
www.reading.org/downloads/positions/ps1048_technology.pdf

National Council of Teachers of English. (2005). Multi-Modal Literacies. Guideline
www.ncte.org/about/over/positions/category/media/123213.htm

The Miss Rumphius Award for Classroom Websites
www.reading.org/resources/community/links_rumphius_info.html

Leu, D. J., Kinzer, C. K., Coiro, J., & Cammack, D. W. (2004). Toward a theory of new literacies emerging from the Internet and other information and communication technologies. In R. B. Ruddell & N. J. Unrau (Eds.), *Theoretical Models and Processes of Reading* (pp. 1570–1613). Newark, DE: International Reading Association.
www.reading.org/Library/Retrieve.cfm?D=10.1598/0872075028.54&F=bk502-54-Leu.pdf

Chapter 9

Writing

By the usual method of teaching to write, the art of writing is totally distinct from reading or spelling. On the new plan, spelling and writing are connected and equally blended with reading.

—Joseph Lancaster (1808)

Children's early written products resemble spoken language, but the complexity of the written productions increases steadily through the elementary school years.

—Albert J. Harris & Edward R. Sipay (1990)

. . . writing is a powerful ally and aid to reading. From the very beginning, students need to engage frequently in activities in which reading and writing are paired. . . .

—Michael Graves, Connie Juel, & Bonnie Graves (2007)

Changes and Issues in Writing

Few areas of literacy instruction have undergone more sweeping changes over the past 35 years than writing. Several important trends have characterized this period and have led to a transformation in the way educators have come to view the role of writing.

1. *Emphasis on process.* Insights into the approaches used by skilled writers have led to a refocusing of instruction from the final product to the process through which it was produced. Consequently, *process writing* instruction is now an everyday activity in many classrooms and at virtually every grade level. While authorities differ slightly on the nature of the stages, there is general agreement that they include the following: (1) drafting, (2) revising, (3) editing, (4) proofing, and (5) publishing. Nancie Atwell's approach to the "writers' workshop" has become a popular

means of facilitating children as they move through various stages of the writing process, but there are other viable approaches as well.

2. *Emphasis on learning.* It is now undisputed that writing can cause knowledge to become organized and coherent. Writing is for this reason now recognized as a means of reinforcing and extending learning. The phrases, *writing to learn* and *writing across the curriculum*, are testaments to its usefulness as a learning tool.

3. *Emphasis on reading.* The *reading–writing connection* has emerged as one of the more important insights of the twentieth century. Reading and writing are now viewed not as opposite processes, but as complementary activities. In particular, an early emphasis on writing facilitates learning to read (e.g., Adams, 1990). Through the years, important approaches to beginning reading instruction have made writing a central component. These include Montessori's techniques and the language experience approach. The success of a writing emphasis on the reading development of some children led Patricia Cunningham to make writing one of the "four blocks" in her own highly popular approach to language arts instruction (see Cunningham & Allington, 2007).

4. *Emphasis on word processing.* Word processing software is now firmly established in the workplace and is increasingly evident in classrooms. As some have put it, the most relevant instructional question will soon become not *whether* to incorporate word processing but *how* to incorporate it. Still, hardware limitations have meant that word processing, as an integral part of writing instruction, is a trend that is still in its early stages, particularly in elementary schools.

These trends, which together suggest a heightened interest in writing instruction, have given rise to a host of issues. The following list captures some of the more important controversies, though other issues could undoubtedly be added. Those that follow underscore just how difficult these issues tend to be.

1. *Time.* Granted, writing can help young children learn to read and can assist other children in organizing and solidifying what they learn. But writing takes time. What is the proper balance between classroom time devoted to writing activities and to other means of engaging learners? And what about the teacher's time? Given that children's writing must be *read*, how much writing can feasibly be assigned and evaluated?

2. *Attitudes.* Many children lack a natural inclination to engage in writing. In fact, studies suggest a steady worsening of attitudes toward writing into the secondary years (Kear, Coffman, & McKenna, 1997). Good writing is, after all, nearly always taxing. How can teachers effectively motivate their students to engage in meaningful writing?

3. *Assessment.* Evaluating writing is anything but straightforward. Rubric systems, consisting of descriptive rating scales devoted to various aspects of writing are now used extensively and help make the process systematic. However, many questions remain. What is the proper balance between assessing mechanics and content? How can the sensibilities of developing writers be spared the inhibiting effects of candid criticisms?

4. *Electronic transformation.* Word processing has already drastically altered the landscape of writing instruction, and changes are still under way. The use of spelling and grammar checkers, for example, can heavily support a student who is deficient in the mechanics of writing. Will the assessment of writing mechanics be permanently distorted by the use of these devices? As such devices become increasingly part of the preferred method of writing, both at home and in the workplace, does it matter that an individual's mechanical deficiencies may be remedied by their continual use? Moreover, such support extends well beyond mechanics. Access to a variety of electronic sources, such as encyclopedias and Internet documents, now makes copying and pasting from a variety of sources a simple matter. At what point do documents constructed in this way amount to plagiarism? For that matter, will plagiarism continue to have any real meaning in an electronic future? Finally, writing in electronic environments makes options available that have no place in traditional writing. For example, incorporating animation and hypertextual links to other documents are changing what it means to write. How must writing instruction change to accommodate these options?

Research on Writing Instruction

Unlike reading, for which an abundance of research evidence is available, writing suffers from a dearth of research—some would say neglect. However, a recent report of the Carnegie Corporation (Graham & Perin, 2006) identifies eleven elements of instruction for teaching children in the upper elementary grades and higher:

1. *Writing strategies*, which involves teaching students strategies for planning, revising, and editing their compositions.
2. *Summarization*, which involves explicitly and systematically teaching students how to summarize texts.
3. *Collaborative writing*, which uses instructional arrangements in which adolescents work together to plan, draft, revise, and edit their compositions.
4. *Specific product goals*, which assigns students specific, reachable goals for the writing they are to complete.
5. *Word processing*, which uses computers and word processors as instructional supports for writing assignments.
6. *Sentence combining*, which involves teaching students to construct more complex, sophisticated sentences.
7. *Prewriting*, which engages students in activities designed to help them generate or organize ideas for their composition.
8. *Inquiry activities*, which engages students in analyzing immediate, concrete data to help them develop ideas and content for a particular writing task.
9. *Process writing approach*, which interweaves a number of writing instructional activities in a workshop environment that stresses extended writing opportunities, writing for authentic audiences, personalized instruction, and cycles of writing.

10. *Study of models*, which provides students with opportunities to read, analyze, and emulate models of good writing.
11. *Writing for content learning*, which uses writing as a tool for learning content material. (Graham & Perin, 2007, pp. 4–5)

The Carnegie Report may be downloaded free of change. See the Online Resources section of this chapter for details.

As You Read

Michael Moore, editor of NCTE's journal, *English Education*, is a national authority on approaches to writing instruction and assessment. He wrote this article at our request, and it captures the chronology of how these approaches have evolved. We think readers will appreciate not only his insights but his personal experiences and honest admissions about his own teaching. Karen Bromley then elaborates on Moore's final theme, the influence of technology. She discusses this influence and raises important questions that must be addressed if we are to be effective teachers of writing. As you read, keep these questions in mind:

1. What are the major trends in writing research, writing instruction, and writing assessment?
2. What future projections seem likely in these areas, especially given the advent of technology?
3. Are high-stakes assessments causing a pendulum swing back to the product mentality, or will process and product remain merged?

References

Adams, M. J. (1990). *Beginning to read: Thinking and learning about print.* Cambridge, MA: MIT Press.

Cunningham, P. M., & Allington, R. L. (2007). *Classrooms that work: They can all read and write* (3rd ed.). Boston: Allyn & Bacon.

Graves, M. F., Juel, C., & Graves, B. (2007). *Teaching reading in the 21st century* (4th ed.). Boston: Allyn & Bacon.

Harris, A. J., & Sipay, E. R. (1990). *How to increase reading ability: A guide to developmental & remedial methods* (9th ed.). New York: Longman.

Kear, D. J., Coffman, G. A., & McKenna, M. C. (1997, December). *Students' attitudes toward writing: A national survey.* Paper presented at the meeting of the National Reading Conference, Scottsdale, AZ.

Lancaster, J. (1808). *Improvements in education.* London: J. Lancaster.

Issues and Trends in Writing

MICHAEL T. MOORE

• • • • •

Those of us who lived through the days when writing process/composition theory was still developing all have our own particular stories. Each of us sees this history in a unique way, through the lens of context. It is my hope that sharing my own story will help crystallize key issues and trends in the teaching of writing.

As an English and reading teacher in the early seventies, I am still amazed at how inadequately prepared I was to teach writing. I can think of no college course that even mentioned the teaching of writing in my undergraduate teacher preparation. In retrospect, I intuited how to teach writing from my personal experiences, first as a student in public school and later in college. These experiences were remarkably similar. They involved writing reams of compositions, submitting them to be graded, and receiving each one back, hideously scarred with red ink that eerily resembled war wounds. A cycle of subsequent rewrites then began (when rewrites were allowed), and with each revision there seemed to be less "blood." I was a journeyman, or apprentice, at what seemed a highly technical craft governed by arcane rules. I learned about comma splices and fused sentences by committing these errors (first as a high school writer and later as a college freshman), having my transgressions pointed out to me, and then doing the appropriate penance. As I grew more adept at anticipating what was expected, I became a better academic writer. I intuited what each teacher wanted through the inevitable cycle of revisions.

The lessons I learned in red were the lessons that I passed along to my own students when I became a teacher. As a beginning classroom teacher, I had no idea that I would live through a paradigm shift that would substantially change the way we conceptualize and teach writing. When I now reflect, I am amazed at what we did not know as a field when I started teaching, and what we now take for granted and that is, in fact, part of every teacher education program. I didn't know about process, free writing, journals and writing logs, topic choice, multiple perspectives, multiple drafts, the effect of audience, the many ways writing could be assessed (holistic evaluation, primary trait scoring, the effect of audience on writing, peer editing, and portfolio assessment), the effect of topic on writing, or even the many kinds of writing that could exist in school. I could not have predicted the trends that I would see

Reprinted with permission of author, Michael T. Moore.

develop from this shift in emphasis. The study of process over product would spawn the writing process movement, the Bay Area and National Writing Projects, workshop approaches to teaching writing, a reappraisal of revision in writing, and a new focus on writing assessment.

The first inkling I had that change was in the wind for writing instruction was when I joined the National Council of Teachers of English in 1973 and read an article in *English Journal* by Toby Fulwiler on the subject of journal writing and its implications for multiple drafts. This was the first time I had ever considered a form of writing other than a formal essay. During this time, I became a writing teacher at the middle school, high school and college levels, as well as a writing researcher.

A Brief History of Writing Research

It is difficult to separate writing from rhetoric since composition/writing grew out of the 19th-century topic of Rhetoric. In fact, this tradition has returned, as indicated by a quick review of the tables of contents in such leading writing journals as *College Composition and Communication* and *Written Communication*. Further evidence is in the number of university departments that have broken from literature studies to form new departments or programs often named Rhetoric and Composition Studies or variations of these terms. This division has implications for both elementary and secondary schools, where composition has always played a subordinate role to literature study and where writing is typically viewed as supporting reading or English. At the postsecondary level, more fragmentation exists; composition and rhetoric are often found in a separate department offering support courses for all majors and including minors in writing, creative writing, technical writing, and so on. Before 1830, the notion of writing as composing did not really exist, and writing instruction focused on penmanship and transcription (Monaghan, 2003). This instruction occurred in grammar schools. Eventually, reformers influenced schooling to the extent that students were permitted to self-actualize their experiences through writing (Woods, 1985). Continued reform moved the notion of writing as a matter of mental gymnastics involving grammar toward a model of practice-while-doing. Ironically perhaps, schools were much more innovative than universities in this movement (Schultz, 1999).

The acknowledged view from the late 1930s until recently stemmed from a "formalist" view of literature instruction that originated with the "New Critics." This group included Robert Penn Warren, John Crowe Ransom, Allen Tate, and others who advocated that the meaning of a text could only be determined by a close reading. It was the text alone that counted—not the writer or the circumstances that surrounded the creation of the text. In other words, any text should stand alone. Everything we needed to construct meaning was in any given text. This view wended its way from literary critics to college classrooms and soon to public school English curricula. Thus, writing for students meant that their written products were subject to the same kind of close reading used to read published texts. Accordingly, texts were subject to rigid structural guidelines in the four traditional modes of discourse: description, narration, exposition and argument (Young, 1978).

This model entailed a close study of grammar. This "classical" model held that the importance of an education was to train one's memory and one's reasoning ability (Applebee, 1974). English itself held little interest as a subject, but grammar had two things going for it. Students had to learn rules and how to apply them—tasks that lent themselves to explicit curricula and concrete assessments. Grammar instruction became great preparation for college but was not necessarily a college subject.

Interestingly enough, 1874 marked the first time that composition became a prescribed course at a university (Harvard). English study as a discipline in our public schools traces its own beginnings to 1958, when funding from the Ford Foundation coincided with righteous curricular squabbling involving both the Modern Language Association and the National Council of Teachers of English (Applebee, 1974). As a field matures, a worldview emerges from the accumulation of research, and this view becomes dominant. Paradigm shifts occur when the previous stance is no longer tenable. A paradigm shift in the teaching of writing began in the early sixties. In 1963, Braddock, Lloyd-Jones, and Schoer, writing in *Research in Written Composition*, identified a list of 504 studies, and the "worldview" became evident. Only two of these studies dealt with the process of writing; the rest were grounded in a very different perspective. Specifically, what existed prior to 1962 was what Young (1978) called a concern with the composed product, the analysis of discourse, and a general preoccupation with the essay form and the term paper. The studies reviewed by Braddock et al. in 1963 focused on curricula, textbook making, rhetoric, teaching by television, writing vocabulary, handwriting, typewriting, among others. Thus, North (1987) dates the birth of modern Composition (with a capital *C*), to 1963 and the seminal review by Braddock et al. of written composition research to that time. Over the next ten years, a distinct shift in stance would be very apparent in Janet Emig's book, *The Composing Process of Twelfth Graders*, James Moffett's *Teaching the Universe of Discourse*, Donald Murray's *A Writer Teaches Writing*, Peter Elbow's *Writing without Teachers*, and Ken Macrorie's *Telling Writing*. Also during this period, NCTE began plans for a bulletin soon to become the journal, *Research in the Teaching of English*, first edited by Richard Braddock and N. S. Blount. This new journal became a forum for composition research (Gere, 1985). Cooper and Odell (1978) in *Research on Composing: Points of Departure*, their sequel to *Research in Written Composition*, challenged researchers to examine the nature of writing competence, successful writing practices, characteristics of competent writing teachers, and to develop new methods or procedures suited to studying these questions.

Kuhn (1964) calls a "paradigm" a system of widely held beliefs, values, and supporting elements that form a discipline or a worldview. In his influential book, *The Structure of Scientific Revolutions*, Kuhn (1964) called into question the standard view of science. He critically examined previous approaches and encouraged new interpretations of previous research and new research embracing new approaches. By 1973, writing research therefore had the theoretical underpinnings to explode in several new directions, most notably into questions of process and assessment. Cooper & Odell's challenge clearly signaled the end of the previous paradigm and the ushering in of a new paradigm in the teaching of writing.

Writing as a Process

The birth of the process writing approach arguably occurred in 1971 with the publication of Janet Emig's dissertation, *The Composing Processes of Twelfth Graders.* North (1987) called it "the single most influential piece of Researcher inquiry—and maybe *any* kind of inquiry—in Composition's short history" (p. 197). Emig's study was a venture away from product examination and it focused on how writers actually wrote. Her study spawned a plethora of similar investigations that looked at college writers, children learning to write, the causes of writing failure, the role of the teacher, and other issues. Emig's study also served to condemn public school writing instruction, which she called "a neurotic activity" (p. 99). She wittily observed:

> A species of extensive writing that recurs so frequently in student accounts that it deserves special mention is the five-paragraph theme, consisting of one paragraph of introduction . . . three of expansion and example . . . and one of conclusion. This mode is so indigenously American that it might be called the Fifty-Star Theme. In fact, the reader might imagine behind this and the next three paragraphs Kate Smith singing "God Bless America" or the piccolo obligato from "The Stars and Stripes Forever." (p. 97)

I encountered Emig's work in 1973 as a graduate student and first-year middle grades teacher. She described the writing process as both "laminated and recursive" and claimed that there was a "blending" of identifiable writing behaviors she had observed, such as "planning, starting, stopping," and so on. Over the next thirty years, composition research on process would flourish to the extent that most universities now support composition studies as a distinct discipline. Writing research is published regularly in both liberal arts and education venues. The Bay Area and later the National Writing Project were partially funded by the federal government. Writing Across the Curriculum as a movement has been with us almost as long as research on composing. Growing scholarship on writing assessment and technology has identified new areas of research on writing. However, old habits die hard, and although most teachers know "process," a regular observer of schools might note that a wide gulf continues to exist between research and practice (Burhans, 1983). One does not have to travel far to find that the five-paragraph theme is alive and well, and indeed flourishing, in our nation's schools.

One of the earliest process-writing proponents was Donald Murray and especially influential was his 1968 book, *A Writer Teaches Writing.* Although this book has undergone several editions, I have always found that his first edition most clearly conceptualizes what we mean by process. Murray later crystallized his view of this process as "Collect, Plan, Develop" (Murray, 1985), but it is in his description of the writer's "seven skills" that I began to understand what Emig was referring to as a "recursive process." Murray's seven skills were simply these: A writer "discovers a subject, senses an audience, searches for specifics, creates a design, writes, develops a critical eye, and rewrites" (pp. 2–12). Although missing from subsequent editions, these seven skills became the way I understood process to work and what it might mean for a new teacher. The term *recursive* means that we are not quite sure when a particular process is happening. That is to say, writing is not a lock-step affair; while there is a general order, the steps are occasionally repeated and feed back to each other. A writer might be developing a topic at any time, including when he/she is developing a critical eye or editing. Editing itself might be occurring as the writer is discovering a topic or sensing an audience.

The purpose of instruction shifted from teacher to student. The implications for instruction were that writing was about student choice. Students wrote to clarify and understand their own thinking. Writing was no longer only formal; personal and narrative forms of writing were encouraged. Multiple drafts became part of the process and we kept student writing in writing portfolios, a device borrowed from artists.

James Moffett published *Teaching the Universe of Discourse* in 1968 as a companion to his *Student Centered Language Arts Curriculum, Grades K–13: A Handbook for Teachers* (1983). He proposed a highly interactive curriculum that stressed drama, writing for different audiences, peer review, and editing and adaptation over formal writing assessment. Moffett also wrote about the reading-writing connection in *Active Voice: A Writing Program across the Curriculum* (1992). The "role of the teacher, then," wrote Moffett, "is to teach the students to teach each other" (p. 196). Moffett put his theory into practice by publishing the highly controversial "Interaction" series through Houghton Mifflin. This series was an integrative curriculum that promoted trade books containing real literature and students' responding to literature through a process approach. This series actually led to rioting in Kanawha County, West Virginia. This account is chronicled by Moffett (1989) in *Storm in the Mountains: A Case Study of Censorship, Conflict, and Consciousness.*

Today, writing process is seen to comprise a number of events (not always agreed upon). They include talking, reading, planning, idea generating, detail generating, collaborating, drafting, editing, reenvisioning, proofing, sharing, publishing, responding and revisiting. Students choose their own subjects, they become part of a community of writers, they write to explore, they have something to say to us and each other, and they publish what they write. Standard Five in the *IRA/NCTE Standards for the English Language Arts* (1996) reads: "Students employ a wide range of strategies as they write and use different writing process elements appropriately to communicate with different audiences for a variety of purposes." Unfortunately, in too many writing classrooms the emphasis is still on the product, and the primary goal is that students learn to write academically acceptable exposition. Traditions die hard.

Process and the Writing Development of Children

As a new college professor, I became a consultant to a local school system interested in implementing a writing process approach. We decided to begin our program with kindergarten. During the summer, the kindergarten teachers and I discussed process writing and the approaches they might use. We decided we would implement journals and guided writing assignments at the beginning of the school year. On the first day of school, students found nicely bound journals on their desks, colorfully decorated and embossed with each student's name. Children were invited to write in their journals with their teacher as part of each morning's routine. I then observed what I had only read about in research journals (Dyson, 1981; Graves, 1981; Gundlach, 1981). Given a brief daily prompt to write about their families, pets, school, or favorite things to do, children proceeded to write or imitate behaviors they'd observed to be associated with writing. In other words they opened their journals and began to write, moving from left to right and top to bottom. Most of what we observed were squiggly lines that imitated writing. Along with the "writing" were drawings, the beginning of letters and other curious symbols. There were a very few children who could actually write some words. However, most could only vaguely imitate writers; thus, they attempted to produce something that they thought resembled a text. When children were invited to sit in the "Author's Chair" and share their writing, they then imitated readers reading a text. When interrupted and asked exactly where certain words occurred in their writing, the children were able to point without hesitation to certain lines confidently. If stopped early on, they pointed to "words" near the top of the page. If asked to stop later, they pointed to words correspondingly farther down. This behavior reflects the complex and hierarchical nature of the symbol system of written language. Children appear to have an almost intuitive grasp of written syntax in much the same way that they quickly assimilate spoken syntax and often feel free to experiment with it. As students wrote daily in their journals, with their teachers, and shared every day, we noticed that students soon became frustrated by what they couldn't produce. We began to see more attempts at letters and comments like, "That's a *T* and it goes in Brittany, but I don't know how to make that." As children learned the symbol system, the alphabetic nature of writing, journals became much harder for them to write, but the production of written language began to grow.

We also noted a greater concern for accuracy when children wrote cards or other such work destined to go home—to a different audience. We began to see closer attention to real text production. We noticed that most of the children learned the letters of their names first and that connections started to build between these letters and other words with the same letters. Dyson and Freedman (2003) suggest that teachers listen closely to children's talk at this stage to gain insight and to help them reflect further on all aspects of thinking and writing. We also noticed that children's knowledge of narrative structure was more advanced than we thought it would be. Children knew how to tell stories and knew enough about basic plot, character and action to wish to reproduce these in their writing.

Children in this project engaged in all aspects of the writing process as we knew it at the time. We focused on making writing a daily activity, we sought to encourage the recursive aspect of the process and not promote the process as linear. We had children writing for real audiences and we gave them opportunities to share their writing. Our aim was to continue with these same students from grade to grade so that they would have the benefit of a consistent model.

Outgrowths of the Writing Process Movement: The Bay Area Writing Project and the National Writing Project

Tracing its roots directly to the outgrowth of writing/composition theory was the 1974 inception of the Bay Area Writing Project (Bay Area Writing Project Web site) in the

Graduate School of the University of California at Berkeley. The Bay Area Writing Project would later become the flagship site of the National Writing Project. Writing projects abound and are firmly entrenched as summer institutes in most states. A teacher-teaching-teachers model is used, in collaboration with a university writing program. The Bay Area Writing Project's stated goals are:

- To improve student writing abilities by improving the teaching and learning of writing in Bay Area schools.
- To provide professional development programs for classroom teachers.
- To expand the professional roles of teachers.
- To increase the academic achievement of the Bay Area's diverse student population. (Bay Area Writing Project Web site)

The Bay Area Project like the National Writing Project embraces the following principles:

- Writing is fundamental to learning in all disciplines.
- Writing deserves constant attention from kindergarten through university.
- Teachers are the key to educational change.
- The best teacher of teachers is another teacher.
- Effective literacy programs are inclusive, reaching all teachers in order to reach all students.
- Universities and schools accomplish more in partnership.
- Exemplary teachers of writing write and use writing themselves.
- Excellent professional development is an ongoing process. (Bay Area Writing Project Web site)

Each year, close to 4,000 teachers participate in the Bay Area Project alone. Different sites set their own programs, but among the areas of focus are: process, theory, workshop approaches, writing across the curriculum, emergent writing, publishing student writing, coaching models for teaching writing, among other strategies. At each project, teachers learn to teach writing by first becoming writers themselves. Teachers become immersed in all aspects of the process and become convinced (as they will soon convince their own students) that they are real writers with all the rights and privileges thereof.

Writing across the Curriculum/Writing in the Disciplines

The WAC/WID movement is a broadly based pedagogical practice that grew from the process movement. Most WAC/WID programs stemmed from faculty workshops in 1970 as an outgrowth of the writing process movement and were started on university campuses across the country. This became a reform movement over the next thirty years. Although not as widely based in public schools, WAC/WID programs hold the premise that writing is important in all academic areas, not just composition classes.

Additionally, students use writing as a bridge from what is known to what one expects to learn, and writing is a means of making sense of a discipline. Most sites urge that all courses include a writing component, but a popular model is one in which a number of courses are deemed by the university as writing-intensive courses. Thus, students know in advance that writing will be an important aspect of the course. Often, writing-intensive courses are listed as such on student transcripts.

Workshop Approach

An outgrowth of both writing projects and of the whole language movement in the early eighties was the implementation of the Writers' Workshop approach. Since writing projects saw it as their job to convince teachers that they were real writers, teachers next had to convince their students that they also were real writers. Writing and reading workshops grew out of the concept of writing retreats, where writers worked on their own materials and came together to share, discuss, criticize, and edit. The person who captured teachers' imaginations about how writing workshops could be organized for instruction was Nancie Atwell (Atwell, 1987). Atwell showed teachers that workshops could be highly organized and could function smoothly. Atwell describes her approach to the workshop as having principles that serve to inform both teaching and learning:

1. Writers need regular chunks of time—time to think, write, confer, read, change their minds, and write some more.
2. Writers need their own topics. Right from the first day of kindergarten, students should use writing as a way to think about and give shape to their own ideas and concerns.
3. Writers need response. Helpful response comes during—not after—the composing. It comes from the writer's peers and from the teacher, who consistently models the kinds of restatements and questions that help writers reflect on the content of their own writing.
4. Writers learn mechanics from context, from teachers who address errors as they occur within individual pieces of writing, where these rules and forms will have meaning.
5. Children need to know adults who write. We need to write, share our writing with our students, and demonstrate what experienced writers do in the process of composing, letting our students see our own drafts in all their messiness and tentativeness.
6. Writers need to read. They need access to a wide-ranging variety of texts, prose and poetry, fiction and nonfiction.
7. Writing teachers need to take responsibility for their writing and teaching. We must seek out professional resources that reflect the far-reaching conclusions of recent research into children's writing. And we must become writers and researchers, observing and learning from our own and our students' writing. (Atwell, 1987, pp. 17–18).

Atwell showed teachers how to respond to student writing in a workshop format, how to negotiate grading, and how to implement instruction through "writing mini-lessons." She clearly articulated the roles of teacher and student. As a student, you knew what you were supposed to do on a daily basis and how to go about doing it. Teachers also let students know what they themselves were responsible for and allowed students to hold teachers responsible for their obligations in the workshop. Atwell's book, now in its second edition, remains very popular with whole language teachers and graduates of writing projects.

Whole Language

Although more thought of as a reading movement, Goodman (1989) does trace the theoretical underpinnings of whole language to composition theorists such as Alvina Burrows, Donald Graves, James Britton, and the National Writing Project. A decade later Daniels, Zemelman and Bizar (1999) analyzed 60 years of research to conclude that support exists for wholistic, literature-based approaches to writing.

Trends in Writing Assessment

Writing assessment has largely followed the same trends as reading assessment. As reading assessment shifted from a focus solely on the text to a focus on how students read, much the same has happened in writing. Previously, writing assessment was purely textual analysis. Teachers focused on errors, how many and how often. Writing assessment has shifted to interpretation and process. One element of this shift has been from sentence-level correctness to revision as reformulation (Hull, 1984). In *Errors and Expectations: A Guide for the Teacher of Basic Writing*, Mina Shaughnessy (1977) wrote: "Errors count but not as much as most English teachers think" (p. 120). Error analysis now serves as an analytical tool that helps teachers to understand student thinking and to help students develop strategies that lead to better writing. Unfortunately, errors still count. Formal assessment in all aspects of education is growing, and writing assessment in many states focuses solely on grammatical accountability. For writing, this debate focuses on direct and indirect assessment. Proponents of indirect assessment view writing as a means of communicating ideas while proponents of direct assessment view writing as the construction of meaning (Williamson, 1993). In fact, it is only in recent years that formal testing of writing has moved from a multiple-choice examination to a holistic evaluation of students' actual writing.

Holistic Assessment

Perhaps the most common form of informal assessment is holistic scoring. Many state competency tests and college placement tests in writing favor an open topic structure; these tend to produce more errors in student papers (see Smith et al., 1985) and thus tend to make it easier for evaluators to place students. Basically, in holistic evaluation, two readers rate each paper on a four- or five-point scale (most use a four-point scale because differences are easier to resolve). If the raters are in agreement, then a third rater is not needed. If raters are not in agreement, then a third rater is used to resolve disagreements. Another way of conducting holistic evaluation is to have three readers read each student essay then average their ratings. In a holistic evaluation, where readers have been trained, error is one of several factors that influence raters. Other factors might include, format, content, vocabulary and spelling. However, since the mid-seventies, holistic evaluation has attempted—through carefully posed topics, scoring guides and sample papers for raters to use for uniformity and attention to reliability and validity—to rate student papers for placement and minimum competency as accurately as possible. The downside of holistic evaluation is its prohibitive cost both in time and money, especially in large-scale assessment.

Portfolio Assessment

Portfolio advocates make a strong case for using portfolios in large-scale assessment. They argue that a portfolio is much more reliable as a measure of growth and ability. It really is not quite accurate to call portfolios a means of assessment, however. Portfolios are a means of collection. Some sort of holistic evaluation would need to be conducted in order to judge the content of the portfolios. Questions must be decided about what to include in portfolios as well as the purpose of the portfolio in the first place.

Primary Trait Guides

Another form of writing assessment is the use of primary trait scoring guides. A primary trait guide focuses specifically on a few key aspects of student writing. A primary trait guide might focus on errors, especially particular types of errors. Another guide might focus on paragraph patterns or topic sentences. Although generally viewed as unsuitable for large-scale assessment, primary trait guides are very useful in classroom settings, especially those advocating a workshop format.

Issues in Writing Assessment

The current political climate for assessment means that large-scale writing assessment is likely to continue. The shift from using multiple-choice measures to evaluating student-produced essays has turned the corner, however. As of this writing, even the venerable SAT now includes a writing sample scored by rubrics. However, issues of reliability and validity will continue to persist. Work by Smith (1993) has questioned exactly what the difference is between a 3 and a 4 on a 4-point scale and especially between a 2 and 3, since the rater is likely to realize that the rating given might affect a student's being placed in a remedial program or, in extreme circumstances, not graduating from high school.

Technology and Writing

Most would readily agree that technology has greatly affected the teaching of writing. Students routinely use classroom computer stations for much of their writing, and these tools now have their own applications for error study and analysis, fluency, and organization. Information and Communication Technology (ICT) has expanded the notion of writing instruction, but it has decidedly not replaced or supplanted it. Cutting-edge research in writing might focus today on multimodal literacies and digital technologies. Some researchers are beginning to distance themselves from these new technologies in order to study their impact on us (Swenson et al., 2006). Leu (2005) reflected that the Internet as well as evolving technologies are not technological issues but literacy issues. While digital texts can take forms similar to their print counterparts, we also see how profoundly different these can be. "Many digital texts are dynamic, their content updated and revised continuously. Such content is typically multimodal, incorporating visual, auditory, and other non-verbal elements" (Swenson et al., 2006, p. 354). These new digital arrays, collectively called *hypermedia*, change the ways we read and how we connect texts to texts. Of course, this affects how students then produce writing—and what counts as writing (see Bromley, this volume). As Postman (1992) warns us, it is "a mistake to suppose that any technological innovation has a one-sided effect" (p. 4).

However, it is not as if we educators are blazing a technology trail for our classes since our media-saturated students spend an average of 6.5 hours per day with media (Roberts, Foehr, & Rideout, 2005). Interestingly enough, while our students are text messaging, blogging, using multiple forms of digital texts on MySpace.com, the national emphasis on accountability, standardized tests, and the writing prompt on the SAT have had an ironically reductionist effect on the teaching of writing, as evidenced by such programs as 6+1 Writing Traits (2003) and America's Choice Writer's Advantage, both programs that encourage formulaic approaches to student composing. Heilker (1996) cautions that such formulaic approaches encourage students to not think critically or innovatively. Curiously, students' written communication in school may consequently prove to be vastly different from written communication in non-school settings.

Conclusion

Nothing these days is more a political hot button than literacy in general and "readin' and 'ritin'" in particular. Interest in writing is not likely to flag any time soon. To be sure, the focus on the product and on students' ability to produce academic writing will remain in the forefront of educational reform. Clearly, process is part of this reform, as is writing for real audiences and writing for personal understanding. How process and product will play out in this era of high stakes assessment is anyone's guess. More importantly, though, the lessons learned over the last thirty years are that writers get better at writing by writing. Good teachers find ways of motivating students to produce their best writing by paying careful attention to *both* process and product. Surprisingly, technology has not had the effect one would have imagined on writing.

Surely, computers have made writing easier to edit and revise. Teachers can take far less time to edit student's papers, and publishing no longer relies on justifiers and professional publishers. It is the rare school where students do not have access to word processors for at least final drafts. So, while the nature and applications of writing are evolving, and while instructional approaches continue to mature over time, the future is far from certain.

References

Applebee, A. N. (1974). *Tradition and reform in the teaching of English: A history*. Urbana, IL: NCTE.

Atwell, N. (1987). *In the middle: Writing, reading and learning with adolescents*. Portsmouth, NH: Boynton Cook/Heinemann.

Braddock, R., Lloyd-Jones, R., & Schoer, L. (1963). *Research in written composition*. Champaign, IL: NCTE.

Bay Area Writing Project. Retrieved June 24, 2002, from http://bawpblogs.org.

Burhans, C. S. (1983). The teaching of writing and the knowledge gap. *College English, 45*, 639–656.

Cooper, C. R., & Odell, L. (1978). *Research on composing: Points of departure*. Urbana, IL: NCTE.

Daniels, H., Zemelman, S., & Bizar, M. (1999). Whole language works: Sixty years of research. *Educational Leadership, 57*(2), 32–37.

Dyson, A. H. (1981). Oral language: The rooting system for learning to write. *Language Arts, 58*, 776–784.

Dyson, A. H., & Freedman, S. W. (2003). Writing. In J. Flood, D. Lapp, J. R. Squire, & J. M. Jensen (Eds.), *Handbook of research on teaching the English language arts* (2nd ed.). Mahwah, NJ: Lawrence Erlbaum Associates.

Elbow, P. (1973). *Writing without teachers*. New York: Oxford University Press.

Emig, J. (1971). *The composing processes of twelfth graders*. Urbana, IL: NCTE.

Gere, A. (1985). Empirical research in composition. In B. W. McClelland & T. R. Donovan (Eds.), *Perspectives on research and scholarship in composition* (pp. 116–124). New York: MLA.

Goodman, Y. M. (1989). Roots of the Whole Language Movement. *Elementary School Journal, 90*, 113–127.

Graves, D. (1981). *A case study observing the development of primary children's composing, spelling and motor behaviors during the writing process* (Final report to the National Institute of education). Durham: University of New Hampshire.

Gundlach, R. (1981). On the nature and development of children's writing. In C. Fredericksen & J. Dominic (Eds.), *Writing: The nature, development and teaching of written communication: Vol. 2. Writing, process, development and communication* (pp. 133–152). Hillsdale, NJ: Lawrence Erlbaum Associates.

Heilker, P. (1996). *The essay: Theory and pedagogy for an active form*. Urbana, IL: National Council of Teachers of English.

Hull, G. A. (1984). The editing process in writing: A performance study of experts and novices. (ERIC Document Reproduction Service No. ED 245254.

Kuhn, T. S. (1964) *Structure of scientific revolutions*. Chicago: University of Chicago Press.

Leu, D. J., Jr. (November 2005). *New literacies, reading research, and the challenge of change: A deictic perspective*. Invited presidential address to the National Reading Conference, Miami, FL. Retrieved September 6, 2006, from http://www.newliteracies.uconn.edu/nrc/don_leu_2005.html.

Macrorie, K. (1970). *Telling writing*. Rochelle Park, NJ: Hayden.

Moffett, J. (1992). *Active voice: A writing program across the curriculum*. Portsmouth, NH: Boynton/Cook.

Moffett, J. (1989). *Storm in the mountains: A case study of censorship, conflict, and consciousness*. Carbondale, IL: Southern Illinois University Press.

Moffett, J. (1968). *Teaching the universe of discourse: A theory of discourse: A rationale for English teaching used in student-centered language arts curriculum.* Boston: Houghton Mifflin.

Moffett, J., & Wagner, B. J. (1983). *Student-centered language arts and reading, K–13: A handbook for teachers.* (3rd ed.). Boston: Houghton Mifflin.

Monaghan, J. (2003). The uses of literacy by girls in colonial America. In J. E. Greer (Ed.), *Girls and literacy in America: Historical perspectives to the present* (pp. 53–80). Santa Barbara, CA: ABC Clio.

Murray, D. M. (1985). *A writer teaches writing: A complete revision.* Boston: Houghton Mifflin, College Div.

Murray, D. M. (1975). *A writer teaches writing.* (2nd ed.). Boston: Houghton Mifflin.

Murray, D. M. (1968). *A writer teaches writing: A practical method of teaching composition.* Boston: Houghton Mifflin.

North, S. M. (1987). *The making of knowledge in composition: Portrait of an emerging field.* Upper Montclair, NJ: Boynton/Cook.

Postman, N. (1992). *Technopoly.* New York: Knopf.

Roberts, D. F., Foehr, U. G., & Rideout, V. (2005). *Generation M: Media in the lives of 8–18 year olds.* Menlo Park, CA: Kaiser Family Foundation.

Shaughnessy, M. (1977). *Errors and expectations: A guide for the teacher of basic writing.* New York: Oxford University Press.

Schultz, L. M. (1999). *The young composers: Composition's beginnings in 19th century schools.* Carbondale, IL: Southern Illinois University Press.

Smith, W. L., Hull, G. A., Land, R. E., Moore, M. T., Ball, C., Dunham, D. E., Hickey, L. S., & Ruzich, C. W. (1985). Some effects of varying the structure of the topic on college students' writing. *Written Communication, 2,* 73–89.

Smith, W. L. (1993). Assessing the reliability and adequacy of using holistic scoring of essays as a college composition placement technique. In M. M. Williamson & B. A. Huot (Eds.), *Validating holistic scoring for writing assessment* (pp. 142–205). Cresskill, NJ: Hampton Press.

Standards for the English language arts. (1996). Urbana, IL: IRA/NCTE.

Swenson, J., Young, C., McGrail, E., Rozema, R., & Whitin, P. (2006). Extending the conversation: New technologies, new literacies, and English education. *English Education, 38,* 351–369.

Williamson, M. M. (1993). An introduction to holistic scoring: The social, historical and theoretical context for writing assessment. In M. M. Williamson & B. A. Huot (Eds.), *Validating holistic scoring for writing assessment* (pp. 1–44). Cresskill, NJ: Hampton Press.

Woods, W. F. (1985). The cultural tradition of nineteenth-century "traditional" grammar teaching. *Rhetoric Society Quarterly, 15*(1–2), 3–12.

Young, R. E. (1978). Paradigms and problems: Needed research in rhetorical invention. In C. R. Cooper & L. Odell (Eds.), *Research on composing: Points of departure* (pp. 29–48). Urbana IL: NCTE.

Technology and Writing

KAREN BROMLEY

Rapid changes in information and communication technology (ICT) require regular redefinitions of literacy. Many of us can no longer consider ourselves "literate"; rather we must accept the continuing need to "become literate" (Gee, 2003; Leu, 1997; Leu & Kinzer, 2003). New technology related to writing requires constant change in our literacy to adjust to word processing software upgrades, new computer programs, and new composing concepts (e.g., e-zine, html, e-book, WEB editors, filters, ALT text, synchronous and asynchronous communication). For many of us, becoming literate is a social endeavor, and how we acquire literacy has changed. Often, we interact with others to learn how to use a new word processor, create a web page or html, use e-mail, or participate in a discussion board. We are only recently beginning to recognize the possibilities ICT has for enhancing communication and exploring language and literacy (Reinking, McKenna, Labbo, & Kieffer, 1999).

Today, perhaps more than ever before, technology is transforming writing. Instead of replacing one kind of writing with another however, we are adding to our repertoire of process and product tools (Bruce, 1998). Past notions of writing that included paper, pencil, standard conventions, and the isolated writer are changing in dramatic ways for students, parents, educators, researchers, administrators, and policy makers. This chapter provides a brief overview of the technology-writing relationship, trends in writing related to technology, and questions for future research.

The Technology-Writing Relationship

Technology has enhanced the basics of effective teaching and learning about writing and it has made the writing process easier. Technology has changed our ways of writing, thinking, and communicating, and it has affected both what is written and how it is written (Daiute, 1985: Farnan & Dahl, 2003). Because much computer-based writing never becomes words on a printed page, but rather is read directly from a video screen, the computer has become "a new communications medium" that facilitates traditional paper-based writing and allows other forms of writing as well (Bruce & Levin, 2003). Writing with technology allows for combining the use of paper and pencil with use of

Karen Bromley, Technology and Writing. From M. C. McKenna, L. D. Labbo, R. Kieffer, & Reinking, D. (Eds.), *International handbook of literacy and technology* (Vol. 2, pp. 349–353). Mahwah, NJ: Lawrence Erlbaum Associate Publishers. Reprinted with permission.

the computer and wireless technologies. For example, a writer may refer to handwritten notes or an outline and several Web sites to compose a draft using a word processor on a wireless laptop. A colleague's suggestions for revision may be done on paper or may appear as comments in the margins of an e-mailed file. As well, writers can now send text accompanied by images, graphics, sound, and video with fonts in different languages and text displayed in different orientations. Technology has extended the concept of audience and users routinely write to each other using not only paper, pencil, and pen, but also via instant messaging (IM), e-mail, discussion boards, chat rooms, and listservs.

Technology also affects who is writing. Many more technology users are writers because of word processors, presentation software, WEBpage programs, desktop publishing, and Internet publishing. In a recent study of schools, 75% reported a majority of teachers use computers daily, 77% reported a majority of teachers have school-based e-mail addresses, and two-thirds said a majority of teachers use the Internet for instruction (Cramer & Smith, 2002, p. 10). Student writing with word processors has become a "commonplace fixture in language arts classrooms" (Bruce & Levin, 2003). Since 87% of classrooms have at least one Internet computer and 85% of schools have Internet access (National Center for Education Statistics, 2002), there are also many more opportunities for students to write online for their peers and sharpen their writing skills as they do so (Kehus, 2003; Smolin & Lawless, 2003). The writing of students with disabilities is motivated and facilitated with enhanced word-processing programs that include multimedia, speech synthesis, word prediction, and online dictionaries (Kamil, Intrator, & Kim, 2000).

Research suggests computers have a positive impact on student writing. Students using computers tend to write longer compositions, add more to their writing, and revise more (Daiute, 1985; Farnan & Dahl, 2003). Because technology makes it easier to compose and revise, identify problems with text, and share texts, students learn to be better writers and readers (Bruce & Levin, 2003). In addition, student collaboration seems to occur more frequently when compositions are accessible for reading on computer screens (Baker & Kinzer, 1998), and variety and complexity of language use increases during creative writing projects on the computer (Kamil, Intrator, & Kim, 2000). Online writing centers provide access to writing resources, offline centers, e-mail links, and handouts, and students can submit papers for online tutoring (Leander, 2003). There are hundreds of word-processing programs, myriad software tools for planning and organizing for writing, and text editors make revising easier. Spell checkers and grammar checkers give feedback more quickly than a teacher can, thus freeing the teacher to support the writer's idea development, clarity, and style. Of course, the ability to cut and paste from multiple sources may enhance both creative thinking and plagiarism, but online sources make it easier to identify a writer's use of others' ideas without giving credit (Kehus, 2003).

However, there are some caveats related to technology-enhanced writing. Schools in many urban and rural high-poverty areas do not have computers or workable computers. Many families living in poverty do not have computers. Many schools do not provide technology support to help teachers use technology to enhance writing. Technology may foster a product-oriented approach toward writing as students focus on presenting work attractively using clip art and animation, rather than focusing on content, and frustration with software may inhibit planning and revising (Baker & Kinzer, 2003). The cost of technology that permits writing with the full complement of hypermedia and ICT may not be reflected in benefits to student learning and achievement. And, because technology changes so rapidly, it is expensive for schools with meager resources available for instructional resources to remain up-to-date (Bruce & Levin, 2003). Reading and editing from a video screen may not be as comfortable for the eye and may be less efficient than from paper (Kamil, Intrator, & Kim, 2000). Of course, factors such as keyboarding skill, complexity of word processors, motivation, attitudes, audience, the process used for writing with technology, and teachers' instructional goals affect how and what writers compose.

New Directions

Technology-enhanced writing will be visible in more K–12 classrooms in the future. The IRA's position statement, *Integrating Literacy and Technology in the Curriculum* (2001), recommends that instruction and assessment in reading and writing include the new literacies of ICT. It exhorts teachers to integrate Internet and other ICT into the literacy curriculum because "Proficiency at using the new literacies of networked information technologies has become critical to our students' success in the workplace and their daily lives" (p. 2). Reading and writing assessments need to include ICT literacies because research shows that many students prefer to use word processors to complete writing assignments, and research suggests that 20% more students will pass state writing assessments if they can use them (Russell & Plati, 2000).

As literacy instruction and ICT converge, the central role teachers play in guiding student learning will increase, not decrease (Leu, Kinzer, Coiro, & Cammack, 2003). "Teachers will be challenged to thoughtfully guide students' learning within information environments that are richer and more complex than traditional print media, presenting richer and more complex learning opportunities for both themselves and their students" (p. 58). Thus, work that examines authentic cases and practical classroom applications (Karchmer, 2001; Richards & McKenna, 2003; Teale, Leu, Labbo, & Kinzer, 2002) will be needed to help teachers conceptualize and structure integrated lessons using technology-enhanced writing. And, more teachers will begin to connect out of school literacies with classroom writing (Alvermann, Moon, & Hagood, 1999; Grisham in Pailliotet, 2003).

Other new directions in writing are emerging as a result of technology's influence. Changes in notions of authorship and text will continue as new ways of collaborating and writing across distance and time emerge. More online publishing will undoubtedly occur, providing the benefit of quicker access to information as well as the need for critical literacy. Online texts such as *Education for an Information age: Teaching in the Computerized Classroom* (Poole & Jackson, 2003) available at http://www.pitt.edu/~edindex/InfoAge4index.html and electronic journals will augment paper texts like *Linking Literacy and Technology: A Guide for K–8 Classrooms* (Wepner, Valmont, & Thurlow, 2000) and paper journals like *The Journal of Computer Assisted Learning*.

Other changes in the form of writing will continue to occur. One example is IM, a quick way to communicate online using acronyms that require fewer keystrokes than conventional English. The message, ***wu with w and ict 2day*** (*What's up with writing and information and communication technology today?*) illustrates how technology and audience have affected writers' spelling, punctuation, and form. IM users have created a new language (accessible in online acronym dictionaries) for use with computers, cell phones, or personal digital assistants (PDAs). As this type of informal writing finds its way into student journals, assignments, and tests, it will require teachers to rethink standards for writing and the form of classroom writing in relationship to ICT.

Another result of technology-enhanced writing is global access and an ever-shrinking world. The Web offers teachers access to the work of other teachers around the world and opportunities to share their own creative work. Connections established among students within our country and around the world through electronic networks will continue to bring students closer together. The creation of personal web pages by students and teachers throughout the world that include photos, stories, music, and graphics makes users more public and accessible (Bruce, 1998). These connections can help erase cultural, ethnic, linguistic, and economic barriers as users come to know each other through technology-enhanced writing.

Directions for Future Research

Research is needed to better understand the complex nature of technology-related writing. Questions posed by researchers include the following. What will it mean to compose in the 21st century (Yancey, 2004)? How will traditional literacy contribute to the new literacies of the Internet (Len & Kinzer, 2002)? What are the consequences for reading and writing instruction as the boundaries between author and reader disappear (Bruce & Levin, 2003)? How do text preparation and presentation, including graphics, hypermedia, and layout, affect meaning making (Kamil, Intrator, & Kim, 2000)? How do current copyright laws need to change to address new forms of disseminating information electronically? (Reinking, 1996). What is the role of facilitative devices on students' writing processes and writing quality (Farnan & Dahl, 2003)? How do age, cognitive development, and writing style impact technology-related writing (Daiute, 1985)? Other questions arise as well, e.g., How does technology-related writing affect student learning? How do student–student interactions and student–teacher interactions in writing conferences change as a result of writing with ICT? How can technology-enhanced writing better serve students from diverse backgrounds? In what ways should curriculum, instruction, and assessment change to incorporate technology-related writing? What factors cause shifts in teacher thinking about writing with ICT? How can teachers' instructional goals be met using technology-enhanced writing? How can teacher education programs prepare preservice teachers to integrate technology with writing? How will the English language continue to change as technology and writing co-mingle? These are but a few of the questions educators will undoubtedly need to seek answers to in the future in order to better understand the complex nature of technology's impact on writing.

References

Alvermann, D. E., Moon, J. S., & Hagood, M. C. (1999). *Popular culture in the classroom: Teaching and researching critical media literacy.* Newark, DE: International Reading Association.

Baker, E., & Kinzer, C. K. (1998). Effects of technology on process writing: Are they all good? In T. Shanahan & E. N. Rodriquez-Brown (Eds.). *Forty-seventh yearbook of the national reading conference* (pp. 428–440). Chicago, IL: National Reading Conference.

Bruce, B. C. (1998). Learning through, expression. *Journal of Adolescent and Adult Literacy, 42*(4), 306–310.

Bruce, B., & Levin, J. (2003). Roles for new technologies in language arts: Inquiry, communication, construction, and expression. In J. Flood, D. Lapp, J. R. Squire, & J. M. Jensen (Eds.). *Handbook of research on teaching the English language arts, 2nd ed.* (pp. 649–657). Mahwah, NJ: Lawrence Erlbaum Associates.

Cramer, S., & Smith, A. (2002). Technology's impact on student writing at the middle school level. *Journal of Instructional Psychology, 29*(1), 3–14.

Daiute, C. (1985). *Writing and computers.* Reading, MA: Addison Wesley.

Farnan, N., & Dahl, K. (2003). Children's writing: Research and practice. In J. Flood, D. Lapp, J. R. Squire, & J. M. Jensen (Eds.), *Handbook of research on teaching the English language arts, 2nd ed.* (pp. 993–1007). Mahwah, NJ: Lawrence Erlbaum Associates.

Gee, J. P. (2003). *What video games have to teach us about learning and literacy.* New York: Palgrave Macmillan.

Integrating literacy and technology in the curriculum: A position statement of the International Reading Association (2001). Retrieved on January 6, 2004 from http://www.reading.org/resources/issues/positions_technlogy.html

Kamil, M. L., Intrator, S. M., & Kim, H. S. (2000). The effects of other technologies on literacy and learning. In M. L. Kamil, P. B. Mosenthal, P. D. Pearson, & R. Barr (Eds.). *Handbook of reading research, vol. III* (pp. 771–788). Mahwah, NJ: Lawrence Erlbaum Associates.

Karchmer, R. A. (2001). The journey ahead: Thirteen teachers report how the Internet influences literacy and literacy instruction in their K–12 classrooms. *Reading Research Quarterly, 36,* 442–466.

Kehus, M. J. (2003). Opportunities for teenagers to share their writing online. In B. C. Bruce (Ed.). *Literacy in the information age: Inquiries into meaning making with new technologies* (pp. 148–158). Newark, DE: International Reading Association.

Leander, K. (2003). Laboratories for writing. In B. C. Bruce (Ed.), *Literacy in the information age: Inquiries into meaning making with new technologies* (pp. 222–232). Newark, DE: International Reading Association.

Leu, D. J., & Kinzer, C. K. (2002). Toward a theoretical framework of new literacies on the Internet: Central principles. In R. C. Richards & M. C. McKenna (Eds.), *Integrating multiple literacies in K–8 classrooms: Case commentaries and practical applications* (pp. 18–38). Mahwah, NJ: Lawrence Erlbaum Associates.

Leu, D. J., Kinzer, C. K., Coiro, J., & Cammack, D. (Forthcoming). Toward a theory of new literacies emerging from the Internet and other ICT. In R. Ruddell & N. Unrau (Eds.), *Theoretical models and processes of reading, 5th ed.* Newark, DE: International Reading Association.

Leu, D. J. (1997). Caity's question: Literacy as deixis on the Internet. *The Reading Teacher, 5,* 62–67.

National Center for Education Statistics (2002). *Internet access in public schools and classrooms: 1994–2000.* Retrieved on January 6, 2004, from http://nces.ed.gov/pubsearch/pubsinfo.asp?pubid=2002018

Pailliotet, A. W. (2003). Integrating media and popular-culture literacy with content reading. In R. C. Richards & M. C. McKenna (Eds.), *Integrating multiple literacies in K–8 classrooms: Case commentaries and practical applications* (pp. 172–189; Grisham pp. 180–181). Mahwah, NJ: Lawrence Erlbaum Associates.

Poole, B. J., & Jackson, L. (2003). *Education for an information age: Teaching in the computerized classroom, 4th ed.* Retrieved January 6, 2004, from http://www.pitt.edu/~edindex/InfoAge4index.html *Reading online.* Retrieved January 6, 2004, from http://www.readingonline.org

Reinking, D., McKenna, M. C., Labbo, L., & Kieffer, R. (Eds.). (1999). *Literacy for the 21st century: Technological transformations in a post-typographic world.* Mahwah, NJ: Lawrence Erlbaum Associates.

Reinking, D. (1996). Reclaiming a scholarly ethic: Deconstructing "intellectual property" in a post-typographic world. In D. J. Leu, C. K. Kinzer, & K. A. Hinchman (Eds.), *Literacies for the 21st Century: Research and practice* (pp. 461–470). Forty-fifth Yearbook of the National Reading Conference. Chicago, IL: National Reading Conference.

Richards, J. C., & McKenna, M. C. (Eds.). (2003). *Integrating multiple literacies in K–8 classrooms: Case commentaries and practical applications.* Mahwah, NJ: Lawrence Erlbaum Associates.

Russell, M., & Plati, T. (2000). *Mode of administration effects on MCAS composition performance for grades four, eight, and ten.* Chestnut Hill, MA: National Board on Educational Testing and Public Policy.

Smolin, L. I., & Lawless, K. A. (2003). Becoming literate in the technological age: New responsibilities and tools for teachers. *The Reading Teacher, 56,* 570–577.

Teale, W. H., Leu, D. J., Labbo, L. D., & Kinzer, C. (2002). The CTELL project: New ways technology can help educate tomorrow's reading teachers. *The Reading Teacher, 55,* 654–659.

Wepner, S. B., Valmont, W. J., & Thurlow, R. (Eds.). (2000). *Linking literacy and technology: A guide for K–8 classrooms.* Newark, DE: International Reading Association.

Yancey, K. B. (2004). Made not only in words: Composition in a new key. Keynote address. Conference on College Composition and Communication. San Antonio, TX. Retrieved January 16, 2004, from http://www.ncte.org/profdev/conv/cccc04/featured/114905.htm

Classroom Implications

1. How can *both* process and product concerns best be addressed in your instructional setting?

2. How can you contend with the time required for the process approach?

3. What are ways that the writing curriculum might be revised to acknowledge the role of technology? Or should it?

For Further Reading

Ellis, R. A. (2006). Investigating the quality of student approaches to using technology in experiences of learning through writing. *Computers and Education, 47,* 371–390.

Engle, T., & Streich, R. (2006). Yes, there "Is" room for soup in the curriculum: Achieving accountability in a collaboratively planed writing program. *The Reading Teacher, 59,* 660–679.

Fisher, D., & Ivey, G. (2005). Literacy and language as learning in content-area classes: A departure from "Every teacher a teacher of reading." *Action in Teacher Education, 27,* 3–11.

Levy, G. A., Gong, Z., Hessels, S., Evans, M. A., & Jared, D. (2006). Understanding print: Early reading development and the contributions of home literacy experiences. *Journal of Experiemental Child Psychology, 93,* 63–93.

Manning, M. (2006). Celebrations in reading and writing: Be true to yourself. *Teaching Pre K–8,* 68–69.

McDonald, N. L., & Fisher, D. (2006). *Teaching literacy through the arts. Tools for teaching literacy series.* New York: Guilford.

Ostrosky, M. M., Gaffney, J. S., & Thomas, D. V. (2006). The interplay between literacy and relationships in early childhood settings. *Reading and Writing Quarterly, 22,* 173–191.

Peterson, S. S., & Kennedy, K. (2006). Sixth-grade teachers' written comments on student writing: Genre and gender influences. *Written Communication, 23,* 36–62.

Scheuer, N., de la Cruz., M., Pozo, J. I., Huate, M. F., & Sola, G. (2006). The mind is not a black box: Children's ideas about the writing process. *Learning and Instruction, 16,* 72–85.

Smith, L. A. (2006). Think-aloud mysteries: Using structured, sentence-by-sentence text passages to teach comprehension strategies. *The Reading Teacher, 59,* 690–697.

Vincent, J. (2006). Children writing: Multimodality and assessment in the writing classroom. *Literacy, 40,* 51–57.

Online Resources

Graham, S., & Perin, D. (2007). *Writing Next: Effective strategies to improve writing of adolescents in middle and high schools—A report to the Carnegie Corporation of New York.* Washington: Alliance for Excellent Education.
www.all4ed.org/publications/ReadingNext

The Literacy Hub: Connecting Reading and Writing. Don Leu's site at the University of Connecticut.
www.literacy.uconn.edu/writing.htm

The Nation's Report Card: Writing. Results of the National Assessment of Educational Progress.
http://nces.ed.gov/nationsreportcard/writing

Name Index

● ● ● ● ●

Subject Index